They Never Go Back to Pocatello

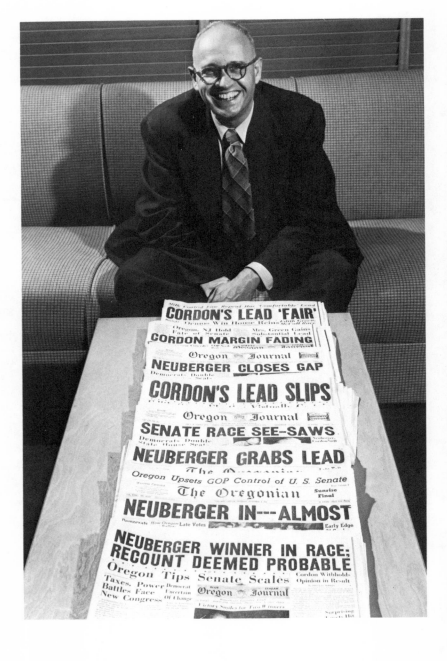

THEY NEVER

The Selected Essays of

GO BACK TO

RICHARD NEUBERGER

POCATELLO

Foreword by Maurine D. Neuberger

Edited & Biographical Introduction by

STEVE NEAL

OREGON HISTORICAL SOCIETY PRESS

FRONTIS: *The almost United States Senator from Oregon, Richard Neuberger the night of November 3, 1954.*

(BURT GLINN, MAGNUM PHOTOS, INC.)

The Oregon Historical Society would like to thank Magnum Photos, Inc., for the Burt Glinn photo of Richard Neuberger, Ray Atkeson for the generous use of his Richard Neuberger photos, Paul Pitzer for permission to use his bibliography on the writings of Richard Neuberger, and Maurine Neuberger for her support of this project.

Library of Congress Cataloging-in-Publication Data

Neuberger, Richard L. (Richard Lewis), 1912–1960
  They never go back to Pocatello: the selected essays of Richard Neuberger / edited by Steve Neal.
    p.   cm.
  Bibliography: p.
  Includes index.
  ISBN 0-87595-201-1
    1. United States—Politics and government—1933–1945.   2. United States—Politics and government—1945–1953.   3. United States—Politics and government—1953–1961.   4. Politicians—United States—History—20th century.   I. Neal, Steve. 1949–   .
II. Title
E806.N414   1988
973.9'092'2—dc19   88-17935

This volume was produced and designed by the Oregon Historical Society Press.

Printed in the United States of America.

for Jane Neuberger Goodsell

Contents

Senator Richard and Maurine Neuberger on the Capitol steps. 1955.
(VERA SPRINGER COLLECTION)

Foreword

A S I FORMULATE my ideas for a foreword to this anthology of
Dick's writings, I must caution myself about making it too
autobiographical. I accompanied him on many trips to seek
out stories, and I helped with research to verify the facts he was using. When he sought political office, I drove the car while he slept, I
carried the notebook where relevant facts were kept, and I watched
for audience reaction after a campaign appearance. Though we
worked closely together in his political life – in the Oregon Legislature and in his U.S. Senate office – when I began conferring with
Steve Neal about this anthology, we decided that the book should be
more about Dick's writing and his journalism than about his Senate
career. Rereading these articles, from his first one published ("The
New Germany," 1933) to his last ("Should a Public Man Write?"
1960) I see that it is impossible to separate his writing from his sense
of politics, yet his political sensibilities did not come to fruition until
he ran for the state legislature in 1940.

In his book *Integrity: The Biography of Senator George Norris*,
written in collaboration with Stephen Kahn, he writes about the
American conception of a politician.

A large expansive smile and an enthusiastic handshake. His
pockets crammed with a battery of cigars which he passes out

freely. He is all things to all people, and he never disagrees with anyone. For his home state he has nothing but praise and his constituents are noble, warm-hearted souls whom it is an unrivaled honor to represent.

He knows a myriad of persons by their first names. He never takes a stand on any issue he can straddle, and he balances himself between the two sides of a burning issue as expertly as a tightrope artist walks a wire.

He belongs to all the service organizations. He controls a patronage machine that assures him of reelection. He seeks publicity as eagerly as a Northwest Mountie stalks his prey. In short he is responsible for the disparaging tone of voice in which millions of Americans say, "Oh, he's a politician."

He immediately points out that his description of a politician was the antithesis of George Norris, who refused to compromise on any issue and took a forthright stand on all public questions.

Dick was proud to call himself a politician and tried to instruct readers and listeners to his radio broadcasts of the importance of politics as it affected their daily lives. He pointed out in "I Run for Office" and in his book *We Go to the Legislature*, how the deliberations of these "politicians" determine the kinds of schools our children attend, the kinds of roads we drive on, even the cleanliness of the water we drink and the air we breathe.

When I once expressed disappointment that my local League of Women Voters chapter had refused to take a stand in supporting a provision to reapportion our state legislature, Dick pointed out to me that the way to accomplish such a reform was not only to go to meetings about it but to participate in the legislative process, to run for elective office. I had never thought of being a "politician" myself, but that convinced me. A few weeks later I filed for election to the Oregon Legislature.

Dick was concerned with the importance of state government. He knew that state legislature was closer to the people and therefore he was also interested in reforms such as the above mentioned need for reapportionment, and the need to revise constitutions so legislative bodies could be free from "picayune restrictions dating from a century ago."

As he approached the idea of running for the United States Senate, Dick became personally aware of the influence of money in seeking political office; how to raise money for opening an office, for advertising, and for travel that raises the money to raise more money? He often said, "When is a bribe not a bribe? When the money is a campaign contribution!" That might be followed by the adage: He who pays the piper calls the tune.

Through his many published articles, Dick was known to be a conservationist. That meant preservation of forests and protecting wildlife. This often brought disfavor and, hence, no campaign contributions from some of the big timber operators. He was a proponent of public power and felt that the profit from harnessing our rivers should benefit all of the people rather than the utility companies and their stockholders. Thus, no contributions from the private power companies in Oregon.

He occasionally sought advice from lobbyists to find out how a particular segment would be affected by pending legislation. Since his articles had put him in the position as having taken a stand on various issues, he was less subject to pestering by lobbying groups hoping for his vote. A resident of a southern Oregon community who owned property in the area to be incorporated in the proposed Oregon Dunes National Recreation Area came into Dick's Senate office and said threateningly, if he persisted in promoting the Area, "I'll see that you stay home after the next election." To which Dick replied, "Home has no terrors for me."

Dick had a life-long love and admiration for Thomas Jefferson. Jefferson showed him what being a politician could mean. Through Jefferson's vision and perserverance, he persuaded the Congress to appropriate two thousand dollars for the journey of Meriwether Lewis and William Clark. Dick's study of Jefferson led to reading *The Journals of Lewis and Clark* which tell of the trek that led them over the Lolo Pass and eventually down the Columbia River to Fort Clatsop on the shore of the Pacific. From his awakened interest in these explorations he was inspired to follow the Lewis and Clark

Trail himself wherever it was feasible and practical. From this experience came his children's book, *The Lewis and Clark Expedition*.

His writing continued after he was elected to the United States Senate in 1954. From the time he was elected to the time of his death in March 1960 he wrote almost two hundred articles. This collection of some of Dick's articles will give the reader a feeling for the journalist and the conservationist, as well as insight into the art of politics.

MAURINE NEUBERGER
United States Senator, Oregon
1960–1966

Editor's Note

IN A CAREER that was cut short in 1960 with his death at the age of forty-seven, Richard Lewis Neuberger left a rich literary legacy: a half dozen books and more than four hundred articles in national journals and magazines. From the Civil War through the dawn of the Space Age, Oregon has produced other notable journalists, including Homer Davenport, from Silverton, who became the most celebrated political cartoonist of the 1890s on William Randolph Hearst's San Francisco *Examiner* and New York *Evening Journal*; John Reed, the romantic revolutionary whose *Ten Days That Shook the World* is a classic of war correspondence; and William Lambert, who won a Pulitzer Prize for his investigative reporting on the *Oregonian* in the 1950s and achieved national prominence in the 1960s as *Life* magazine's chief investigative reporter. But Neuberger was the Oregon journalist most identified nationally with the Pacific Northwest.

Growing up in Oregon in the 1950s, I was an avid reader of Neuberger's writings. I began gathering his articles in 1962 and have been collecting them ever since. This volume is a representative collection of some of Neuberger's best and most enduring writings. I am indebted to his wife Maurine for granting permission to publish these writings; to the late Martin Schmitt of the University of Oregon Library's special collections department for assistance with the Neuberger papers; and to the staff of the Oregon Room at the Oregon State Library.

In choosing articles for inclusion, I sought those of compelling historical or regional interest; profiles of notable political personalities; and reporting that dealt with Neuberger's political activities and his writing career. I have worked with Adair Law of the Oregon Historical Society Press in deciding what material to use. Notes that appeared in the original articles are shown by an asterisk. Numbered notes have been added for explanation of names, events, and phrases that are less familiar today.

As always, I am indebted to my wife Susan and our daughters Erin and Shannon for their support and thoughtful suggestions.

Richard Neuberger working in his home in Portland.   (RAY ATKESON)

Biographical Essay

RICHARD LEWIS NEUBERGER was among the master reporters of the twentieth century. For a generation, he informed the American people about the Pacific Northwest, its politics and social trends, mysteries, and scenic wonders. Whether exploring the Alaskan wilderness or his beloved Columbia Gorge, Neuberger wrote with verve and narrative force about America's last frontier. William O. Douglas observed that Neuberger did more than anyone in American history to teach the nation about their native region. A man of abundant talents, he excelled as a political analyst, social critic, magazine writer, scholar, historian, liberal commentator, and literary critic. Neuberger was always in motion. His indefatigable energy awed his contemporaries almost as much as the hydroelectric power generated by the Columbia River.

Senator Ernest Gruening of Alaska described him as perhaps the greatest journalist of his time. Governor Adlai E. Stevenson of Illinois said that Neuberger was the most articulate and eloquent voice of the Northwest. Governor Tom McCall of Oregon predicted that Neuberger's writings would prove to be as enduring as the journals of Neuberger's favorite biographical subjects, Lewis and Clark.

Neuberger roared out of the Pacific Northwest as a journalistic prodigy in the 1930s. He was twenty years old when he created a sensation with his chilling firsthand account of Nazi Germany for *The*

Nation in October of 1933, just eight months after Adolf Hitler had gained power. Leading American pundits were portraying Hitler in favorable terms, suggesting that the replacement of the Weimar Republic by Hitler's Nazi regime was a welcome change. Walter Lippmann of the New York *Herald Tribune*, then America's most influential journalist, described Hitler on May 19, 1933 as "the authentic voice of a genuinely civilized people." But unlike Lippmann, Neuberger did not accept Hitler's propaganda at face value. In the summer of 1933, Neuberger went to Germany and deliberately went off the path to which more prominent American journalists and tourists had been directed by their Nazi hosts. The grandson of German Jewish immigrants, Neuberger was appalled by Hitler's police state. He wrote about the gangster tactics of Nazi stormtroopers, the burning of more than twenty thousand volumes written by major Western writers, and the violent persecution of German Jews. Six years before Hitler launched the Second World War, Neuberger had exposed him as a brutal tyrant, a force for evil.

Back at home, Neuberger chronicled the formidable political movement of Western populism; the impact of Franklin D. Roosevelt's New Deal in the Far West; and the emerging power of organized labor. He co-authored a book with Kelly Loe entitled *An Army of the Aged*, that deflated the reputation of one of the Depression's most successful demagogues, Dr. Francis Everett Townsend, whose revolving pension plan for the elderly had galvanized a national movement. Neuberger effectively demonstrated that Townsend, in spite of his kindly image, was a tent-show con man. In a national magazine, Neuberger exposed vice conditions in his hometown of Portland. The denials of local officials were so vehement that Neuberger was forced to defend himself on the radio airwaves. Not only was Neuberger more convincing than his critics but he had the crucial advantage for winning the battle for public opinion in that his charges were true. Neuberger was among the first major political commentators to speak out against the red-baiting assault on civil liberties of Senator Joseph R. McCarthy in 1950. Long before there was an environmental movement, Neuberger was shedding light on the conspiracies of special interests to plunder forests, streams, and other natural resources. Neuberger's writings were a powerful force in the creation of a postwar progressive movement in the Pacific Northwest, with conservation and public power as the major issues. With the zest of a crusader, Neuberger fought the good fight.

Browsers at newstands could find a half dozen Neuberger bylines in different publications at the same time. His name was almost everywhere. He wrote for the *Saturday Evening Post*, *Harper's*, *Life*, the *New Republic*, *The Nation*, *The Progressive*, *Reader's Digest*, the New York *Times*, the *Oregonian's Northwest Magazine*, and the *Ford Times*.

For three decades, Neuberger knew the nation's movers and shakers. Before he was thirty, Neuberger was a friend and confidant of Franklin D. Roosevelt. An admirer of Neuberger's writings, FDR dispatched his eldest son, James, to invite Neuberger to the White House. Senate Republican leader Charles L. McNary of Oregon and Senator William E. Borah, the legendary Lion of Idaho, also became Neuberger friends. Supreme Court Justice William O. Douglas, from Washington state, and Governor Adlai E. Stevenson of Illinois were Neuberger hiking and camping companions. Senator George Norris of Nebraska, perhaps the greatest of the western progressives, and Roosevelt were Neuberger's first political heroes. But in the 1950s, Neuberger worshipped Stevenson, whom he had watched grow into national prominence. Neuberger was buried with a Stevenson campaign button pinned to the inside of his lapel.

In the tradition of Lincoln Steffens and Upton Sinclair, Neuberger played the dual roles of writer and political activist. As a political figure, Neuberger was elected to the Oregon Legislature at the age of twenty-seven in 1940, one of the few Democrats to win in a Republican stronghold. In his early thirties, Neuberger served as a military aide to the American delegation to the 1945 San Francisco Conference that created the United Nations, a position to which he had been appointed by Secretary of State Edward R. Stettinius. Just a year later, Neuberger was offered the Democratic nomination for governor of Oregon. Sensing that it would be a Republican year, Neuberger turned it down. Though he lost a bid for the Oregon State Senate, Neuberger led the Democratic ticket in populous Multnomah County. In 1948, Neuberger was elected to the Oregon State Senate.

Neuberger's partner in fact as well as in name was his wife, Maurine Brown Neuberger, who shared his liberalism and his devotion to the Pacific Northwest. Tall, witty, and highly intelligent, Maurine was the granddaughter of Oregon pioneers and the niece of *Oregonian* editor Paul Kelty, one of Dick Neuberger's journalistic mentors. Neuberger met Maurine Brown in 1939 when she was teaching English at Portland's Lincoln High School. During the Second World War, she managed her brother's farm. When Neuberger got out of the Army in 1945, he married Maurine. She became Neuberger's chief journalistic collaborator, accompanying him in his travels, shooting the pictures to illustrate her husband's articles for national magazines, and writing her own profiles for major publications, including a study of Portland's Mayor Dorothy McCullough Lee for the *New York Times Magazine*. In 1950 Maurine was elected to the Oregon House of Representatives, making the Neubergers the nation's first husband-and-wife legislative team. "Maurine is the real campaigner in the family," Dick Neuberger proudly declared. He took positive joy in her substantial political accomplishments. Her election in 1960 to succeed him in the Senate carried on the Neuberger legacy.

Through the force of his personality, Richard L. Neuberger ended Republican domination of Oregon, sparking a mid-century revival of the Democratic party. He became a rarity among historians, a history-maker, in 1954 when he scored a stunning political upset to become Oregon's first Democratic United States senator in forty years. His election sent thunderbolts to the East because it shifted the balance of power in the Senate, restoring the Democratic majority that had been lost in the 1952 Eisenhower landslide. In his first month as a senator, Neuberger was featured on the cover of *Time* magazine.

Despite the brevity of his term in the Senate, Neuberger had major impact. His Senate colleague, Wayne L. Morse, nicknamed him "Mr. Conservationist" because of Neuberger's high profile as a guardian of natural resources and the most persistent and articulate critic of the Eisenhower administration's public land, timber, and power policies. Neuberger's tenacity proved highly effective. The Eisenhower White House modified its resource policies in response to the public outcry generated by Neuberger's opposition. In the field of civil rights, Neuberger was an outspoken champion for racial minorities and for women. Neuberger gained national attention for his civil rights leadership in 1957 when he sought to prod Eisenhower to show more commitment to ending racial discrimination. Lyndon B. Johnson, then serving as majority leader, relied on Neuberger as among his valued lieutenants. Although Neuberger was considerably more liberal than the Johnson of the 1950s, he also recognized that it was sometimes necessary to settle for three-fourths of a loaf if the alternative was nothing. He joined John F. Kennedy in calling for France to withdraw from Algeria. JFK sought Neuberger's advice in the preparation of his Pulitzer Prize-winning book, *Profiles in Courage*. Had the book been written four years later, it is quite possible that Neuberger might have been among Kennedy's courageous subjects. Kennedy and his colleagues were deeply moved by Neuberger's brave struggle against cancer.

Neuberger knew how to get things done for his Oregon constituents, and for the Pacific Northwest. Morse had so many enemies within the Senate and the Eisenhower administration that his name was almost legislative poison. The Neuberger style was reminiscent of McNary, who taught Neuberger that achievement in the Senate required the formation of blocs and coalitions. Morse never played the game. But Neuberger soon became a legislative master by practicing the art of compromises and delicate trades. A Republican governor, Tom McCall, said that Neuberger did more for Oregon in his five years than any other senator in the state's history. Neuberger was the driving force for the preservation of the Oregon Dunes as a National Scenic Area, and for National Park historic status for Fort Clatsop, Lewis and Clark's camp, near Astoria. More than anyone else, Neuberger blocked the giveaway of the timber and wildlife marshes of the Klamath Basin to private lumber and mining interests. He secured federal funding for the development of Yaquina Bay harbor at Newport and for the University of Oregon's medical research center. As he planned his bid for reelection in 1960, Neuberger outlined an ambitious agenda for his state as a second-term senator. But he never got the chance.

If Neuberger had lived into the 1960s, he would probably have returned to journalism. Shortly before his death, Neuberger told his longtime friend, J. W. Forrester, Jr., editor of the Pendleton *East Oregonian* that he intended to serve just one more term in the Senate. "Another term," wrote Forrester, "and then he was coming home to Oregon to spend the rest of his years writing and enjoying life with close friends."

"I am by no means clear in my own mind that I will be a candidate again," Neuberger wrote Wayne L. Morse in January of 1957. "I have enjoyed my service here, ... But I value my ability and talents as a writer, and I feel that this ability has scant chance to show itself now. I am not becoming any younger, and if I am to write some of the things which I aspire to undertake, it can only be done my making literary work my sole career and leaving fulltime political activity to others."

Returning to Oregon was Neuberger's fondest ambition. At the time of his election to the Senate, Neuberger's family had lived in Oregon for almost a century. His grandfather had immigrated to Oregon from Southern Germany in 1870. Richard L. Neuberger was born on 26 December 1912 in the midst of the Progressive Era. His parents, Isaac Neuberger and Ruth Lewis, owned a popular Portland restaurant, The Bohemian, and the family lived comfortably in Westover, one of Portland's more fashionable neighborhoods. In his youth Neuberger attended Stanley's kindergarten, Couch and Chapman elementary schools, and Lincoln High School. He was reared in the Jewish faith in a state with one of the smallest Jewish populations in the nation. Neuberger's mother, Ruth, dominated the family, ran the restaurant, and was the major influence in her son's formative years. Isaac Neuberger was affable and well-liked but squandered so much of the family's money on his gambling debts that he lost control of the restaurant. Partly because of his father's experiences, Richard L. Neuberger abhorred gambling and was frugal with his own earnings.

Even as a youngster Neuberger wrote with flair. As a sportswriter for the Lincoln High School newspaper he impressed L.H. Gregory, the sports editor of the *Oregonian*. On Gregory's recommendation, Neuberger was hired for a summer job as a copy clerk for the *Oregonian*, and was quickly promoted to reporter. When Neuberger graduated from high school, in 1930, Gregory hired him as his assistant. The crusty Gregory taught Neuberger "how to grapple with the English language" and other fundamentals of journalism. Throughout his career, Neuberger listed Gregory as his journalistic mentor.

Entering the University of Oregon in the fall of 1931, Neuberger promptly became sports editor of the school paper, the *Daily Emerald*. Neuberger struck up a close friendship with Dr. Clarence W. "Doc" Spears, the Oregon football coach. And, with the backing of the university's sports establishment, Neuberger was chosen as editor of the *Emerald* as a sophomore, breaking the precedent that the post went to an upperclassman. Neuberger was politically conservative in 1932, a defender of the status quo. As the new editor, he proclaimed: "The *Emerald* will be conservative in whatever it does. Radical opinions and bolshevik tendencies will have places in neither its news or editorial columns. It is the opinion of the writer that a paper can oppose an existing order without turning radical in doing so." In a front-page column, Neuberger endorsed Herbert Hoover, Republican conservative, for reelection to the presidency in 1932 over Democratic challenger Franklin D. Roosevelt. Neuberger was not yet old enough to vote.

One of Neuberger's greatest strengths was that he was always open to new ideas. His college roommate, Stephen Kahn, with whom he would later write a critically acclaimed biography of Senator Norris (*Integrity: The Life of George W. Norris*), encouraged Neuberger's conversion from placid conservatism to liberal activism. By Neuberger's sophomore year, half of the student body had dropped out of school because of the Great Depression. It was Kahn who introduced Neuberger to such progressive journals as *The Nation* and *The New Republic*. "I lured him down to the local Salvation Army yard to watch men splitting wood for a meal," Kahn later recalled. "Again, we visited a nearby cooperative farm where awkward city folk were trying to wring enough to eat from their own over-mortgaged acres.

Dick sat down and ate the meager stew from a rough-plank table, and tasted his first margarine. It made Dick realize there were hungry women and children a couple of miles from his comfortable dormitory."

Influenced by Kahn, Neuberger became a voice for reform and at times, a lonely dissenter. In his editorials, Neuberger wrote favorably of FDR's New Deal initiatives; called for the proceeds of the Oregon–Oregon State football game to be used to feed the poor; and denounced fraternity parties and homecoming pageantry as trivial pursuits in a time of social upheaval. Neuberger also editorialized against compulsory fees, making the argument that students who could not afford textbooks should not be forced to subsidize the athletic department and frivolous student dances. Thwarted in this effort by the Oregon legislature, Neuberger successfully pushed for a statewide referendum and the compulsory fees were abolished by an overwhelming vote in a special election.

Neuberger's causes were unpopular among the student establishment. A "Send Dickie Home" campaign was undertaken by the fraternity crowd. Posters with coin boxes suddenly appeared on telephone poles and on tree trunks along Eugene's 13th Street, the major thoroughfare of the Oregon campus. Neuberger was unmoved by their protest.

Between his sophomore and junior year at Oregon, Neuberger traveled to Europe with his uncle, Julius Neuberger, a Navy physician. Neuberger visited France and England but it was Germany, his family's Old Country, that made the sharpest impression. Neuberger, sensing the story of a lifetime, spent his days in Germany interviewing citizens and local officials, and gathering his own observations about Hitler's first year in power. "Dick reported realistically what he had seen after going, with his great intellectual curiosity and his characteristic determination to ascertain the truth," said Ernest Gruening, then editor of *The Nation*, who published Neuberger's historic article. "It was the first realistic firsthand revelation in any American magazine of what was taking place in Nazi Germany. It was an epoch-making article."

Following the publication of "The New Germany," Neuberger's

talents were in much demand. Within a short time, he wrote articles for *Harper's*, *Current History*, *Collier's*, and *Esquire*. His first byline appeared in the New York *Times* in 1934. From 1936 through his election to the u.s. Senate in 1954, Neuberger served as Northwestern correspondent for the *Times*. Neuberger was also a regular contributor to the St. Louis *Post-Dispatch*.

For a brief time, Neuberger considered a career in law. But he was an indifferent student in his first year of law school at the University of Oregon and dropped out. Neuberger later studied law in Portland but concluded that he preferred a life in journalism and politics. Although Neuberger attended the University of Oregon for six years, he was too involved in outside activities to complete credits for his degree in journalism. Neuberger later donated his literary and political papers to the University's special collections library. It rankled some of Neuberger's college contemporaries that he was considered one of the school's most distinguished alumnus. Despite a formal education that was limited by his energy and ambition, Neuberger was proud that his legislative memoirs *Adventures in Politics: We Go to the Legislature* were published with much fanfare by Oxford University Press.

With a growing national reputation and the publication of three books prior to his twenty-sixth birthday (*An Army of the Aged*, 1936; *Integrity: The Life of George W. Norris*, 1937; *Our Promised Land*, 1938), Neuberger was recruited in 1940 by *Life* magazine. Founded just four years earlier by publishing mogul Henry R. Luce, *Life* was the richest and most powerful magazine in America, a dominant cultural and political force. In the era before television, the mass-circulation, weekly photomagazine had the effect, wrote David Halberstam, of "opening a window on the entire world." Neuberger was a specialist in the in-depth profiles that *Life* showcased with dramatic photos of people and events. In this period among the newsmakers whose faces were splashed across the *Life* cover were Winston Churchill, Benito Mussolini, Cordell Hull, Eleanor Roosevelt, Bette Davis, Gary Cooper, Franklin Delano Roosevelt, Wendell L. Willkie, Joe DiMaggio, Ginger Rogers, and Tom Harmon. Neuberger had written the cover article about Charles L. McNary when the

Oregon senator was nominated for the vice presidency. Neuberger was seriously tempted by an offer from *Life* that would have doubled his income and broadened his journalistic horizons. But Neuberger opted to remain in Oregon where he enjoyed his status as the region's best-known journalist.

Another reason for Neuberger's reluctance to leave Oregon was that he was becoming a major player in the state's political scene. Clinging to FDR's coat-tails, Neuberger was elected in 1940 as a state representative from Multnomah County, a member of the legislature's Democratic minority. An ardent Roosevelt supporter, Neuberger established close ties with leading members of the national administration. "I suppose he is the best-known young journalist on the Pacific Coast," Interior Secretary Harold L. Ickes wrote of Neuberger in his diary in 1941, "and for one so young he has been making great headway and building up quite a reputation."

In the meantime, Neuberger had learned that it was good business for a western journalist to build up the reputations of leading western political figures. The more prominent his subjects became, the more demands there were from national publications for Neuberger's by-line. His favorable coverage of McNary in the 1930s was a factor in the Oregon senator's nomination for the vice presidency in 1940. Neuberger also promoted the national political fortunes of Supreme Court Justice William O. Douglas, Senator Burton K. Wheeler of Montana, Governor Earl Warren of California, Senator Mon C. Wallgren of Washington, and fellow Oregonians Charles A. Sprague and Wayne L. Morse. With his typewriter, Neuberger also could be cutting in his depiction of old-style conservatives. His portraits of Oregon's conservative Democratic governor, Charles H. Martin, in the 1930s and Interior Secretary Douglas McKay and Senator Guy Cordon, Oregon's top Republicans in the 1950s, seriously tarnished their national reputations and their political standing at home. Cordon, who shunned publicity and distrusted the news media, grumbled that it was impossible to effectively counter Neuberger's polemics.

As a freshman legislator in 1941, Neuberger was widely recognized for his leadership on conservation issues. He sponsored legislation regulating logging in the state's forests and worked closely with Governor Sprague's administration in shaping a landmark forestry code. Six months after the Japanese attack on Pearl Harbor that pushed the United States into the Second World War, Neuberger resigned from the legislature and enlisted in the Army as a second lieutenant.

During the war, Neuberger served as the chief aide to General James A. O'Connor, whose headquarters were at Whitehorse in the Yukon Territory of Canada. O'Connor's division built the Alaskan military highway that connected American airfields in Alaska with Canada. Neuberger fell in love with Alaska and became an early and outspoken advocate for statehood, which was finally achieved during his term in the U.S. Senate. In 1944 Neuberger was transferred to Washington, D.C., and his wartime service ended soon after his assignment to the San Francisco Conference of 1945. It was in San Francisco that Neuberger gained the friendship of Adlai E. Stevenson, then serving as an adviser to the United States delegation to the United Nations. Neuberger wrote an article for the *Oregonian*'s Sunday magazine on another participant in the San Francisco Conference, Carlton Savage, an Oregon native who had been the senior adviser to Secretaries of State Cordell Hull and Edward Stettenius. Savage said that he sensed at the San Francisco Conference that Neuberger was destined for political prominence in the postwar era.

Following the war, Dick and Maurine were married in Missoula, Montana, then settled in a huge, old house in Portland Heights. They did not have children but were second parents to their three nieces, the daughters of Jane Neuberger Goodsell. Neuberger dedicated his children's biography of Lewis and Clark to his nieces. As U.S. senators, both of the Neubergers gave up some of their patronage prerogatives in order to be able to name Oregon students as Senate pages. One of their proudest accomplishments was attracting a new generation of Oregonians into politics in the postwar years.

The Neubergers were a remarkable team. They had limitless energy and vitality, a passion for the outdoors, and for their professions of journalism and politics. Politicians and journalists have more crumbling marriages per capita than any other occupations, but the

Neubergers were different than most political couples because they drew strength from each other, and also because they did not have grandiose pretensions of their importance. Dick Neuberger recognized that Maurine was his peer in intellect and drive, and was always careful to give her much of the credit for his successes. The Neubergers made considerable sacrifices for each other. She would accompany him on trips to distant corners of the Northwest to provide him assistance for an article and companionship. "Writing is an often lonely discipline," Maurine recalled years later, "and I knew that it helped Dick for me to be there."

With Maurine's support and encouragement, Richard L. Neuberger prospered as a free-lance contributor for the nation's best magazines in the postwar years. His wartime experiences in Alaska and Canada provided him with a wealth of background for his writings. Pulitzer Prize-winning reporter William Lambert, a Neuberger friend, quipped that the Alcan Highway should have been renamed for Neuberger because of the reams of publicity that he brought the road. One of the reasons that Neuberger managed to earn a comfortable income as a free-lance writer was his penchant for selling an article to one national magazine, then revising the same material for three other publications.

Writing came easily for Neuberger. He was a natural storyteller with a novelist's sense for detail and an ability to synthesize complex issues and material into highly readable prose. "Other writers marveled that he could toss off three or four thousand words without an erasure or reference to notes and with scarcely a pause in the rattle of the keys," said Malcolm Bauer, former associate editor of the *Oregonian*, who attended the University of Oregon with Neuberger. "He kept his own complex filing system, much of it in his head. He could bring forth statistics, anecdotes, precedents at will. He could talk on a plane with the experts in such diverse and intricate fields as American history and forest conservation."

Neuberger's daily regimen began at 7:30 A.M. with breakfast. By 8:30, he would be working in his study, where he typed on his latest project or gathered research until mid-afternoon. He read five newspapers daily and maintained correspondence with a wide range of political and journalistic associates. Neuberger always read manuscripts that were mailed to him by beginning writers, and offered constructive criticism.

In Portland's literary community, Neuberger and Stewart Holbrook were the reigning lions. A transplanted New Englander and former lumberjack, Holbrook was a generation older than Neuberger, and the author of more than thirty books. Less politically active than Neuberger, Holbrook was much less controversial. Despite his undisputed status as the dean of Northwestern writers, Holbrook viewed Neuberger as an up and coming rival. When New York publishing titans such as Alfred A. Knopf or Bennett Cerf were in Portland, it was a tradition that they dined with Neuberger and Holbrook on different nights. On a trip to the Northwest, Cerf signed Neuberger and Holbrook as authors for Random House's much-acclaimed Landmark Book Series, studies of American history for young readers. Both men were gifted writers. Holbrook wrote with more humor and a somewhat lighter touch than Neuberger. But Neuberger demonstrated a keener grasp of historical forces and his articles had greater political impact than Holbrook's. Neuberger envied Holbrook's productivity of best-selling books and hoped eventually to fill a shelf with his own books.

Neuberger, though, was becoming so entwined in Democratic politics that there was much less time for long-range writing projects. Elected to the Oregon State Senate in 1948, Neuberger began pushing for a revision of the state's outdated constitution. Working with former Governor Sprague, Neuberger helped defeat a loyalty oath for Oregon teachers that was a product of the McCarthy era. In 1950, Maurine was elected as the only woman member of the Oregon House of Representatives. "I decided," she said later, "that I might as well be speaking for my sex in the House of Representatives as knitting socks and sweaters while I watched Dick from the Senate gallery."

Dick Neuberger often said that his wife was the more popular member of their legislative team. Maurine rolled up her sleeves and got her legislative colleagues to repeal the ban on the sale of colored margarine by demonstrating on the House floor the difficulty imposed on housewives by having to mix food coloring with margarine. The men voted her down at first but public opinion rallied behind Maurine. With her husband, Maurine successfully fought to establish Portland State University, to improve the state's workmen's compensation laws, to further protect Oregon's wildlife and streams, and to strengthen civil rights laws. The Neubergers were more popular than the Democratic party. In 1952, they were the only candidates to receive more votes in Multnomah County than General Dwight D. Eisenhower. In writing about state politics, Neuberger chronicled their joint accomplishments, with the emphasis on Maurine.

As a keen student of political trends, Neuberger believed that the timing was right in 1954 for him to seek major political office. For the third time, Neuberger declined the opportunity to challenge a sitting Republican governor. Having served in the legislature, Neuberger knew the formidable powers of incumbency and name recognition held by a governor. Neuberger thought that it was within the realm of possibility that he could successfully challenge Senator Guy Cordon, a ten-year Republican incumbent, who was powerful in the corridors of Capitol Hill but was a shadowy figure to most Oregonians. Neuberger had been offered the Democratic nomination to oppose Cordon's bid for a second term in 1948 but had been doubtful whether he had the political credentials to win statewide office or that he could raise sufficient funds to make a credible race. By 1954, Neuberger had gained much confidence in his political skills and had built a strong political following. Neuberger portrayed Cordon as a looter of the public domain, the architect of the Eisenhower administration's resource policies that diminished the federal role in resource development and preservation and favored special private interests. He also ripped Cordon for his leadership in the Senate on the transfer of offshore oil rights from the federal government to the states, noting that the tax receipts would have benefited American education instead of the oil monopoly.

Shortly before Neuberger made his candidacy official, he conferred over a luncheon of Chinook salmon with *Harper's* editor Bernard De Voto, a noted conservationist and historian of the West. "We knew that I would confront the opposition of nearly all the press, of most of the campaign funds. My adversary was to be the incumbent senator, who had sponsored the surrender of the oil tidelands, the relinquishment of public grazing and timberlands and the yielding up of Hells Canyon."

After De Voto walked down the steps in front of Neuberger's house, he turned and ran back up to the porch. "Be of good cheer, my friend," De Voto told Neuberger. "The American people have never yet voted to abandon their natural resources when the issue was understood by them – and they never will. Everything's going to be all right. I'm just about sure of that."

Neuberger's message was powerful and compelling. To a remarkable degree, he succeeded in turning the 1954 Senate election into a referendum on the Eisenhower administration's controversial resource policies. An overconfident Cordon did not return to campaign until a month before the election. By then, it was apparent to the Republican high command that Cordon was on the ropes. President Eisenhower, Vice President Nixon, House Speaker Joseph Martin, and Interior Secretary Douglas McKay were among the Republican leaders who campaigned for Cordon. Their efforts reinforced Neuberger's arguments against Cordon. On election day, Neuberger scored what was considered the state's biggest political upset in a half century, and Maurine was reelected to the Oregon House by the largest vote ever cast for a legislative candidate.

In the Senate, Neuberger created a stir by attacking Nixon in his presence for his slashing campaign tactics in the 1954 midterm elections. He embarrassed Eisenhower by accusing the White House of trapping squirrels that had been digging up Ike's practice putting green. Neuberger tagged the Interior Secretary with the nickname of "Giveaway McKay" that led to his eventual political exile. The Oregon senator's efforts also prodded the Eisenhower administration to modify its resource and development policies.

Neuberger, midway through his term, made a choice to become a legislator rather than a personality in the Morse mold. For all of Morse's eloquence, he was not effective in representing home state constituencies. Neuberger's performance contrasted so sharply with Morse's that he gained immeasurably among independents and Republicans, while retaining his Democratic support. There was little doubt that Neuberger would have easily won a second term in 1960.

In his final bout with cancer, Neuberger inspired the nation and his state with his courage and resolve. He focused national attention on the disease that would kill him through articles such as "When I Learned I Had Cancer" and galvanized support for medical research. When Neuberger died on March 9, 1960, Senator Gruening arranged for a fitting tribute. A 6,749-foot peak in Alaska was named for Neuberger who had done so much to promote statehood. With the spirit and vision of a pioneer, Richard L. Neuberger was a man to match the mountains of the Pacific Northwest.

Richard Neuberger (left) and Steve Kahn (right) in Hells Canyon ca. 1936. Kahn, a college roommate of Neuberger's, collaborated with him on the book Integrity: The Life of George Norris, *published in 1938.*

JOURNALISM

The New Germany

The Nation, 4 OCTOBER 1933

This was Neuberger's first contribution to a national magazine, and it established his reputation as a journalist. *Time* magazine described Neuberger's firsthand report of Hitler's Germany as nothing less than a sensation. Leading American commentators had shown a remarkable insensitivity to Hitler's persecution of Jews and intellectuals. Walter Lippmann, who, like Neuberger, was of German-Jewish ancestry, had even suggested in the spring of 1933 that Hitler wasn't entirely at fault in his dealings with German Jews. Neuberger's article was a major corrective. Throughout his journalistic and political careers, Neuberger was a defender of human rights and civil liberties.

ISIT the New Germany," the American tourist reads in the advertising columns of Paris editions of American newspapers. Embellished with photographs of picturesque scenery and stately cathedrals, the advertisements strive to persuade the tourist that Hitler's "new Germany" is virtually identical with the old Germany of charm and *Gemütlichkeit*. That the advertising often appears in issues which carry front-page accounts of Nazi violence has been harmful but, surprisingly, not fatal to the purpose of the costly displays. Despite a falling off in the tourist trade, foreigners return home frequently with tales of the peace and contentment that prevail under the Nazis. They stay at the Hotel ———— in the larger cities and blandly report that "they saw no outrages," and pay tribute to the "new spirit" engendered by Hitler. Of this type is Mayor James M. Curley of Boston. It is more surprising, however, to find a supposed scholar like Dean Henry Wyman Holmes of the Harvard Graduate School of Education, who returned on September 10, reported by the Associated Press as saying: "I think the reports of Hitler's oppression of the Jews have been exaggerated. Some action may have been necessary"; "it is something Germany needed"; "Germany has regained self-respect." This noted educator, the author *inter alia* of "The Path of Learning," arrived at these conclusions, he admits, in France and "from talking with people on the voyage home" (aboard the German liner *Berlin*), and *without visiting Germany*.

For a week in Paris I listened to tourists who described Hitler's Germany in rosy colors. On questioning, however, I found that they had visited only the places featured in the advertisements. Not one had strayed to a town off the beaten track. I determined to make a different sort of trip to the "new Germany," and visit the hamlets and villages of the Black Forest and the Rhine country, places where Americans are not expected. The officials at the border were courteous. On the main streets of the large tourist centers I too saw no violence. Then I left the tourist highway and headed for a little village in the hills west of the Neckar River. I was thirty kilometers from the railway. Only a twisting automobile road penetrated the hills and forest surrounding it. The inn, at which I was the only guest, was run by an old Catholic woman. She was easily led into conversation and told me how her little business had been ruined by the Nazis. It was not difficult to make a person of her political misfortunes my ally, and I persuaded her to introduce me to other victims in the little community.

In a ramshackle house near the outskirts of the hamlet I met a distraught old woman. Two nights before, a troop of brown-shirted Hitlerites had taken away her two sons, partly because they were Jews, partly because their political affiliations had been with the Social Democrats. "Say goodby to your mother, you may never see her again," ordered the Nazi leader. For forty-eight hours she had waited for word of her sons. They were her only kin. She had spent all of a small life-insurance policy educating one for law, the other for medicine.

It was not in my power to console this frantic gray-haired widow, but I tried to find some trace of her boys. The search did not last long. The next day the two young men, whose "crimes" had been their race and their belief in a government for the majority of the people, were sent home – in plain board coffins. The Nazis asserted that the boys had died of tuberculosis, though neither had been ill when taken from his home. Their mother was compelled to sign a paper agreeing not to open the coffins; the undertaker and the rabbi had to collaborate in this promise. "Otherwise," admonished the Nazi chief, "we will dispose of the bodies ourselves."

But in that village was a young Jewish doctor, a war veteran, and one of the few undaunted victims of the Hitler persecution whom I met. Despite Hitler's promise to exempt Jewish ex-soldiers from discrimination, the young man's entire practice had been taken from him by the burgarmaster and he had been beaten up at the local "Brown House." But he was unafraid. He said to me: "I'll open those coffins if you will help me to get out of the country." I promised. (Today he is in France.) That night, by candlelight, he opened the oblong boxes. Every major bone in both bodies was broken. The flesh was terribly lacerated; the boys had suffered horribly before they died.

The next afternoon the young men were buried in the Jewish cemetery. Over their coffins the old rabbi, his beard blowing in the summer breeze, spoke a few words of praise. For the offense of eulogizing the two dead boys, the rabbi was beaten at the local Nazi headquarters, and the local newspaper – a mere bulletin – which printed some of his words, was suppressed for three months. The mother was sent to a sanitarium by the young physician, her mind clouded by the catastrophe. Thus I was introduced to the "new Germany," the Germany advertised as "less expensive, but otherwise unchanged."

After that I was better prepared for what I saw and heard. I saw new mounds in virtually every Jewish cemetery, marking the resting places of victims of "Nazi tuberculosis." Still hoping they can fool their own citizens and the rest of the world, the Hitlerites camouflage their murders. The victim either "committed suicide," "was shot while trying to escape," or "died from tuberculosis." Announcements are printed in the newspapers accordingly. Always the bereaved families are compelled to promise that they will not open the coffin.

Before I left that little town I met the families of two Jewish girls, both of whom had been smuggled across the border to a hospital in Switzerland. Their parents spoke in whispers of a night when the Nazis had come for the girls. They had been stripped and beaten and made to dance naked before their tormentors. Under the threat of death to themselves and their families, they had been compelled to accept the advances of their captors. The girls were only eighteen. In the morning their families found them, bleeding and senseless, in a meadow near the Brown House.

I put that town behind me like a bad dream. But it proved to be not exceptional. From there I went to Neckargemünd, a small community near the Neckar River.* I arrived on a Saturday afternoon, the Jewish Sabbath. At the home of the rabbi I found a portion of his small congregation. The hands of the men were swathed in bandages; the women were sobbing and crying. The rabbi told their story. During the services the Nazis had broken into the synagogue. They had thrown the Torah and other implements of the church into the street. The women they had ordered to clean the town hall, with the command, "It's about time you dirty Jews were doing some work." While the Jewish mothers and daughters scrubbed the floors on their hands and knees, the storm troopers stood over them and beat them with whips. The men underwent worse torture. At gun point they were lined up before the synagogue. Red flags, supposedly symbols of communism, were placed in their hands and set afire by the Hitler troopers. The flags burned down to their hands, but the men were not permitted to drop them until their fingers and knuckles

---

* In order to protect his informants the author has switched the names of the small towns mentioned in this article. – Editors THE NATION

were seared. One old man whose trembling hands dropped the burning rags was shot through the shoulder.

I stayed three days with those forlorn people. At night they sat in total darkness, trembling lest the Nazis come and inflict further punishment. By day they stayed in their homes, afraid to venture on the streets. Slowly they watched their savings dwindle, knowing the day would come they would no longer have money to buy food.

Next I went to Heidelberg. Surely, I thought, that citadel of German culture, the site of the famous university could not be the scene of such brutalities as we had witnessed in the Neckar country. The train was crowded with Brown Shirt troopers. The streets were dense with men in uniform. Every building flew the swastika flag. Even on the street cars Nazi banners fluttered. The occasion was the appearance that night of Dr. Alfred Rosenberg.[1] Britain had given him an icy reception, but he was a hero in Heidelberg. A vast throng jammed the amphitheater of the historic castle to hear him. Its howls of approval as he denounced democracy and urged purification of the Aryan race echoed along the cliffs below the ancient walls.

The next day I visited the university. The first thing apparent was that Heidelberg had gone "football" in a big way. All incentives to culture, intelligence, and independent thought had been removed. The laboratories, where experiments had enabled Otto Warburg, expelled for being a Jew, to discover the difference between cancer cells and normal epithelial cells, were deserted. But the dueling ring was not. Before Hitler ascended to the chancellorship dueling had been forbidden for several years at Heidelberg. Now it is the rage. Youths with fresh scars on their faces, courtplaster on their cheeks, and swastikas on their arms have replaced the thinkers and scientists to whom Heidelberg owes its reputation.

I also noted the paradox of the one new building at Heidelberg – the Robert Schurman lecture hall. It was built largely through the generosity of American Jews, but Jewish professors may not mount its rostrum. On the bronze plate which lists the donors are the names of such prominent American Jews as William Fox, Julius Rosenwald, Mortimer Schiff, Adolph Zukor, and Samuel Sachs. Also included is the name of William H. Woodin, secretary of the treasury.

I wanted a photograph of the plate and opened my kodak. Uniformed attendants wearing swastikas came running. "Kein Bild, kein Bild!" they cried. I was hustled from the building. A young Nazi with a bayonet at his side and a revolver in his belt forbade my reentrance.

In Heidelberg I talked with many brilliant scholars, most of them non-Jews. They deplored the havoc Hitler has wrought in the university and confided the fear that the once great school was ruined forever as a center of culture. One old man, a Socialist and liberal, raised his voice louder than the rest. For forty-four years an instructor, he had been dismissed summarily for his political views. "America must help us," he said. "This is not alone a fight of the Jews. It is the battle of everyone who believes in democracy and freedom. You will do a great service if you carry this message to the liberal and fearless men in your Congress." The old man continued to talk freely on the cause of democracy all the time I was in Heidelberg. When I left there I promised to help him obtain a visa for America. But it was not necessary. Three days later the Nazis invaded the professor's home at night. In the morning his wife found him at the foot of the stairs, his skull crushed in.

From Heidelberg I turned again to smaller communities. Everywhere I saw evidence of cruelty, violence, and death. At Landau a Catholic merchant and his Jewish secretary, whom he had refused to discharge after five years faithful service, were paraded through the streets. About the girl's neck was hung a sign, "I have been this man's Jewish prostitute for five years." In the same town three Jews and two non-Jewish Socialists were dragged from a cafe in the middle of the afternoon and beaten in an adjacent lot with whips of hose and steel cord. I saw their lacerated and torn backs. At Durkheim an old Jewish butcher from whom my friends occasionally purchased cold meat or sausage paid with his life for his refusal to obey a Nazi command to close his shop. One morning we found the store closed. The old man was in a hospital, bleeding from a score of wounds inflicted by clubs. His case was diagnosed on the chart as the result of a "fall downstairs." Three days later he died.

Hitler and his lieutenants must smile behind their hands when they watch tourists leave Germany with stories of the courtesy and fine manners of Nazi officials. In the August issue of *The National Geographic Magazine* Alicia O'Reardon Overbeck describes Freiburg as one of the most *gemütlich* cities of Germany because of the "friendliness of its people." In Baden Baden we met a score of refugees from this haven of peace and tranquillity. One of the refugees was a lawyer who had dared to say in public that the people should run the government. While he was away on a brief trip to plead a case, Nazis entered his home and sold at auctions all his possessions – his law library, his files, valuable art treasures, his furniture. He and his son protested; the latter was fatally wounded and the father had to flee to avoid arrest. He was at Baden Baden under an assumed name and with his appearance disguised. The others who had fled from Freiburg, the most gemütlich of cities because of the "friendliness of its people," were Jews, several of them schoolboys burned on the legs and feet. Their Nazi schoolmates had forced them to run through a bonfire of burning books!

It is difficult to comprehend how any tourist with the slightest knowledge of German can return from the Third Reich with praise for the Hitler dictatorship. Hitler's *Mein Kampf*, approximately 800 pages of the Chancellor's egotism and hatred, is on sale at all book-shops, available to visitors and citizens. Listen to this brief excerpt from its pages:

If the Jew wins ... his crown of victory is the death wreath of humanity, and this planet will again, as it did ages ago, float through the ether, bereft of man.... While I defend myself against the Jews, I fight for the work of the Lord.

The black-haired Jewish youth lies for hours in ambush, a devilish joy on his face, for the unsuspecting girl whom he pollutes with his blood and steals from her own race.... By every means he strives to wreck the racial basis of the nation ... He deliberately befouls women and girls ... it was and is the Jew who brought Negroes to the Rhine, brought them with the ... intent to destroy the white race ... by continual bastardization, to hurl it from the ... heights it has reached ... he deliberately seeks to lower the race level by corruption of the individual.

It is this book which has filled the vacancies left on the library shelves by the destruction of volumes by Heine, Thomas Mann, Remarque, Feuchtwanger, Einstein, Sinclair, and London. The Chancellor's unrelenting fanaticism is reflected in the cruelty of his followers. Not once in the score of small communities we visited did we see a Nazi show mercy or understanding toward the objects of his hate. Even small children are victims of the brutality. We saw one little Jewish girl come from school with a great welt on her forehead. Between sobs she told her mother that the son of a Nazi had hurled an inkwell at her, and the teacher, a man in S.A. uniform, had commended the act.

Horrible as these systematic persecutions are, there is another equally ominous aspect to the "new Germany." It is Hitler's obvious intent to lead the country into war sooner or later. He is converting Germany into a fortress bristling with hate and martial fervor. The saber rattles more loudly than under the Hohenzollern. In the parks and public squares one hears military bands and the tread of marching feet. The Nazi troopers are armed with bayonets and revolvers. They have official permission to carry firearms, a privilege denied to those they persecute. The children also are active participants in martial revival. In the foothill districts of Bavaria and Württemberg we saw boys – none of them more than fifteen years old – parading in review with wooden spears on their shoulders, and children of six practicing the throwing of hand grenades, crawling on their stomachs as to a trench attack.

Despite the contention of Walter Lippmann or any other erudite authority that Hitler's May peace address was sincere and "the authentic voice of a great people," no one who looks behind the barrier of censorship and deceit in Germany can doubt that one of the major premises of the Nazi movement is intense preparation for a war of aggression. I wish those who were deluded by Hitler's peace speech before the Reichstag could have been with me one afternoon on the train between Frankfurt and Munich and overheard a high officer in the Reichswehr talking to a friend:

"Yes, we're fooling the French and Poles all right. We're only supposed to have 100,000 men under arms according to the treaty, but we're training 250,000 new ones every three months. At my camp I command a squad of lawyers – the Chancellor now makes all new lawyers enter a training camp. Then we have the s.a. and the s.s. men and the Reichswehr. We'll have 2,000,000 in arms in another year, besides all the children we're teaching to fight for Germany. Then watch us conquer again."

It is the old story of "Deutschland Über Alles" but under worse auspices than before. No ingenious means for inflaming and arousing the people has been overlooked. In cabarets I heard the music of the "new Germany." The masterpieces of Strauss and Wagner have been subordinated to the Nazi marching song and filthy ditties denouncing the Jews. I saw the official Nazi propaganda film, "s.a. Mann Brand." Its appeal was based largely on military enthusiasm. Communists were portrayed as brutes who spent their time shooting down little children or lolling in luxurious apartments with scantily clad women. The villain was a Semitic-looking merchant who discharged his employees for trivial reasons, but was made to atone for his deed when Hitler came into power. But the Nazis – ah, they were pictured as the very flower of German manhood. Sir Lancelot in search of the Holy Grail could have appeared no more noble and courageous than the stalwart Apollos who portrayed Herr Hitler's gentle disciples.

Daily publications fan the fire of hatred and bitterness. In Nürnberg a notorious Jew-baiter named Julius Streicher publishes *Der Stürmer*, a newspaper devoted entirely to anti-Semitic propaganda. Every Jew who achieves prominence, among them such Americans as Governor Lehman of New York and Samuel Untermeyer, is denounced as a murderer and a criminal. Across the bottom of the paper each day is written in black inch-high type: "Die Juden sind unser Unglück!" (The Jews are our misfortune.) Frequent bulletins from Goebbels's office put more kindling on the funeral pyre of culture and tolerance.

Much else that I saw in the "new Germany" further substantiates the conclusion that those who believe in liberty are finished in Hitler's Reich. Jewish merchants, professional men, and humble workers and their families are facing slow starvation. Jewish children live in an atmosphere they cannot understand, in which they are persecuted by their schoolmates. Jewish families are afraid to venture on the streets; they have no protection, no rights. Jews are barred in many towns from the public swimming pools. Jewish athletes can belong to no sports clubs, which makes the German efforts to retain the 1936 Olympic Games in Berlin on the ground that there will be no discrimination, one more piece of hypocrisy. Socially and economically, as well as politically, the Jews have been ruined. Those who have not suffered physical violence are experiencing mental torture almost as severe.

The fate of those who sponsored the cause of the masses has been equally terrible. Labor-union officials, Socialists, and liberals have been murdered and their homes plundered. Under the guise of saving Germany from the Communists Hitler has crushed ruthlessly all "left" tendencies. He poses as the savior of the laboring man, but the staunchest advocates of the workers' rights have suffered most at his hands. Thus we see the "new Germany" as a land in which a racial and religious minority has been sacrificed on the altar of political expediency and intolerance, in which democracy and civil rights have been abolished, from which culture and independent thought have been expelled, which is preparing its children to be cannon fodder on the battlefields of a future war.

But ruthless and relentless as Hitler and his lieutenants are, there is one weapon they fear. The Nazi mayor of a large German town told me his party dreaded economic pressure. At pistol point the storm troopers have forced their victims to deny all stories of atrocities in an attempt to lessen the indignation abroad. They realize a tight international boycott can kill even the monster they have created. A boycott which shuts out German merchandise, reduces the passenger lists of German liners, and keeps tourists out of Germany can soon write an end to the most gruesome chapter of modern history by dethroning Hitler and Hitlerism.

This is not alone the battle of the Jews – I saw intellectuals, liberals, pacifists, Social Democrats, almost as badly off. It is the fight of everyone who believes in personal liberty and civil rights, a fight for the principles on which America was founded. For that reason it is depressing on returning to the free and wholesome air of America to find such a concern as R.H. Macy and Company, chiefly owned and operated by Jews, purchasing merchandise in Germany – because it is cheaper. One of the store's principal owners is Jesse I. Straus, American Ambassador to France, who ardently voiced his belief in democratic principles in an Independence Day address in Paris. Actions speak louder than words, however. The Strauses might better follow the example of their Christian competitor, Lord and Taylor, which recalled its buyers from Germany shortly after Hitler inaugurated his reign of terror, and regardless of price established the policy of not buying one pfennig's worth of Nazi goods.

Hells Canyon, The Biggest of All

Harper's, APRIL 1939

Neuberger was closely identified with the deepest gorge on earth, both as a writer and political figure. More than anyone else, it was Neuberger who gave the canyon its name. Until Neuberger began writing national articles about Hells Canyon, the gorge had also been known as Seven Devils Gorge, Box Canyon, and the Grand Canyon of the Snake. The Oregon Board of Geographic Names had battled the use of the name Hells Canyon for more than twenty years, but Neuberger's prolific writings about Hells Canyon made the name stick. Eventually, the board accepted the term. In the 1950s, Hells Canyon was a battle cry for public power, with Neuberger leading the charge against the Eisenhower administration, which favored private development of the Snake River's hydroelectric power. Fifteen years after Neuberger's death, Congress passed and President Gerald R. Ford signed the Hells Canyon National Recreation Area into law, fulfilling Neuberger's dream of preserving the spectacular gorge.

FOR NEARLY A CENTURY now it has been axiomatic that the Grand Canyon of the Colorado River is the deepest cleft on earth. That this is not true is a fact which geographers are just beginning to recognize. The Grand Canyon is not so deep as the basalt and granite gash made by the Snake River between the States of Oregon and Idaho in the Pacific Northwest. Along a mountain-serried stretch where the brawling waters of the Snake twist northward, Hells

Canyon averages 5,510 feet in depth for 40 spectacular miles. Here 6,000-foot expanses are not uncommon. At one point the canyon is 7,900 feet deep: a mile and a half from rim to river. This considerably exceeds the 6,100-foot maximum depth of the Grand Canyon.

The canyon hollowed out by the Colorado River is 217 miles long; that by the Snake River, 189 miles. The Grand Canyon is 15 miles from rim to rim at its widest point; Hells Canyon, 10 miles. The famous Bright Angel Point towers 5,650 feet above the Colorado; the bluff of White Monument, an equal horizontal distance from the Snake, is 5,922 feet higher than the river. In the Grand Canyon the Colorado River drops approximately ten feet a mile; the Snake in Hells Canyon descends about twelve and a half feet a mile.

Both chasms are built of many levels. These levels rise terracelike above the rivers. From the water only the first rims can be seen, but there are many rims beyond until the last embayments are reached.

Peculiar to the Grand Canyon are its lavish coloring and its array of buttes, mesas, rock temples, and flat-topped hills. The walls eroded by the Colorado are more or less uniform; they are long sheer cliffs approximately 1,500 feet high to the level directly above the river.

The Snake, however, is flanked by shale slides, then by timbered slopes, and finally by granite and lava precipices. Where Hells Canyon spreads out below Hat Point its sides consist of countless evergreen hills and bare basalt crags piled on top of one another in magnificent disordered array. A few miles downstream the scene changes sharply, and waterworn granite and basalt sweep down to the Snake in majestic stratified escarpments amazingly like the buttes that typify the Grand Canyon of the Colorado.

Dr. Otis W. Freeman of the American Geographical Society, one of many authorities who concede the greater depth of Hells Canyon, says that it is certainly "both the narrowest and the deepest gash in the North American continent." The Geological Survey has lately called attention to it as one of the great scenic resources of the nation. Why, then, has it been overlooked?

Only its remoteness and inaccessibility can account for the fact that Americans are almost completely unaware of its existence, that encyclopaedias and atlases and other sources of general information scarcely mention it, and that the thorough *Britannica* accords it only passing reference.

II

The name of this chasm is symbolic. The frontiersmen of years ago called it Hells Canyon because of its sinister splendor. Escarpments of granite rise from the river like gloomy battlements. On wet, windy days wraiths of clouds swirl and break around the jagged basalt crags far above. No gulf anywhere has rougher rock surfaces. Bluff is piled on bluff in huge torn chunks of black and gray lava. Sheer and rugged walls are interspersed with slides of shale and ragged hillsides of cheat-grass. Creeks tumbling down long gullies add their pittance to the river. The Snake surges an angry white through much of the abyss. At a dozen rapids its foam-topped waves are still wearing away the rock. "*La maudite rivière enragée!*" exclaimed the early French-Canadian voyagers, and the pioneers of the Oregon Trail paraphrased them in English: "The accursed mad river." Here and there in the canyon, hackberry bushes and ponderosa pines and Douglas firs, growing tenaciously on steep slopes and fringelike bars, provide contrast for the harsh bleakness of the precipices.

The sun's rays reach the waterway at the bottom of the chasm only a few hours each day, particularly in the winter months. The nocturnal tones of the cleft are broken only when sunlight softens the rim rock and the shadow from one bluff gently blankets the opposite wall. Then Hells Canyon seems filled with a thin blue haze; seen from afar up its craggy trench, it is like the background of one of the painted fantasies of Maxfield Parrish. In such interludes, brief though they are, the reaches of the mountain river show themselves clean and clear, and the canyon takes on enough color to lose some of the ominous aspect that in 1812 brought this quaintly worded report from Robert Stuart of the Pacific Fur Company to his chief, John Jacob Astor.

The whole body of the River does not exceed 40 yards in width and is confined between Precipices of astonishing height, Cas-

cades & Rapids succeed each other, almost without intermission,
and it will give a tolerable idea of its appearance were you to
suppose the River to have once flowed subterraneously through
these mountains, and in the process of time, immense bodies of
Rocks were detached occasionally from the ceiling till at length
the surface of the Heights descended into the Gulph and forms at
present the bed of this tumultuous water course. Mountains here
appear as if piled on Mountains and after ascending incessantly
for half a day, you seem as if no nearer the attainment of the
object in view than at the outset.

Hells Canyon has not the bright glory or magnificent mesas of the
cleft of the Colorado. Its grandeur is the majestic mystery of sheer
size. The bottom of the canyon is a pit of unbelievable depth. From
it the rim seems studded with tiny green bushes – until Forest Ranger
Fenton Whitney says they are ponderosa pines 100 feet high. Up the
side ravine dug by Deep Creek a wanderer with stout wind can climb,
after hours of terrific effort, to the top. The Snake, way below, is now
a slender strip of green; white flecks indicate rapids with waves as
high as breakers. Upward, rim succeeds rim to a horizon dim and far
off. The climber seems standing in the core of the world, like Astor's
courier of long ago who too made the heartbreaking ascent of
"mountain ... piled on mountain."
    Ages ago there was no Hells Canyon. The events directly respon-
sible for its creation began in the Cenozoic Era, just as the remote
forerunners of man were coming on the planet.
    Over the granite uplands of what is now the Pacific Northwest
poured the Tertiary lava flows. They inundated dales and valleys and
came to rest against peaks and ridges like water shoving at a dam.
The liquid basalt buried some hills completely. Much of the rugged
topography thus covered had been reared up in earlier epochs by vol-
canic activity. In numerous places the spread of lava was 6,000 feet
thick. Then, with more than a mile of basaltic rock quilting the land,
the crust of the earth began to stir again. The Wallowa Mountains
were jolted 10,000 feet into the sky near where the border of Oregon
now is. The Seven Devils range was wrinkled almost as high along

the present boundary of Idaho. After this rampant vulcanism, ice sheets moved out of the north and sheathed the region. They gouged out lakes and began U-shaped dips that would later be canyons. One of these dips was between the outlying ramparts of the Wallowas and Seven Devils. Then the ice melted and receded. Into the jumbled mass of granite and lava a river pushed, the Snake.

The river is still pushing today. A mile through the hardened lava flow the Snake has cut, and into a thousand feet of the granite bedrock besides. The foothills of the Wallowa Mountains lie along the western rim of the chasm. The steep slopes of the Seven Devils form the opposite wall.

A college friend of mine named Amos Burg is one of the few men who have risked going by boat through both Hells Canyon and the Grand Canyon. Some of his observations are significant. He says that to look up from either the Snake or the Colorado at the rim rock so far above makes one dizzy. Despite its murky and forbidding appearance as compared with the Grand Canyon's splurge of color, Burg calls Hells Canyon "a more hospitable abyss." This is primarily because of regional characteristics. The Grand Canyon is part of the arid Southwest. Its vegetation is negligible. No soil cloaks the rocks. The Colorado River is full of silt and sand and practically devoid of fish life. It carries a million tons of Dust Bowl sludge through the canyon each day.

The somber Hells Canyon, by contrast, is typical in many respects of the lush Pacific Northwest, although it is outside the rain belt of that fertile region. Trees dot the bars and upper slopes. There are trout and sturgeon in the Snake and occasionally even a giant Chinook salmon from the mouth of the Columbia 500 miles away. The defiles that merge with Hells Canyon are gloomy and narrow, but through them pour clear mountain creeks. Deer introduced artificially into the Grand Canyon frequently die; bighorn sheep and deer and elk lived in the chasm of the Snake before the white man came. So, paradoxically, the very qualities that give Hells Canyon its grim aspect actually make it more a land of the living than the gayly tinted canyon of the Colorado.

The Grand Canyon is cut through a desert plateau. That is why it is easy to get to and why the many rims of the canyon are as level as a railroad grade. Hells Canyon penetrates two mountain ranges. That is why it is difficult to reach and why its rims are irregularly broken.

III

The Snake River is the least-known major waterway of the continent. Millions of Americans have never heard of it, yet it is more than three times as long as the Hudson and its drainage area is eight times as great – including nearly all of Idaho and parts of Washington, Oregon, Wyoming, Utah, and Nevada. Only three rivers in the United States – the Columbia, the Colorado, and the Tennessee – excel it in hydroelectric power potentialities. Compare its 18,081,000,000 kilowatt-hours of latent energy with the 3,017,000,000 available in the Potomac River, for example. The Snake is 1,038 miles long and the principle tributary of the vast Columbia River system, which is second in the country only to the network formed by the Missouri and Mississippi.

The Snake is primarily a wilderness river, more so than any other stream in the nation. It drains our last great frontier. Its basin, though twice as large as the State of New York, contains considerably fewer people than the city of Buffalo. The biggest population center in the basin is Boise, the Idaho capital, with 21,500 inhabitants. There are about 4 persons per square mile in the Snake River basin; in Massachusetts each square mile has 528 persons, and even in rural Iowa there are 44. From its origin just west of the Continental Divide to its meeting with the Columbia, the Snake flows through a lonely hinterland.

After rising near Yellowstone National Park, it courses through Jackson Hole in Wyoming and then rushes toward Idaho in a chasm half a mile deep. The chasm bisects the Teton Range and is called the Grand Canyon of the Snake River – a name conferred by men who knew nothing of the infinitely greater canyon 600 miles downstream. Continuing into Idaho, the Snake cuts a wide valley for 65 miles and then flows on to the soil-mantled rock of the Snake River Plain. Here is one of the principle irrigated sections of America. Four million acres need only moisture to produce almost any crop. Two Federal

dams span the river and plenish the canals which crisscross the
120,000 acres of the Minidoka potato and beet-sugar project. This
important chore requires huge draughts of water, but the hard rock
underneath the reclaimed land returns to the river nearly all the water
used. So the Snake as it leaves its peaceful plain is at full force for
the grim business ahead.

It moves faster now. Into it pour the Thousand Springs, the outlet
of prehistoric creeks that got lost beneath the lava ages ago. These
subterranean streams constantly add to the Snake enough water to
provide each inhabitant of the nation's cities with 120 gallons a day.
At the hamlet of Milner the river begins a gorge through the basalt
plateau. By this time it is a chute of foam plunging over a succession
of cataracts and crashing down the 212 feet of Shoshone Falls. At
Huntington it touches the Oregon boundary. Here the outlying palisades of the Wallowas and Seven Devils begin to enclose the waterway. Passengers on the Union Pacific get a tantalizing glimpse of the
head of the canyon as its trains clatter across the Snake and use two
locomotives to climb out of that frowning terrain. Sixty miles down
the river from Huntington the practically deserted mining colony of
Homestead is the lone settlement along this wildest stretch of all. Below Homestead the ever-rising slopes straighten into the crags of
Hells Canyon. This is the river's supreme achievement.

Hells Canyon falls away near the Idaho town of Lewiston. There
the river, at last free of its granite and basalt shackles, flows westward across 141 miles of Washington wheatland. At its ending in the
Columbia it is a mighty waterway with a greater average flow than
the Colorado or the Rio Grande. The rivers meet about midway between the huge dams which the government is constructing on the
Columbia at Grand Coulee and Bonneville.

How little we know about this country of ours! No room for the
German refugees, we say almost categorically – yet the Federal government owns more than half the land of the vast State of Oregon.
Are the unemployed going to be on our backs forever? we ask in de-
spair – yet Grand Coulee Dam will make fertile a potential farming
section twice as large as Rhode Island. There is no place for the surplus population to find sanctuary, we lament – yet the National For-

ests alone in the Snake River Basin are as big as the whole State of Maine, and one rural county in Washington with a handful of inhabitants is as big as Delaware, Connecticut, and Rhode Island combined – and there are 10 people a square mile in Oregon and 6 in Idaho, against 537 in New Jersey and 214 in Pennsylvania!

White space on the United States census map means fewer than two persons a square mile. The only white space east of the Mississippi River is a tiny patch indicating the swampy Everglades of Florida. But white space almost predominates in the great basins which the Columbia and Snake Rivers have carved in the Pacific Northwest. In these pages not long ago, Carl Dreher wrote that the outpost regions, "always an avenue of escape" from the dilemmas of civilization, have been closed. Yet Congress recently authorized Secretary Ickes to open for settlement in the Far West five-acre tracts of public land equal in aggregate size to the State of Texas; and the Secretary has just quarreled with the Governor of Washington over whether a new National Park shall encompass a million or only 600,000 acres. Perhaps the frontier is gone as the force in our national development which Frederick Jackson Turner considered it – yet can we wholly forget that the wilderness is still so boundless that in it many of our geographers and encyclopaedists have lost track of the deepest canyon in America, if not on earth?

IV

Only once did the most famous exploration in American history ever turn back. That was when Lewis and Clark encountered the "miles of white water and snow-covered mountains" of the Salmon River Canyon, which enters the Snake in Hells Canyon. "This formidable barrier," as Captain Clark called it, proved too much for them. Wearily, they climbed out of the main tributary of the Snake and sought another route through the fastnesses. They finally reached the Snake itself near Lewiston and paddled down it to the Columbia. Hungry and exhausted, they sent Sergeant John Ordway up the river to look for fish and the roots of kouse plants. He was the first white man to see Hells Canyon. Meriwether Lewis, in that autumn of 1805, had been the first to see the river and Captain Clark named it for him. But today other rivers honor the explorer's name, and whether the Snake is named for the Snake Indians or because of its serpentine windings no one is certain.

Not so many years ago a hunter on the river unearthed the great frontiersman's branding-iron:

U.S.
Capt. M. LEWIS

John Jacob Astor corresponded with Jefferson and read the journals of Lewis and Clark. He decided that it might be profitable to own a string of trading posts between the Plains and the Far Northwest. The Pacific Fur Company was organized and Astor dispatched a ship, the *Tonquin*, to the mouth of the Columbia by sea. The principal party of 64 men he sent overland in 1811 under the leadership of Wilson Price Hunt, who was in charge of the venture in the field. This was the first push toward the sundown after Lewis and Clark. The trek was uneventful until the party stood on the banks of the Snake River. Against his better judgment, Hunt agreed to follow the churning waterway to the Columbia. It was a fatal blunder. Near the present village of Milner the expedition lost five canoes and its best voyager, Antoine Clappine. A Scotchman, saved by clutching at a rock, named this vortex the Caldron Linn, meaning boiling water.

The adventurers continued on foot. Uplands turned into mountains and the men were in Hells Canyon. The bluffs became so steep they could not get down to the river for water. They dropped kettles on ropes, an experiment which frequently failed. When they tried to follow the Snake, "it passed through such rocky chasms and under such steep precipices that they had to leave it and make their way, with excessive labor, over immense hills, almost impassable." It was a winter of famine, the Indians said, and the men were driven to munching on moccasins and beaver pelts. Once they were spared starvation only by a chance shot that killed a bighorn sheep. The Devil's Scuttle Hole they called a particularly ominous part of the cleft, and Ramsay Crooks, who years later became president of the American Fur Company, attempted to lead a handful of men over the wall of this dreadful place. After a day of slippery climbing the famished wayfarers "found they were not half way to the summit, and that mountain upon mountain lay piled beyond them in wintery desolation." They crawled back into the chasm.

A third of the way through Hells Canyon, Hunt disconsolately gave the order to turn back. He had lost two more members of the party and a third had gone mad. Others refused to brave the chasm any farther. Astor's hopes and plans never survived that ordeal. The morale of the expedition was gone. The men who eventually reached the Pacific Ocean in February of 1812 were not the confident voyagers who five months earlier had neared the Caldron Linn. Disaster capped disaster; the crew of the *Tonquin* was massacred by Indians and the stockaded settlement was finally abandoned. Today Astoria, at the mouth of the second greatest river of the United States, is a salmon-fishing colony.

For twenty years after Wilson Price Hunt's tragic journey no white men peered into Hells Canyon. Then westward trudged a romantic, vagabonding army officer in the fur trade, Captain Benjamin L.E. Bonneville, on whose possible secret military mission Bernard De Voto speculated some months ago in this magazine. It was characteristic of Bonneville that he wanted to find out for himself if Hells Canyon could not be made a route to the Columbia. Yet he confessed to trepidation when he saw the Snake twisting between "tremendous walls of basaltic rock that rose perpendicularly from the water edge, frowning in bleak and gloomy grandeur." Two horses stumbled in swift eddies and were swept away; the riders saved themselves by grabbing hold of rocks. The cliffs loomed higher and steeper, in places overhanging the river. At last Bonneville, like Ramsay Crooks before him, tried to climb over the walls, and after ascending to what appeared to be the summit, "found the path closed by insurmountable barriers." Daylight showed Bonneville and his followers that "although already at a great elevation, they were only as yet upon the shoulder of the mountains." For the first time in his life the soldier of fortune admitted discouragement. He led the way back into the gulf in search of another exit.

A week of struggle and effort eventually got the party out of the canyon. As he sat on the last rim and looked down on the Snake far below and remembered four years of wandering across the nation, Bonneville wrote in his journal:

> The grandeur and originality of the views presented on every side beggar both the pencil and the pen. Nothing we had ever gazed upon in any other region could for a moment compare in wild majesty and impressive sternness, with the series of scenes which here at every turn astonished our senses and filled us with awe.

That was the end of Hells Canyon as a way to the rich valleys of the Oregon Country. The oncoming settlers shunned it, and the covered wagon trains forded the Snake above Huntington and creaked away from the Wallowas and the Seven Devils. A few bold pioneers traveled to the head of the canyon but none attempted to pick a trail through its depths. Some called the cleft Box Canyon and others referred to it as the Seven Devils Gorge, but mostly they spoke of it as Hells Canyon and agreed that the name was appropriate.

v

A century has passed since the days of Bonneville, yet the canyon of the Snake River is still remote and difficult of access.

Only about 175 people live in the hinterland between Homestead and Lewiston. Some of these are ranchers back in lonely draws in the hills. Others are cowpunchers with scattered herds of cattle to watch. Along the river itself a prospector here and there sifts the gravel bars for gold which Mr. Roosevelt's government will buy at thirty-five dollars an ounce. On narrow flats in the upper canyon an occasional dilapidated barn or gaunt cabin tells where a settler retreated before so hostile an environment.

Some of the backwoods inhabitants have radio sets operated by batteries, but it is 100 miles to the nearest doctor and as far to a store bigger than the two-by-four tobacco-and-bean counter which Bill Rolfing keeps in the post office at Homestead. A sure-footed pony can cut down the distance. The WPA Guide for Idaho blames the inaccessibility of the section for the fact that the Seven Devils range, "potentially one of the richest mineral regions in the world," has yet to be tapped for its resources.

There is no railroad. About a decade ago the people of Lewiston began clamoring for rail connections with the lower part of the State. Why not a line through Hells Canyon? The Union Pacific made a survey and learned that a right-of-way, if it could be hewed out of the rock at all and maintained between avalanches from above and sudden rises in the river from below, would cost $198,434 a mile. This initial investment was prohibitive, decided the Interstate Commerce Commission.

If there are no rail lines, automobile roads are not much better. Down the Oregon bank to Homestead a careful driver can get, and even a few miles farther on a narrow road to the abandoned Red Ledge Mine. Over the Idaho wall opposite Homestead a spine-tingling road creeps. It is wide enough for one car, there is no railing. In several places where it is 2,000 feet above the river the road switches back sharply; the motorist must reverse a few feet to make the turns, with his gasoline tank and spare tire hanging out over space. This is not a pleasant drive.

Other methods of getting about are similarly circumscribed. The region is without level tracts that might serve as airplane landing fields. "Never again!" swore the World War aviator who in 1927 flew the length of Hells Canyon taking aerial photographs for the Union Pacific.

River travel is equally hazardous. Under favorable water conditions a pair of experienced boatmen, Press Brewrink and "Cap" MacFarlane, can coax their flat-bottomed *Idaho* 95 miles upstream from Lewiston. There, beneath slopes more than a mile high, the rocks block further navigation. On a sandy bar the *Idaho* unloads its cargo of mail and supplies for prospectors and settlers and scoots back to civilization. Other rivermen have not attained this comparative success. Several boats have been lost in the Snake in recent months. Amos Burg twice had his canoe sloshed out from under him on his trip through the chasm. Two engineers drowned when a railroad survey was made. The Salmon River, also in a cleft deeper than the Grand Canyon, is even more unmanageable. It is called "The

River of No Return" because of the impossibility of bucking its current. A National Geographic Society expedition termed it "the wildest boat ride in America."

Even on foot this wilderness is traversed with difficulty. Listen to the leader of the railroad survey as he testifies before the Interstate Commerce Commission: "Little that is good and much that is bad can be said of the river and ravine trails. For the most part they are extremely narrow, winding, difficult, steep, and ill-kept."

A hundred years earlier Wilson Price Hunt had told Washington Irving almost the same thing about the Indian paths. That suggests how superficially time has touched Hells Canyon. This remarkable abyss is virtually unknown even to people living comparatively nearby. Sixty miles away at the Cornucopia Gold Mine, the girl who kept books said she had heard vague talk of a great chasm beyond the Wallowas. Had she ever been there? She shook her head. Had any of the men at the mine? She knew of none.

All over the Northwest the story is the same. In the Oregon town of Baker, 105 miles from the canyon, the men playing cards in the biggest poolhall in town had scarcely any better idea where it was. And, buying post cards in a Baker drugstore, another newspaperman and I assumed heroic stature in the clerk's estimation when with proper modesty we admitted to him that our tattered appearance was the result of a trek to Hells Canyon.

This wilderness has a folklore all its own. There is the yarn of the Squaw Creek hermit who fed his chickens on flour and water until they were blinded by paste – and the fable of the deer on Studhorse Creek that knew so little about men that a hunter could measure them with a tape before shooting.

And in Homestead Bill Rolfing told me about the "wheelbarrow woman." A middle-aged woman had come down the rutted road from Huntington lugging a massive bundle. She had set it down in the dust and gone back up the road for another just like it. That was more than Bill could stand. He resurrected a rusty wheelbarrow from his cellar and presented it to her. She disappeared in the fastnesses on the Oregon shore.

Twelve miles down the Snake from Homestead, forest Ranger

Robert Harper pointed across the river. On a sloping bench of Hells Canyon a cabin perched precariously: "Who lives there?" I asked. Harper pointed again. Across an open space on the bench – I swear it! – a woman pushed a loaded wheelbarrow. After that I was ready to believe the story about the prospector in the Salmon River Canyon who had conferred with Captain Meriwether Lewis the night before election and been advised to vote a straight Democratic ticket!

How *do* these people vote? The Smith Mountain precinct in Oregon gave 22 votes to President Roosevelt, three to Mr. Landon, one to Mr. Lemke, and none to Mr. Thomas. It voted for a public power bill 10 to 8, and endorsed the Townsend Plan 11 to 6. Although overwhelmingly for the President, it inconsistently approved 12 to 2 an anti-labor initiative measure which the A.F. of L. claimed would destroy trade unions in the State. At the Iron Dyke precinct in Homestead, with a smattering of labor sentiment left over from the bygone mining days, sentiment for Mr. Roosevelt was about the same; but the public-power scheme and the Townsend Plan were voted down and opinion on the anti-union bill was equally divided. Across the canyon in Idaho the backwoods voters of the Cuprum precinct favored the President over the Governor of Kansas 33 to 8, and gave Senator Borah a 5-to-2 majority over his Democratic opponent.

Foreign affairs are not discussed with particular zeal by these people. After all, the dark pit below White Monument seems a long way from Seattle and Portland and Salt Lake City, let alone Berlin and London and Shanghai. I would not like to be the recruiting officer who has to convince Herb Potsch that he must sail for Europe to defend his canyon shack on Deep Creek from fascist aggression.

Yet perhaps the dwellers in the hinterland are not so different. As Fenton Whitney and I walked down toward the Snake at night, a radio blared loudly in one of the four or five farmhouses in Homestead. We listened. From New York City over a national hookup a synthetic cowboy was singing "Home on the Range."

VI

As soon as winter relaxes its grip on Hells Canyon the National Park service will begin an investigation of the region. Should the canyon and the adjacent territory be added to the nation's public parks? If the report of the service is favorable Senator McNary of Oregon will sponsor a bill in Congress. Borah may help him. Both these men are ardent conservationists and both are extremely influential. McNary is the Republican spokesman. They may have the assistance of the President, for Mr. Roosevelt likes the hinterland.

But should Hells Canyon be a National Park? Why not leave this bit of unknown scenic splendor for those willing to be incommoded to see it? Who wants it cluttered up with professional tourists, tired business men, junketing politicians, knickknack peddlers, and glamour girls and boys? Surely it merits a happier fate than that. The acquisitive instinct is powerful, but Bill Rolfing assured me emphatically that he has no desire to turn his country store into a tourists' hotel. Idaho has Sun Valley; Oregon has the sumptuous Timberline Lodge which Mr. Hopkins' WPA built for the wealthy; let these resorts take care of the dude ranchers and the sightseers and the Tyrolean-clad ski artists. Why not leave the Snake River and its chasm for those who would see the West almost as it was when Lewis and Clark arrived? The Forest Service has just set aside 223,000 acres on Eagle Cap above the Canyon as a primitive area to be untouched by man; only enough trails for forest fire protection will invade it.

Eventually, to be sure, Hells Canyon will probably be a National Park. There is something to be said for the argument that America's natural wonders should be available to everyone. I have a hunch, however, that the forthcoming report this summer may be adverse. Railroad connections are 50 or 60 miles away over rugged terrain, and adequate highways would require generous chunks of public money. Washington is not in a spending mood right now unless the spending pertains to national defense; and Hitler can hardly be said to have Freeze-out Saddle as his next objective.

For awhile, at least, Hells Canyon will probably remain a sort of American Erehwon, tucked away beyond the ranges. Yet what a paradox this is! The palisades of the Hudson, the Virginia Natural Bridge, a dozen other scenic centers would be only rock deformations down there among that dark conglomeration of bluffs and crags and hills and mountains. From the last rim the Snake looks like a rivulet, like the river one sees on a panoramic map made from an airplane flying high. How could the nation have overlooked this mighty cleft, particularly when it was discovered and explored at so great a price in suffering? Down there is where the frontiersmen struggled and froze and starved and turned back. And down there the champing waterway is still at work on its job of erosion.

On windless days the only sound from Hells Canyon is the roar, faint and far off, of the mountain river, gnawing at the rocks the earth spewed up long ago.

The Columbia

Holiday, JUNE 1949

The Great River of the West was a dominant theme of Neuberger's
writings. Neuberger had a lifelong passion for the Columbia, which he
listed as the top of what he liked about America. As a reporter, he covered
the construction of the great New Deal-era dams, Bonneville and Grand
Coulee, that harnessed the mighty river's hydroelectric power and transformed barren landscape into fertile farmland. Although the early
opposition from the private utility monopoly is forgotten a half century
later, Neuberger was a strong voice for public power. He was also a leader
in the movement to protect the Columbia Gorge, and his wife Maurine
has maintained their tradition as a prominent advocate for the Friends of
the Columbia Gorge. There have been numerous changes along the
Columbia since Neuberger's mid-century report. The Hanford atomic
plant, no longer a novelty, is a matter of much controversy in Washington
State. In February of 1988, the decision was made to shut down Hanford.
The controversy continues over what to do about the nuclear waste
materials.

A MUSTACHED LITTLE ENGLISHMAN stood hip-deep in a
snow-fed tributary which foamed into the Columbia River.
Working his rod and reel, he filled his creel with salmon.
Later he wrote of his experience:
"I have lived! The American Continent may now sink under the

sea, for I have taken the best that it yields, and the best was neither dollars, love nor real estate."

Rudyard Kipling's enthusiastic outburst was inspired, perhaps, only by the fighting fish. But more likely it was the atmosphere of the Columbia – the distant snow-capped peaks, the nearer hills luxuriant with Douglas fir, the canneries and sawmills peeking from the verdure, the immensity of the ponderous torrent that begins in the Canadian sub-Arctic and ends in the blue Pacific.

Only two or three generations of settlers had been living along the Columbia when Kipling saw it. Less than a hundred years had passed since the Yankee skipper, Robert Gray, sailed up the timbered mouth in 1792, to identify the deluge as a river for the first time and name it for his good ship *Columbia*. Even today the expedition of Lewis and Clark, the first white men to paddle downstream on the Great River of the West, seems hardly remote in time. True, the crude logs of Fort Clatsop, where the explorers spent the historic winter of 1805–1806, have vanished; and archaeologists are already prodding the soggy ground for traces of the wilderness structure. But the Columbia as the last major waterway discovered and developed in the United States, remains our youngest river. It is one of our last frontiers, still in the dawn of its impact on civilization.

Nowhere else in the nation do backwoods and metropolis mingle so promiscuously as along the Columbia. The great fortress of Grand Coulee Dam stands athwart the river in the heart of Washington State's Inland Empire. Its thundering waterfall approaches Niagara in volume; its lofty battlement could hold four *Queen Marys* stern to bow. Yet this mightiest source of hydroelectricity on the planet made its first delivery of power not to one of the new aluminum plants sprawling at tidewater but to Ernestine Nanamkin, a squaw from the Nespelem Indian Agency, who had purchased a washing machine just for the occasion.

This titan among United States rivers, second only to the Mississippi in volume, locks within its watershed 42 percent of the nation's potential hydroelectric power. It drains an area of 259,000 square miles, and totes down to the sea more water than all the other rivers of our Western seaboard combined. To tame the wild torrent and put it to work, President Truman early this year called for a Columbia Valley Authority.

The organization would be similar to TVA, but different in one vital respect. When all the proposed dams are built on the Columbia and its major tributaries, they will be capable of generating 33,000,000 kilowatts, or roughly half as much electric energy as is produced by all our present sources.

Physically and economically, the Columbia dominates the vast American Northwest. Though high mountains wall off the Pacific seaports from inland cities, the Columbia Gorge, a twenty-mile slot carved through the lofty barricade, provides the only water-level outlet for the agricultural, mining and timber riches of the interior. Where land is fertile but climate arid, the Columbia alone offers hope of irrigating immense basins now claimed by sagebrush. In an area with no oil wells and only a few thin veins of coal, its waters are the sole source of energy for lighting cities, running factories and mechanizing farms.

Along the 1,214 miles of its flow, the Columbia is many rivers in one. Crammed between granite walls, it becomes a hissing dragon like the Colorado. As it flattens out in the lowlands, it is a turgid replica of the Mississippi. Where it twists through the gaunt plateau of Eastern Washington, it takes the shape of a Yangtze bisecting an inland desert. In the neighborhood of the damp Pacific, spattered with 100 inches of rainfall blown from the Aleutians, the Columbia is a massive Amazon, flowing between banks matted with green foliage.

In places the Columbia trills and splashes merrily, its clear waters revealing trout and salmon against the scrubbed gravel of the river bottom. Elsewhere, many fathoms deep, it will foam over a steep slant with a sinister roar, as if the lanyards of a hundred cannon were being pulled at once.

For those who are brought up beside it, the Columbia holds a fascination that is seldom shaken off. Justice William O. Douglas, a son of the Northwest who sits on the United States Supreme Court, returns loyally every summer to Oregon's Wallowa Mountains, where he and his wife make their home in a cabin of tamarack logs above the Columbia. "It has become awfully important to me," he explained recently, "to spend some time in the Columbia Basin each year. President Roosevelt once told me that whenever he was able to come to the Northwest he felt like Antaeus, the mythical giant who gained strength by touching the ground. I think I feel that way when I see the Columbia River."

There is also a strange finality about the Columbia. Where it flows between Oregon and Washington, it serves not only as a boundary but as a barrier between two kinds of landscape and two ways of thinking. Oregon is more pastoral, more Arcadian; dairy herds dot its green meadows, barns and silos are its hallmarks. Washington has more smokestacks, more railroad sidings and 700,000 more people in spite of its lesser area. Oregon seems satisfied with its frontier fringe along the Columbia; Washington, across the river, yearns for greater industrialization.

While public ownership of the river's power burgeons in Washington, it languishes in Oregon. Electricity from the same generators at Bonneville is sold through a co-op in Washington but by a private company in Oregon. When transmission lines were strung on steel towers rooted in the Columbia's cliffs, men in Washington bought electrical appliances and waited for the juice. Minnie Yandle, wife of a Washington stump rancher, wrote an ebullient poem titled *There's Power at the Dam*, which the late Sen. George Norris included in the *Congressional Record*. But Oregon's people are wary of the endless kilowatts humming out on the wires. They know that power means factories, and factories mean boisterous cities, and they are not at all sure that these things are desirable.

Washington has been predominantly Democratic since 1900, while Oregon, only the width of a channel away, is as Republican as its neighbor is not. At the polls last November, Washington gave Truman a margin of well over 80,000 votes, but Oregon stood alone among the eleven states west of the Continental Divide in going Republican. The split was equally sharp in other issues. Washington's voters expressed a clear desire to legalize the sale of liquor by the drink, but the people of Oregon refused to allow such things as highballs and daiquiris to be consumed in public places.

The cleavage can be traced to the opposing philosophies brought in by early settlers. Washington attracted Swedes and Norwegians, rugged loggers and fishermen with a background of co-operatives and public ownership. The fields of Oregon were planted to wheat and orchards by self-reliant individualists from New England and Iowa. The two groups might have mingled, but both were stopped by the Columbia. Always too deep and too swift to ford, the river kept the two streams of Northwest development in separate flumes until each had formed its own pattern.

As a boat enters the Columbia from the sea, the river itself claims more attention than the cultures it divides. The brackish entrance is dotted with trawlers dragging gill nets to harvest the Columbia's fabulous salmon crop. One of the biggest reapers is Nick Bez, a Yugoslav whose fortune totaled $1.50 when he landed in New York in 1910. His Columbia River Packers Association netted $1,123,428 in a single recent year, and the burly salmon tycoon had won the distinction of rowing the boat in which his good friend, Harry Truman, went fishing in Puget Sound.

Most of Bez's fishermen are recruited from the Finnish colony at Astoria, the last town on the river's course. The Finns are on the clannish side, clinging to the language of the old country and preferring their dried-cod lutefisk to the flaky pink meat of the Chinooks they drag in from the Columbia. On the other hand, they have made Astoria famous in the Northwest for statuesque blondes who win beauty contests and for tireless basketball squads which run opponents off their feet.

Upstream from Astoria, Tongue Point flicks out its long bulwark into the river. This is the wooded promontory named by Capt. George Vancouver in 1792, when he spied it from the deck of His Majesty's sloop *Discovery*. Today a vast moth-ball fleet rides at anchor behind the ancient landmark – Liberty ships, aircraft carriers, tankers, hospital ships and destroyers, all left over from modern war. The steel vessels are lined up hull to hull, like cigars in a box, seeming somehow incongruous in a wilderness river where herons wade in the shallows and fishhawks swoop overhead. But the Navy has not forgotten that Japanese submarines shelled Fort Stevens, at the mouth of the Columbia, in 1942, nor that this storm-lashed jetty lies only 2,700 miles from Soviet soil.

Beyond the swaddled naval vessels the river surges sluggishly through fertile lowlands. This is the Columbia's mildest, most meandering interlude, where grass reaches to a cow's belly, and Douglas fir, the Northwest's great tree, crowns the hills. The current is lazy, and salt clings to the water's taste. Rainfall and overcast rule the weather. The damp hills are streaked with tributaries. Canneries perch on the steep banks. Farms and dairies are scattered among the sawmills and logging camps. Cigar-shaped rafts of logs float to the mill docks, towed by straining tugs. The river muffles the screech of saws as timber giants are turned into planks and shingles.

Here the "bull cook," down from a logging camp, stands beside a rusty branch line of the S.P.&S. in his yellow slicker and rubber shoepacks. He is not the chef but the chore boy, waiting for the mail and two dozen copies of the *Oregonian*. As the train rattles by, the package comes flying out of the express car. It lands neatly in his wheelbarrow, and the boy takes off with it through the dripping woods to the bunkhouse. The Columbia's bunkhouses, incidentally, are clean these days, and the lumberjacks no longer subsist on greasy salt pork and johnnycake. Breakfast still comes at six A.M. but the loggers sit down to two or three kinds of fruit, ham and eggs with hashed browns, toast and biscuits and quantities of coffee "strong enough to float a steel cable." In the Scandinavian mills on the Washington shore, the meal will probably be crowned with ample helpings of Danish pastry.

The Columbia still lingers uncertainly between backwoods and pavements in this stretch, its wilderness status not seriously changed. Compared to the Mississippi, the Missouri or the Hudson, it carries a mere cockleshell of water traffic. In two average months the Mississippi teems with more tonnage than the Columbia receives in a year. Yet a change is clearly on the way. More than 3,000,000 tons of cargo ascended the Columbia in 1938, and this figure was doubled in the decade that followed.

The main ingredient in the change is power – the incredible electric wealth of the Columbia. The town of Longview, Washington, spotted where the river narrows perceptibly, has been rejuvenated by this force. Founded twenty-six years ago as a model lumber town, it faced an ever slimmer future as its forest resources went down before the ax. Now, thanks to huge loads of current created by the river, an aluminum plant keeps the townspeople busy turning out 5,000,000 pounds of the strategic metal per month.

Thirty-nine miles upstream, where Vancouver hugs the north shore, an even larger plant adds 14,000,000 pounds a month to the amount produced on the Columbia, which comes to nearly half the nation's supply. Yet when President Roosevelt issued his call for "fifty thousand planes a year," not an ounce of aluminum was manufactured west of the Mississippi.

Across the river from Vancouver lies Portland, another changeling of the past decade. The Oregon metropolis, which once lay idyllically relaxed along the lower Willamette, grew turbulent with shipbuilding during the war. Industrial workers streamed in, swelling the city till it reached the brink of the Columbia at the suburb of Vanport. And when the war ended, many of them stayed. When the big river, heaving with the runoff from record snowfalls last year, clawed through Vanport's dikes and crushed its temporary houses to kindling, the refugees remade their home in trailer camps, still in sight of the Columbia.

Such loyalty can be partly accounted for by the "eternal fascination" of the river. Portland's gracious ways, too, must have attracted many transient workers to become residents. But the most realistic explanation lies in the wires strung down from the Columbia Gorge, forty miles upstream, where the piers of Bonneville Dam set their massive shoulders against the torrent. Here man has built the world's highest lift locks, which can raise a ship sixty-six feet to admit it to the waters below. Here man and the river generate 518,400 kilowatts – a stupendous charge which promises industrial jobs and fat pay envelopes.

Between Portland and Bonneville, the river runs a scenic course. The cloudy domes of Rainier, Adams, St. Helens and Hood squat on the horizon like hooded goblins at a council fire. Waterfalls tumble in slender white Corinithian columns from the Oregon crags. The pulse of the distant tide is feeble now, and the current swifter. Its waters combine, as Henry Villard, builder of the Northern Pacific, observed, "the characteristics of a brook with the volume of a flood."

Beyond the dam and the basalt gorge through the Cascades, a subtle transformation overtakes the Columbia. The railroad tracks, hidden for miles in a dense cloak of foliage, come gleaming into view on both banks. The underbrush thins out and disappears. No more Douglas fir mantles the bluffs. The ominous gray overcast of the seaboard gives way to harmless white streamers, and presently the streamers vanish in a sky of dazzling blue. The rainfall spawned in the Aleutians cannot cross the mountains. The Columbia has breasted the Cascades, and the climate has changed.

In its new environment the river flows past the town of Hood River, Oregon, which is being developed into a Salzburg of the Northwest by its 3,500 music-minded residents. Last August they launched an annual music festival with four days of big-time programs, the talent being provided by some 400 enthusiasts of the mid-Columbia regions, topped off with visiting artists like Ezio Pinza. The spark came from Boris Sirpo, a Finnish conductor stranded in Portland by the war. He found the Northwest had abundant room in which to wave his baton, and now Hood Riverites pay out more cash per capita than Portlanders for music of the "good" variety. In planning concerts, Sirpo's rule is firm: "No woogie-boogie."

Above Hood River the Columbia blocks navigation with a stormy stretch of narrows and rapids. Upstream traffic ends abruptly at The Dalles, on the Oregon side, where the river roars through a narrow chute with terrifying speed. The rough channel begins at Celilo Falls, eight miles above, where Indians still pull salmon from the churning waters with spears and dip nets, as their ancestors were doing when Lewis and Clark came by. The white men who followed, intent on opening avenues of trade, by-passed the bad spot, first with a portage railroad and later, in 1915, with a canal. Now they propose to build a taller dam than Bonneville at The Dalles.

The river becomes a wide green belly of water beyond Celilo. Sunlight bathes rounded hills and bare rocks. Days are hot but the general run of summer nights is bearable, and the mild climate helps anchor people to the region. One of its most devoted residents spent many years insisting that this strip of riverbank was one of the most healthful spots on earth, blessed with something to be called "air flow" and life-giving winds.

The enthusiast was Samuel B. Hill, son-in-law of the man who built the Great Northern Railroad. Sam Hill, besides being a millionaire and an advocate of good highways, was an intense admirer of Marie of Rumania. His enthusiasm for the queen and the Columbia was combined into a single gesture in 1926, when he converted Maryhill, his home, into a museum and had Her Majesty pronounce the dedication. Sam Hill, who felt a man might live forever in this region, passed away five years later. Maryhill still squats on the arid Washington shore, its garish Byzantine furniture symbolizing a bygone Balkan kingdom that is half a planet removed from the water and rock and sky of the Columbia.

Some 250 miles from the Columbia's mouth, the river bed abandons its prevailing east-west course to veer sharply northward. As a boat rounds the bend and moves up the narrrowing channel, the $347,000,000 Hanford plant rises from the sagebrush like a desert fort. This is the cradle of Plutonium 239 – the establishment which is absorbing one fifth of the Atomic Energy Commission's funds – and here the Columbia plays a dual role. Upstream at Grand Coulee, its thaw-born waters charge 230,000-volt transmission lines to Hanford, providing the tremendous energy required to break up uranium into other radioactive elements. The same waters, reaching Hanford a day or so later, absorb the heat generated by the huge chain-reaction machines, which turn out several pounds of deadly plutonium each day.

In the vast upland fastnesses of the Columbia, the men who work at Hanford are a group apart. They dwell in the nearby towns of Kennewick, Pasco and Richland, all in Washington, but their neighbors know as little as their families about the jobs they handle. Tilling the soil and felling trees are undertakings in the Columbia's tradition, which the old-line residents can understand and talk about. But the mysterious doings at "The Works," as it is called by scientists and laborers alike, are something alien to the land. Even today, four years after nuclear fission performed its first devastating miracle, store-keepers in the Hanford area look with a certain awe on customers wearing Hanford badges.

Grand Coulee Dam bestrides the river half-way along its plunge to the sea from the glacier-gouged peaks of Canada. The concrete be-hemoth, weighing twice as much as the entire United States popula-tion, impounds the rushing waters to form Lake Roosevelt, which stretches clear to the edge of Canada, 151 miles away.

Thus deepened and slowed down, the Columbia allows ships to cross the border northward and sail another 200 miles to Revelstoke, B.C. Yet the dam controls the level of the lake so delicately the backed-up waters never surge into the Canadian territory. When the river flow turns heavy, Grand Coulee's engineers simply open the 500-ton drum gates on the crest, and the excess goes tumbling over the spillway.

The Columbia does its heavy work deep inside the dam, close to the thirty-acre plot of riverbed the structure stands on. The torrent, entering through submerged intakes on the upstream side, spins the largest turbines in the world. Above the turbines, safely over the downstream level of the river, giant generators raise their high-pitched wail. Needles swing obediently across their dials, reporting how much of Grand Coulee's potential of 1,944,000 kilowatts is being delivered to the Columbia Basin. The enormous powerhouse already has a record of flashing out more than 15,000,000,000 kilo-watt-hours during the war, a fund of energy that could be matched, in terms of human labor, only if a million men worked eight hours a day for seventy-eight years.

The most spectacular of the Columbia's blessings will come from the Grand Coulee itself, the dried-up river bed which gives the dam its name. The ancient channel has been sealed off by separate dams, erected twenty-seven miles apart, and turned into a mammoth stor-age tank, pumped full from the Columbia's copious supply. Its con-tents will be fed out across the gaunt mesas of the Big Bend country, irrigating more than a million acres of wasteland. Eventually this acreage will grow a wealth of grain and produce. It will feed, according to estimates by agricultural experts of the Department of the Interior, 307,000 dairy cattle, 190,000 sheep, 40,000 beef cattle, 70,000 horses, 350,000 feeder lambs, 180,000 hogs, 200,000 turkeys and 2,000,000 chickens. When in full swing, the Columbia Basin Project will wrest 17,000 fertile farms from the desert and provide 80,000 farming folk with a productive livelihood. At least 170,000 others, according to the u.s. Bureau of Reclamation, will be needed in nearby towns to run shops and newspapers, give legal counsel or medical care or haircuts, and furnish the myriad services required by the burgeoning new civilization.

All this is progress, certainly, but progress begets problems, and the Columbia has not been spared. Old-timers in Oregon still mourn the recent day when no factory windows looked out across the river, and a man might slake his thirst at the water's edge without fear of typhoid or dysentery. Factories, they claim, mean not only pay rolls but also slums and racial prejudices and potential relief rosters.

Whether this yearning for yesterday can hold back tomorrow is dubious, yet backward-looking sentiment is strong along the river. President Roosevelt voiced the feeling as early as 1937, when he dedicated Bonneville Dam to the industrial future of the Columbia Basin, but at the same time warned against "another Pittsburgh, a vast city of swirling machinery."

Once, all the people on both banks were dirt farmers, lumberjacks, salmon fishermen – inhabitants of the frontier. The war brought shipyards and plutonium to the Columbia, and a rush of oddly assorted workers. Many came from industrial centers on the West Coast; others were Negroes from Harlem, carpenters from Georgia, furnace men from Akron, mechanics from Detroit, girl clerks from Philadelphia. They brought with them many of the social problems which plague other sections of the country. At Pasco, for example, near the Hanford works, there are 2,000 Negro families today, compared to the handful that lived there before the war. Of the white families brought in to build the plant, nearly half are from the South. The result is that ugly racial tensions, once unknown in this arid wilderness, are now firmly transplanted.

In Oregon, a bigoted migrant may well believe that Indians are "a lesser breed without the Law." The state has not yet passed a civil-rights statute outlawing discrimination in public places as Washington has done, although the Oregon legislature recently enacted a fair employment practices law. Signs proclaiming We Do Not Cater to Native Trade have begun occasionally to appear. Outside a hamburger stand on Oregon's scenic Columbia River Highway, you may meet a salmon fisherman in dark braids. He will tell you that his grandmother, at whose knee he was brought up, saw the great captains in buckskin come down the river in 1805, bringing the flag of freedom. You blush, for he is forbidden to enter and sit at the counter with white men.

But the Indians of the Columbia have even more at stake than their idyllic past. Tommy Thompson, eighty-five-year-old patriarch of the Celilo tribe, is one of those convinced that dams and factories have diminished the quantity of fish on which his people live. He shakes his head in distress. Did not the white soldiers make a treaty long ago, promising that Indians could spear and net salmon at the falls as long as "the grass grew on the hills and the sun set in the sky?" But what if there are no fish? What happens then to the promise made by a forgotten regiment?

Flora Thompson, the chief's gray-headed squaw, sets her jaw and tightens her lips. "Many years ago there were more fish than we could use," she says. "There are not many now. The poor things come up here with their noses bent this way and that way, and covered with oil and scratches. The dam at Bonneville hurts them. The factories cover them with filth."

The Columbia River salmon is one of the most amazing wild creatures on the American continent. No one knows exactly where it spends its four-year life span in the Pacific, but when spawning time comes it returns to fresh water. A subtle instinct leads it to the one among the Columbia's myriad creeks and rivulets, sometimes a thousand miles from the sea where it first drew water through its gills. The cycle is finished when the female lays her eggs and the male squirts milt to fertilize them; the parents die soon afterward. But if they fail to reach the headwaters, if their spawning grounds have been choked off, the biologic process ends in frustration. The salmon die in the upstream struggle without reproducing.

This hardly ever happened before civilization laid its grip on the Columbia. In 1883, the year the Northern Pacific thrust its rails across the Continental Divide and down the river on a shelf of lava, white men had been fishing commercially on the Columbia for perhaps a dozen years. The salmon catch that year, although limited to the superior spring run, came to a whopping 42,799,000 pounds. Today, more than half a century later, this figure remains the all-time high. Fishermen in 1948, going after the inferior autumn run as well as the remnants of the lush spring pilgrimage, pulled in 15,524,998 pounds of salmon. The decline of the Columbia's traditional industry has been relentless.

The story is detailed on two maps in the Portland offices of Al Kemmerich, veteran biologist of the Fish and Wildlife Service.

One map shows the tributaries available for spawning along the Columbia in 1883. The second reveals where salmon can spawn today. The tale is grimly clear. Two thirds of the original stream beds in the Columbia Basin have been blocked by dams, or polluted with sewage, or clogged with silt of flash floods.

Al Kemmerich, a tall, intense scientist whose life's work is the protection of fish, refuses to assign the blame primarily to dams. "Bonneville Dam was not completed until 1938, Grand Coulee was not until 1942," he points out. "Dams certainly don't help the salmon, but overfishing with 2000-foot seines at the mouth of the river has contributed materially to the diminution of the runs. So, too, has the shameful pollution of the Columbia as it passes Portland. The Columbia is still the most uncolonized of America's principal rivers, but even a fragmentary kind of civilization threatens its continuance as our number one fish stream."

One of the bigger fragments of civilization, Bonneville Dam, was built with the salmon problem in mind. Nearly a tenth of the $80,400,000 budget went into the construction of hydraulic locks and miniature waterfalls known as fish ladders to help upstream migrants scale the barrier, and special by-passes to keep ocean-bound young fingerlings out of the churning turbines. As a check on these devices, Civil Service employees were trained to actually count the teeming fish as they struggled up the ladders after their 140-mile journey from the coast. One of the counters, Mrs. Roxy A. Hill, once ticked off 3,451 Chinooks, 2,004 steelhead trout and 1,200 "scrap-fish" in a single hour.

Mrs. Hill, who is the wife of the Bonneville paymaster, performs her job in a doghouselike structure suspended above the ladders, as do the ten other women who work with her. They are kept warm in the raw winds of the upland gorge by electric heaters, the coils of which are made to glow by a couple of the kilowatts produced in the powerhouse only an outfielder's throw away. The figures currently turned in by Roxy Hill and her associates indicate Bonneville Dam has not spelled the doom of migratory fish on the Columbia. In 1939, the first full year devoted to this unique census, the counters recorded 286,236 Chinooks, 121,922 steelhead trout and 73,382 bluebacks. The 1948 tally, far from dwindling, reported 419,555 Chinooks, 139,062 steelheads and 131,541 bluebacks.

What about Grand Coulee Dam, which rises to the height of a 40-story building? There seemed no way around the problem of this massive roadblock, impassable to salmon headed for some icy rivu-let far upstream. The spawning beds above Grand Coulee were blockaded forever, and fish hatched and nurtured there would never spawn elsewhere. A solution appeared only recently, when the Fish and Wildlife Service completed a biological experiment conducted on a heroic scale.

A decade ago, Al Kemmerich and his staff began to trap all salmon headed for Grand Coulee. The fish were transferred to enormous hatcheries and artificially relieved of eggs and milt. The resulting fin-gerlings were then released in tributaries which enter the Columbia *below* the dam. Patiently the scientists sweated out the years until the first generation of transplanted salmon were on the way home as ma-ture fish. Would they head for Coulee, as their parents had done, and end their lives buffeting $195,000,000 worth of steel and concrete? The fish supplied the answer by swinging off obediently up the Methow, the Entiat, the Okanogan, the Wenatchee – each to its own adopted home in a white-watered tributary uniting with the Columbia below Grand Coulee. For once, man had masterminded the salmon's breeding habits.

Encouraged by this success, Al Kemmerich predicts that ultimately the entire Columbia River salmon population, of which the Coulee run was only a fraction, may have to be moved downstream. Roughly a dozen other dams have been proposed or authorized in the Columbia watershed and all will act as major obstacles to homing fish. A dam like McNary, whose eighty-eight-foot spillway will tower higher than its downstream neighbor at Bonneville, would crush tender fingerlings as they plunged over its crest toward the ocean. It seems clear that the migrations have to be diverted, but Kemmerich is not certain the scheme will always work. The characteristics of lowland streams, close to the salty ocean, are vastly different from the clear, cold headwaters beneath the glaciers of Canada. "How much can you monkey with nature?" the biologist asks.

His question draws a happier answer from the young farmers near Pasco, Washington, where a year or so ago the first parcel of land was irrigated with Grand Coulee water. "This old river has meant a brand-new chance for me," says Olden C. Gillum, a broad-shouldered Navy veteran and former Big Ten intercollegiate wrestling champion, as he surveys the eighty-five acres on which he will raise choice turkeys. His gratitude is echoed by Bill Lovercheck, an ex-paratrooper wounded in the invasion of Normandy, whose 124 acres of wheat are thriving as a trickle from the mighty Columbia gurgles through the canals. These men have felt the lure that first drew settlers westward, yet the soil on which they labor lies almost within sight of the chimneys and retorts of the Hanford plant.

Gillum and Lovercheck are only the vanguard of what promises to be a vast migration under the Columbia Basin Project. A rush reminiscent of the Klondike already is on in nearby towns. Lots that once went begging for eighty-five dollars sold recently for as high as $4,500. Fortunately for the colonizers, land to be irrigated has been pegged by Congress at the price it brought before the river waters multiplied its worth. The Project, of course, offers no free handouts; there will be no homesteading in the old-fashioned sense. The ex-

G.I.s, who get preference under the law, and other qualified settlers who come in must buy their land. (Officials urge each family to have at least $7,000 available before applying, since normal expenses include a modest house and the first crucial preparation of the soil.) But at least Congress has guarded their pocketbooks against the ravages of speculation, which otherwise would balloon dangerously each year, as 50,000 more acres of barren land are transformed into flourishing fields.

As this new civilization begins to spring out of the dead desert, even the men who first envisioned it are slightly dazed. They are Rufus Woods, an exuberant newspaper editor of seventy-one; Gale Matthews, a surveyor; and Billy Clapp, a backwoods lawyer. The idea was given to Woods on a hot July afternoon in 1918, as he and the others were sitting together over a soda pop. Through his *Daily World*, of Wenatchee, Washington, he issued the first proposal to build a stupendous dam across the Columbia at the Grand Coulee. Warming up to the suggestion, all three men dug into slender bank accounts to enlist the talents of Jim O'Sullivan, a fiery Irishman who carried the crusade direct to the Congress in Washington, D.C.

That was three decades ago. Jim O'Sullivan died in February, just after Secretary Krug had dedicated O'Sullivan Dam to hold back the waters coursing through the Columbia's old bed. Woods, Matthews, and Clapp, old men now, survive to see the dream beginning to come true. They like to stand beside the great green curtain of Grand Coulee, where the Columbia thunders over a spillway twice as high as Niagara Falls. The noise rolls across the upland desert. The old men cannot talk. Their frail voices would be drowned by that toppling maelstrom. After a while, they turn and silently walk away.

Above the dam and the broad river, spray hangs in the air like a cloud. Through the misty plumes, sheep often plod across the high concrete arches on the long dusty trek to distant mountain pastures. A herder in greasy denim pants, his shirt open at the throat, looks up at the transmission towers that stretch like a metallic centipede off toward Hanford. In him the simpler ways of the frontier abide along the Columbia, whether its waters split the atom or dwarf Niagara. Here, progress and the primitive dwell side by side.

Bloody Trek to Empire

American Heritage, AUGUST 1958

One of Neuberger's favorite magazines was *American Heritage*, founded in the 1950s by Columbia University historian Allan Nevins and Civil War historian Bruce Catton. Had Neuberger lived to return to his writing career, it is likely that he would have become a frequent contributor to *American Heritage*, which provided a new outlet for popular history about the Pacific Northwest.

OREGON COMMEMORATES in 1959 the one hundredth anniversary of its admission as a state of the Union. Oregon today contains the country's greatest reserve of standing timber and produces far more lumber than any other state. Oregon was first in the nation to provide for election of United States senators by popular vote, and it pioneered in introducing to the New World such governmental reforms as the initiative, referendum, and recall.

Yet the earliest attempt of white men to found a permanent settlement on this frontier of majestic solitudes and swift rivers was attended by death, destruction, and massacre. Lives and dollars were strewn recklessly across a vast expanse of the globe – from Manhattan Island to the distant island of Oahu. Almost half the participants in this effort were to perish, some on the spray-spattered ocean reefs and others in the darkness of mile-deep mountain chasms. The founder of one of America's great fortunes was dealt a stunning financial setback, and the U.S. Navy suffered a blow to pride and prestige which was not forgotten for decades.

And yet, despite all the suffering and agony and failure, no other thrust westward was so important to American sovereignty over the immense Columbia River basin. Although a larger portion of its personnel died on land and sea than during any other expedition to the Pacific Coast, the undertaking proved to be the anchoring claim to Oregon; so President James K. Polk was to declare at the time of the historic international crisis of "Fifty-four forty or fight" more than a generation later.

It all started bravely enough as the bark *Tonquin* sailed from the New York Harbor in the late summer of 1810. The frigate *Constitution*, Old Ironsides herself, escorted the *Tonquin* to the open sea.

With the *Tonquin* went the hopes of the new nation along the Atlantic seaboard. Lewis and Clark had returned from the western solitudes only four years before. Their startling reports of limitless forests and prairies had been avidly read, but behind them the valiant explorers left no outpost symbolizing American rights to the region. Now the spectacularly successful German-born merchant John Jacob Astor, had organized the Pacific Fur Company to build a settlement at the mouth of the legendary Columbia River.

This would be the first American colony on the shores of the Pacific Ocean, and Astor had no doubt it would be the beginning of a fabulous empire. Were not the creeks and marshes of the West alive with beaver? Beaver pelts were the standard symbol of wealth. Astor owned half the 100 shares of stock in the company, and guaranteed its expenses up to $400,000. His partners divided ownership of the other fifty shares. One of the principal partners, Alexander McKay, who had been to the Arctic with the intrepid Sir Alexander Mackenzie, sailed in the *Tonquin*. Another, a gentle and pious New Jersey-born businessman named Wilson Price Hunt, was to lead an expedition overland across the continent to occupy the fort which the *Tonquin*'s passengers and crew would erect.

The enterprise had the full blessing of the American government. On orders of President Madison himself, the Navy furloughed Lieutenant Jonathan Thorn to take command of the *Tonquin*. Thorn had been cited by Stephen Decatur for gallantry under fire at Tripoli. He was considered one of the Navy's most promising junior officers. But he had a jaw of granite and a stubborn arrogance, and he tried to bring to a trading vessel the discipline of a warship.

The top royals of the *Constitution* had barely disappeared over the horizon when those aboard the *Tonquin* learned what manner of man their captain was. Thorn ordered all lights doused by eight o'clock; he cursed the crew for chanting a ditty and told McKay he considered him "the most worthless human who ever broke a sea biscuit" because he demurred at some of the ship's fare.

"I fear we are in the hands of a maniac," McKay wrote that night in his journal by the flicker of a candle lit surreptitiously beside his bunk.

This fear was confirmed when the *Tonquin* replenished its supply of fresh water at the bleak Falkland islands, off the coast of South America. Five of McKay's business associates were a few minutes late getting back to the beach; so Thorn lifted anchor without them. The five, sure they were to be left behind to perish as castaways, rowed frantically after the Tonquin for three hours. Thorn obstinately refused to stop even when one of Astor's younger partners, Robert Stuart, threatened him with a brace of pistols. Later Thorn wrote Astor that only the opportune waning of the wind, which left the *Tonquin* becalmed, enabled the five wretched men to overtake the bark. They clambered up her side to deck, where they lay gasping and vomiting. This experience terrified all on board.

The *Tonquin* rounded Cape Horn and scudded northward with no civility or conversation between Thorn and the members of the Pacific Fur Company. On the island of Oahu in the Hawaiians, the Captain sneered at the display of Highland plaids and kilts which McKay and his Scottish aides put on for the admiring native girls.

And then at last, on March 22, 1811, half a year after clearing New York, this cargo of tensions and rivalries stood off the Columbia's surging mouth. There on that timbered shore, with distant snowcapped mountains framing the scene, was to be laid the cornerstone of Astor's Northwest empire.

But where was the course across the tossing bar? Thorn commanded Ebenezer Fox, the first mate, to put out in a whale boat to find the passage into the river. The captain arbitrarily ordered him to man the boat with French-Canadian *voyageurs* instead of with sailors from the crew. The *voyageurs* had been brought along to paddle canoes on riffled mountain streams. They knew nothing of this churning maelstrom of salt water. Fox appealed to McKay over the Captain's order. "I am to be sent off," protested the mate, "without seamen, in boisterous weather, and on the most perilous of missions."

When McKay remonstrated with him, Thorn thundered defiance. "I command here!" he shouted. "Mr. Fox, do not be a coward. Put off!"

As the whaleboat disappeared into the gloom, the mate looked up once again at the Captain in silent dismay. The boat with its five occupants breasted the heavy breakers and slid sideways over the long spit. It bobbed violently like a log in a waterfall. Then the boat was seen no more. The waves had swallowed it. The next day two Hawaiian oarsmen, far from the sunny homeland where they had been recruited by Captain Thorn, also drowned attempting to locate the elusive passage.

When the *Tonquin* finally was anchored in a deep bay of the Columbia, eight men had perished on the bar. To Alexander McKay it was an ominous start. Lewis and Clark had crossed the whole continent and returned with the loss of only one man.

Now began the construction of Fort Astoria, the first settlement ever built by Americans on the great ocean they would one day dominate in peace and in war. It was an agonizing task. Two months passed before a single acre of ground was cleared. Tools were crude and inadequate. Three men were killed by marauding Indians, and three more painfully injured by falling fir trees. Through an incredible oversight, Astor had not included a doctor in the expedition. The men bandaged their own wounds and cuts with unsanitary poultices. Blood poisoning attained alarming proportions.

Thorn, waiting impatiently aboard the *Tonquin*, wanted to sail northward along the coast on a trading voyage. Perhaps he could pick up some valuable furs for Mr. Astor. McKay decided to accompany the ship, leaving behind a small company at Astoria. Just before the *Tonquin* braved the bar again, Thorn had an angry quarrel with the only surviving mate and banished him to shore. "If you ever see us again, it will be a miracle," the despondent McKay told his friends at Astoria.

The miracle did not occur. Instead, there befell the *Tonquin* a disaster which today, nearly a century and a half later, still is whispered around the council fires of coastal tribes from Alaska to the California border. Thorn put in at Clayoquot Sound and commenced trading with the Salish Indians. Soon he had brutally struck a chief in the face with an otter pelt for demanding what Thorn considered a hard bargain. A grim surliness spread over the Indians, who swarmed aboard the *Tonquin* in ever-increasing numbers. McKay became frightened. He called to the Captain's attention a stern sentence in the instructions from Mr. Astor:

"Under no circumstances admit more than a few natives on the ship at a time."

Thorn brushed aside the warning. He who had bested the Tripoli pirates could take care of these fish-eating savages. The Indians began trading for knives rather than for beads and blankets. This, too, alarmed Alexander McKay, but he had no time to communicate his fears to the Captain. At a high, shrill, sudden shout from Shewish, the son of a chief, the Indians fell on the outnumbered white men with their new knives and with clubs they had concealed in bundles of furs.

McKay was first to die. An Indian pushed him over the rail into a war canoe, where waiting squaws cruelly killed him with their cooking utensils. The imperious Thorn, who had brought doom to himself and his vessel, fought ferociously in his final few moments of life. This, at last, was the task for which the great Commodore Decatur had recommended him. He was no merchant captain; he was a fighting man of the U.S. Navy. When Thorn went down beneath a torrent of brown bodies, the deck around him was strewn with dead Indians. One of the victims, the Captain's clasp-knife buried in his chest, was Shewish. So the man who had planned the massacre did not live to share in the loot.

It was an unequal battle. Soon Indians stood alone on the *Tonquin*'s bloody deck. The natives quit the ship at sundown, intending to return the next day to claim the greatest prize ever won by any tribe. Did not the vessel bulge with trade goods? Salish warriors would possess guns without number. They would rule all the tribes of the North. But in the bowels of the *Tonquin* one desperately wounded white man still lived. Long afterward, the remnant of the *Tonquin*'s company, left behind at Astoria, decided from vague descriptions of him that this man was James Lewis, the ship's quiet and inconspicuous clerk.*

At dawn Lewis dragged himself to the rail and motioned in friendly fashion for the Indians to come aboard. Then he staggered back down the companionway. The savages hesitated. They had been sure all the white men were dead. But the temptation of guns and trinkets was too great. They raced up the sides of the *Tonquin*. In an hour the ship was covered with Indians, who crowded shoulder to shoulder snatching booty from each other's hands.

Suddenly, with a dreadful shiver, the 290-ton *Tonquin* blew up. The clerk, in a final sacrificial act, had fired the magazine. The explosion was deafening. A great column of smoke rose above the bay. A few fragments of timber, floating in the red-stained water, were mute reminders of a millionaire's dream of empire and an Indian tribe's plot for conquest. The mutilated bodies of natives were washed upon the shore for a fortnight. The tribe along the waters of Clayoquot never recovered from the terrible revenge taken by the ship's clerk. It disappeared almost as completely as had the shattered *Tonquin*.

Months passed and the isolated settlement at Astoria heard no word of the ship on which they depended for contact with the distant world of cities and supplies and manufacturing. Rumors drifted along the wooded seacoast of a great and searing holocaust that involved a white man's vessel. Indian campfire rumors were notoriously unreliable, but McKay's interpreter, one Kasiascall, had been

---

* Among historians there is still some discussion as to the identity of the wounded crewman. Some say he may have been Stephen Weekes, the *Tonquin*'s armorer.

on shore at Clayoquot Sound when the *Tonquin*'s magazine was fired. Being a native, he had survived the massacre. Only whites had been slaughtered aboard ship. Eventually, it was Kasiascall who brought to the lonely outpost of the Pacific Fur Company authentic news of what had befallen Mr. Astor's proud bark.

The Astorians realized they were a solitary outpost in a vast wilderness, many miles from other white men and nearly a continent removed from the country whose flag of seventeen stars flew over their log stockade. Of the *Tonquin*'s original company of 53 men, 37 were dead. Gravest of all, one of the missing was the canny Scotsman McKay, the veteran of the Arctic who had been selected by Astor to found the Pacific Fur Company's trade in skins and metals. Gone, too, were most of the goods and supplies, for Captain Thorn had neglected to unload cargo before sailing the *Tonquin* off to its destruction.

Sole succor for the only American settlement on the world's greatest ocean now rested with the Astor overland party led by Wilson Price Hunt.

But it was a question of who needed help the more – the beleaguered men at Astoria or the starving ragamuffins of the overland expedition, chewing on the soles of their moccasins in the 6,000-foot abyss of the Snake River.

To avoid the hostile Blackfeet, Hunt had led his party of 64 on a route south of that advised by Lewis and Clark. On this trek Hunt had crossed the famous South Pass over the Rocky Mountains, some day to be followed by the Oregon Trail and charted by the Union Pacific Railroad. But on the headwaters of the Snake River, west of the Continental Divide, the irredeemable blunder was made.

The *voyageurs*, tired of razor-backed horses and trudging on foot, wanted to journey to the Columbia by water. This was their natural element. They insisted on discarding their mounts and building long canoes. Hunt had grave doubts, but the New Jersey merchant lacked the implacable will of the dead mariner, Jonathan Thorn. He reluctantly assented to the plan. They turned over their horses to a Shoshone tribe and embarked in fifteen canoes.

It was a mistake from the beginning. They had been on the Snake only two days in the autumn of 1811 when they bitterly regretted abandoning their horses. The river commenced to brawl and fret. It snatched at the boats with white-capped talons. One of the canoes capsized and two men were swept away in the foam. *"La maudite rivière enragée!"* it was called by the French-Canadians: "The accursed mad river."

The hills along the Snake stiffened into cliffs. Above the cliffs loomed white mountains with pinnacled summits. Now the expedition was in a prison of granite and lava rock. Return upstream was impossible. The river slanted through the gorge like a thing alive. Snow began to fall, plugging the side canyons which opened on the Snake. Precipices almost a mile high frowned down on the dark moat. This was Hells Canyon, deepest of all chasms on the continent, although the Argonauts could not know it at the time. No game fell to their rifles. It was a winter of famine, and they boiled their buckskin footgear and drank the fetid broth. Two more *voyageurs* were swallowed up by rapids and another went mad.

That more of the members of the party did not crumple may have been due, in Hunt's opinion, to a remarkable Indian woman. The only female on this prodigious trek, she was the willowy Iowa wife of the half-breed interpreter, Pierre Dorion. With her were their two small sons. After ten days in the gloomy canyon with only a few crumbs of food apiece, the men endured their hunger impassively because this dark young Indian woman with long braids and lithe legs had uttered no word of complaint. "She is as brave as any among our group," Hunt confided in his notes.

But escape from the abyss they must. To remain in its depths meant starvation or death in the brawling river. It took three desperate attempts to find a way over the slippery crags. And when at last, half-frozen and exhausted, they looked down on Hells Canyon, they had left behind in the yawning crevice practically all their trade goods, weapons, and tools. With barely enough strength to drag themselves up that terrible perpendicular mile, they had dumped their employer's loads before they reached the first rim. But Dorion's squaw had a cargo she could not jettison. Up the canyon wall she carried her two-year-old son and helped along the four-year-old by the hand.

Winter shrouded the land and still there was no food. Deer had fled the region, and fish did not rise to the lures the men desperately dropped through the ice. Hunt decided that in small parties they had a better chance of finding game. So they scattered in this uncharted wilderness, hoping to meet at the Columbia's distant mouth.

One by one, in January and February, 1812, the members of the overland party tottered into the log outpost at Astoria. Some were so emaciated their friends could not recognize them. Now the remnants of the two shattered expeditions struggled to salvage something from their disasters on land and sea. A small schooner was built of fir timbers, the first ever launched on the Pacific Coast. It was named *Dolly* for the wife of John Jacob Astor. They sailed up the Columbia and trudged into the back country. Small trading posts were established on the sites of such present cities as Boise, Salem, and Spokane.

One of these expeditions brought a grim ordeal to Dorion's squaw. Her party was attacked on the trail by Snake hostiles. She and the children escaped only because they were in camp at the time. Her husband perished with the nine white men.

Somehow, the slim squaw and the two little boys survived in a Wallowa Mountain defile for three months. She built a lean-to of pine boughs and butchered a horse stolen from the Indians. She crept out only at night to avoid the murderous Snakes. Many times she watched the slayers of her husband filing past to hunt. But her woodcraft exceeded theirs. Her hiding place was not found. When spring unlocked the fastnesses, she and the children picked their way silently down the tumbling creeks and so eventually came to the domain of the friendly Walla Walla tribe.

Wilson Price Hunt, eager to trade with the far-off Russians, had gone northward along the mountainous coast to New Archangel and was entertained by the czar's high-living emissary, Lord Baranof. The horrified American merchant saw Indians wilt at the stake under the knout and their half-naked women fondled in the barbaric court which the Russian governor maintained. Hunt was shocked by the cruelty of the Russians, but impressed by the riches of the land of which New Archangel was the capital. He referred to it as *Alakh-Skhah*; today we know it as Alaska.

Despite the lack of trade goods, skins were piling up in the crude warehouses of Astoria. The Astorians looked at them by lantern light – glistening bales of wealth. Perhaps, after all the tragic reverses, the Pacific Fur Company might yet succeed. Astor, learning of the loss of the *Tonquin* a year after its destruction, had not been dismayed. "Would you have me weep for what I cannot help?" he thundered to a friend. The Navy Department had been more stunned than the owner of the lost vessel. It could not believe the follies committed by Jonathan Thorn, protégé of the illustrious Commodore Decatur.

But further misfortunes were still to occur. England and the United States went to war in 1812. British ships of the line now cut off the long sea lanes to Astoria. John Jacob Astor, however, was one to take a gamble. He sent out a speedy, full-rigged merchantman, the *Lark*. Ironically, the *Lark* ran the British naval blockade, but capsized in a hurricane off an island in the Hawaiians. Five more men lost their lives in this disaster.

With the sinking of the *Lark*, Astoria was without supplies or communication with the nation to which it owed allegiance. It also was at the mercy of the British Northwest Fur Company, whose factors in 1813 forced Astor's representative virtually at gun point to sell $200,000 worth of furs for less than $80,500. Then His Majesty's ship *Raccoon* anchored at Astoria, the Stars and Stripes came down, and the Union Jack went up. Astoria was renamed Fort George.

Captain William Black of the *Raccoon* looked at the pitiful collection of crumbling log buildings where Americans had founded their first settlement on the shores of the Pacific Ocean. "Is this," he exclaimed, "the great Fort Astoria I have heard so much of around the world? Good God, I could batter it down with a four-pounder in two hours!"

Astoria was lost and the Pacific Fur Company abandoned. The death of 65 men, prolonged suffering on the part of many more, and the expenditure of a vast amount of money seemed to have arrived only at a dead end. But in his Virginia home, Monticello, Thomas

Jefferson gazed at the uncompleted map of the continent. British possession, he felt, was not to be permanent. The former President wrote reassuringly to John Jacob Astor:

"I considered, as a great public acquisition, the commencement of a settlement on that point of the western coast of America, and looked forward with gratification to the time when its descendants should have spread themselves through the whole length of that coast, covering it with free and independent Americans...."

So into the Treaty of Ghent, which concluded the abortive War of 1812, was written a clause which in effect restored Astoria to the sovereignty of the United States. On a bright August afternoon in 1818 the American sloop of war *Ontario*, Captain James Biddle commanding, stood off the green headlands which so many adventurous men had died to win. In the Captain's leather case were instructions from President James Monroe "to assert the claim of the United States to the adjacent country and especially to reoccupy Astoria, or Fort George."

This time it was to be Astoria permanently, and this time the American flag was there to stay. It snapped brightly at the halyards, while the marines from off the *Ontario* came to a salute. The notes of the bugle echoed back from the wooded hills. Some day that flag would have three new stars – for Oregon, Washington, and Idaho, states carved out of a domain made secure for America by the Argonauts who voyaged through the dark gorges or manned the luckless *Tonquin*.

Guarding Our Outdoor Heritage

The Progressive, JANUARY 1959

Neuberger wrote this half century review of the American conservationist movement, in which he had played a major role as advocate, legislator,
and reporter, to commemorate the fiftieth anniversary of *The Progressive*
magazine. Founded in 1909 by Senator Robert Marion La Follette of
Wisconsin, the magazine then as now, was a journal that interpreted the
great events of the day and offered an agenda for social reform. Beginning
in the 1930s, Neuberger was a frequent contributor to its pages, most
often on issues dealing with protection of natural resources. Supreme
Court Justice William O. Douglas said in 1960 that Neuberger had done
more than any living American to teach his generation the need for
conservation and the need for the preservation of the woods, lakes, streams,
and meadows of North America.

AFTER AX AND SAW and blasting powder had laid waste the
green groves of the Great Lakes states, wise men in America
feared that the same desolate fate awaited the upland forests
mantling the foothills and mountainsides of the Far West. These were
next in the ruthless path of the primitives in the lumber industry, who
thought only of profits rather than of future generations. The bearded
naturalist, John Muir, had warned that, while only God could grow
a tree, only Uncle Sam could save a tree. This meant positive action
by the federal government if the great watersheds of the Rockies,
Cascades, and Sierras were not to be stripped bare – with eroded

slopes, flash floods, starved wildlife, and stranded fisheries as the inevitable result.

On March 4, 1907, President Theodore Roosevelt signed the Forest Reserves Act. It was an epochal event. It signified that the American government suddenly cared about its natural resources. It heralded an eventual end to what the geographer, J. Russell Smith, has described as "the American cycle of cut, slash, fire, and land abandonment."

Gifford Pinchot, that determined woodsman with handlebar mustaches who became President Roosevelt's chief forester, later wrote of this era: "We had the power, as we had the duty, to protect the Forest Reserves for the use of the people, and that meant stepping on the toes of the biggest interests in the West. From that time on it was fight, fight, fight."

This was the atmosphere during the years from 1907 through the end of Theodore Roosevelt's two terms in the White House, in 1909. The modern conservation movement was just being born. Indeed, President Roosevelt had called the first Governors' Conference on Conservation at the White House in May of 1908, and there he said to the chief executives of 46 states: "The wise use of all our natural resources is the great material question of today.... These resources are the final basis of national power and perpetuity. It is ominously evident that these resources are in the course of rapid exhaustion."

So it was that national anxiety over the preservation of timber, soil, water, minerals, and wildlife came into existence at just about the time that one of Theodore Roosevelt's associates in the Progressive political movement, Robert Marion La Follette, Sr., of Wisconsin, was founding the forerunner of *The Progressive* magazine. The career of *The Progressive* during the past half century has paralleled the great surge of concern among Americans for the future of their outdoor heritage.

Such concern was throughly justified. It came about after many decades of plundering and exploitation. Wastelands of stumps in New England and in Michigan and Wisconsin told dramatically what would happen along the Columbia, Colorado, and Snake Rivers if government were not galvanized into bold action. Nobody had worried over the future. America's hardwood forests had lasted barely a generation. Wasn't there always another horizon ahead where the booty was unlimited? Could resources in such profusion ever thin out?

After Lewis and Clark had come with the flag, Americans moved tempestuously westward. They plowed the prairie, cleared the slopes and settled the valleys. Grasslands were turned over and planted to wheat and corn. Railways and wagon roads threaded out through the solitudes. Wild animals were slaughtered indiscriminately to make way for domestic herds. At least 50,000,000 bison had thundered across the plains at the time of Lewis and Clark. Their fate meant so little that wranglers drove them over cliffs in order to save expensive ammunition. Whole animals were slain so merely the tongue could be eaten. Travelers on the first overland railroads fired at the shaggy beasts from Pullman windows. Visiting European potentates rode furiously all day to learn how many animals they could kill between dawn and sunset. The carcasses rotted on the plains. Settlers migrating into the vast Northwest set virgin forests on fire to hasten the clearing of the land, burning a crop which had taken centuries to mature so they could sow seeds that would blossom during a season. And when the lumber industry finally got under way in the Northwest, almost as much lumber was left to rot on the ground, in stumps and slashings, as reached the market in boards and beams and ship's decking. It was an era of profligacy.

Tragically, people often could not discern where their own genuine welfare lay. In Oregon, greatest of the tree-growing states, the legislature memorialized against Pinchot's program for Forest Reserves. Pinchot himself frequently speculated on the sad fact that much of his opposition came from the West, where were concentrated the natural resources which he and his President sought to save. It was a question of the looters being present in the West, too, and they sometimes could dictate to state legislatures, which in that period also had the authority to appoint United States Senators.

In the end, after all, there are only the land and the people. And the land means natural resources – all of them. Without these resources, America could be as bereft as the Middle East, as hard put as China, as reliant upon imports as Western Europe. A nation can become "have not" almost overnight.

There were voices in our nation for conservation – voices like those of Teddy Roosevelt, Robert Marion La Follette, John Muir, George W. Norris, Stephen T. Mather, Franklin K. Lane, and others. The Pacific Ocean had been reached. The frontier was closing. No more was there another untrammeled valley just beyond the next hill or mountain peak. Americans realized they had to survive on what they had. They had seen the entire inventory. Now it was their task to preserve it – or else.

Theodore Roosevelt and his associates ushered in the modern era of conservation. Never again would Americans deal so cavalierly with their resources. This did not mean that conflict between exploiters and the public was over – far from it. Indeed, such controversy had only just begun. But no longer would the citizenry as a whole look on with drab indifference when forests went unprotected from fire, when rivers were turned into cesspools of sewage and offal, when big game and fisheries and waterfowl could be decimated without regard for the future survival of their species. An Idaho Senator said forest fires were of no particular importance, because there were always more trees where the burned ones had come from. His constituents retired him.

The Forest Reserves became known as the National Forests, eventually encompassing 181,000,000 acres. These now contain 33 percent of the country's commercial timber, a large part of the summer range for the Western livestock industry, and some 70 percent of the big game of the West. Nearly every major city in the West, the fastest growing realm in the nation, receives its drinking supply from watersheds safeguarded behind the boundaries of National Forests. These include Denver, Portland, Los Angeles, San Francisco, and Seattle. In fact, many of the lumbermen and logging operators, who originally opposed creation of the Forest Reserves, now depend almost totally upon these federal sanctuaries for their own sources of timber. National Forest receipts from the sale of timber stumpage, in the 11 Western states alone, amounted to nearly $90,000,000 during 1957. These trees were prudently harvested under the watchful vigi-

lance of trained forest rangers, so that each year the allowable cut
would be kept in permanent balance with new growth.

National Parks also came into abundance in the years that the forests were being saved. Yet great natural wonders like the Grand Canyon, the Yosemite, and the "rain forests" of the Olympic Peninsula
were not spared for forthcoming generations without angry political
battles. Ranchers claimed that the high terraces of the Colorado's
chasm were more useful for grazing than for sight-seeing. Lumbermen wanted the borders of such parks as the Olympics and Crater
Lake kept to narrow proportions so that few forested stockades
would be taken out of lumber production. But, gradually, some
14,500,000 acres of matchless outdoor grandeur were swept into National Parks and Monuments. Yellowstone, the first park, had been
set aside as early as 1872. Now, the National Park system began to
contain many companion pieces during the period that Senator La
Follette's magazine was beginning its demands for great adherence
to the public welfare in this and numerous other fields. Few such decisions ever were regretted. In my own state of Oregon, for example,
there is only pride in the gleaming blue majesty of Crater Lake,
which occupies the deep cauldron of a volcano that blew off its summit in geological times.

In our time about 55,000,000 people visit the National Parks each
year and at least 52,000,000 trek to the National Forests. The park
system is for recreation and scenic enjoyment alone. The forests,
however, are managed according to what Gifford Pinchot described
as "multiple use." This means that camping, lumbering, mining,
grazing, fishing, dam-building, and hunting all take place simultaneously under rules and regulations prescribed by the u.s. Forest
Service. In the Pacific Northwest, last great citadel of commercial
lumbering, the allowable annual cut within the National Forests has
leaped from 577,000,000 board-feet in 1940 to nearly
3,000,000,000 today. Yet the principle of perpetual supply is pre-
served. The proportionate increase in recreation is not far behind.
Visits to the forests have gone up 113 percent since only 1950. James
B. Craig, editor of *American Forests* magazine, has written: "The
cry of 'no more land' is something new to Americans only one gen-

eration removed from pioneering ancestors ... Healthy recreational outlets should have a high priority on any planning totem pole."

As public lands came to be used for the general welfare rather than for private plundering, fluctuations of course occurred in the pace of conservation. The complacent 1920s saw scant progress. Under President Harding, Republican politicians from the Southwest connived at the looting of Wyoming oil lands dedicated to the use of the Navy. Reclamation reservoirs, storing the precious waters of the arid inter-mountain states, received little encouragement from the parsimonious regime of Calvin Coolidge. But in 1933 Franklin D. Roosevelt brought into the White House a fondness for his own private arboretums, a keen appreciation of the wide open spaces, and a philosophy of government which envisaged great social responsibility.

Boys were taken off the streets of Eastern cities, where unemployment and crime had been rampant, sent into the solitudes of the West as the Civilian Conservation Corps. They built trails and roads, improved campgrounds, and developed ski bowls. Never before had recreation in the fastnesses benefited by so intensive a program. The CCC boys also cut in half the previous losses from forest fires, as they erected lookout towers and other equipment. Fire hazards have never again been quite so grim as in the days before the CCC. President Roosevelt also authorized the construction of huge river projects for hydroelectricity, navigation, flood control, and irrigation. These were symbolized by the Tennessee Valley Authority and by Grand Coulee Dam. One rehabilitated a wide section of the Southeastern states. The other became mankind's largest power plant and, at the same time, furnished water to reclaim 1,200,000 acres of upland desert.

In addition, the modern Fish and Wildlife Service came into existence during the long Roosevelt Administration. A network of refuges for game and birds was expanded. The first director of the service, Dr. Ira N. Gabrielson, was instrumental in negotiating agreements with Canada to protect the millions of ducks and geese traveling nomadically the prodigious flyways between the Arctic and the tropics. Preservation was intensified for vanishing species like the California condor and the whooping crane. Farmers were encouraged to provide wetlands where migratory birds could breed and find sanctuary.

The New Deal had come into office at a time of widespread unemployment. At first, with hunger and misery to alleviate, men had been put to work raking leaves – anything for jobs. But more lasting benefits resulted from the Public Works Administration, and many of these projects advanced the cause of conservation. Billions of cubic feet of water had been escaping wasted to the sea. As the source of cheap hydroelectricity, these impounded reaches of our rivers not only saved countless tons of exhaustible oil and coal but made possible the pioneering atomic developments at Oak Ridge in the Tennessee Valley and at Hanford on the banks of the Columbia. The most eternal source of power, falling water, was serving to unlock the riddles of the universe. And water pumped for irrigation brought about thousands of new farm homesteads, which produced specialty crops that were not surplus. GIs from America's wars enjoyed priority in settling on the reclaimed lands. The upland desert was being made to bloom, and this helped to encourage a vast migration westward to California, Arizona, and other Western states.

Nor was it government alone which motivated the conserving of resource. Great lumber companies like Weyerhaeuser and Crown-Zellerbach now realized that the era of "cut out and get out" had to end if their industry were to survive. They began to duplicate the sustained-yield policies practiced by the Forest Service. They hired professional foresters of their own. "Tree farms" began to dot these private holdings – wide areas where reforestation was carefully nurtured. Some of the timber companies began operating free public parks for the benefit of hunters, fishermen, and campers. This was a happy contrast to the era in which federal forest rangers had been warned off the holdings of some companies at the point of a gun. In fact, a number of lumber corporations adopted with much heraldry the Pinchot philosophy of "multiple use," and they announced that their lands could produce game, water, and scenery as well as 2 × 4 s and plywood. They had "got" religion and it was an opportune development.

Another contrast in the field of conservation occurred early in 1953, when the Eisenhower Administration took office. The New Deal and Fair Deal of the Democrats had brought to new heights the resource concept of a Republican, Theodore Roosevelt. But now a Republican regime set back the conservation clock.

In 1912 President Taft's Secretary of the Interior, Richard A. Ballinger of Washington state, had said:

> You chaps who are in favor of this conservation program are all wrong. You are hindering the development of the West.... In my opinion, the proper course to take is to divide it up among the big corporations and the people who know how to make money out of it, and let the people at large get the benefit of the circulation of the money.

The Eisenhower Administration, four decades later, began somewhat along this theme, albeit a little less blatantly. The great multipurpose damsite at Hells Canyon, on the Snake River, was surrendered by the government to the Idaho Power Company. Three small dams, capable of barely half the output of energy, replaced what might have been a high barrier equal to the lofty Hoover Dam on the Colorado River. Herbert Hoover, often considered the epitome of Republican conservatism, had authorized this great structure while he sat in the White House, but the Eisenhower Cabinet was opposed to a comparable federal dam along the Snake.

At other natural damsites, the soldier President recommended that the public pay for such non-revenue-producing features as navigation locks and fish ladders, but that private utilities be privileged to install the valuable powerhouses. As a result, the federal dam-building program lagged. Still worse, pressure was placed to choose alternate sites where great peril was involved to migratory salmon runs – particularly on the Salmon River watershed of Idaho. Furthermore, the Interior Department licensed wholesale oil drilling on wildlife refuges under its protection. This touched off a House investigation, which condemned such a policy as inimical to the basic conservation purposes of the game and waterfowl sanctuaries. Funds from "duck stamps," considered by hunters as inviolate to develop game refuges, were diverted for purely administrative expenditures. Termination of federal supervision over Indian tribes was legalized, without any real heed to the fate of timber, wildlife, and other natural resources that had received prudent custodianship while the tribes were under government protection.

Yet every disease frequently produces its own antidote. The adverse policies of the Eisenhower Administration stirred new militancy and determination in the ranks of national outdoor groups. They rallied to the to the programs jettisoned by the President and his counselors. These groups, such as the National Wildlife Federation and the Wildlife Management Institute, mobilized public opinion so vigorously that the President had to drop his Cabinet officers who had been the most aggressive about abandoning conservation policies of long standing. The Izaak Walton League conceived the bold idea of a National Outdoor Recreational Resources Review Commission, which would inventory all the country's possibilities for rest and fun beneath the open sky. In Oregon the public became thoroughly alarmed over the prospect that the great ponderosa pine forest of the Klamath Indians might be exploited and clear cut. The outcome was an enlightened bill for alternative federal purchase of this vast and rich reservation that I introduced at the request of the Eisenhower Administration, which by 1958 had learned something of a lesson regarding the fervent interest of the American people in their natural resources.

And so half a century after the setting aside of original Forest Reserves by Teddy Roosevelt and Pinchot the citizens of the United States are thinking more zealously than ever about the fundamental importance of conservation. It is my personal hope that their thoughts tend in the direction of such policies as these:

1   Strict adherence to the long-standing National Park tradition of no commercial impairment or invasion, plus recreational development of the Parks under the splendid "Mission 66" program.

2   No substantial diminution in size of either National Parks or of Wilderness Areas within the National Forests. Some segment of America should remain as it was before the white men came.

3   Protection of wildlife refuges and waterfowl sanctuaries from oil-drilling and similar exploiting activities.

4   Continuation of the wise multiple-use program of timber management, grazing, mining, and recreation within the bulk of our National Forests.

5   Authority in the office of the U.S. surgeon-general to levy penalties against industries or communities which create a menace to health by dumping sewage and waste into our rivers and streams.

6   Sufficient Congressional appropriations each fiscal year to keep on schedule "Operation Outdoors," by which the Forest Service hopes to rehabilitate many of the recreational projects started by the CCC troopers nearly a quarter of a century ago.

7   Legislation to prevent the commercial sale of trees on National Forest land that has been patented as the result of mining claims.

8   A law forbidding the Federal Power Commission to license either a public or private dam on a river inhabited by migratory fisheries, unless the Fish and Wildlife Service approves the fish ladders and similar protective devices.

9   Legislation modifying the authority of the Federal Power Commission and other agencies to disregard the views of state conservation bureaus in licensing projects on rivers wholly within the borders of one particular state.

10   Greater attention to scenery and natural grandeur and aesthetics, such as keeping billboards off our highways and making inns, lodges, and other facilities more in keeping with the natural terrain.

It seems evident that one of the prolonged conservation controversies, during the next 50 years of *The Progressive*, will be how much of the public lands in the American outdoors to leave as primeval wilderness and how much to adapt to supervised use. Both sides already have mounted strong and convincing arguments regarding a Wilderness Preservation Bill, now before Congress. One persuasive theme threads through my own mind. Once wilderness is mined or grazed or logged, it never can be true wilderness again. This should induce Americans to proceed slowly when they alter the character of their few remaining primitive realms, because such a process inevitably becomes irreversible.

Nature has done well by our United States. It is man's part which needs constant attention and improvement.

From the left, presidential candidate Adlai Stevenson, Sen. Wayne Morse, Sen. Richard Neuberger, and Rep. Edith Green at a Democratic rally in Portland on 11 October 1956. (OHS NEG. CNO 14737)

PROFILES OF POWER

The Lion of Idaho

Coast, NOVEMBER 1939

William Edgar Borah (1865–1940), named by *Time* magazine in 1950 as the most important senator of the first half of the twentieth century, was the most compelling stage presence in American politics, a thundering orator of the old school. Neuberger liked and respected Borah, though he disagreed with his isolationist views and thought that the Idaho senator underestimated the threat of Nazi aggression. Only weeks before Hitler's invasion of Poland, Borah wrote Neuberger that "we need not be disturbed" by the events in Europe.

DOWN IN THE DARK MAW of Idaho's Hells Canyon a prospector on one of the Snake River's gravel bars said to me, "We hadn't ought to have any truck with them European countries. What reason have we got to be messin' around over there? It'll only mean trouble and misery. Look at last time."

This philosophy of the Idaho frontier, translated into sharp, dramatic prose, is presented to America and the world by William Edgar Borah, who may rank in history as the most typically Western of all the statesmen and politicians yet produced along the Pacific seaboard.

The great regret of Borah's career is that he voted for America's entry into the World War. Of all the votes he has cast in 32 years of membership in the United States Senate, he would like most to go back and change that one. Perhaps this impulse has impelled his leadership of the group which now insists that under no circumstances shall the nation participate in the present European conflict.

Idaho is a vast state, nearly twice as large as England. Yet it is known principally because of its senior senator. Persons who do not know whether Idaho is north or south of California have heard about Borah. Maybe this is all right, for Borah conforms to his constituency. A few years ago Chester H. Rowell of the San Francisco *Chronicle* observed that only 49 people from Idaho had applied for passports to go abroad, "These, of course," he wrote, "do not include Idaho's most famous citizen."

Like the rest of the residents of Idaho, Borah is not particularly interested in visiting Europe or Asia. A clairvoyant once told him to beware of the water, for he might die at sea. It is not impossible that this has something to do with his decision. Notwithstanding that he has never set foot on an ocean liner, he is more widely read and quoted in Europe than Americans who have been President, and Shaw once said of him: "Borah is the only American whose brains seem properly baked; the others are either crumbs or gruel."

The playwright's estimate of Borah's mentality is not unsupported. Oswald Garrison Villard once made a similar remark. And recently *Life* asked the Washington correspondents to rate the members of the Senate according to integrity, intelligence, industry, and influence. In intelligence Borah led all the other senators by a big margin. Aggregately, he ranked second to George W. Norris of Nebraska, who *did* vote against America's participation in the World War. The correspondents virtually put Norris and Borah in a class by themselves, the rest of the Senate trailing far behind.

Borah, who has served longer as a Senator than any living man, is essentially a Western homebody. William S. Hart and later Will Rogers were his favorite movie actors. The Bible is his favorite book. In the evenings he reads and studies. Social events have little attraction for him. He likes plain food. He eats lots of vegetables and prefers spinach to the others. Mrs. Borah is always seeking new recipes for onion soup, which is her husband's special dish. Mrs. Borah is a great baseball fan, but the Senator is not interested in athletics. He sometimes wonders if intercollegiate football is as wonderfully worthwhile as its promoters claim.

In Boise, Borah and his wife live at Owyhee Hotel. It is not the most modern hotel in town. He spends a lot of time in their plain, unpretentious rooms reading Emerson, Hawthorne, and Milton. Emerson's essay on self-reliance frequently bolsters him in a fight for a lost cause. He has a vast fund of information. Gadgets do not interest him, but knowledge does. He cannot drive an automobile, yet can quote facts and statistics on peonage in Liberia, railroad trains in Canada, agricultural labor in California , and co-operatives in Sweden. He speaks extemporaneously on almost any subject. Once he debated against Nicholas Murray Butler on prohibition without even referring to notes.[2]

In Idaho in the summers, Borah often rents a car and driver and travels all over the state. He knows hundreds of farmers by their first names. He has the faculty of being democratic in his personal relationships. He never talks down to people. He can chat with Pullman porters, bus drivers, and prune pickers with complete simplicity. He is a legend in Idaho, yet thousands of Idaho farmers have sat on cracker boxes with him and argued political questions. The loftiest point in Idaho is Borah Peak's 12,655 summit, but the man for whom the mountain is named often stands diffidently in line at a Grange meeting on the plateau below it and awaits his turn for the lunch of chicken fricassee and biscuits.

When Senator Key Pittman, chairman of the Senate Committee on Foreign Relations, looks around the long, ash-littered conference table, he calls Senator Johnson of California "Hiram" and Senator Harrison of Mississippi "Pat." But Borah is "Senator." This respect is commanded as much by appearance as attitude. Borah is neither arrogant nor austere. Some people think he is shy. On his regular walks in a park he once met another elderly man. They walked together many times after that. The other man never learned who his companion was.

Borah's face is strong without being harsh. His stubborn chin with its deep cleft is as hard as a granite cliff but it is softened by blue eyes with a kindly twinkle. His voice is mellow and it cushions the general sternness of his countenance. The Senator's most distinguishing characteristic is the long mane of hair which falls back almost to his collar, giving him the appearance of a lion quietly watching the world. The mane blends with his little bow-tie and his high Stetson hat, and they combine to make him resemble an actor who has just stepped off the stage of a 19th-Century political drama.

Borah neither drinks nor smokes; he was opposed to Repeal, and he voted against legalizing beer. This may have something to do with his dislike of organized athletics, especially inasmuch as football is not entirely disassociated from liquor and carousing. On the table in the Borah living-room is usually a bowl of pears and apples, and nothing stronger. The Senator, in short, believes in temperance, and almost three decades ago, the Anti-Saloon League in Idaho was lauding his attitude.

A William S. Hart thriller which would bore the average sophisticate can still entertain Borah, yet at the same time he is a profound student of the classics.[3] He is an authority on Milton and Dante and regards Shakespeare's characterizations as phenomenally prophetic. He can enjoy himself at a Farmers' Union meeting in the afternoon and read Balzac and Swift in the evening.

In 1924 Coolidge was threatened by the Progressive movement organized by the elder La Follette. He felt that with Borah as his running mate the Progressive menace would subside. He asked Borah if he would like a place on the Republican ticket. Borah looked at Coolidge coldly. "Which place, Mr. President?" he asked.

Once after Borah had been speaking at the University of Idaho, two lumberjacks from the Coeur d'Alenes came to the home of the University president. They wanted to see Borah, they said. Their ramshackled car had broken down on the way and they had missed the speech. From the parlor Borah listened to them. "Come on in," he called, and the three of them talked all afternoon.

Borah was born in a village in Illinois and practiced law on the Kansas prairie. But his viewpoint is the viewpoint of Idaho, where he settled in 1891, three months after that outpost state had become the forty-third star in the American flag. He is suspicious of the intrigues and maneuvers which take place in Europe. He feels no great cultural bond with England, and he condemns tryanny in Egypt and Ireland as readily as tyranny in Ethiopia and Czechoslavakia. He thinks the people of India are as entitled to independence as are the people of Poland.

Diplomacy Borah sees from beneath the shaded hand of the frontiersman rather than through the bifocals of the cosmopolitanite. Although he is frequently provincial, this freedom from any preconceived notions of policy has led to amazing prophecies on his part. He was first to say the Versailles Treaty had in it "the seeds of many wars." He claimed the treaty sanctified imperialism. In 1919 and again in 1931 he contended the problem of the Polish Corridor would have to be settled. He also said the World War reparations schedule had to be adjusted to give the German Republic a chance for survival.

Borah has worked with Hiram Johnson in opposing foreign entanglements, he has collaborated with Norris and La Follette in crusades for economic reform, and he has cooperated with Vandenburg and Glass and Wheeler in defense of the Supreme Court. Yet fundamentally he is a lonely man. He and Johnson are the country's most zealous isolationists, but they are not warm friends. Borah has no children; some people believe this is the sorrow of his life, for little children instantly claim his attention. In the days when he used to ride horseback along Boise's byways, youngsters would time his coming and wait for him to jog past. Frequently he would dismount to sit with them; listening sympathetically to the story of a broken dolly or lost baseball bat. One day at an Idaho rural fair Borah bought merry-go-round rides for all the children on hand.

The Senator is 74 years old now, but he is still the most impressive orator in Congress. Correspondents playing poker in the press rooms drop their cards and hurry to the Senate gallery at the cry of "Borah's up!" As a lawyer in Idaho, before his election as a senator in 1906, Borah earned big fees, some say as much as $75,000 annually. He prosecuted Big Bill Haywood, radical leader of the old iww, charged with the murder of former Governor Steunenberg – strange beginning for a man who later led the campaign for American recognition of the Soviet Union. Clarence Darrow was counsel for the defense. Long after the trial in the Idaho hinterlands, Darrow wrote,

"Few men that I ever met in a courtroom contributed so much industry, learning and natural ability to his cause as Mr. Borah."

Haywood was acquitted and Borah has in general been more successful as a defender than as a prosecutor. One of his clients was Jim Lusk, a logger who had used a wrench to knock out a 250-pound giant accused of insulting a lady. The behemoth claimed the blow had permanently damaged his memory and Jim was brought to trial. In court Borah placed Jim beside the towering bruiser.

"And now," said he, "please show the jury just how you would strike a man much taller than yourself high on the head with a wrench." He took from his pocket a small bicycle wrench and put it in Jim's hand.

Immediately the giant bellowed, "That ain't the wrench he hit me with!"

"Indeed?" cried Borah. "Tell us about it."

"It was fourteen inches long. Many times I have seen it in Jim Lusk's – "

"But your memory, what about your memory?" inquired Borah.

Jim Lusk was turned loose in five minutes.

It is obvious that the struggle to keep the United States neutral in the second World War has only just begun. Now, Borah magnificently leads the forces resisting foreign alliances. Where will he be as the fight sharpens and the chips are really down? William T. Evjue, editor of the Madison, Wisconsin, *Capital-Times*, contends the elder La Follette once said to him, "Borah is a fellow who grabs the limelight before the battle starts, but when the battle is on and the fighting becomes hot, you look around in vain for Borah. He is usually missing."

This story may or may not be apocryphal. The elder La Follette is not alive to pass judgment on it. Perhaps Borah himself admits he fails to carry through the campaigns which he often starts. He is opposed to war, but voted for the World War. He is an insurgent, but did not take the stump for the insurgent movement of 1912 and 1924. He has positive ideas on government and economics, but remained silent during the critical Presidential contests of 1932 and 1936.

Yet who can accuse Borah of lack of courage? In 1899, three years after he had married Mamie McConnell, the daughter of the Governor of Idaho, Borah was prosecuting a criminal charged with shooting a man from on top of a freight car. The defense contended the stretch of track in question was too rough and twisting to permit such a feat.

The next day Borah left the courtroom, got a rifle and mounted a freight train starting out on its run. Around curves and across trestles rattled the long chain of cars. Borah was jostled and bumped, but clung to his swaying perch. At the end of the run, he climbed down from the box-car and returned to the courthouse black with dirt and soot. He took along the train crew as witnesses. The defendant was convicted.

Not long before Borah was elected to the Senate for the first time, he was sitting in a Boise hotel lobby one afternoon when he heard that a frightened Negro was threatened by rioters in the town of Nampa. The colored man was a bootblack from Boise, whom Borah knew. The mob suspected him of shooting a police officer. Borah rushed to the Union Pacific yards and persuaded an engineer to start immediately for Nampa with a locomotive and coach. Railroading in the Far West was not as formal then as it is now!

As the abbreviated train lurched along the rocky roadbed, Borah walked through the car pulling down all the shades. The train ground to a halt near the Nampa jail, where several hundred attackers were battering at the doors. Inside quavered the terrified Negro. Borah pushed his way to the front of the mob. Ascending the steps he shouted, "Do you want the fair name of Nampa stained by a lynching?" Some one in the crowd hooted, and again the mob pushed forward. Borah pointed dramatically to the train. "No lynch law shall hold sway here!" he challenged. "We have men on hand to prevent it. We have brought the militia from Boise."

The mob looked apprehensively at the dark and silent car. It eyed the firm jaw of the young attorney. Then it broke. Borah strode into the jail and grabbed the trembling bootblack. They walked unmolested back through the crowd and boarded the ominously shuttered coach. The train began the 22-mile return trip to Boise.

In 1920, shortly after the Republican victory at the polls, Harding asked Borah to be the administration leader in the Senate. "Mr. President," Borah replied, "You can get along without me, but I cannot get along without my views."

The United States today is split into two groups confronting the European crisis. One believes America should help remove the menace of Hitlerism from the world. The second says, "No foreign entanglements!" Borah is the principle personal symbol of the latter faction. He also is the symbol of the hinterland state which stretches from Canada to the Boise Basin, from Hells Canyon to the Rockies, Idaho is a long way from Chicago, Philadelphia, and New York, let alone Paris, London, and Berlin. Boatmen on the Snake River and potato growers near Arrowrock Dam would not be good subjects for a recruiting sergeant enlisting men to make the Old World safe for democracy.

From 1932 until 1938 Idaho had a senator who advocated the League of Nations, the World Court, and other instrumentalities for collective security among the countries: James P. Pope. Borah never said much about this colleague who so directly challenged his own opinions. Only in the summer of 1935 was he induced to comment. Pope was abroad, making frequent observations on conditions there. Most of his observations concerned Mussolini's intentions toward Ethiopia. As Borah descended from his Pullman car at Boise, a reporter sought his estimate of Senator Pope's activities.

"If Senator Pope can avert war between Italy and Ethiopia," Borah said wryly, "he is certainly entitled to a great deal of credit."

Last year Pope was defeated in the Democratic primaries by D. Worth Clark, who promised Idaho's people that his conduct in foreign affairs would be determined by the example of Senator Borah. In the Senate, Clark watches Borah and does likewise when international questions are at issue. He is a young man exactly half Borah's age, 37.

Borah may rank for a long time as the Far West's most distinquished contribution to the American Congress. Many historians think that three Senators of recent years deserve to compare with Clay, Webster, and Calhoun of the past – the elder La Follette, Norris, and Borah. This seems to be the consensus among the Washington correspondents, who, in the *Life* poll mentioned above, gave Norris 297.5 points and Borah 287 and then left more than a 25-point gap before any other senators were listed.

There are still pioneers in Idaho who remember when a young lawyer from Kansas, with $15.77 in his pocket, got off a day-coach at Boise – it was Boise City then – to build up a legal practice. The old argonauts of Idaho take Borah's career in matter-of-fact fashion. They are not phased by the fact that he is the most famous senator and will appear in the history books. But some of the second and third generation citizens are a little awed.

There is a celebrated story in Idaho of the young farmer who was digging potatoes in the field when his six-year-old son romped up to him and said he had been in Boise with his mother, and there they had seen the great Senator Borah. They had heard people in the street greet him by the impressive title of Senator.

This young farmer straightened up. "Son," he chided. "Those big city people were trying to fool you and mother. What would a man like Senator Borah be doing in a place like Idaho?"

A Politician Unafraid:
George W. Norris,
Senator from Nebraska

Harper's, OCTOBER 1937

George W. Norris (1861–1944), senator from Nebraska from 1913 through 1943, was Neuberger's first political hero and a role model for his own career. Norris, father of the Tennessee Valley Authority, was arguable the most innovative legislator of his era. Neuberger admired the Nebraska Republican's political independence, his intellect, and creativity. When Norris told Neuberger in 1942 that he did not plan to seek reelection that year, Neuberger responded, "Senator, you cannot retire. You are a soldier on the field of battle and you must fight until the war is ended." Norris took the advice and sought another term but was defeated. His autobiography, *Fighting Liberal*, was published a year after his death. Neuberger referred to Norris in his writings more than any other political figure.

ON FEBRUARY 12th of this year newspapermen in Washington asked prominent political leaders what policies Lincoln would advocate if he were abroad in the land once more. With a solitary exception the statesmen on Capitol Hill took the occasion of the one hundred and twenty-seventh anniversary of the Emancipator's birth to engage in verbal bombardments praising or condemning the New Deal. The exception was Senator George W. Norris of Nebraska. His gaunt, sad-eyed face was lighted by a quizzical smile as he told his interrogators, "Lincoln would be just like me. He wouldn't know what the hell to do!"

Such a reply from a newcomer to politics would have been regarded as inexcusably naive. Politicians are not supposed to be frank with the voters. The hypothetical return of Abraham Lincoln is a subject to be considered – at least for public consumption – with due reverence and pomposity. Yet George William Norris has been breaking political rules and maxims in this fashion for two generations and he has served in Congress longer than any other living person. Into the hurly-burly of American public life this gray-haired, seventy-five-year-old prairie philosopher has brought a candor and sincerity which once prompted the "Topics of the *Times*" to declare: "Norris has many critics, but no criticism of him has ever included the charge that he is what is known in politics as a 'trimmer.' His insurgency has never been confined to the period between elections. It is not lulled by favor, flattery, or White House breakfasts, or fear of consequences with the voters."

The New York *Times* does not favor the social and economic reforms advocated by Senator Norris. Its admiration of his probity is admiration for an opponent. This respect for Nebraska's senior Senator among his adversaries is not confined to the *Times*. His unwillingness to indulge in the customary equivocations and hypocrisies of politics has made him virtually a national institution. In an era in which it is common to identify public figures with certain qualities – Roosevelt with personality, Borah with oratory, Hoover with efficiency – Senator Norris, practically alone of all the nation's statesmen, is identified with honesty. Lewis Gannett remarked of him in 1926: "George Norris is the only honest man in political life in America."

By all the accepted standards of modern political combat, the voters of Nebraska should have retired Norris long ago to his little house at McCook. He has consistently refused to submit to the various pressure clans which roam the arena of public affairs, looking for wayward statesmen to terrify. He has denounced political patronage as an unmitigated evil and has never solidified his following with the disbursement of government jobs. He has often bolted the Republican party in Presidential years. He does not attend White House receptions and other social festivities which the public reads about so avidly. He and his wife have disagreed publicly as to political policy. He belongs to no church. He has never surrounded himself with the hocus-pocus atmosphere of aloofness and Olympian wisdom dear to most statesmen. He has not hesitated to antagonize important men, whether they be captains of industry, cabinet members, or residents of the White House. He has obtained recognition on the floor of the Senate to read satiric doggerel about the Vice-President then presiding over the upper-chamber. He has been so apparently indifferent to obliteration at the polls that the Nebraska *State Journal* once intimated that martyrdom is an inseparable characteristic of his personality.

Since 1902 Norris has represented his State in the national capitol. He spent his first ten years there in the House of Representatives. He was elected to the Senate in 1912 and is now completing his fourth term in that body. During these thirty-four years he has been so free of the fears to which most politicians pay homage that Senator Arthur Capper of Kansas recently said, "George Norris is a living, perambulating Declaration of Independence in human form." Here is a singular and remarkable career – one of the longest in the history of Congress – which offers vivid proof that there can be an occasional rare exception to the truism expressed a century ago by the prophetic Frenchman, De Tocqueville, "A political aspirant in the United States begins by discriminating in his own interest."

As significant as Norris's direct approach to issues is the fact that he behaves like a human being. His unruffled course through the turmoil of public life is a challenge to the widely prevalent belief that politicians – like royalty – cannot remain in power if they act like normal persons. They must be clever clowns, providing entertainment for the populace, or oracles solemnly mouthing pompous truisms, or their mouths must be perpetually wrinkled in gay, cavalier smiles. They must attend church faithfully and make frequent allusions to the Scriptures in their public utterances. There can be no subject on which they are not seemingly posted. They must pose as authorities on everything from garden spades to light cruisers. They must never be mistaken; if they blunder, some subordinate must shoulder the blame.

This pretentious and frequently hypocritical way of living, though it is the price which many men are willing to pay for high public office, has not been the price of the longest tenure in Congress. Norris lives as simply as if politics had never removed him from the humdrum routine of legal practice among McCook's seven thousand inhabitants.

Most American families disagree as to political opinions – and so do the Norrises. In 1928 the Senator announced he would support Alfred E. Smith for the Presidency. Mrs. Norris promptly said she could not reconcile Smith's advocacy of repeal of the 18th Amendment with her own dry views and would scratch her ticket, voting for neither Smith nor Hoover. For a time the country was treated to the unusual spectacle of a wife collaborating in the possible political embarrassment of her husband because they honestly disagreed on an issue of the campaign. Many ministers in Nebraska said the "good people" of the State were ashamed of Norris, particularly as he had been a dry all his life. The Senator answered that he still believed in Prohibition, but that he considered economic questions such as taxation and public ownership infinitely more important than the liquor problem. This performance was repeated on a modified scale in 1932 when Norris supported Roosevelt, another advocate of repeal.

Despite their occasional political differences, the Norrises are among the most devoted couples in Washington. They love to walk together and to drive their inexpensive sedan. They shun social affairs and are together whenever the Senator is not participating in public events. More than fifteen years ago a Washington newspaperman remarked of Norris, "He has not any of the things which Senatorial hearts most crave: social position, influence in his party, or companionship of the cocktail-drinking, poker-playing good fellows." In the summer months the Senator and Mrs. Norris motor to Wisconsin, where they have a little forest cabin he built with his own hands. Crowds and lavish functions are distasteful to them, and no shoe salesmen and his wife travel more obscurely than this couple who have been in the national capitol since almost the turn of the century.

In Washington the Senator and his wife spend the evenings at their apartment. They have three daughters, all married, and one of Norris's sons-in-law is his secretary, John P. Robertson. The Senator is a voracious reader. His library is lined with books on social and economic problems, many of them with his own penciled notations of salient points. He devotes long hours to analyzing reports on hydroelectric power, armaments, and other subjects which draw his attention. Rostand's *Cyrano de Bergerac* is his favorite book and the militant challenges of that hero have a deep emotional appeal for him. He has always associated the cadences of stirring poetry – which he loves to read aloud – with the deeds of his friend, the elder La Follette, and he quoted at length from William Ellery Leonard and other poets in his memorial address when the Wisconsin Senator died in 1925.

In his offices Norris is accessible and unassuming. He is no desk-pounder, no thundering oracle bellowing like the throat of Vesuvius. He frequently will tilt his feet on the desk and let the visitor carry the brunt of the conversation. A corncob pipe and a plentiful supply of cigars are his chief enjoyment and he generally has them arrayed on the blotter in front of him. Like Borah and two or three other Congressional veterans, he dresses in dark baggy suits. Most of the time he wears a stubby, tightly-knotted shoe-string tie. Norris makes his only concession to sartorial correctness when the humidity of the Washington summers drives him to linen clothing. He is eager for information and wants to know what is taking place in the country and what the people are talking about. Tales of poverty and distress move him immeasurably. He is naturally sad and heavy-eyed and his face – beneath his white hair and dark brows – is touched by sorrow whenever visitors tell him of the misery prevalent in many parts of the country.

It is one of the anomalies of Washington that this grave old man, whose very appearance is melancholy, should move into debate with sardonic humor as one of his principal weapons. Capitol Hill has not yet forgotten the letter which Norris publicly addressed to Secretary of State Stimson seven years ago when the controversy over Dolly Gann's social status was at its height. Here is an excerpt:

> The League of Nations, the World Court, the maintaining of a big Navy … are all important and may affect the peace of the world, but sink into insignificance and fade into oblivion when compared with the great question that is now agitating the whole world as to where the Vice-President's sister shall sit at the dinner table.

Another Vice-President was the target of Norris's shafts of satire when Charles G. Dawes rushed from the Willard Hotel to reach the Senate in time to vote with the conservatives on an important bill. Into the *Congressional Record* Norris read a rhymed parody, comparing Dawes' pell-mell rush through the Washington streets with Sheridan's ride to Winchester:

> Up from the east out into the day
> Bringing to the Willard fresh dismay
> The affrighted air with a shudder bore
> Like a herald in haste to the chieftain's door
> The terrible grumble and rumble and roar
> Telling the battle was on once more
> And Dawes fully fifteen blocks away.…

One summer during the Coolidge administration Norris was run down by an automobile and slightly injured. The Senate was anxious to adjourn and escape from the heat of the capitol, but Norris limped into the room and declared, "I am ready to stay here all summer and I think the farmers … have a right to demand that we all stay. I am in good shape; when that automobile struck me the grinding and crunching of the wheels simply massaged and invigorated me."

Norris's colleagues were indignant, but they remained in Washington for several weeks to consider the tariff. The good-will and friendly companionship of the majority of his fellow Senators has never been anything but an incidental objective with Norris. Content to be a lonely anchorite, over a period of three decades he has angered virtually every Congressional adherent of the party system. Political discipline and party patronage are his *bêtes noires*. He is so suspicious of political alliances of any sort that he has not even agreed with other liberals in their demands for a new party. In 1924, when appeals for a Progressive party were coming from the hinterlands, Norris threw cold water on the proposal: "I have small faith in a new party. There is too much belief in parties in this country. Unless its leaders were Christlike men – in which case they would not be political leaders – its candidates would be dictated by a few bosses conferring in private, just as in the old parties." This mistrust of political factions prompted Norris to insist last year that the constitutional amendment giving Nebraska a unicameral legislature contain a provision calling for non-partisan election of the members.

It gives Norris considerable amusement to relate to his visitors how he became convinced of the futility of party discipline and ties. On February 22, 1904, when he was a young Congressman with a drooping mustache and faith in the infallibility of the Republican party, the Democratic whip in the House moved to adjourn in tribute to the memory of George Washington. Norris was the only Republican to support the motion. He was severely reprimanded by the floor leader of his party, who explained that Republicans positively could not endorse legislation introduced by Democrats, no matter how worthy it may be.

Several months after this episode, the forty-three-year-old Representative from Nebraska delivered a five-minute speech opposing an increase in pay to a door-keeper whom he regarded as merely a customer at the political pie-counter. This insurgency offended the members of both parties. Norris, later looking back on his service in the House, declared, "Although I was a member of the House for ten years, and eight years of that time my party was in control, I never received a single piece of patronage ... I doubt whether there ever has been an instance where a man has served that long in the House ... and has never been given a single solitary appointment of any kind."

Unwillingness to court the support of his party made each of Norris's campaigns for reelection a hazardous undertaking. His eminent fellow-Nebraskan, William Jennings Bryan, would come into the district every two years to stump for the Democratic candidate. In 1908 Bryan delivered more than thirty speeches in behalf of the Democrat, and Norris kept his seat by a margin of only twenty-two votes. After the election was over Bryan told Norris he was glad he had won and that he frankly preferred him to the Democrat whose victory he had urged. On the way back to Washington, Norris said he wondered what explanation could be made of Bryan's course.

This experience with party lines impelled Norris to attempt what the capital then regarded as impossible: the overthrow of Uncle Joe Cannon's rigid rule over the House. "The Speaker is in control of the political guillotine," Norris contended. He demanded that the Committee on Rules, instead of being composed of five members selected by the Speaker, should consist of fifteen members appointed by the House. "This is anarchy under the color of law," Cannon thundered. But in 1910 Norris was the spearhead of a carefully-timed insurrection which stripped Cannon of the power he had wielded so long without question or challenge. Only three votes decided the battle.

II

Two years later Norris successfully fought both the Democrats and the Republican regulars and was elected to the Senate. He was nearing fifty-two when he entered the upper chamber in March of 1913. He took his seat branded as a political insurgent, but he had not yet acquired a reputation as a rebel in the economic field. Most of his efforts in the House had been directed toward political reforms. He had attacked the stilted procedure of the electoral-college method of electing the President and he had condemned political deals and alliances. But in the economic sphere his exploits had not been daring. If anything, he had inclined toward caution. When most of Red Willow County in Nebraska had flirted with the Populist movement, Norris and one other attorney were the only lawyers to resist the clamor. A roamer in far political pastures, until his advent into the Senate he had held relatively conservative economic beliefs.

In the upper chamber, however, Norris found himself in intimate contact with two men whose influence greatly shaped his life. One of these was Robert M. La Follette of Wisconsin, a Senator since 1906.

La Follette was voicing the demands of the workers and the farmers of the Northwest for industrial and agrarian reforms, and was opposing the railroads, the banks, and Wall Street. Norris soon found himself increasingly in agreement with the man from Wisconsin. The other Senator who met a sympathetic ally in George Norris was Harry Lane of Oregon. Lane frankly called himself a "philosophical anarchist." The Oregon Senator and Norris – newcomers to the Senate – became constant companions. Both social recluses, they spent long hours walking along Washington's byways.

La Follette, Norris, and Lane became the nucleus of a little group of Senators and Representatives who endeavored in vain over a period of two years to prevent American participation in the World War. Each of the trio had thought he saw in Wilson a President who would be susceptible to La Follette's economic reforms, to Norris's political ideas, and to Lane's social beliefs. Yet as the country moved inexorably toward entanglement in the conflict raging in Europe, they became the President's most implacable opponents, and he in turn denounced them as few Chief Executives have ever denounced members of the nation's highest legislative body. By the middle of 1916 the lines were tightly drawn and Norris, La Follette, and Lane were marshaling a tiny unit of a dozen Senators to protest the demands for increased military appropriations.

These men insisted that the Government manufacture its own munitions, and Lane angrily predicted that the young men enrolled in compulsory military training would eventually be used as strikebreakers. The trio of Norris, Lane, and La Follette led a long debate for an amendment to forbid the intervention of American troops in Central American countries, but at the showdown could muster only five votes in addition to their own. La Follette condemned the Administration bitterly as he described how he and Norris and Lane, while riding in a street car, had overheard Federal employees complain that they had been coerced into marching in the Preparedness Parades. Norris accused Wilson of saying to the members of Congress, "You shall not express your opinion if it conflicts with mine."

In the midst of the vain struggle to avert participation in the War, Lane's health broke down. Physicians diagnosed his ailment as

Bright's disease and warned he had not long to live unless he avoided all possible excitement and strain. They besought him to withdraw from the stubborn little pacifist bloc, but one afternoon he told his daughter Nina that he "would rather die tomorrow than not go down the line with George Norris." Between the two Senators there was a deep bond of friendship. Long after Lane's death, his family described how Norris sat at his colleague's bedside night after night when Lane was too weak to attend Senate sessions.

The most furious of the storms of derision broke over these men when their filibuster prevented passage of the armed-ship bill at the 1917 short term of Congress. Patriotic organizations excoriated Norris, La Follette, Lane, Stone of Missouri, and a handful of others as "twentieth-century Benedict Arnolds." Wilson denounced them as "a little group of wilful men." The abuse was so vehement in Nebraska that Norris decided to offer to resign and stand for reelection. Even La Follette advised against such a course, pleading that the people could act in the heat of war hysteria as they would not act in the calm aftermath of later years. But against the counsel of his friends, Norris returned to Nebraska, rented the largest hall in Lincoln, and announced he would explain his position to his constituents. No one would volunteer to preside as chairman of the meeting and Norris received several messages threatening his life. When he finally walked on to the platform, a lonely figure in a baggy suit, he faced a grim crowd which packed the auditorium in ominous silence. "I have come home to tell you the truth," Norris began.

Slowly, painstakingly – step by step – he described to the people who had sent him to the Senate the reasons for his opposition to America's entrance into the War. Then he returned to the capital and was one of six Senators who to the end maintained their stand against the War resolution. On the final day of Senate debate – April 4, 1917 – Norris brought down upon himself the wrath of pulpit, press, and patriot by exclaiming, "I feel that we are about to put a dollar stamp on the American flag." As the full import of this challenge struck his colleagues, James A. Reed of Missouri cried that Norris had bordered on treason.

Norris replied, "The Senator from Missouri has said something that at some time he will regret, I believe."

Alone of the 6 dissenters,* Norris was still in the Senate in 1925 when Reed described the minority vote against the War as "the most superb act of courage this century has witnessed."

Few Americans ever have been called upon to endure a barrage of ridicule comparable to that which was hurled at the Senators who opposed the War resolution. They were castigated as "skunks," "traitors," and "copperheads." Congress was deluged with petitions insisting that they be expelled from the Senate and even banished from the land. Lane died six weeks after the vote in the upper chamber. Norris crossed the continent to attend his friend's funeral, and as he was leaving the newly-covered grave in the Oregon hills, he remarked to Lane's daughter, "Well, Nina, your father's gone. He gave up his life for peace, I guess a few of us can risk our political careers."

Norris faced reelection in 1918, but dared to challenge the Espionage Act and other Administration measures. The Democratic Senatorial nominee was supported by Nebraska's Senior Senator, Gilbert M. Hitchcock, the sponsor of the War resolution. Although the election was held in the last few days before the Armistice – when enthusiasm was running high over Allied victories on every sector – Norris defended his War position and defeated John H. Moorhead by 21,000 votes out of a total of 220,000 ballots.

Assured of a second Senatorial term, Norris continued to oppose Wilson's demands. He condemned the Treaty of Versailles and threw himself into the fight against the Japanese claims to Shantung. Japan's aggression in China has always aroused his indignation. It is still rumored in Washington that Borah won over Norris to the isolationists' refusal to ratify World Court membership two years ago by emphasizing to his colleague the inability of the League of Nations and the Court to prevent Japanese imperialism.

---

* The other 5 were La Follette, Lane, Stone of Missouri, Gronna of North Dakota and Vardaman of Mississippi.

When Harding replaced Wilson in the White House in 1920, and the Republicans gained a majority in Congress, Norris became chairman of the Senate committee on Agriculture. A year later Henry Ford submitted his famous offer to buy Muscle Shoals and Norris was plunged into the hydroelectric power problem. This has been the great, consuming interest of his life. He has analyzed and explored it from every perspective. Engineers say he is as conversant as they are with the technical details of the question. Since Ford first focused attention on Muscle Shoals as a national issue, Norris has been the country's most tenacious advocate of public power development.

In 1921 Henry Ford was near the crest of his popularity. He even was mentioned frequently as a possible Presidential candidate. His Muscle Shoals offer, including as it did a provision to manufacture nitrogen for fertilizer at not more than eight percent profit, was hailed with enthusiasm in rural districts. A majority of Congress was inclined to favor the proposal. President Harding was sympathetic. But Norris declared, "the magic name of Henry Ford seems to have dulled all the reasoning faculties of thousands of farmers;" and for three years he carried on a desperate campaign to prevent Muscle Shoals from being sold. On several occasions he was barely able to avert favorable action on Ford's bid, although in 1922 Norris had strengthened his forces by assisting Robert Howell to replace Gilbert Hitchcock as his Senatorial colleague from Nebraska. So soon had the sponsor of the War resolution fallen by the political wayside!

Finally in 1924 Ford withdrew his offer. Yet two years later both Houses of Congress passed the Underwood bill to turn over Muscle Shoals to private operation. With his tenacious fight apparently lost, Norris made an eleventh-hour thrust and blocked the Underwood measure on a point of order when it was already submitted as a conference report. After this almost unbelievable recovery on the brink of defeat, Norris marshaled his support to block the proposal permanently. As a result the $46,000,000 Wilson Dam at Muscle Shoals today is still the property of the Federal government.

Here, then, is Norris's background in the power problem. Here, possibly, is the reason why President Roosevelt is the first occupant of the White House to be supported vociferously by the gray-haired

Senator from Nebraska. Here is the reason for the excitement in Norris's voice when – during the debate last year on the "death sentence" bill – he proclaimed, "Holding companies constitute the greatest evil of our civilized age!" Power looms large in his vista of national affairs; once when a prominent editor asked him for a statement on an important foreign policy, he confessed to having spent so much time in study of the hydroelectric issue that he was not even conversant with the other problem.

Unanimity on the power question is the stoutest chain holding Norris to the New Deal. On a number of subjects the President and he have disagreed: the limitation of crops, the increases in Naval armaments, Farley's patronage methods.[4] But Mr. Roosevelt has accepted a generous portion of the Senator's power advocacies. Pressure from the White House recently drove through Congress an ultimate $400,000,000 allotment for rural electrification. Federal power "yardsticks" in the form of giant dams are under construction on the Columbia River and other streams. In the South the Tennessee Valley Authority constitutes the New Deal's most remarkable experiment in social planning. All this has been the partial fulfillment of a dream to Norris and he has assured the President of unqualified support in the coming election.

Some of Norris's admirers are afraid that the implacable Senatorial foe of Wilson, Harding, Coolidge, and Hoover has been spellbound by Roosevelt's personality. But of one fact there is no doubt – on the power issue the President has been more consistent and tenacious than in the pursuit of any other objective. When the holding company bill was at stake, he refused to give ground in the face of rebellion within his own Congressional ranks. He has kept political considerations out of the appointments of Dr. A.E. Morgan and David Lilienthal to head the TVA and of Morris L. Cooke to manage the Rural Electrificaton Division. The TVA has moved forward so vigorously that individuals as far apart economically as Norman Thomas and the editors of *Judge* have hailed it as the most significant achievement of the Roosevelt Administration.

Senator Norris is largely responsible for this escape from the customary halts and compromises of the New Deal. He has followed every phase of the power problem with the relentlessness of an Indian trailer. He communicates constantly with persons on the scenes of operation at Chattanooga, Tennessee; Bonneville, Oregon; and other power centers. During the debate on the holding-company legislation, he took complex charts and graphs to the floor of the Senate and suspended them from a portable blackboard. Using a pointer like a pedagogue drilling a group of schoolboys, he explained the intricacies of utility combinations to his colleagues. He feels so intensely on the issue that several times he has assailed Comptroller-General McCarl's detailed questioning of TVA expenditures, despite the fact that McCarl was once his secretary. Norris told newspaper correspondents he would have been heartbroken if the Supreme Court decision in the TVA case had gone against the Government. And when the development of some phase of the power program is not satisfactory to him, he generally stalks over to 1600 Pennsylvania Avenue to see the President about it.

III

Between the fifty-four-year-old occupant of the White House and the seventy-five-year-old veteran of the Senate there is a unique friendship. From George Norris the President has accepted rebukes and criticisms he would not tolerate from any other person. Almost without cessation, Norris has condemned the patronage empire of Jim Farley. His hatred of the spoils system prompted him to support the late Huey Long's resolution authorizing an investigation of the Postmaster-General. When the Democratic political forces opposed the reelection in 1934 of Senator Shipstead of Minnesota and the late Senator Cutting of New Mexico, Norris branded the action as "gross ingratitude" and scathingly added that it had been undertaken with the "knowledge and consent of the President." He and five other liberals stalked indignantly from the Senate chamber when Cutting's Democratic successor, ex-Congressman Chavez, was sworn in. Norris has always voted against and denounced the Naval appropriation bills – bills marked "must" by the President. The orthodox New Dealers have found it impossible to harness Norris to political strategy, and in an election year, with the Administration anxious to dodge the Constitutional issue, he has called the Supreme Court a "continual Constitutional convention" and has sponsored a measure to curb its powers. "I do not intend to avoid this issue," he recently telegraphed a friend.

Mr. Roosevelt does not cherish people who question his favorite policies. The one exception is Senator Norris. The venerable Nebraskan can denounce a New Deal Naval allotment as "militaristic" in the morning and at an afternoon press conference the President will reiterate the hope that "Uncle George" can be persuaded to serve another term in the Senate. On a recent speaking tour in the Middle West Mr. Roosevelt referred to Norris as one of the greatest of all Americans. It was the President's express wish that the key unit of the TVA be named "Norris Dam." He also has put his relations with the Senator on a personal as well as an official basis. For the first time since Norris came to Washington, he finds himself an occasional visitor at the White House for an evening discussion in the Lincoln study. After one of the Presidential cruises to Central America, Mr. Roosevelt jocularly remarked that a happy result of the voyage was a Panama hat he brought back as a Christmas gift for "Uncle George" to replace a dilapidated Stetson the Senator once lost at the White House.

Liberal critics of the New Deal have been disturbed by Norris's support of the Administration. They intimate that the dean of the Progressive bloc has overlooked the fact that frequently the Roosevelt deeds do not accord with the Roosevelt promises. They feel it is a mistake for Norris, an outspoken foe of large armaments, to aid an Administration engaged in gearing the war machine to its highest peace-time pitch. They do not want the nation's most forthright liberal to be attached to the New Deal, should it eventually fail – as they believe it will. Let the Senator answer these complaints in his own words, in a letter addressed to a constituent in April of 1935.

> … The President was confronted with difficulties which had never before confronted any living man. He had no precedents to follow. He had to guide the ship through uncharted seas…. In some respects it seems to me that President Roosevelt has been

one hundred percent right. In other respects, he has failed.... I
could never believe that it was right to destroy food products
when so many people were suffering for the necessities of life....
Yet I have believed it was my duty to go along with any program
which was honestly conceived with a view of bringing better
conditions.

This confidence of Norris in a Democratic President is a sharp
contrast to his attitude toward the Chief Executives of his own party.
For twelve years his verbal forays on the Senate floor aroused the
wrath of Harding, Coolidge, and Hoover. When the Republicans rebuked him for sponsoring a resolution calling for an investigation of
the Tariff Commission and its relations with Coolidge, Norris
snapped back, "No man owes a duty to his party that in any way conflicts with the duty he owes to his country." Once, while speaking of
Coolidge, Norris blurted out, "He thinks he is a little Jesus Christ."
The clerk tactfully changed the sentence in the *Congressional Record*
to "He thinks he is the embodiment of perfection."

This sort of verbal recklessness is almost without parallel in public
life. Nine hundred and ninety-nine politicians out of a thousand balk
at all except the most discreet approach to religion and its institutions. Yet during a discussion of Japan's subjugation of the Chinese
Norris stated, "I am not a member of any church; I am not a member
of any religious organization...." He went on to describe himself as
"one of the followers of the religion proclaimed by Abou Ben Ad-
hem ... who loved his fellow-men."

It requires both courage and simplicity of character to make a declaration like that on the floor of the United States Senate in these days
when newsreel photographs show every public figure parading in and
out of church.

So Nebraska's senior Senator plods through the arena of American
politics – a mild, soft-spoken old man defying every orthodox rule
for success in public affairs. See him in the Senate chamber quiet and
unobtrusive, his head cocked to catch what is taking place. His white
hair contrasts vividly with the black mop of his forty-one-year-old
colleague, Bob La Follette, Jr., who sits back of him. When he

speaks he does so in subdued, almost-conversational tones. Norris has none of the thunder of Borah, little of the eloquence of Ham Lewis, none of the histrionics which characterized Huey Long. Sometimes his colleagues and listeners have difficulty in hearing him. He is inclined to be long-winded on certain subjects and occasionally he is dry and monotonous. The New York *Times*, in discussing the possibilities of a filibuster against the War resolution in 1917, prophesied, "For the others (outside of La Follette) only Norris is likely to be lengthy." Norris's speeches are not adapted to rabble-rousing. The word-music of contemporary political oratory – composed largely for radio distribution – is not the Senator's style. He does not cram his addresses with frantic appeals to God, Home, and Mother. Maps, statistics, and charts are his ammunition and he will fill pages of the *Congressional Record* with tables which relatively few of its readers bother to analyze and understand.

IV

How far to the left is Norris? Of course he is listed in the *Red Network*. If for no other reason, his presence in that extraordinary roster of the supposed enemies of the republic would be assured by his sponsorship of the Lane Pamphlet attacking compulsory military education. He is willing that the principle of public ownership be applied not only to power, but to other basic industries such as coal. He is an advocate of co-operatives and he has sponsored anti-injunction bills and other labor legislation. These and similar proposals are aimed at the modification of capitalism – and the Socialists are enthusiastic over the TVA – but Norris has not given outright support to the Production-for-use program of the Farmer-Labor party of Minnesota. He is not a money radical, although he has backed some of the Frazier-Lemke farm assistance measures. He voted against Father Coughlin's banking bill when it was before the Senate, and he turned down flatly the threats of the Townsendites, terming the OARP [Organization of American Retired Persons] transactions levy a "pyramided sales tax." He has continually contended:

> I do not believe we can ever have a permanent recovery until we take some steps which will bring about a more equal distribution

of wealth and property. I believe the saving of the situation and even of civilization depends upon something of this kind.

Along such a course also ran the beliefs of Huey Long. But whereas Huey reduced the answer to a simple Share-the-Wealth formula, labeled with Biblical metaphors and put in attractive bottles for the peasants of the South, Norris has proposed more steeply graduated income and inheritance taxes, using graphs and statistics to bolster his arguments.

For nearly two decades Norris has hammered away at this theme. Now he is ready to retire. He sees younger men like Black of Alabama, Nye of North Dakota, Bone of Washington, La Follette of Wisconsin, Holt of West Virginia, and Pope of Idaho coming up in the ranks to take his place. He wants to withdraw to the little town of McCook, where he has had his home ever since he entered politics. Norris did not file in the Republican Senatorial primaries this year, and if he decides to run again, he must do so as an Independent candidate. He has received thousands of letters from every State urging him to remain in public life. The President has repeatedly requested him to seek another term in the Senate. Nebraska's Democrats at their recent convention adopted a resolution which said, "The need for his (Norris's) return to his undiminished work in the Congress outweighs all consideration of party regularity and transcends all fair regard for the political aspirations, however worthy, of any individual." At this writing a movement is under way in the State to nominate Norris by petition, regardless of whether he gives his consent.

On two previous occasions the Senator determined to retire, but each time circumstances forced him to remain in the arena. Twelve years ago, discouraged by the inevitability of Coolidge's victory over La Follette, he declared, "I have been bucking this game for twenty years and there is no way of beating it. Now I'm through." But his friends suppressed his telegram declining the nomination, and he was reelected by a decisive majority. He listed his campaign expenses as "Postage, two cents." Again in 1930 he wanted to withdraw; but Republican regulars ran against him in the primaries a grocer who was also named George W. Norris, and the Senator, aroused by this trick, again won the Republican nomination and in the general election opposed Gilbert M. Hitchcock, the wartime Senate leader who was attempting to come back in politics. Hitchcock pointed to his long record for patriotism and was supported by the Republican conservatives as well as by the Democrats. Norris said, "There is nothing which has given me so much suffering or of which I am so proud as my vote against the World War." The result was Norris, 247,000 votes; Hitchcock, 172,000.

Two years ago Norris won a victory in his State even more notable than his 1930 triumph. Nebraska's voters adopted by an overwhelming margin his amendment to the State Constitution providing for America's only one-house legislature. It was a score for the Senator over most of the old-line politicians in the state. And three years ago he won another notable triumph. He became one of the few men in history almost solitarily responsible for a change in the Constitution. Four times he had hammered through the Senate his amendment abolishing "Lame Duck" sessions of Congress, only to see it killed by the House; but he persisted, and finally his proposal became the twenty-first amendment to the Constitution. Next year it will result in the Presidential inauguration being held in January.

George W. Norris is ending his career – a career which began amidst the poverty of eighty acres of stumps in Sandusky County of Ohio – in an era of unrivaled political demagoguery. It has become expedient for the ambitious statesman to demand governmental economy in one breath and twenty-four-billion-dollar old-age pension programs in the next, to espouse a balanced budget and cash payment of the bonus, to praise the Civil Service while constructing a mammoth patronage machine, to insist upon higher tariffs on products from his own district and free trade for goods manufactured by the other fellow's constituents. Tolerance and honesty in public affairs are at a greater premium than ever before. Appeals to hatred and ignorance are legion. To millions of Americans "humbuggery" has become a virtual synonym for politics.

Yet in this age of expediency at least one man has proven that success and sincerity in public life are not necessarily incompatible. In George W. Norris the nation has produced a unique figure: a politician who can act like a human being, express his convictions, and yet survive at the polls. There are those who contend he is unduly suspicious; others claim that his hatred of the "power trust" and "the interests" amounts to an obsession; but not even his most aggressive foes question his integrity.

Frequently harsh in his mistrusts, sometimes wrong in his views, the silver-crested Gentleman from Nebraska has been on Capitol Hill more than thirty years, and the hour is yet to come when he will mince words on a public issue. It is encouraging that the most forthright member of Congress is the member whom the people have kept there the greatest length of time. On all issues except where the Senator is concerned the voters of Nebraska are relatively conservative. Respect rather than agreement is responsible for his thirty-four-year tenure.

Perhaps intellectual honesty is not an unappreciated virtue after all.

William Simon U'Ren and the "Oregon System"

The Oregonian, 1959

William S. U'Ren (1859–1949) was arguably the most effective reformer in Oregon's political history. Lincoln Steffens described him as "The Lawgiver." As the father of the direct election of U.S. senators, the primary election, the initiative and referendum, U'Ren was among the true giants of the Progressive Era. Neuberger was an ardent defender of the Oregon system and a friend of U'Ren.

FEW STATES, even those dating back to Colonial times, have made as great an original contribution to government in the United States as has the state of Oregon.

In fact, the "Oregon system" may well be the most decisive landmark associated with our state during its entire eventful history to date. The term "Oregon system" refers to certain basic governmental reforms known as the initiative, referendum and recall. In addition, it encompasses the direct election of United States Senators, for Senators were appointed by legislatures until Oregon became the first state in the nation ever to choose a member of the upper chamber of Congress by popular vote.

Following Oregon's leadership, at least 28 other states of the Union have adopted the initiative and referendum in varying degree. The recall is part of the constitution of even more states. And the 17th amendment to the Federal constitution provides for all 49 states what

Oregon was first to undertake in only one state – the election of U.S. Senators at the ballot box rather than in legislative halls.

After the 17th amendment had been adopted, the famed Senator William E. Borah of Idaho had this to say: "The original work for this amendment was done in the state of Oregon by the same man who drafted Statement No. 1."

This man was a frail, determined migrant from Colorado with fervent ideals and a propensity for inducing other people to share his burning faith. The man's name was William Simon U'Ren. He was of English and Dutch ancestry, the son of a blacksmith.

Between the years 1900 and 1910 U'Ren sponsored and promoted many sweeping governmental reforms which were destined to make Oregon a laboratory for testing the wisdom and sovereignty of the electorate. Indeed, whenever I speak on a college campus or before a group of political scientists, I am asked more questions about U'-Ren and his "Oregon system" than on any other phase of activity involving our state. And the name of U'Ren is listed in the history books and the civics texts with the greatest frequency of any Oregon political figure. Lincoln Steffens long ago described U'Ren as "The Law-Giver" and the description has stuck.

What did U'Ren do?

U'Ren came to Oregon in 1889, full of a reformer's zeal. In a Rocky Mountain mining camp, he had read Henry George's epic "Progress and Poverty." The book convinced him that the single tax could solve most of the economic ills of mankind. While changing from a boat to a train at Oakland Pier, U'Ren picked up a frayed pamphlet about the initiative and referendum, as they had been adapted from the ancient *Landesgemeinden* in the cantons of Switzerland; this was where all the men in an alpine district made the local laws.

In Oregon, the newcomer threw himself fanatically into the crusade of the Australian Ballot League, helping Oregon to pioneer among the states in guaranteeing a secret ballot. But U'Ren's real goal was the single tax. He knew the single tax never would be enacted by the conservative Oregon legislature. But what about the people at the polls? U'Ren enlisted such groups as the Farmer's Alliance, the Oregon Knights of Labor and the State Grange to join him in promoting the initiative and referendum. His task was made comparatively easy by the fact that under the proposal known as the initiative, the signatures of 8 percent of the registered voters could place any suggested law on the ballot for the people to decide with their ballots. The referendum was slightly different; it provided that 5 percent of the voters could force a plebiscite at the polls on any proposition enacted by the legislature. Both ideas were based on the widespread circulation of petitions through city marketplaces and along rural roads.

U'Ren crusaded, agitated and conferred. As secretary of the League on Direct Legislation, he distributed 50,000 copies of a pamphlet in English explaining the proposed reforms and 15,000 in German. This was an enormous number in a state which had a population of only about 400,000 in 1900, particularly when it is remembered that this was prior to the period of women's suffrage. But U'Ren, by now 41 years of age, felt he could leave no loophole permitting failure.

U'Ren worked closely with men as far apart on other issues as Harvey W. Scott of the *Oregonian* and W.S. Vanderburg of the Knights of Labor. He embroiled himself in jockeying and trades at the legislature over the appointment of U.S. Senators. And once he admitted: "All the work we have done for direct legislation has been done with the single-tax in view, but we have not talked single-tax because that was not the question before the house."

Gradually but inexorably, public opinion mobilized behind U'-Ren. The legislature could resist his importuning and lobbying no longer. In 1901 the legislature at last submitted to the voters a proposed constitutional amendment embodying the initiative and referendum. At the elections of 1902, it was adopted overwhelmingly – 62,024 votes in favor and a trifling 5,668 against it. U'Ren's cup runneth over....

Yet, for him, the millenium had not arrived. Several times U'Ren and his followers used initiative petitions to place the single-tax on the ballot, but the voters rejected his cherished panacea for economic woes. However, there were political woes too. At the legislature U'-Ren had been horrified over the deals and trades which determined who would represent Oregon in the Senate of the United States. Yet what could be done about it? The situation seemed hopeless, for the national constitution stipulated that Senators in each state should be "chosen by the legislature thereof..."

U'Ren's imaginative mind created an idea known as proposition No. 1 – the proposition to which Senator Borah had referred as breaking ground in the nation for Senators to be elected by popular vote. Proposition No. 1 was a pledge asked of each candidate for the legislature; this was how the pledge went:

"I further state to the people of Oregon, as well as to the people of my Legislative District, that during my term of office I shall always vote for the candidate for u.s. Senator in Congress who has received the highest number of the people's votes for that position."[5]

U'Ren's initiative method next was employed to place on the ballot, at the election of 1908, a law instructing the legislature to support the people's choice for u.s. Senator. Decisive approval followed – 69,668 votes in favor and only 21,162 in opposition. Some celebrated men thus came to the Senate by popular selection through the devious but effective "Oregon system" worked out by the fertile ingenuity of U'Ren. These included Jonathan Bourne, Jr., a wealthy New England Republican who had reached Oregon via a shipwreck off Formosa, and Democratic George E. Chamberlain, who had become chairman of the key Senate Military Affairs Committee during World War I.

With one state electing its Senators at the polls, the old appointment form had no chance of surviving elsewhere. The contrast was too great. In 1913 the 17th amendment was ratified, thus spreading from sea to shining sea William S. U'Ren's conviction that the u.s. Senate should represent the sovereign will of the people as expressed at the ballot box.

The recall of public officials also was added to the Oregon constitution in 1908 as part of U'Ren's arsenal of reforms. According to the Library of Congress, all these varying governmental devices are known generally as the "Oregon system" because they had their American origins in Oregon and because they have been used more often in Oregon than in any other state. This is particularly true of the initiative and referendum, although during recent decades California has had a larger number of proposals put on the ballot by petition than the state where the "Oregon system" was cradled.

And William S. U'Ren, founder of the "Oregon system," what became of him?

He lived to be a very old man, dying in Portland on March 8, 1949, at the age of 90. For many years he had a small office in the bygone *Oregonian* building. I frequently visited him there, listening to the tales of the great days when Oregon under his prodding had become the fountainhead of new governmental ideas for the whole United States. As he grew older, he became more cautious and conservative politically. Yet occasionally one glimpsed the crusading fire which had made him tell Steffens: "I would go to hell for the people of Oregon!"

To the last, U'Ren defended the initiative and referendum. The "Oregon system" was his Bible and Koran. My wife Maurine and I went to see him at his suite in the Ambassador apartments a few months before his death. His wife lived there with him.

U'Ren scoffed at suggestions that the initiative and referendum should be jettisoned because the voters had passed some unwise laws. "Some mighty weak men have been put into high public office," he said to me, "and yet no one talks of curtailing the right of every man and woman to vote."

And he insisted that the initiative and referendum had been a success and of permanent value to Oregon. His voice was faint and weak. He was nearing the end of very long trail. His dim blue eyes seemed tired and groping for brighter vision. Maurine and I said goodbye to him for the last time. We looked back at U'Ren in the darkened apartment, with its massive furniture and brocaded tapestries.

Norman Hapgood, the editor of *Collier's*, had written that U'Ren, alone among men, had once changed the brilliant and stubborn mind of Woodrow Wilson. The 27th President had been adamantly opposed to the initiative and referendum, until he heard U'Ren talk fervently in his study in defense of the "Oregon system." Wilson not only revised his views but apologized publicly for his earlier hostility to the initiative and referendum. What other resident of Oregon could claim so persuasive an influence on a President?

In the gloom of the somber living room, William Simon U'Ren's shock of white hair stood up like a plume – a knight's plume.

Charles Linza McNary:
Oregon's "Charlie Mac"

The Progressive, 20 MARCH 1944

Charles Linza McNary (1874–1944) was a major part of Neuberger's Pacific Northwestern political beat during his first decade as a journalist. As Republican leader of the United States Senate, McNary was a dependable newsmaker. Neuberger was a frequent grest at Fir Cone, McNary's Salem farm. In 1940, Neuberger touted McNary as presidential timber in *Life* magazine. When McNary was chosen for the vice presidency, Neuberger wrote *Life*'s cover article. Neuberger supported FDR over the Willkie-McNary ticket but twice voted for McNary's senatorial candidacy despite their different party labels. This tribute, written while Neuberger was serving in World War II, appeared in *The Progressive*.

HE WAS ONE of the last links with the old progressives of the great tradition. William Borah is gone and so are Tom Walsh and the elder Bob La Follette. George Norris is in retirement. And now Senator Charles McNary, of Oregon, is gone, too.

He was essentially a kind man. He was moved by generous impulses and by deep human sympathy. He had few preconceived social and economic beliefs. This was one of the reasons for his unrivaled personal popularity among men of all political faiths. He was no breast beater, no table pounder. He neither proclaimed nor declaimed. He never looked down from Olympian heights. He did not aspire to rule or sovereignty or power.

Charles Linza McNary, for 26 years United States Senator from Oregon, was happy in that position. He declined many opportunities to be Governor of his State. He was a reluctant candidate for Vice President. Once his friend, Senator Jim Couzens, of Michigan, wanted to contribute $100,000 to a campaign fund to back McNary for the Presidency.

McNary smiled and little crow's-feet appeared at the corners of his eyes, as he scrawled on the back of the restaurant menu:

> The Presidential bee is a deadly bug.
> I've seen it work on others.
> O Lord, protect me from its hug,
> And let it sting my brothers.

McNary's beliefs and convictions stemmed from kindness and tolerance. In basic philosophy he was neither a liberal nor a conservative. His views spanned both sides. He was for public ownership of water power but he was skeptical of Government bureaucracy. He voted against extending the draft, but he favored the original lend-lease bill. He backed up much of the criticism which his running mate, Wendell Willkie, directed against the New Deal, but he did not go along with all of Willkie's comments on foreign affairs.

He liked people. His friends were universal. He liked the President immensely, and this regard Mr. Roosevelt reciprocated. Bob La Follette and Senator Arthur Capper were among McNary's closest cronies. General George C. Marshall was another intimate of the Oregon Senator. They first met when Marshall was a brigadier general in command of the historic old post at Vancouver Barracks.

There was a rectitude about Senator McNary which no events could wear away. He was Republican minority leader, but when he felt the administration was moving in the right direction, he went along with administration policies. He was Willkie's running mate, but when he could not agree with Willkie's views he said so. He and President Roosevelt were good friends, on warm, personal terms, but he did not hesitate to challenge the President on many issues.

McNary's family went back a long way in Oregon history. He once told me, "I go back a long way too, Dick." He was acutely conscious of the events behind him. He knew that his grandfather had crossed the continent in a covered wagon and floated, hungry and tattered, down the Columbia River on a raft.

His farm, Fir Cone, held for him memories of his grandmother Linza, and of his other pioneer predecessors. Fir Cone was one of his conversation pieces. "I want to see Fir Cone," said Bob La Follette as he arrived in Oregon for the funeral. "Charlie never got tired of talking about Fir Cone."

Senator McNary was wise and cynical and urbane, yet he delighted in chatting with his farm neighbors in the Willamette Valley. He liked people and people liked him. He always was to Oregon what Jefferson must have seen to Virginia. Fir Cone was for a quarter of a century Oregon's Monticello. Without bias, malice, or personal ambition he studied the questions which affected his native State. Many things which unscrupulous politicians might have wanted to do, they did not do because of fear of him and his influence.

Oregon was proud of Harry Lane, and later of Harry Lane's successor. When Senator Lane died, the elder La Follette quoted, "He added to the sum of human joy, and if everyone to whom he had done some loving service were to bring a blossom to his grave he would sleep tonight beneath a wilderness of flowers."

That could have been said about Harry Lane's successor. "Charlie Mac" was the best-loved Member of the United States Senate, and he was almost a final link with the men who 20 years ago fought for equality for agriculture and to retain Muscle Shoals for the people.

Oregon is not represented in Statuary Hall in the National Capitol at Washington, D.C. A number of States are represented by former Senators – New Hampshire by Daniel Webster, South Carolina by John C. Calhoun, Wisconsin by Robert M. La Follette, Sr., Louisiana by Huey P. Long, Missouri by Thomas H. Benton. Someday Charles Linza McNary may be there, too.

Mr. Justice Douglas

Harper's, AUGUST 1942

William O. Douglas (1898–1980) served a record thirty-six years on the United States Supreme Court and may have been the most controversial justice in its history. Throughout his tenure, Douglas reflected the Populist tradition of the Pacific Northwest. Douglas grew up in Yakima and headed East after graduation from Whitman College, to attend Columbia University Law School, then to become a law professor and chairman of the Securities and Exchange Commission in the 1936. A champion of the small investor, Douglas forced major reforms by the New York Stock Exchange. In 1939, Roosevelt named Douglas to the Supreme Court. Douglas met Neuberger as a young reporter and they became close friends. They frequently took mountain trips in the Wallowas and the Cascades, floated Fall River and the McKenzie, and hiked the trails along the Columbia Gorge. "There was no greater passion in Dick's life than the preservation of the wilderness," said Douglas, who shared Neuberger's enthusiasm for the outdoors.

THE DICK WHITTINGTON TALE of the New Deal is that of William Orville Douglas. Sixteen years after he jounced eastward out of Yakima, Washington, on the brake rods of a Northern Pacific freight train he was sworn in as the youngest member of the United States Supreme Court since President Madison appointed thirty-two-year-old Joseph Story in 1811. Mr. Douglas was not quite so precocious. He took his seat on the Supreme Court at the ripe old age of forty. When he had learned on a March morning in 1939 that he had been selected to succeed one of the heroes of his legal career, Justice Louis D. Brandeis, he told his wife that he felt just like the fellow who received the first message ever sent over the telegraph: "What hath God wrought?"

Yet there are many people in the national capital who believe this success story is not ended. They think Douglas will surely become President some day, perhaps comparatively soon. At the time of his appointment to the Court, New Dealers in Congress publicly predicted that he would be the 1940 nominee of the Democratic Party if Mr. Roosevelt did not run again. Mr. Roosevelt ran again. The same men still make the same prediction, but with the date revised to 1944 or left indefinite.

Meanwhile there have been constant demands that the youngest of the Justices be enlisted actively in the war effort. No important position is vacant for long without vociferous suggestions being heard that Mr. Douglas occupy it. He has been mentioned in the recent past for such assorted jobs as WPB [War Production Board] director, head of man-power mobilization, and Secretary of War. Most of this talk originates with men convinced that the sternness and executive competence which Douglas demonstrated as chairman of the Securities and Exchange Commission should not be interned on the Supreme Court during one of the gravest crises of American history. "When is the President going to send in the varsity?" asks a Wall Street banker who, although lisagreeing with Douglas on economic questions, believes his talent for getting things done is sorely needed in the Government.

But the recurring talk about Douglas stems also from another source, a source that has a lot more to do with his personality and background than with his ability. Probably through sheer coincidence, of the twenty-five or thirty people closest to the President in the war effort not one comes from the Far West. This rankles in a region which has had blackouts, and air raid alarms, and radio silences for forty-eight hours at a time, and which feels itself on the frontier of the fighting in the Pacific, particularly since the Japanese threat to Alaska materialized. When he was in Los Angeles several months

ago Walter Lippmann detected strong sentiment for greater considerations to regional needs. And Governor Culbert L. Olson of California, although he is a supporter of the Administration, contends
that the capital "fails to understand the problems of California, the
Pacific Coast in general, and Alaska." All along the seaboard, from
the British Columbia line to Mexico, one man is put forward as the
person to close this breach: Mr. Justice Douglas.

Congressman John M. Coffee, an all-out New Dealer who represents the Puget Sound seaport of Tacoma, recently demanded
the presence in the nation's high war councils of "a man with a Far
Western background, familiar with the Far West, and with an understanding of its difficulties." He recommended Douglas. But this suggestion comes not alone from New Dealers. It is repeated in such
conservative newspapers as the Portland *Oregonian* and the Los Angeles *Times*. Editorials advocating Douglas for a top war position are
put into the *Congressional Record* by the Republican minority
leader, Senator Charles L. McNary of Oregon. Some of these editorials ask the President to give Douglas a leave of absence from the
Court so he can accomplish the dual task of jacking up the war effort
and assuring the Far West a larger measure of participation. Whenever even a potential opening looms in the Government, Washington
is bombarded with petitions, letters, and resolutions from Denver on
west, all insisting that Douglas is the man.

To understand this agitation it is necessary to understand something about William Orville Douglas.

Pussyfooting and shifting loyalties are unfortunately prevalent in
American public life. The most striking characteristic of Mr. Justice
Douglas is that he has never been accused of either of these. His performance as head of the SEC [Securities and Exchange Commission]
was distinctive for bluntness and courage. He took over the chairmanship in 1937. "Under Joe Kennedy," said the new chairman,
"the gains made toward protecting the rights of investors through
President Roosevelt's legislative program were consolidated. Under
Jim Landis we were taught how to get things done. *And now we're
going to go ahead and get them done.*" Douglas stalked into the

Bond Club of New York and delivered the most extraordinary speech ever heard there. After announcing that "the economic utility of continuity of banking relationships is of unestablished value to anyone except the banker," he further startled the assembled brokers by maintaining that the directors of a collapsing corporation owed first allegiance to the stockholders rather than to themselves.

Some way had to be found, he said, of "obtaining directors who will represent the public interest." He wondered about the propriety of one man serving as a director on many different boards. Perhaps the basis of directors' compensation ought to be overhauled. Might not "so-called public directors" be a solution? Certainly there was no excuse for centralizing, under the stress of emergency, all of a corporation's powers in the hands of a few men. "These voting trusts," he charged, "are the apotheosis of the process of divesting the stockholders who own the company from control or voice in the affairs of the company. They afford promoters convenient devices for eating the cake and having it too. They merely make the stockholder an easier prey to pressures brought upon him by management or other dominant groups, whose power the stockholder is rarely in a position to challenge. In sum the voting trust, as currently observed, is little more than a vehicle for corporate kidnapping."

The title of the speech was "Democracy in Industry and Finance." When Douglas sat down there was barely a handclap. His audience stared at him in hostile silence. Wall Street had been told off, straight to its collective face, by a rangy thirty-eight-year-old upstart from Yakima, Washington, who looked something like Gary Cooper playing a hayseed role. A banker nudged a director of the Northern Pacific who was sitting at the table and whispered hoarsely, "I understand he used to ride your trains, blind baggage."

The heads of the Stock Exchange visited Douglas's office to determine whether these words would be followed by action. He motioned them to be seated, lifted his long legs on to the desk, squinted as though he were peering at the sun, and delivered an ultimatum: "Gentlemen, the job of regulation has got to be done. It isn't being done now, and damn it, you're going to do it or we are. All you've

given the Commission is the run-around. If you'll produce a real program of regulation I'll let you run the Exchange. But if you just keep
on horse-trading I'm going to step in and run it myself."

Hope dies hard and the Exchange tried to compromise with Douglas on a list of halfway reforms. Douglas put on the five-gallon Western hat he invariably wears and went to see W.H. Jackson, counsel
for the Exchange.

"Negotiations are off," said the SEC chairman, striding in. "Letting
the boys in the Street throw a perpetual party isn't going to help recovery. The proposals given the Commission are phony clear
through."

"Then I suppose you'll go ahead with your own program," Jackson
murmured cautiously.

"You're damn right I will."

"Well, when you take over," said Jackson, "remember that we've
been in business a century and a half. There may be some questions
you want to ask."

Douglas leaned across the table and looked at Jackson. "There's
just one question I'd like to ask," he said. "Where do you keep the
paper and pencils?"

The Exchange could no longer doubt that the legislative ammunition provided by Congress for its subdual would be used. The new
chairman had shown he was ready to empty the whole arsenal. The
Exchange reorganized. For the first time a paid outside president administered trading – William McC. Martin, Jr., who later joined the
Army as a private. Three governors were installed to represent the
public. What was left of the old system which had permitted pools
and manipulation and the rigging of securities passed out. The Street
itself clamped down on overspeculation. The "death sentence" of
the Wheeler-Rayburn Act was applied to utility holding companies,
bringing to bay, among others, the squirming Mr. Hopson of Associated Gas & Electric.[6] In Douglas's words, "the casino element was
being removed from what should have been an old-fashioned open
auction." And investors voted in a special Gallup poll that their faith
in stocks and securities had increased since the reorganization
began.

These changes were by no means revolutionary, yet even the skeptical *Nation* agreed that the new chairman of the SEC had found "the New York Stock Exchange a private club and made it a public institution." The important element in all this is that the Exchange moved slowly and unwillingly toward reform of its own basic practices until it bumped into an SEC chairman whose bluff it could not call because he was not bluffing. Douglas was the third chairman of the SEC but the first to venture a genuine showdown with high finance.

In the midst of his stubborn battle for Government operation of Muscle Shoals, Senator George W. Norris once observed that a man cannot accomplish a lot for the people unless he is willing to risk being destroyed in the process. Douglas put his entire career on the line when he went to the mat on the question of the reorganization of the Stock Exchange. John T. Flynn attributed his ultimate success to the fact that he had "no extraneous ambitions, no hankering for either wealth or honors." These are qualities which Douglas's friends emphasize now as they urge him for a key role in our war effort. They contend that in both the industrial and military fields the hour demands a departure from old notions and practices and that a young man who was unawed by the mightiest American bankers will not pay undue homage to gold braid from cuff to elbow. They insist that no assignment, regardless of its magnitude, could make him lose his nerve or abandon his convictions.

II

One of the most revealing facts about this youngest Supreme Court Justice, who will be forty-four in the fall, is that the same people are boosting him today for a place in the war Cabinet who at the start of his public career backed him for the SEC, then for its chairmanship, and finally for the Supreme Court. In the intrigue of Washington, friends and political alliances melt like slush. Lewis breaks with Murray; Hopkins and Ickes do not speak; Hull and Moley hunt each other's scalps; Congressional colleagues come to the parting of the ways.[7]

Douglas has always been backed by four groups: (1) The original young liberals of the Roosevelt Administration headed by Tommy

Corcoran and Benjamin V. Cohen. (2) New Deal Democrats in Congress like Claude Pepper, Lister Hill, Frank Maloney, John M. Coffee, and Walter Pierce. (3) The independent progressives such as Senators Norris, La Follette, Borah, and Bone. (4) The Far West in general.

This support has been constant. One reason is that Douglas has warmly reciprocated it even when it was not expedient for him to do so. Although isolationists are out of favor in Washington now and although Douglas himself was a pre-Pearl Harbor adherent of the President's foreign policy, he often associates with his old friends, Bob La Folette and Homer Bone. Tommy Corcoran has been under heavy assault for some of his recent legal fees, but Douglas endorsed him for the post of Solicitor General. Some of the intellectuals in the Administration see this "my friend, right or wrong" attitude as a flaw in Douglas. They mistrust his admiration for the late Senator Borah of Idaho, whose speech hailing Douglas as the choice of the West came at a time when his appointment to the Court was in doubt.

These loyalties have weakened Douglas in certain circles. They feel he should have dumped Corcoran for ethical reasons and men like La Folette and Bone for their opinions. Yet his faithfulness is also a source of strength. In the loosely knit alliance that is the Democratic Party a leader must win the liberals through his views and the politicians through his behavior. Such a leader is Mr. Roosevelt. Few others possess these special qualifications. McNutt has the support of the politicians but not of the liberals; Vice-President Wallace, of the liberals but not of the politicians. Both factions, however, support and trust Douglas.

Loyalty is a basic factor in politics. Jim Farley has always put a top premium on it. Douglas is known in Washington for one of Mr. Roosevelt's weaknesses – a tolerance of shortcomings in his friends. In fact, despite the difference in their backgrounds, there is considerable similarity between the President and his youngest Supreme Court appointee. Both are liberals and definitely not radicals, and both lack the pomp and Olympian aloofness customarily associated with high office. Douglas fervently admires Mr. Roosevelt, whom he calls "the boss" and considers one of our three greatest Presidents along with Jefferson and Lincoln.

A hostess in the Capitol once told her friends that "that young Mr. Douglas is certainly not a fit person to be on our Supreme Court." She had seen the Justice scratch a match on the seat of his trousers while eating lunch at the Hay-Adams House. Had she heard him talking to his companions she might have been shocked further. Working in logging camps, taking bands of sheep to market in boxcars, and bunking with migratory farm laborers are experiences which contribute words to a man's vocabulary found in no dictionary. Justice Douglas remembers most of them. Some of his critics fear he is not sufficiently dignified to be a member of America's highest Court, but he has given many average Americans their first direct contact with an institution long identified in the public mind with beards, ritual and stuffiness.

After Douglas had visited some of the railroad workers in the Union Pacific yards at La Grande, Oregon, a leathery engineer on No. 26, the Pacific Limited, said: "He looks and acts a hell of a lot more like my fireman than a Supreme Court judge." And after Douglas had crowned the queen of the Wenatchee Apple Blossom Festival, one of his critics grumbled, "He acts more like a candidate for county commissioner than a Supreme Court Justice." Another critic said, "Douglas ought to fish or cut bait. If he wants to be a Supreme Court Justice he should behave like one. But if he wants to behave like a small-town politician he should get off the Supreme Court."

Never before has the Supreme Court had a member quite as plebian as Mr. Justice Douglas. Douglas and his dark-haired wife and their two namesakes, Mildred, who is eleven, and Bill, Jr., who is eight, have driven across the country in an inexpensive sedan when Court has adjourned each summer. On the way to their twelve-hundred-dollar cabin in the Wallowa National Forest of Oregon they have put up for the night at "motels" and tourist camps. Not many landlords along U.S. 30 would believe that the angular young man with unruly hair and blue eyes who loped in and bargained for a bungalow for four was one of the fabled "Nine Old Men." His signature,

"W.O. Douglas, Silver Spring, Maryland," was never much of a giveaway in this land of first names. This let him sit on a hardtack box and freely acquire local gossip about weather, politics, and crops. (The transcontinental drive is out this summer, for Douglas and his family are traveling by train because of gasoline and tire shortages. He did not apply for an X card.)

The fact that few people ever call Douglas anything except Bill affords a pretty accurate estimate of his personality. Palmer Hoyt, publisher of the *Oregonian*, took him fishing on the Columbia River a year ago and found that the Justice, having been there the season before, was nonchalantly addressed as Bill by Indians, storekeepers, and Forest Rangers. Douglas was brought up along the rim of the frontier by a family which lived on the sagebrush side of the N.P. right-of-way, and he still can throw a diamond hitch on a packhorse and cut down a ponderosa pine twenty-four inches thick. Keith McCool from the McGraw Creek Ranger Station reports that Douglas is the best woodsman ever to camp in his district, even including a troupe of movie heroes noted for outdoor roles.

In Washington the Douglases seldom attend social functions. He does not like to dance and enjoys most of all sitting around with highballs and smoked Chinook salmon sandwiches (made with fish which he caught and smoked himself), talking politics, government, and war with some of his cronies – Under Secretary of the Navy James V. Forrestal, Justices Hugo L. Black and James F. Byrnes, Jerome Frank, Ferdinand Pecora, Lowell Mellett, Governor Ernest Gruening of Alaska, Secretary Ickes, Eliot Janeway of *Fortune*, and Robert A. Lovett, Assistant Secretary of War for Air. At a reception last winter Mrs. Douglas noticed that her husband had been missing nearly an hour. She found him outside, trying to extricate Congressman Knute Hill's car from a snowdrift.

Douglas is seldom inhibited by formality. He does practically all his own driving, helped out once in a while by his Negro handy man Rochester. Supreme Court attendants twitch remonstratively when the Justice leaves Washington on the train. He trudges the seven or eight blocks from the Court to the station carrying his own valise.

Sprawled out with his feet on the desk, pencil behind his ear, surrounded by a redoubt of law books, Douglas derives a steadying assurance from the fact that he is Brandeis's successor. On a trip to Boston on SEC business in 1936, Douglas wandered into shops looking for a good etching of Brandeis. The one that he bought hung over his desk at home for three years, until he could take it down and hang it in Brandeis's old chambers. One of the great moments of his life was when Brandeis greeted him after the Senate had confirmed his nomination 62 to 4. "I wanted you to be here in my place," Brandeis said.

Perhaps some of Brandeis's faith in him stemmed from their mutual mistrust of excessive size in both bureau and corporation. Douglas believes the war effort should be decentralized so that decisions affecting farflung localities are made regionally rather than in the nations capital. As chairman of the SEC, he proposed a chain of Federal loan banks to lend funds exclusively to small mercantile and industrial enterprises, but the proposal was blocked by Jesse Jones.

"Bigness," Douglas told an audience of Chicago business men, "taxes the ability to manage intelligently. The needs of a small Middle Western community are apt to be better served by a banker at the head of a small local bank than by the same banker at the head of the nation's biggest bank. Bigness concentrates tremendous economic and financial power in the hands of a few. The growth of bigness has resulted in ruthless sacrifices of human values. The disappearance of free enterprise has submerged the individual in the impersonal corporation. When a nation of shopkeepers is transformed into a nation of clerks enormous spiritual sacrifices are made. Service to human beings becomes subordinate to profits to manipulators."

This sounded like Brandeis. In fact, Douglas began the speech by quoting from *The Curse of Bigness*. Today he is extremely conscious of the fact that he occupies Brandeis's seat on the Court. In his own handwriting he carries on a voluminous correspondence with the friends of his predecessor. He asks questions about the problems in which Brandeis was interested – State insurance, co-operatives, health and safety standards in industry. He maintains close contact with the Brandeis family. "We all think," said Elizabeth Brandeis Raushenbush recently, "that father could have had no better successor, especially in an appreciation of the dignity and identity of the common man." Smallwood, Brandeis's graying Negro messenger, continues to work for Justice Douglas. From his vantage point Smallwood has decided that both "my Justices" have been plain, kindly men. "'Course," he qualifies, "there's one big difference. Justice Brandeis – he used to bring a sandwich from home in his pocket. But Justice Douglas, he eats more. He sends me over to the Methodist Building cafeteria to fetch him a whole lunch."

III

The story of William O. Douglas is unique in the New Deal. It is one of the paradoxes of this Administration which has done so much for the laboring man that most of its leading officials have come from prosperous homes. The President himself, Francis Biddle, Henry Wallace, Frances Perkins, Henry Morgenthau, Jr., Robert H. Jackson, William C. Bullitt – all grew up in well-to-do or comfortable households. Bill Douglas was born on October 16, 1898, in the threadbare flat of a Presbyterian "home missionary" in the town of Maine, Minnesota. His father, who sang hymns in the brogue of his native Nova Scotia, moved to Yakima in 1900 and died when Bill was six. Bill's mother, of Scotch ancestry from Vermont, was left with a small girl, two small boys, and $1,800 in life insurance.

The $1,800 paid for an old house. After school Bill sold the arch-Republican Yakima *Republic* on street corners and ran errands for Falkenburg's jewelry store for ten cents an hour. Bill attended Yakima High, where the *Annual* predicted of him (along with virtually every other member of the class) that he was "sure to succeed." But he was valedictorian and won a one-year scholarship to Whitman College at Walla Walla in the Palouse wheat hills. He pedaled the one hundred and thirty-one miles from Yakima on an old bicycle and landed a job on the campus washing windows and waiting on tables. To save dormitory rent so he could send money home, he pitched a tent in a nearby grove of trees and lived in it throughout his college career. During the summers he picked fruit, and drank water out of the irrigation ditches with the Okies, and shared their mulligan stews. The only luxury he allowed himself at Whitman was membership in Beta Theta Pi.

Douglas left college in 1918 at the age of nineteen to enlist in the Army. He emerged with a sergeant's chevrons and went back to Whitman and graduated with a Phi Beta Kappa key. He taught history and English at Yakima High for two years and worked for the Forest Service putting out fires in July and August. At the end of this time he had less than $75 in the bank, so he decided on a different profession. He threw everything he owned into an ancient family trunk and shipped it on ahead to Columbia University Law School in New York City. Then on a dark night he swung silently aboard a long freight train as it threaded through the Yakima yards. He arrived in Manhattan dusty and gaunt, with six cents in his pocket

Law school was a struggle and twice he was locked out of his room in the dormitory for failure to pay rent. He finally got some money in his wallet by brashly annotating and editing a course for a correspondence law school, although he was barely under way in his own legal studies. This paid $600 and, thus affluent, he returned to the Northwest, in a day coach this time, and married his campus sweetheart, Mildred Riddle, who was teaching school in La Grande. He graduated from Columbia second in his class and editor of the *Law Review*. On a tip he invested every cent he could scrape together in a stock selling at $9. It soared to $28.75 and he sold at a big profit. Three days later the stock was back at $9. This was his sole personal flier in Wall Street.

He went to work for the crack corporation law firm of Cravath, de Gersdorff, Swaine, and Wood and taught at Columbia on the side. For a period he returned to Yakima to practice law on his own, then hurried to New York again to teach full time at Columbia. He resigned in protest when Nicholas Murray Butler appointed a new Law School Dean without first consulting the faculty. "That's not democracy," he complained. A few weeks later at a party he met Robert M. Hutchins, then Dean of Law at Yale. Hutchins and Douglas retreated into a corner and talked all evening. In three days Douglas had been hired to teach at Yale. He set about preparing a course which would discuss the facts as well as the theories and fancies of business and finance.

Along with his teaching Douglas studied corporate bankruptcy procedure. Soon he was one of the highest-paid professors in the country, earning almost $20,000 a year altogether. Many businesses employed him as a consultant in reorganizations. On the side he dabbled in Connecticut politics and was one of the campaign managers for a liberal Democrat from Meriden named Frank Maloney, who was elected to the United States Senate in 1934. That year Douglas took nearly a fifty percent reduction in income to go to Washington and begin a series of corporate studies for the SEC. He was offered the job by Joe Kennedy and they are still good friends, another contact for which Douglas is criticized by some of the interventionists.

In 1936 it was practically automatic for a vacancy on the Commission to go to Douglas, and he got the chairmanship by default after Landis resigned in the fall of 1937. The New Deal had just been returned to power, the liberals were riding high, and there was no other important candidate. His first press conference as chairman of the SEC was historic. A reporter asked what sort of fellow he was. "What kind of bird am I?" began Douglas with the inevitable lifting of his feet to the desk. "To tell you the truth, I think that I am really a pretty conservative fellow from the old school, perhaps a school too old to be remembered. I am the kind of conservative who can't get away from the idea that simple honesty ought to prevail in the financial world. I am the kind of a fellow who can't see why stockholders shouldn't get the same kind of fair treatment they would get if they were big partners instead of little partners in an industry."

As a member of the Temporary National Economic Committee Douglas met Senators Joe O'Mahoney of Wyoming and William E. Borah of Idaho. Borah in particular was strong for him, and in 1932 Borah had been the main influence in President Hoover's appointment to the Supreme Court of Benjamin N. Cardozo. When Brandeis resigned Borah said that Douglas was a natural for the post. The West wanted a judge. Brandeis had been a liberal, a militant opponent of monopoly and privilege. Douglas satisfied all the qualifications. He was appointed by President Roosevelt in March of 1939 and took his seat on the bench April 17th, approximately sixteen years after he had ridden the rods out of Yakima.

Felix Belair of the New York *Times*, looking through the records of the Court, discovered that the new Justice was not a member of the Supreme Court bar. On the way up he had not had time.

IV

Large in the tradition of the United States Supreme Court is the phrase "Justices Holmes and Brandeis dissent." It is too early to tell whether the dissenting team of Justices William Orville Douglas and Hugo La Fayette Black will occupy as famous a niche in American judicial history. They are the new liberal minority on the liberalized Court selected by Mr. Roosevelt. Sometimes they swing enough of their colleagues to speak for the Court. Sometimes they are joined in their dissents by Justices Murphy and Reed. But they are almost invariably together, on the left of decisions involving fundamental social and economic issues. During the recent session Douglas dissented twenty-seven times and in twenty-one of these dissents he was allied with Black. Even when agreeing with the majority decision they have gone beyond their colleagues in strength of argument.

Justice Douglas's score of dissents during the 1941–42 session was higher than that of any other member of the Court. In a few cases his disagreement was based on technicalities, but more often it resulted from his feeling that the Court was interfering unduly with the Federal agencies created by Congress and was thus whittling down the gains recently won by the average man. His language in these opinions paralleled in some measure that of Brandeis in his great dissent in the Oklahoma ice case of 1932, which held that legislatures, both State and national, had wide power to deal with social and economic ills. "We are not a legislative committee," Douglas several times reminded his colleagues.

When the Court outlawed a California statute forbidding indigent workers to cross the State line, Douglas remembered his Okie pals in Yakima and wrote a special concurring opinion. He held that a State could not "curtail the right of free movement of those who are poor or destitute. To allow such an exception to be engrafted on the rights of national citizenship would be to contravene every conception of national unity. It would also introduce a caste system utterly incompatible with the spirit of our system of Government. It would permit those who were stigmatized by a State as indigents, paupers, or vagabonds to be relegated to an inferior class of citizenship. It would prevent a citizen because he was poor from ever seeking new horizons in other States."

This shows quite clearly the slant of Mr. Justice Douglas's mind. Perhaps he recalled the young vagabond from Yakima who had sought new horizons in 1923. The decisions written by Douglas have pointed toward extension of collective bargaining, toward control of trespassers on the public domain, toward greater power for the Government under the commerce and general welfare clauses of the Constitution. When the Court went only halfway in upholding an NLRB [National Labor Relations Board] order that the San Antonio, Texas, *Express* had to deal collectively with its employees in the American Newspaper Guild, Douglas thought the entire order should have been enforced. In this opinion he stated his philosophy on both labor organization and the power of the judiciary to restrain the verdicts of governmental agencies.

"Take the case," he wrote, "where an employer is playing ducks and drakes with the National Labor Relations Act. He pays mere lip service to the requirements of the Act while intent on blocking in his plant any effective union action. Employees are dropped – perhaps the leaders of the union; labor spies are employed; a company union is sponsored and financed; new employees are selected who promise not to join any outside union. The purpose is to thwart any effective action by that union. Such obstructive tactics could go on apace and yet no 'efforts' of the union 'to bargain collectively' need be denied. The employer could continue the so-called negotiations with the union, and yet in a myriad of ways undermine it if the breadth of the Board's order were delimited."

Should the Supreme Court be able to modify the order of the NLRB? Douglas and Black, joined by Justice Reed, did not think so. "Congress has invested the Board, not us," Douglas went on, "with discretion to choose and select the remedies necessary or appropriate for the evil at hand. Whether the remedy chosen by the Board was reasonably necessary in this case is not for us to determine. Nor is it for us to say what language is adequate to safeguard the labor rights which are in issue. To cut down the language of this order not only substitutes our judgment for that of the Board; it will also result in the creation of a host of uncertainties."

When Justice Frankfurter wrote a majority decision affirming a Texas court's injunction enjoining a strike by a carpenters' union, Douglas was among the dissenters. He joined Justice Reed's dissent against an opinion ruling that the NLRB could not compel shipowners to rehire seamen who had gone on strike while a ship was in harbor. He dissented when the Court, speaking through Justice Frankfurter, vacated an order issued by the Federal Communications Commission. "The Commission, not the courts," wrote Douglas, "is the ultimate guardian of the public interest under this Act." He dissented when the Court held that a redcap's tips could apply on the minimum wage he had to receive from the transportation company. "The tip-paying public," contended the minority, "is entitled to know whom it tips, the redcap or the railroad."

Like the amoeba, the Supreme Court, whether appointed by Roosevelt or Hoover or other Presidents, continually breaks up into subdivisions. David Lawrence's *United States News* regards the present Court, although largely the handiwork of President Roosevelt, as split into three factions: (1) Chief Justice Stone, Roberts, and Frankfurter on the right. (2) Byrnes, Jackson, Reed, and Murphy in the middle. (3) Douglas and Black on the left. Murphy sways toward the liberals, while Byrnes is inclined in the direction of the conservatives. How the Justices at the center make up their minds determines the decision of the Court.

The one case that really shattered this lineup was the celebrated Jehovah's Witnesses verdict of 1940, in which Frankfurter decreed the compulsory salute of the flag and only Harlan F. Stone dissented. Why Douglas and Black at first went along on this decision is still not clear; they later challenged Frankfurter sharply on a number of questions affecting civil liberties. The best guess is that the Roosevelt appointees, then being comparatively new to the Court, were trying desperately to stick together. At all events, after that Frankfurter inched toward the right, Douglas and Black veered left, and the schism was complete. In June of this year, when the Court again restricted the activities of Jehovah's Witnesses, the completeness of the break was clearly shown; in a move without precedent Douglas, Black, and Murphy not only dissented in the case immediately at issue but also declared that the earlier case had been wrongly decided.

Not enough time has elapsed since Douglas's appointment in 1939 to appraise him as a Justice of the Supreme Court. He works hard and puts in long hours, and on his summer fishing trips takes along writs of certiorari and reads them at night by kerosene lamp. Judicial history will probably estimate him and Frankfurter on the same page. The famous professor from Harvard, passionately resentful over the depredations of the Axis, evidently believes that both social reform and a measure of civil rights must be shelved temporarily by the war effort. Douglas, on the other hand, sees the world struggle as all one piece – whether the endeavor of a farm community in Montana to get electric power, or the revolt of a village in Jugoslavia against its Nazi masters. And perhaps history will decide that both of them were right.

V

Ever since the President's speech at Chicago in 1937 urging a "quarantine" of nations which attacked their neighbors, Douglas has been an interventionist.[8] Yet he has believed that America must accompany its military might with a promise of real political and economic freedom for the masses of Europe and Asia. He thinks now that the Atlantic Charter must be specifically applied east of Suez. T. V. Soong and Pearl Buck and her husband, Richard J. Walsh, the editor of *Asia*, are among his closest friends and his sympathy for India, China, and other colonial peoples is well known in Washington. He carried proudly in his pocket a magazine published in Malaya which reprinted a commencement address of his on American democracy. "I wonder how many of the folks there can read English?" he inquired of a friend.

Back of Douglas today is a record of liberaliam on domestic questions and an international outlook on foreign affairs. He is among the few men in public life who might succeed Mr. Roosevelt in the Democratic Party as the leader of the Eastern factory workers and Western agriculturalists who have decided the last three Presidential elections. Who else is there? Many of the progressives have branded themselves as isolationists. Senator Norris is past eighty. Harry Hopkins is chronically in bad health. Under the pressure of a campaign will labor ever accept McNutt after martial law in Terre Haute?[9] It finally resolves down to Henry Wallace – and Douglas.

Douglas himself has never said a word about this, not even to his most intimate friends. If he has any higher ambitions they are secret. Yet no man of his age, with his possibilities, can remain unaware of the role he could play. He has a grassroots personality, a homespun Lincolnesque appearance, and the nearest thing to a log-cabin background there is in American politics today. "Justice Douglas," said a Washington correspondent, "is the kind of fellow that most politicians' press agents wish their politicians were." The Democrats must carry the West solidly to win any future elections in which the Republican Party puts up a candidate of Willkie's stature, and men all over the West are waiting for the chance to start a favorite-son boom for Douglas. He is the first genuine White House potentiality the Pacific seaboard has produced in several generations.

Wayne Morse: Republican Gadfly

American Mercury, JULY 1947

Wayne L. Morse (1900–1974) was a liberal Republican senator when Neuberger wrote this article in 1947. At the time, Morse was facing a serious threat for renomination from Earl Snell, a highly popular Republican governor. But in November of 1947, Snell, Oregon Secretary of State Robert Ferrell, and State Senate President Marshall Cornett were killed in a plane crash while on a hunting trip. Morse won another term as a Republican, in 1950. Two years later, he became an independent, then switched to the Democratic party in 1954 after campaigning for Neuberger. Morse was Neuberger's law professor at the University of Oregon, and advised him to stick to journalism because he would never be a lawyer. Neuberger twice voted for Morse as a Republican senator, then actively campaigned for him in 1956, Morse's first race as a Democrat. Jealous of Neuberger's growing prestige and influence, Morse's bitterness turned into enmity toward Neuberger. Morse vowed to oppose Neuberger's reelection in 1960. The breakup of the Morse-Neuberger alliance was a major national political story. Neuberger believed that Morse was paranoid and more than a few of his Senate colleagues were in agreement.

THE LAST TIME the Republicans controlled Congress it was not the party's stalwarts but its rebels in the Senate who captured the imagination of the country. Although the present GOP rulers of Capitol Hill insist that there is no longer any reason for liberal Republicans to assume the rôle of insurgents, a first-term Senator from

Oregon can be depended upon to demand regularly and loudly that the party's election pledges against reaction, isolationism and special privilege be made good. Indeed, Republican Senators had just had time to adjust themselves to the pleasant occupancy of the high-backed, upholstered chairs of committee chairmen when Wayne Lyman Morse began denouncing their plans for tax reduction and new labor legislation.

Morse is totally unlike the insurgents of the Coolidge-Hoover era whom Senator George H. Moses of New Hampshire dubbed "Sons of the Wild Jackass." He is only forty-six. Before he ran for the Republican nomination for Senator in 1944 he had never stood for any elective office. He has behind him a brilliant academic record, which includes the fourth doctorate in jurisprudence ever awarded by Columbia University.

It is in the Norris tradition for Republican insurrectionists to look venerable and benign. Morse resembles a good deal more the prototype of the vested interests he is harassing. A coed in a criminal law class which Morse taught at the University of Oregon once observed that her professor looked like an "intellectual Simon Legree." Morse's trimmed mustache, thick eyebrows, sleek black hair and dark complexion give him an appearance ill-suited, at least in the public mind, to his rôle as the White Knight seeking to purify the Grand Old Party.

Morse himself is evidently aware that he must be the City Slicker rather than the Country Boy. He boasts of his extensive education, frequently listing for the voters his academic honors. Instead of putting on leather chaps and a ten-gallon Stetson for the campaign photograph so cherished by Western politicians, Morse tempts the scorn of the cattlemen among his constituents by riding in society horse shows clad in balloon breeches and a monogrammed silk shirt.

Despite his disregard for West political shibboleths Morse, who will be in office at least until 1950, has become a significant national figure as the spokesman and strategist of such opposition as exists within Republican congressional ranks to the reigning monarchs of the party. Because of the gag rule which silences all except a few members of the House, this opposition can be effectively voiced only in the unlimited debate of the Senate. The newly dominant Republicans are now on trial before the nation, and it may well be Wayne Morse who restrains them from rushing back to the lush but toxic pastures of the reckless twenties. At least he will make the try.

II

Most of Morse's Senatorial associates were chary of him from the day he took the oath of office, yet no member of the Senate can complain that Wayne Morse has not made at least one bid in his direction. Within a year the junior Senator from Oregon called President Truman a "ham actor" – and backed up Truman's opposition to Republican plans for tax reduction. He demanded the resignation from the government of Chester Bowles – and assailed the "greed and avarice" of Bowles' principal antagonist, the National Association of Manufacturers. He berated "the same old reactionaries" in the national councils of the Republican party – and made fulsome speeches urging the reelection of Oregon's reactionary Republican congressional delegation. He supported left-wing Democratic Senator Pepper on price control one week – and right-wing Republican Senator Wherry the next. He dismissed the Republican platform as "disappointing and a stillbirth of the party's hopes" – and within a month was proclaiming the Republican party as "the instrument for saving the nation from leftists and chaos." He called the last meeting of the Republican National Committee "a flop at which we listened to clichés *ad nauseum*" – but promised to support any candidate nominated by the party for President. He introduced a strong anti-monopoly bill with Senator Hugh B. Mitchell – and then traveled to the state of Washington to deliver speeches which contributed to the victory of Mitchell's Old Guard Republican adversary.

Can a man guilty of such contradictory behavior lead the Republican party out of the morass of reaction? There is an explanation, if perhaps not an excuse, for Morse's whirligig record, and that is the political state of affairs in Oregon. Oregon is the most conservative state in the West, and most of Morse's trimming is in deference to the cautious voters from whom he must seek reelection. By instinct he is a liberal on most public issues. He favors amnesty for wartime consciencious objectors, he has taken the floor of the Senate to speak against bills of attainder which would proscribe government officials for their political views, and he continually opposes those who would come to the aid of utilities by suspending Federal power projects.

In many ways Morse is an old-fashioned trustbuster. He mistrusts big business, as he doubts the wisdom of big government. He believes that business should be scaled down to reasonable size, rather than government be given power to control it. Taxation, he thinks, might be a weapon with which to do the scaling. "Not a single dollar of the war profits now collected under our tax structure should be returned to business men by a tax reduction," Morse insists.

When chided for "backsliding," Morse cites President Roosevelt: "I can only go as fast as people will let me." "My influence as a Senator and as a liberal will be gone," he argues, "if I get so out of step with the citizens of Oregon as to be suspended between heaven and earth like Mohammed's coffin." Morse is no Norris heading resolutely in one direction, regardless of consequences. In political behavior he is more akin to Borah – brilliant in debate but often short in accomplishment. As the attacker, the denouncer of others, the militant critic, Morse has few peers in the Senate. But he himself mixes little mortar to close the breach which he thus exposes. After many blistering assaults on the labor proposals of Taft and Ball, he was able at first to suggest nothing more than a measure to enlarge the National Labor Relations Board and to outlaw jurisdictional strikes, which is comparable to being against original sin.

Again like Borah, Morse is often moved by impulse. It was at the time of the 1946 railroad strike that he leaped to his feet to castigate President Truman as a "ham actor." The same impulsiveness led him to make an apology in the Senate for this reference after the President's speech requesting aid for Greece and Turkey.

Unlike Borah, Morse is no isolationist. He was the first Republican Senator to pledge all-out support for financial aid to Greece and Turkey. He is convinced the United States must participate actively in the affairs of Europe "or Russia will rule the Continent from Vienna to Normandy."

It is in this respect that Morse differs most markedly from his fellow Republican progressive, Senator George Aiken of Vermont. Aiken still inclines toward isolation. He lacks Morse's faith in the United Nations, the World Court and other instruments of international adjustment. But on domestic questions their philosophies are virtually identical. Both believe business monopolies must be controlled or all talk of "free enterprise" becomes largely academic. They advocate conservation of forest, soil and water resources by the Federal government. They have opposed exempting railroads, fire-insurance companies and other corporations from the anti-trust laws. And they have led the fight on the Republican side of the chamber for confirmation of such public officials as David E. Lilienthal and Gordon Clapp.

"Government must protect the econmically weak from the financially powerful or our private-profit economy is not going to survive," declares Morse, and Aiken has concurred.

"George Aiken is the wheel-dog of the Republican progressives," said a correspondent watching them from the gallery, "but Wayne Morse is the leader of the pack. He picks the trail the team will follow."

III

Morse often implies that his presence in the United States Senate is a "political accident." Oregon's conservative Republican leaders are still uncertain how it happened, but they woefully admit that Morse sold them a bill of goods. Suspicious of him as a Roosevelt appointee to the National War Labor Board, they nevertheless let him convince them that in the Senate he would be as safe as the president of the National Association of Manufacturers. As a seller of himself, in other words, Wayne Morse has done very well.

Politicians in general and Republican politicians in particular are notoriously allergic to professors; yet ex-professor Morse has become a force whom Republican politicians must listen to. Thomas L. Stokes has called him "the most insistent voice for progressivism among Republicans in the eightieth Congress." Marquis Childs believes Morse "may be the forerunner of a new liberal movement within the Republican party which will oppose both leftism and black reaction."

Overcoming the handicap of his academic background was not Morse's biggest achievement in getting elected. He broke the tradition that a state's highest offices shall be reserved for the native son, or at least a resident of long standing. Suspicion of the outlander, the newcomer, the *cheechako*, is old in American public life. In the Far West it is nearly as intense as in the South.

Morse had lived in Oregon a decade before anyone suspected him of political ambitions. In that time he stream-lined the university's law school and led a victorious faculty revolt against a chancellor who tried to limit academic freedom. Called to the attention of the Department of Justice by his friend and former teacher, Raymond Moley, Morse hired two thousand workers and spent a million dollars directing a nationwide study of the administration of criminal law. This association with the New Deal increased the belief among the lumber barons that the dean of the Oregon Law school was a radical, but Morse consistently registered as a Republican – possibly because Oregon was one of three states sending only Republicans to the Senate at the zenith of Roosevelt's popularity.

In 1940 Morse delivered an address at a Republican banquet in the logging town of Klamath Falls. He waxed autobiographical and talked more about himself than about Abraham Lincoln, the topic of the occasion. He explained that although he came from Wisconsin he had steadfastly refused to align himself "with the very active La Follette Progressive Club on the University of Wisconsin campus, for La Follette's opposition to the war made it impossible for me to accept him as a party leader." In fact, as a mere stripling Morse had discerned the alleged dangers of La Follettism:

> I was not of voting age but in the family arguments, sometimes for the sake of argument but to a large measure out of youthful conviction, I would contend that a more acceptable political program lay somewhat halfway between the reaction of the Stalwarts and the ultra-liberalism of the Progressive. Thus I suppose it may be said that I have always been a "middle-of-the-roader" in Republican politics.

As plain as smoke signals to a Shoshone, this told Oregon's cautious Republican party officials, reliant on lumber and utility financing, that the spectacular young dean hankered for their endorsement. They expected Morse to enter the lists for public office at once, but instead he accepted an appointment as arbitrator of labor disputes along the troubled Pacific Coast waterfront. It was a perilous job for a man with political ambitions, but Morse carried it off well. Generally pro-labor in his decisions, he nevertheless refused to be bluffed when Harry Bridges announced defiantly that his CIO longshoremen would refuse to recognize one of Morse's decisions. Bridges sought to palaver at the St. Francis Hotel, but Morse took the afternoon train back to Oregon, where he announced:

> The union's failure to live up to its promise to abide by the decision of the arbitrator has destroyed the arbitration agreement and rendered the union's word valueless. The union must answer to public opinion. I herewith tender my resignation.

For once, the arrogant Bridges was trapped. Pressure from the membership of his union compelled him to apologize publicly to Morse, accept the disputed ruling and then ask the law professor to return as arbitrator.

During the term of his service on the National War Labor Board Morse demonstrated the same independence. Ahead of his time, he saw that Federal capitulation to John L. Lewis might become an endless process. When a majority of the Board gave in to Lewis in 1943[10] Morse contended, "This is the surrender of government in the name of political expediency." Harold L. Ickes, trying to cozen Lewis along so the mines would not shut down, accused Morse of playing to the grandstand. It proved to be one of the few tiffs in which an antagonist could match the sulphurous language of the Secretary of the Interior.

"Dear Mr. Secretary," Morse began a letter to Ickes. "Your most recent communication serves only to strengthen and confirm my low opinion of you."

This rumpus altered Morse's career, and probably to Morse's ultimate advantage. When a vacancy occurred on the Circuit Court of Appeals for the Western States, Morse had the backing of many New Dealers along the Pacific Coast. James F. Byrnes, then Director of the Office of War Mobilization, who had also opposed further salaaming to Lewis, endorsed Morse, but at the last minute Ickes hurried to the White House in protest, and Roosevelt scratched Morse's name from the list.

IV

Morse now looked toward the Senate. Rufus Holman, an aged Senate demagogue whose principal theme was an attack on foreign "refugees" in terms that smacked of Anti-Semitism, seemed ripe for the conquest. Morse at first proposed the candidacy of Palmer Hoyt, the sensational young publisher of the Portland *Oregonian*, now editor of the Denver *Post*, but Hoyt decided that newsprint and personal political ambitions did not mix and threw the powerful support of the *Oregonian* to Morse.

It was a bitter primary campaign and Morse was at his best. In challenging speeches he accused Holman of bigotry and prejudice. Holman underwrote the charges by taunting Morse as "perfesser" and contending that he was financed by wealthy Jews. Morse won by a slender margin; Palmer Hoyt said later that only "the most genuinely brilliant and masterful campaign talks ever delivered in Oregon" had overthrown Holman, long a feeder at the political trough.

Having won the Republican nomination as a liberal, Morse reverted to conservatism to demonstrate to Oregon's GOP leadership that he was to be trusted with the Senate seat. New Dealers, to whom he had protested his fealty to Roosevelt when seeking a place on the Federal bench, were astonished to hear him going all-out for Tom Dewey and denouncing President Roosevelt as an advocate of "regimentation and scarcity." Morse's close friends on the University campus, knowing his personal belief in international cooperation, heard him tell rural audiences that the Hull reciprocal trade program had to be abandoned in the interests of "American markets for the American farmer."

Morse was helped by the fact that his opponent, a Liberty League Democrat, also stayed off the Roosevelt bandwagon. Thus, although the President carried Oregon, Morse was elected by the whopping majority of 269,095 to 174,140.

As a member of the United States Senate, Wayne Morse has tried hard to prove that his behavior in the 1944 general election was what the late Wendell Willkie once called "merely a bit of campaign oratory." He has been the least regular of all the Republicans. No sooner had he taken the oath of office from Vice-President Truman, when he voted to confirm the contested appointments of two New Dealers, Henry A. Wallace and Aubrey Williams. Once, when he found himself holding the Senate floor almost alone, Morse tried to slip over a bill abolishing the poll tax, and the frantic Southern Democrats barely got back to the chamber in time. Morse has repeatedly questioned the sincerity of his party's bid for the Negro vote and has suggested that the Republicans pass a measure to outlaw filibusters and so permit a bill to be adopted to outlaw the poll tax despite Southern opposition.

Morse also showed that he had recovered fully from his professed youthful aversion to the La Follettes. He began sending contributions to the La Follette weekly newspaper, *The Progressive*, and he urged Wisconsin Republicans to renominate Senator Robert M. La Follette, Jr.

Morse has a keen sense of personal rectitude. He ended the 1944 election campaign deeply in debt but refused to accept funds from "questionable" sources to pay it off. His intimates claim he turned down utility money and substantial donations from slot-machine operators in Portland. Morse was disturbed when some of his Senate colleagues were reported to be speculating on the cotton market while the life of OPA [Office of Price Administration] was at stake last year. This lay behind his urging that Senators be compelled by law to reveal the source of all income they receive. Nevertheless, at the height of gasoline rationing he drove 3000 miles across the continent with a trailer carrying two thoroughbred horses, Oregana Bourbon and Spice of Life, which he now enters in Eastern horse shows. The prize money they win does diminish the campaign deficit. So do the speeches he delivers for sizable fees. A fluent and forceful speaker, he seems to be talking so often that even his partisans back home hope there will be at least one question before the country on which Morse will not have an opinion.

Morse can be picayunish as well as righteous. When the wife of Senator Langer of North Dakota sat on the Senate floor with her husband during the Bilbo debate, Morse demanded that the sergeant-at-arms expel her. "Why'd you do that, Wayne?" asked Langer after the session. "Because it was against the rules of the Senate," Morse answered coldly.

Like Jack London's derelict attorney who tried hard to dispense gold-rush justice at Whitehorse, reverence for the law is at once Morse's strength and weakness. It has prompted him to undertake lonely and painstaking investigations to ferret out twenty-year sentences handed soldiers by military courts for relatively trivial offenses. It also has instilled in him wrath for the cavalier disregard of congressional appropriation limitations by the Army, Navy and other Federal agencies. "Acts of Congress are to be obeyed and not evaded!" he once shouted at a bureaucrat with whose general aims he was in sympathy.

Detailed immersion in the law marked Morse long-winded and wordy. It took him nearly eight thousand words to defend his opposition to the Taft-Ball labor bills in a letter to an anti-union trade paper in Oregon. "Wayne sometimes forgets the difference between political speeches in the Senate and opinions delivered by the Ninth Circuit Court of Appeals," a colleague from the Far West has observed.

Morse would probably swap his senatorial seat for a chance to be Attorney General or a member of the United States Supreme Court. (The *Herald Tribune*, incidentally, has proposed him for inclusion in the next Republican cabinet.) If he was precocious in deciding not to join forces with the elder La Follette, he was even younger when he decided to be a lawyer.

Morse was born near Madison, Wisconsin, in the fall of 1900, a direct descendant of Samuel F. B. Morse, the inventor of the telegraph. He won all his grade and high school debating contests; he knew a lawyer had to be able to convince a jury. After graduating from the University of Wisconsin, he paid his way through the law school of the University of Minnesota by teaching public speaking. Along the route of acquiring degrees he married Mildred Downie, who taught home economics at Minnesota and was famous for her cakes and icebox cookies. They now have three daughters – Nancy, 16; Judy, 13; and Amy, 12.

Within two years after arriving at the University of Oregon in 1930 Morse was dean of law. Some accuse him of being ruthless in his ascent. Certainly he knew where his own interest lay – but that is hardly a crime in a competitive society.

Morse has always estimated pretty shrewdly what he could and could not get away with. At a tense moment in the 1944 primaries one of his campaign managers urged him to stress the fact that he was born on a farm. Morse looked in the hotel room mirror at his dark, sophisticated face, with an almost Oriental cast to eyes and cheek-bones. He shook his head emphatically. "When I was a boy," he said, "I went to a lot of political meetings with my father. I've never forgotten what he said when one candidate presented himself as a farmer. 'A good day's work on a farm would kill that buzzard.'"

v

For many years the dramatic figures in the United States Senate came from the Pacific seaboard and the Middle West. Norris was the symbol but there were others – Borah, Pittman, Hiram Johnson, McNary, Wheeler, Walsh, Costigan, the La Follettes. The Senate may have been run by men from the metropolis, but the vision of the better world-to-be stemmed from cornfield and fir forest.

Virtually alone among the inheritors of the "Sons of the Wild Jackass" tradition, Wayne Morse gives promise of living up to this heritage. Yet the very revolution which has moved the origins of American liberalism from alfalfa field to factory makes it difficult for him to do so. Radicalism in the United States once stemmed from farm and backwoods – the Wobblies of the IWW, the Non-Partisan League, the Farm Holiday Association. Today the progressive influences in the Congress are men from the centers of trade-union strength, from the great cities of the nation. Wayne Morse represents a state which is predominantly rural, and he is trying his best to defy this trend.

Morse is badgered continually by the leaders of his party in Oregon, many of whom are lobbyists for utilities, chain stores, loan companies and gambling syndicates. They confront him with threats; the latest of these is that he will be opposed for reelection in 1950 by Earl Snell, a vapid and timid public official but the greatest gubernatorial vote-getter in the state's history. Despite his sophisticated appearance Morse reacts emotionally to the almost untenable political situation in which he finds himself, and most of his backsliding has occurred after the thumb screws were applied in punishment for some liberal escapade. He stumped the West for a slate of Republican tories when party stalwarts were demanding his scalp because of a sharp attack on Senator Taft. He spoke out abruptly against the New Deal at a time when Oregon lumbermen and bankers were indignant over his criticism of the NAM. On another occasion, Morse believed it desirable to cite the fact that he was quoted approvingly in a book by Eric Johnston, then president of the United States Chamber of Commerce.

Morse's dilemma is an old one in American public life. Should a member of Congress speak for himself or for the voters who elected him? Morris thought "conscience should be the only guide. Otherwise a member of Congress, giving weight to expressed public sentiment, becomes an automatic voting machine." Norris never trimmed, but there has been only one Norris. Morse is too ambitious to be indifferent to reelection.

Speaking at a banquet honoring what would have been the fifty-fifth birthday of Wendell Willkie, Morse said Willkie, had put "country above party" when he refused to campaign against conscription during the 1940 Presidential campaign. Morse implied that he would do the same under similarly grave conditions. Morse probably risks his political life more often than any other member of the present Senate. Were he up for reelection now, the resources of his party would undoubtedly be thrown against him. Taft, Ball, and Wherry are not happy over his warnings against a "return to the tragic economic mistakes made by the Republican party in the twenties." Their plans for the future do not encompass the junior Senator from Oregon, but the junior senator from Oregon will continue to goad and harass them until at least 1950.

"A Republican insurgent from a Republican state takes his political life in his hands when his party holds power in Congress," the elder La Follette said long ago. Morse, who as a boy in Wisconsin shunned La Folletteism, would no doubt cry amen.

Wayne L. Morse: 1956 and Beyond

Fortnight, MAY 1955

Oregon – she flies with her own wings!   STATE MOTTO

HOW RIGIDLY are we Americans laced into the course of party regularity? Can a political figure of conscience and intellect change his party affiliation and still survive at the polls? Is it essential for a man to play the political string through to the bitter end, once he begins a career in one major party or the other? Do people really mean what they say, when they talk of "voting for the man rather than for the party?"

All these questions are likely to be answered in Oregon at the general election of November 1956.

At stake will be the political fate of Wayne Lyman Morse, senior United States Senator from Oregon. Morse, now 54 years old, was originally elected to the Senate as a Republican in 1944, reelected in 1950. But in 1956 he will run as a Democrat.

No other such complete metamorphosis has occurred in American politics in modern times. The illustrious Norris of Nebraska shifted from Republican to Independent – a course likewise followed by Morse – but Norris never went all the way to become a registered Democrat. Theodore Roosevelt moved from Republicanism to the Bull Moose Party, which he himself founded. Robert M. La Follette, Jr. deserted the Republican Party and ran as a Progressive in Wisconsin. Burton K. Wheeler of Montana was a third-party candidate for Vice-President, but returned to the Democrats. Hiram W. Johnson of California served as Teddy Roosevelt's Vice-Presidential nominee on the Bull Moose ticket, but also returned to the party of his origin – the Republican.

Morse's full change-over has been in a class by itself, although all these others abandoned their parties in greater or lesser degree.

The entire GOP strength undoubtedly will muster to discipline a man who supped at the table of Republicanism, but now is enrolled enthusiastically as a Democrat. The outcome will test whether or not a politician's conscience can lead him out of one party and into the rival party. If Morse is punished by defeat in 1956, decades will elapse before another political figure duplicates his example – no matter how compelling the principles at issue.

Oregon has been regarded as a Republican State all during the modern era. True, it voted for Franklin D. Roosevelt four times. Its total of registered Democrats has rarely been far behind the number of registered Republicans. It has a progressive tradition, threading back to William S. U'Ren, whom Lincoln Steffens described as "the law-giver." In 1902 U'Ren made Oregon the first State in the Nation to adopt the initiative and referendum and recall. Under U'Ren's urging, Oregon also led all other States in bringing about the direct election of Senators, one of the most fundamental and far-reaching reforms in American political history.

But U'Ren was a Republican. Indeed, in Oregon you did not count unless you were a Republican. It was the thing to do, like being a Democrat in Virginia or playing golf at Pebble Beach. Until I was elected to the Senate from Oregon in 1954, only one other Democrat ever had become a Senator from Oregon by popular vote – George Chamberlain of Albany, back in 1914, a full four decades earlier.

So, when Wayne Morse ceased being a Republican, became an Independent and, finally, a Democrat, he was blazing no easy path in Oregon. The way led up steep ramparts and around perilous bluffs.

Morse tried manfully to be a loyal Republican. Although he often deserted a majority of his party on key roll-call votes in the Senate, he stumped the country for Dewey in 1944 and in 1948. He spoke for the election of various Republican Senators. He made speeches why he would not be a Democrat. Political enemies in Oregon are said to have these radio tapes, ready for reproduction during the campaign of 1956. In fact, it is an ironic fact that Morse was the first prominent Republican leader in Oregon to endorse Eisenhower for President. He ran for delegate to the Republican National Convention in 1952 as an Eisenhower backer.

Somewhere along the line, Morse became sadly disillusioned. He heard Eisenhower berating Truman for the mistakes which led up to the Korean War. Morse remembered Eisenhower, as Army Chief of Staff, had participated in those mistakes – nay, may even have initiated some. Morse saw Eisenhower endorsing Jenner for reelection to the Senate in Indiana and recalled Jenner had called General George C. Marshall "a living lie" – Marshall, who dubbed Eisenhower "my man," and lifted him from military obscurity to world acclaim. Morse noted that Eisenhower deleted from a Wisconsin speech, at the insistence of Senator McCarthy, favorable reference to General Marshall.

Morse did what politicians rarely do. He changed his mind. He decided he had been wrong, and abruptly endorsed Adlai E. Stevenson. Referring to himself as an Independent, Morse made dozens of speeches for Stevenson.

After Stevenson's defeat, Morse remained an Independent. He had crossed the Rubicon so far as the GOP was concerned. The party disciplined him by taking away his seats on the Armed Services and Labor Committees. Only a few Democrats, led by Senator Clinton P. Anderson of New Mexico, favored giving Morse his committee posts under Democratic quota. Although the Republicans banished Morse, it is significant that Democratic Senators inflicted no similar penalty on Byrd of Virginia for supporting Eisenhower. Which party plays really rough when the chips are down?

Today, Morse has moved out of the twilight zone of "Independent." He is enrolled on the poll books of Lane County, Oregon, as a Democrat.

From my conversations with Morse, I believe it was Hells Canyon which brought the decision.

Where the Snake River has trenched a mile-deep chasm along the boundary between Oregon and Idaho, lies the finest site for hydroelectric power left in the U.S. Not only can vast quantities of energy be developed but also the immense reservoir in Hells Canyon will release water to "firm up" power plants dotting the lower Columbia during the dry season.

Morse believes the resources of Hells Canyon should be tapped with a high multi-purpose Federal dam, in the pattern of Grand Coulee, Bonneville and Shasta. However, Secretary of the Interior McKay favors turning over Hells Canyon to the Idaho Power Company, an absentee-dominated monopoly, which holds shareholders' meetings in Augusta, Maine. Such a precedent could result in relinquishment to private utility companies of most of the choice waterpower sites remaining in the Columbia basin, where lurks 42 percent of the country's potential hydroelectricity.

There is only one way to prevent the Federal Power Commission, now loaded with appointees inclining toward the private-power viewpoint, from accepting the McKay thesis. Congress can pass a bill authorizing Hells Canyon as a Federal dam. Capitol Hill is superior in authority to any administrative or quasi-judicial agency.

Morse and I circulated the Hells Canyon bill through the cloakrooms, corridors and offices of the Senate looking for sponsors. We ended up with a total of 30. In this 30 were 27 Democrats, two Republicans – and Morse.

"That's about the relative liberalism of the two parties," said Morse as we reviewed the list of Hells Canyon sponsors. From the beginning, it had been obvious that we would obtain the names of only a pair of Republicans – Langer and Young, both of North Dakota, where the old Populist strain still runs strong.

This situation, I feel, was foremost in Morse's mind when he entered the Lane County courthouse in February with Howard V. Morgan, the young chairman of the Democratic Party of Oregon, to complete the political conversion commenced when Morse first opposed Eisenhower.

In Washington, D.C., a new realm for me, I've found Morse widely respected by colleagues. Many who disagree with him admire his courage, intelligence and energy. A conservative Republican Senator said to me: "Your colleague's speech against legalization of wire-tapping in 1954 was the most thorough and masterful address I ever heard in the Senate. It did more than anything else to make impossible the passage of Attorney General Brownell's bill to admit in Federal courts the evidence obtained through wire-tapping." This aspect of Morse's ability and integrity seldom gets through to Oregonians.

In Oregon, the big muscle is GOP – press, campaign funds, the dominant business and industrial groups in every community.

There are 21 daily newspapers, their circulation spread-eagled by two big Portland dailies, the *Oregonian* and the *Journal*. Three comparatively small daily papers supported me in 1954: the Medford *Mail-Tribune*, Coos Bay *Times* and Pendleton *East-Oregonian*. In my opinion, Morse can expect no wider backing. His editorial endorsements probably will be confined to this trio of open-minded dailies in communities of about 20,000 population apiece.

Recently a correspondent for a great Eastern newspaper corralled me, asking for a candid estimate of Wayne Morse's 1956 chances. My opinion of my colleague's three leading assets and three major liabilities are:

ASSETS

1   He is one of the best political orators in America, possessed of limitless strength and the capacity for giving an audience a genuine understanding of complex issues.

2   A general feeling has seeped into the political consciousness of Oregon that Morse is "on the level," that he cannot be swayed by fear or favor or by threats.

3   The Hells Canyon and public-power issues, which are being kept alive by Secretary McKay's all-out assault against conservation and public development of resources.

LIABILITIES

1   The fact that Morse is not sufficiently known as a personality but only as a politician.

2   The on-the-record quotes in which Morse, during the past, was critical of his present party.

3   Is there a possibility of another Eisenhower landslide, with its corresponding pulling power for Republican candidates?

My wife Maurine, the top vote-getter in Oregon's legislative history and the only person who told me personally Truman would win in 1948 (which I disbelieved), is emphatic that Morse should be more portrayed as a personality. For example, he and his wife have three dark-haired and attractive daughters. One recently married in North Carolina. The other two are college coeds. The Morse girls are pretty and wholesome. The Senator, to his credit, is unwilling to exploit his family. Yet, another public personage of good will and liberal views, ex-Governor Earl Warren was never hurt at the polls or in reputation by the attention which went to his statuesque blond offspring.

Mrs. Morse is hardly known in Oregon. Yet, she once was a teacher of home economics, is a famous cook and can astutely discuss public issues. The angel-food cake recipe of Douglas McKay's wife has been touted through two State-wide Oregon elections and during the McKay career as a Cabinet official. Morse's friends wager Mildred Morse can bake a cake as good as that of any other housewife in Oregon.

Morse operates at the intellectual level, but many voters judge candidates by personal attributes. My own wife's help was an important factor in the Oregon upset of 1954. Political writers considered Martha Taft a valuable asset of the late Senator Robert A. Taft.

Wayne Morse is a wise and gentle father, but this has not been made evident to Oregon voters.

Because of Morse's campaigning ability, eagerness to challenge him for his Senate seat is not overwhelmingly apparent. He can make eight or 10 major addresses between dawn and midnight and his collar is fresh and stiff, his tie neatly knotted, his double-breasted suit uncreased. A red rose still may glisten in his buttonhole. For an audience of 50 he will answer questions until no more eager hands are raised. Morse never reserves major efforts for big crowds but treats *all* crowds as big.

These items are important in a State of vast dimensions but comparatively small population (1,620,000). To me, Morse's principal advantage in 1956 is his willingness to put ideals above party. He tried his best to make liberalism work in the Republican Party, decided it was impossible and got out. This quality, properly exploited and heralded, should appeal to thousands – Republicans or Democrats.

I am convinced about 20 percent of the members of each party are "solid" and vote a straight ticket, come what may. To them, party fealty is above all else. Political loyalty rates above social and economic issues. They rationalize voting for anyone, if he is a faithful Republican or Democratic wheel horse. But this is only about 40 percent of the electorate.

What of the 60 percent – those who shift back and forth and register in one party but seldom give it complete devotion?

These people, I think, are Wayne Morse's shock troops.

A machine Senator from Indiana once said that there came a time in the life of every politician when he had to rise above principle. The rank and file shun this cynicism. They get starry-eyed about their candidates. They think of men in history who would rather be right than President, or Senator Norris from Nebraska, which was Dry and Protestant and Republican, yet, who defied his party for Al Smith, who was Wet and Catholic and Democratic. This heroism counts with the average American. It will count in favor of Morse in 1956, when he tells Oregon's people he would rather be in a party hospitable to liberalism than reelected.

Something has been happening in Oregon in the past few years which cannot be disregarded. Although Oregon long has been considered "the Vermont of the West," in 1952 the State elected its first Democratic attorney general in half a century, 44-year-old Robert Y. Thornton. In 1954 Mrs. Edith S. Green of Portland, chairman of the "freshman" Democrats in the House of Representatives, became Oregon's first Democratic member of Congress since 1940. At both of these elections my wife Maurine polled more votes than any other candidate for the lower House of the Legislature. Furthermore, Democratic seats in the Oregon House at Salem have soared from only 10 elected in 1952 to 25 in 1954, a 150 percent gain. It was the greatest proportionate increase in legislative posts scored by either party anywhere in the country.

This resurgence will benefit Morse in 1956. No longer is the Democratic Party the "poor relations" in Oregon.

There was a period when Oregon liberals tended to Republicans. This was true of U'Ren, the law-giver. Charles L. McNary, longtime Oregon Senator and public-power advocate, was a Republican. Democrats named McNary Dam in his honor. Charles A. Sprague and Julius Meier, Governors of progressive social views and humane attitudes, were enrolled in the Republican Party. Morse himself was a Republican. Rufus C. Holman, another proponent of public power, served for six years as a Republican Senator.

Today, U'Ren, McNary and Meier are dead. Sprague and Holman were defeated in Republican Party primaries. Morse has become a Democrat. All the leaders of the GOP in Oregon chant in unison with McKay, and the song is a dirge for public-power and resource conservation.

Despite the background of Republicanism, Oregon voters are inherently independent and enlightened. Oregon rejected teachers' loyalty oaths, when these genuflections to conformity were being adopted in Washington State and California. The University of Washington canceled an invitation this spring for an address by Dr. J. Robert Oppenheimer, but the University of Oregon and Oregon State College refused to back down on similar invitations to the famous and controversial physicist. This freedom of spirit will not be averse to Morse in 1956. Along with Fulbright of Arkansas and Flanders of Vermont, he led the fight in the Senate to bring about censure of Joe McCarthy for conduct unbecoming a United States Senator.

Yet Oregon's liberal social behavior contrasts jarringly with special interests' domination in economics and resources. Partially because Oregon has been a one-party State for so long, its record of protecting school timber lands is far less respectable than that of Washington, where the two parties have been closely balanced. Furthermore, Oregon started earlier and thus experienced a longer period of looting. Here is the school-land record of the two States:

	OREGON	WASHINGTON
Acres received	4,203,000	2,298,000
Acres still in trust for schools	765,000	1,756,000
Funds in permanent school account from use of lands	$10,771,000	$49,318,000

Private utilites also have exercised greater influence over politics and legislation in Oregon than in Washington. Power rates are substantially higher in Oregon, although the two States share the Columbia River, the leading source of kilowatts in both the region and the country. Yet every so often, Oregon's people rebel against the utility yoke. The last such revolt was in 1948. The Idaho Power Company sought enactment of a bill suspending portions of the Oregon Hydroelectric Act which permitted the State to take over certain private dams. The purpose was to encourage private development of Hells Canyon on a piecemeal basis. After a compliant Legislature had passed the bill, the State Grange referred it to a vote of the people with referendum petitions. Despite large expenditures for propaganda by the utilities, the electorate defeated the proposal by nearly 100,000 votes.

Such circumstances make a favorable political climate for Wayne Morse. Of course, national political weather cannot be prophesied. The GOP *per se* seems to be declining in popularity. Yet, the President continues his high rating in public-opinion polls. How this anomaly will be resolved on election day, 1956, no earthly prophet can foretell. Eisenhower many not be a candidate or the present "prosperity" may fail to endure.

And what will happen in the field of foreign policy, that most crucial realm? I think the president is completely dedicated to peace. In this matter, I trust him more than on domestic questions. Yet the zig-zagging course of Secretary Dulles does not encourage confidence. We threaten "massive retaliation" in one breath and we appease in the other. "Liberation" is promised to foreign-language groups in big Eastern cities during a political campaign, but no relative is freed of Soviet fetters after the promises have helped win a national election. Yalta is said to be a symbol of Democratic treachery, but the Administration dares not ask Yalta's repudiation by the Congress. The word rarely matches the deed.

These imponderables will be factors in the Oregon election of next year. They may effect a decision which will determine the political performance of American statesmen for generations to come. Wayne Morse shed his Republican garments because they chafed him. He could not reconcile his own honest opinions with those of his party on taxation, labor, public power, resource conservation, Federal regulatory agencies and a host of other essential questions. In doing what he did, he took his political life in his hands.

I feel Morse should tell the people of Oregon exactly why he became a Democrat. He should emphasize Woodrow Wilson's conclusion that no man is obligated to remain in a political party which offends his inner convictions and ideals. He ought to repeat again and again the famous motto attributed to Senator Claude A. Swanson of Virginia: "When in doubt, do right..."

Moral suasion has high value in American politics. Time and again, my wife and I found that independence and fearlessness paid off in the 1954 campaign. Each minor local prejudice need not be catered to if a candidate has a sound and ethical reason for doing otherwise. If I were Wayne Morse, I would repeatedly ask next year:

"Would you prefer to vote for me if I had stayed in the dominant political party in my State, even though I did this at the sacrifice of my own self-respect and basic political convictions? Would you feel better about me if I put party above principle? Would I stand higher in your estimation if the Republican Party were more important to me than a sound program of legislative reform? Which comes first – the public interest or party regularity?"

If Morse asks these questions often enough and with his customary clarity, I believe he will be reelected as a Democrat. If he wants our backing, for whatever it may be worth, my wife and I intend to voice these issues in Morse's behalf when the 1956 campaign is under way.

Should Morse carry off his across-the-boards political conversion,

I have a feeling that the result would warm the heart of Lincoln, who started as a Whig and later was a regular Republican and then a radical Republican. After all, in its bassinet the Republican Party wasn't quite the hide-bound institution which it has become today!

A few successful resignations, such as that now being attempted by Wayne Morse, may be good for a party which has not achieved an electoral majority in America for 26 years, except when it recruited a world-wide military hero.

The Future Senator from Alaska

Reporter, 19 AUGUST 1952

Ernest Gruening (1887–1974), governor and senator from Alaska, is best remembered nationally as one of the two earliest opponents of the Vietnam war. Gruening and Wayne L. Morse were the only senators to vote against the Tonkin Gulf Resolution, Lyndon B. Johnson's declaration of war against North Vietnam. Gruening was a longtime champion of Alaskan and Hawaiian statehood and improved relations between the United States and Latin America. A Harvard Medical School graduate, Gruening shunned medicine for a career in journalism and politics. Gruening, as managing editor of *The Nation*, was an early booster of Neuberger's journalistic career. It was Gruening who bought Neuberger's 1933 article about Nazi Germany, and who encouraged Neuberger to write his biography of George Norris. When Gruening became territorial governor of Alaska in 1939, be became an important source for Neuberger on the Northwestern beat. Gruening viewed Neuberger as the most effective publicist for Alaskan statehood because his articles about Alaska were read by millions of Americans who knew little about the vast territory.

EARLY THIS YEAR when the Senate sent the Alaska statehood bill back to committee by one vote, 45 to 44, a deeply interested observer seated in the gallery predicted that Alaska's fight for statehood would be won next time. That observer had good reason to be confident: He could look back to 1939 when President Roosevelt had appointed him Alaska's Governor, and could measure the progress made since then.

It would be hard to find a more incongruous symbol of Alaska than sixty-five-year-old Ernest Gruening. Born in midtown New York City, before going north he had been occupied through most of his adult life with Latin America. He had studied at Harvard to be a surgeon, won his M.D. degree, and then put aside his scalpel to become an editor of such varied publications as the Boston *Traveler*, *The Nation*, and the New York *Evening Post*.

Who would suppose that the author of a book called *Mexico and Its Heritage* would eventually become the most influential person in Alaskan history since 1867, when Secretary of State William H. Seward paid Russia $7,200,000 for those 586,400 square miles of unpromising territory?

When Gruening arrived thirteen years ago at the most remote seat of government on this continent, wide-spread indignation prevailed in Juneau. Not only was he a New Yorker; representatives of Alaska's many monopolies whispered that he was also a New Dealer. The new Governor's wife even looked like Eleanor Roosevelt. The hostility spread into government bureaus and even to outlying settlements.

If Alaska achieves statehood soon, one of the two United States Senators from the State of Alaska is sure to be Ernest Gruening. Even his bitterest adversaries concede that. "The election wouldn't even be close," one of them in the salmon-packing town of Petersburg told me disgustedly.

Before Gruening's arrival in Alaska, the enormous northern realm reveled in a kind of loose-jointed political anarchy. The territory's bureaucrats, 5,500 miles away from Washington, saw no reason to challenge the men who were draining Alaska's resources. Not a single general tax was levied for Territorial purposes – no sales tax, no income tax, no property tax. "Alaska is the most lightly taxed entity under the American flag," said the new Governor, implying his strong disapproval.

There were certain tangible evidences of this lack of revenue. Alaska had the world's highest death rate from tuberculosis, yet there were few clinics or hospitals to isolate advanced or highly contagious cases. There was not even a full-time Commissioner of Health. Roads were a rarity. A cannery owner could pay a bush pilot $250 to fly him five hundred miles, but a homesteader with a pregnant wife had no doctor or nurse nearer than five desperate days on snowshoes.

Indians and Eskimos and Aleuts made up thirty percent of Alaska's population. Their ancestors had seen George Vancouver arrive in HMS *Discovery*, but now these people had no genuine part in the life of the Territory, and were excluded arbitrarily from many restaurants, barbershops, and hotels.

Gruening moved into a political vacuum. He demanded that the legislature at Juneau enact a civil-rights law. He called for taxes. He pointed out that Federal "regulation" of the immensely valuable salmon industry was in reality no regulation at all. He sought a Department of Health to fight tuberculosis. As a doctor, he could cite with authority the fact that the disease, rampant among the natives was gradually spreading to the white population. Was each restaurant glass to be a potential killer? Natives might be barred from public eating places, but many of them were working as dishwashers. The discrimination was social rather than scientific.

Of course, all the new Governor's recommendations were rejected at first. Gruening had expected this. But he ordered U.S. marshals to place ballot boxes and poll boxes in Eskimo and Indian villages at the next election. He flew into Aleut outposts where no Governor ever had been before. New faces appeared in the legislature. A man who had said the natives were "but shortly removed from savagery" came no more to Juneau. One or two Tlingits with chicory skins and coarse black hair sat in Territorial senate chairs, and a full-blooded Indian, Frank Peratrovich, was elected to preside over it.

A civil-rights bill with teeth became law. "Native heaven" was abolished in the balconies of Alaskan theaters. The Indians and Eskimos could look at Betty Grable downstairs with the white people. Earl Albrecht, a medical missionary, created a Department of Health and recruited doctors and nurses from all over the United States. The *Hygiene*, a converted Navy vessel 125 feet long, cruised into granite fiords and ice-dotted inlets to take chest X-rays among the tribes. In some places the incidence of active pulmonary tuberculosis was twenty percent. Hospitals were hurriedly constructed at strategic points.

At Gruening's bidding, the legislature passed a Territorial income and corporation tax which was fixed at ten percent of the Federal tax. The corporations immediately fought the law in the courts. A few months ago they lost, and their impounded money will flow to the Territorial treasury. New roads are under construction, and the portion of the Alaska Highway that is inside the Territory is being paved. Last year, for the first time, more people traveled to Alaska by land than by sea or air. More than twenty-two thousand reached Fairbanks over the graveled highway with its majestic bridges, and at least six thousand of these stayed in the North. Since 1940 Alaska has had a seventy-seven percent population increase, greater proportionately than even California's. The present inhabitants number 128,000 — more than those of many a state at the time of its admission to the Union.

But Gruening has yet to win his big fight. In his opinion, without statehood Alaska will be helpless to prevent the destruction of its natural resources.

The salmon industry is his principal case in point. To its owners this vast enterprise is worth more than $60 million a year, or nearly nine times the total purchase price of Alaska. Yet Alaskans cannot control this great source of wealth. Fish traps, huge chambers of timber and netting, catch a large share of the salmon. These traps are set near the mouths of rivers up which the fish surge to spawn. Most of them are owned by absentees – packers living in Seattle or widows taking the sun in Santa Barbara or Tucson.

Fish traps have been outlawed by all other geographic sovereignties bordering on Pacific waters where salmon congregate. This includes the States of Washington, Oregon, and California and the Province of British Columbia. Only in Alaska are these ravenous slaughterers of fish still legal. The Territorial legislature, prodded by Gruening and public opinion, would outlaw the traps in twenty-four hours – if it had the power to do so. In 1948, in a referendum, Alaskans voted nearly seven to one for doing away with the devices.

But Congress must decide this issue, as long as statehood does not come to pass. A Territory has no real authority over its own resources. And Congress has pigeonholed innumerable prayers, pleas, and petitions from Alaska to do away with fish traps. After all, the salmon packers in the States can participate in Presidential elections and they can contribute handsomely to Congressional elections. Fish traps are a source of wealth to these men, for they catch salmon without making it necessary to split the take with the crews of trawlers.

For a time some Alaskan newspapers claimed that Gruening was talking through his hat when he said that the Territory favored statehood. But as far back as 1946, the Alaskans overwhelmingly decided by referendum that they did want it.

It remains to be settled in the United States Senate. Much of the opposition has been provided by Southern Senators because they fear that Alaskan members – particularly Governor Gruening – would be strong for civil rights. Senator Taft has opposed statehood on the ground that Alaska is not economically self-sufficient. This year the opposition prevailed. Governor Gruening believes that it cannot prevail for long.

Sprague – Conscience of Oregon

Nation, 26 JANUARY 1952

Charles A. Sprague (1887–1969), one of Oregon's most distinguished governors, made an even larger contribution to the Pacific Northwest as editor for nearly a half century of the *Oregon Statesman*. Neuberger prized his close friendship with Sprague, with whom he shared a special bond as journalist and politician. Although of opposite political parties, Sprague and Neuberger were in agreement more often than not on major issues. Even so, Sprague endorsed Cordon in 1954, citing his seniority advantage. But in 1960, Sprague jumped the Republican party line to endorse Maurine over a former Republican governor, Elmo Smith, as Neuberger's successor in the Senate. Like Neuberger, Sprague had ambitions to become a senator and challenged Cordon for the job. But a decade earlier than Neuberger, Sprague narrowly lost his bid. Neuberger's articles about Sprague, including this one, contributed a great deal to the former governor's national reputation as the prototypical small-town editor.

OREGON is the most solidly Republican of all the Western states. This Republicanism is in the blood, and not even a 40 percent population increase since 1940 has been able to dilute it. Only Oregon, in company with steadfast Maine and Vermont, never elected a Democratic United States Senator throughout Franklin D. Roosevelt's long tenure in the White House. Yet despite its faithfulness to the GOP, Oregon is the single state of the Pacific seaboard which has not enacted a loyalty oath or similar test legislation.

Although the witch-hunting hysteria has been particularly virulent along the West Coast, in Oregon a person applying for a position of public trust still need swear only the time-honored allegiance to the constitutions of the state and nation.

This happy state of affairs is due in the main to the influence of one man, ex-Governor Charles A. Sprague, publisher of the *Oregon Daily Statesman* in Salem. Perhaps because he was born in Kansas, Sprague's admirers compare him to the late William Allen White of the Emporia *Gazette*. Sprague is a Republican who has abandoned – as White did – his party's predominant isolationism to support the foreign policy of the Democratic Administration. Like White a tireless defender of civil liberties, Sprague recently rebuked his party for inviting Senator Joe McCarthy to speak in Oregon. "If the Republican Party is to endorse McCarthyism," said this lifelong regular Republican, "it deserves to be laid in a grave both wide and deep. And to win the Presidency by condoning McCarthy's tactics would be to obtain office under false pretenses."

But Sprague salts such forthright opinions as these with an old-fashioned economic conservatism which makes him mistrustful of federal spending, of exotic figures in high office, and of concentrations of power in either corporations or trade unions. Only recently he criticized utility companies and public-power districts alike for waiting for the government to build dams across the Northwest's swift rivers instead of doing the job themselves. He assails his own community when it urges federal economy in the abstract and at the same time asks for local pork-barrel projects.

Sprague is Oregon's most influential citizen. His impact on the everyday affairs of the state far transcends that of Senator Wayne L. Morse, whom Sprague sustains against a host of reactionary foes. People in many parts of the Northwest subscribe to the *Statesman* in order to read the front-page column which the ex-Governor writes daily under the title "It Seems to Me." When the Chicago *Tribune* tried to read Morse out of the Republican Party last November, Sprague immediately came to the Senator's defense. "Morse is a party maverick, to be sure," he wrote. "But in my judgment he is a better Republican than Colonel Robert R. McCormick. The Mc-

Cormick brand of Republicanism finds expression in blind isolationism, in distortion of facts, and in character assassination after the manner of Senator McCarthy."

Sprague intrudes himself boldly into the local issues that rock Oregon, a field in which Morse always has been extremely cautious. When a Republican state liquor commissioner took a trip at the expense of the Seagram distillery, Sprague at once insisted that he resign, although some Oregon papers which had been indignant about similar transgressions by the Democrats in Washington, D.C., kept silent. Sprague also has hammered constantly at the legalized parimutuel racing that makes a folly of police efforts to restrict less lucrative gambling.

If the Republicans look westward for a Vice-Presidential nominee, as they may have to do if Taft of Ohio or Eisenhower of New York becomes their Presidential candidate, they could do worse than pick this sixty-four-year-old publisher, often called "the conscience of Oregon." Probably few men would make a stronger appeal to the independent voters whom the GOP must annex if it is not to be a permanent minority party. Young Republicans soon may circulate petitions to put Sprague on the 1952 primary ballot as the beneficiary of the state's convention votes for second place on the national ticket.

A strong religious and moral strain in Sprague often determines his stand. He neither drinks nor smokes, and his paper accepts no advertisements for hard liquor. An official of the Presbyterian Church in the United States, he has cited Scripture against local corruption when other leading Oregon Republicans were looking the other way in embarrassment.

Yet Sprague is rarely doctrinaire. He asserted that "Taft can't have intelligence and integrity and have truck with McCarthyism," but he refused to become disturbed when adversaries of McCarthy were unable to round up signatures in Madison, Wisconsin, to a petition upholding the Declaration of Independence. He felt this was a childish way of opposing a sinister thing like McCarthyism. "The right to petition is guaranteed in our Constitution, and that implies also the right not to petition," he wrote in his column in the *Statesman*. "If 111 people refused to sign the reporter's petition, such was their

privilege. That they can do so with impunity is still one of the benefits of our system."

For Sprague, Vermont is a political ideal. "I favor," he says,
"sound, honest Republicanism which doesn't let people get pushed
around." In his view this is epitomized by such individuals as Senator George Aiken, former Senator Warren Austin, the U.N. delegate,
and former Governor Ernest W. Gibson. Indeed, Sprague fought
with such ardor against the teacher's oath because he felt its passage
in the legislature would challenge his boast that Oregon is "the Vermont of the West," a citadel of tolerance and stability.

The bill for a teacher's oath sailed through the state Senate by a
vote of twenty-five to five. The expected Democratic opposition to it
collapsed under pressure from a veterans' lobby; Democrats contributed some of the most raucous speeches in favor of the measure. The
next morning members of the House of Representatives found a nervous, angular man with sparse hair and rimless glasses pacing the
marble corridors like a panther. One by one, the ex-Governor pulled
aside legislators who were his friends or acquaintances. "Oregon has
not surrendered to hysteria, as have our neighbors in Washington and
California," He told these men. "Let's not run down the flag now.
Communists can be rooted out of the schools by positive action on
each case as genuine proof develops. To subject all teachers to an invasion of their personal and academic freedom would be burning
down the house to roast the pig."

And in "It Seems to Me" Sprague added, "Legislation like this is
a product of fear. I have more confidence in the good sense of the
teachers of Oregon and in their loyalty than to think we have to challenge them. There is no public demand for the bill. There is no situation in our schools which calls for this as a bar to employment of
Communist teachers. The House should keep its feet on the ground
and defeat this bill." The House took Sprague's advice. The oath bill
died in the lower chamber. More than one legislator, just setting out
on the rough road of politics, was surprised and flattered to be approached personally by a famous editor and former governor. Several
college professors told their classes, half in jest, half seriously, that

the events at Salem had knocked into the discard their belief that certain historical developments are inevitable, regardless of the efforts of individuals. There seemed to be no doubt that Oregon would have enacted an oath bill had not one particular man been on the scene.

Sprague's choice for President of the United States would probably be Paul G. Hoffman, the president of the Ford Foundation. Perhaps because of his intense interest in the oath fight, he was profoundly impressed by Hoffman's speech on liberty and tolerance at Freedom House a few months ago. His next preference is Eisenhower – with some reservations. He would like to know a good deal more about Ike's views on important domestic problems. He favors Eisenhower because "his nomination would be a renunciation of McCarthyism and MacArthurism." Sprague once gave this friendly warning to the General: "We may expect that if Eisenhower does say he will accept the Republican nomination he will immediately become the target of the pro-Formosa, pro-Chiang, anti-British, anti-Europe entourage whose white knight is Senator Robert A. Taft."

Sprague was governor of Oregon from 1939 to 1943. One of the conspicuous achievements of his administration was the passage of a forestry code in this lumber-producing state. Bills enacted under Sprague's leadership provided that timber operators must leave a certain number of seed trees per acre and that pines of less than a certain circumference could not be felled. Only recently this pioneering legislation has been praised in a significant new book, *American Forest Policy*, by Luther Halsey Gulick.

William Allen White wrote in his autobiography that he was strengthened in "the gymnasium of the woods and field and water." Sprague was trained in the same environment, and perhaps more ruggedly than was possible in level Kansas. Most of the peaks of the Pacific Northwest have felt his crampons. Even the 14,000-foot Mount Rainier is among his conquests. Thirty-six miles from the capital city of Oregon, Sprague and his wife own a chalet-like cabin on the Little North Fork of the Santiam River. They built it in 1945 on public land leased from the Department of the Interior. Sprague chops the wood for the fireplace and takes meditative hikes through the fir forests. He reads avidly, his regular fare consisting of *Time*, the *Saturday Evening Post*, *The Nation*, *Reader's Digest*, *New York Times Magazine*, *Harper's*, *U.S. News*, and *Scientific American*.

Sprague also is a reader of the *Congressional Record*, where he finds, he says, many "unwritten stories." He confesses that being in politics was "so engrossing a game that I seldom got into the goods or magazines that I needed to make me a well-informed person." And he adds that this may be one of the things wrong with American political life today. "Many of the participants become obsessed with rival personalities and with political animosities. As a result they lose sight of the tremendous impact on mankind of the decisions which they perforce must make."

Sprague's newspaper is partisan. But when he moves from candidates to issues, his party tie shackles him only slightly. No paper in the West encouraged Truman more consistently on the entire MacArthur question than the *Statesman*. Of MacArthur's recent public addresses Sprague has written, "His innuendoes are evidence more of the warping of his own mind than of Truman's malfeasance."

Perhaps because he is comparatively unfettered, Sprague occasionally ends up to the left of the Administration in Washington, which of course has its own groove. He has been chairman of an advisory commission on the administration of extremely valuable federal timber tracts in southwestern Oregon, part of an abandoned railroad land grant. A few months ago certain large and influential lumber companies forced the retirement of the regional director, a young economist named Daniel L. Goldy. Sprague championed Goldy and criticized the Interior Department for succumbing to the companies' pressure.

Sprague would probably return to public life only with considerable reluctance. He relishes the freedom of being a private citizen. He types his own letters, rarely making use of one of the *Statesman*'s stenographers. When some Catholics canceled their subscriptions because the paper published news stories and photographs of Paul Blanshard speaking at a Catholic School in Mount Angel, Oregon, Sprague took the calls himself and patiently explained that it was the policy of the *Statesman* to print all the news without exception.

A religious man himself, particularly in a philosophical sense, he feels that disregard of spiritual values has led to a worship of money in the nation. Last Easter he devoted his column to Joseph of Arimathea, who asked Pilate for the body of Jesus. Sprague's own desire to be a free spirit and to decide great questions without fear or prejudice shone through the piece. "Most of us," he said, "are prisoners of our class, our creed, our associations. We tend to conform, adapting ourselves to whatever level we move in. Joseph was one of those rare souls who refused to be such a prisoner. The instinct of human charity broke through the restraints of narrow sectarianism. We might almost say that this Joseph was the first Christian. In a Christendom riven by multitudinous and contentious sects he has left too few descendants."

Stevenson The Man

Frontier, SEPTEMBER 1952

Adlai E. Stevenson (1900–1965) had just won the 1952 Democratic presidential nomination when Neuberger wrote this account of their early friendship. Maurine told Stevenson that she hoped he would not run against General Eisenhower because the race was hopeless. After Eisenhower's landslide victory, Stevenson said that it was rather like running against George Washington. In the 1950s, the Neubergers were among Stevenson's closest friends and political allies. They actively supported his successful bid for the 1956 Democratic presidential nomination and sought to persuade him to make another attempt in 1960. Neuberger favored a ticket of Stevenson for president and John F. Kennedy for the vice presidency. Stevenson, though, never formally became a candidate and his hopes for a convention draft were dimmed by Kennedy's ascent to power.

THE TIME TO SIZE UP a famous man is before he becomes famous. After he has achieved a great reputation, every trifling nuance assumes hidden and often synthetic meaning. Lavish interpretations are placed on a mere gesture or an act of simple courtesy which would be commonplace in anyone else. A candidate for high office becomes a grand fellow personally because he gave his golf caddy a playful slap on the back.

But to someone living in a remote realm like the Pacific Northwest it rarely is possible to swap jokes or trade alpenstocks with a person destined for immortality. The celebrities generally stick close to Broadway and 42nd Street or to a phone call from "Meet the Press."

The first time I remembered our guest in the Cascade Mountain fastnesses was when I read in the newspapers during the 1948 political campaign that Gov. Dwight H. Green of Illinois has referred to his Democratic opponent as "a State Department cooky-pusher in striped pants and morning coat." The man running against Green was a Chicago lawyer named Adlai Ewing Stevenson.

In the scene which came to my mind Stevenson was not wearing striped pants and a morning coat. He was in khaki shorts and a pair of grotesque boots. Dirty wool socks peered from the clumsy footgear. We were looking down a steep white apron of icy snow on the ramparts of Mount St. Helens. At the bottom of this chute, ugly boulders waited with sabre-toothed fangs. The forest ranger and I hesitated so that we could get our bearings. Was there some safer way around the shoulder of the 10,000-foot mountain?

Adlai Stevenson plodded out onto the slippery gables of St. Helens and began kicking out footsteps for his wavering companions.

"Come on, Neuberger," he scoffed. "Do you want to live forever?"

This is my most vivid impression of the man whom the Democrats have nominated for President of the United States. It doesn't tell anything about his stand on foreign policy or the Taft-Hartley Law, but it tells me something about Stevenson himself. I have read that this man is an intellectual. Unquestionably this is so. Does he not deliver speeches which say something? Even more miraculous, does he not write them himself?

Stevenson may be an intellectual, but he has none of the physical timidity which frequently characterizes the intellectual. In the solitudes of the Gifford Pinchot National Forest, he was splashing and snorting in the glacial-fed lake at dawn. He alone wanted to continue on to the wind-swept summit of the mountain when the ranger warned that we had neither the equipment nor enough hours of daylight for so perilous a venture. And he walked across ravines on narrow logs just a little less reluctantly than anyone else in the party.

Had all these things occurred after he became a Presidential pos-

sibility, I would have ascribed his conduct to a conscious effort to emulate Teddy Roosevelt's "rugged life." But in 1947 Stevenson had
not run for as much as precinct committeeman or the State Legislature. In fact, around a campfire which waved and tossed like a ballet
dancer, I suggested that he ought to go into politics.

I have since checked his answer with my wife and the forest
ranger. Stevenson's reply was non-committal: "Do you think I'd be
good at politics? I'm not so sure. I get awfully short of patience some
times."

Was his interest in the outdoors superficial and a fancy of the moment? In the cramped log cabin we played a game called "Guggen-
heim." Each participant was allowed to pick a category. Then the
contest was to think up five examples in that category beginning with
five selected letters of the alphabet. Stevenson selected as his categories "Cabinet Members in History" and "Peaks of the Alps." No
earth-shaking significance there, regardless of how intently you analyze it, but this is not what I recollect so clearly from five years ago.

The quiet ranger chose two categories. They were "Types of
Grasses" and "Wild Animals Indigenous to North America." Second to the ranger in filling out both categories was neither my wife
nor myself, who are Westerners born and bred, but Adlai Stevenson,
the lawyer from Chicago.

Many citizens have an impression of Stevenson as something of a
dilettante. I did not see Ike whipping the white waters of the Arapaho
National Forest in Colorado, yet I believe I would match Stevenson
against him as an angler, sight unseen. Politics was far out of mind
when Stevenson came to the Northwest in 1947 and trolled for
salmon off Salt Spring Island in British Columbia and cast for rain-
bow trout in the solitudes of Oregon and Washington.

I first met Stevenson at the San Francisco conference which inaugurated the United Nations Organization. As an Army captain recently returned from duty in Alaska and the Yukon, I was one of a
number of aides on the staff of Secretary Stettinius. Stevenson was a
leading policy-maker of the American delegation. I was a long way
from these upper levels of strategy but, both being comparatively
early risers, we used to meet for breakfast in the coffee shop of the

Fairmount Hotel. We grunted peremptorily, as people will do at 7:30 A.M., and then buried ourselves in the special San Francisco edition which the New York *Times* then was publishing as a convention feature.

One morning the *Times* was late and, to make conversation, I remarked casually that I was taking advantage of a long weekend to visit Yosemite. I added that I had heard the great waterfalls were in full throat.

Stevenson said: "I'm going with you. I've always wanted to see them, ever since my grandfather told me about Yosemite long ago." I bought Stevenson a shirt at the Army PX and we were off by Santa Fe day coach for Merced, although he never did tell me that the grandfather to whom he referred so cavalierly had been a Vice-President of the United States.[11]

I remember a few things about that visit to Yosemite. Stevenson had an insatiable curiosity about the wonderful valley. He asked questions of park naturalists and park wardens – questions about trees, wildflowers and stream flow. He never sat down. When I was limp and fagged out, he blithely proposed a five-mile trudge to Nevada Falls. Although I realize he could have afforded the best, he must have known that the pay of an Army captain had its limitations. We ate hamburgers and drank milk shakes and stayed away from exclusive lodge dining rooms.

And when we stood at Glacier Point, with its perspective of the valley from 3,000 sheer feet, I noted that Stevenson got slightly closer than anyone else to the giddy void beyond the frail fence.

"Nasty drop," he observed casually.

In that instance he reminded me of a British-born inspector I had known in the Royal Canadian Mounted Police in the Yukon. This man had some of the same sardonic references to his own prowess as had Stevenson, and in the outdoors he was mundane and matter-of-fact about the most valiant exploits.

I doubt if anyone ever will get him in a Sioux or Blackfoot war bonnet. Should he succumb to such a campaign gesture, he probably will look silly and, still worse, incongruous. Yet clothes do not make the man and neither does a feathered hat. Hip-deep in a rushing stream, at the 8,000-foot ledge on a dizzy peak far off in the green reaches of a fir or pine forest, the sophisticate from Illinois will hold his own with the five-star General from Abilene – or else Ike has some Davy Crockett traits which his publicity managers have not yet exploited.

In the coming campaign, an effort undoubtedly will be made to emphasize the fact that Stevenson has no kinship with such problems as forestry, reclamation, water power and Indian reservations.

I am not an intimate of the Governor of Illinois. I know his views on such matters as have been vouchsafed to the rest of the general public – nothing more. I have seen him only twice, and then but briefly, since he entered into politics as a candidate.

But it was my opportunity to know Adlai Stevenson during several periods when he was in the Far West. To a man of his social position as well as of his influence in the American Delegation to the UN, no door of social prominence in San Francisco was closed to him. Yet he chose on two week-ends to go to Yosemite. So that his companions could economize, he made no protest about riding in railroad coaches. On another week-end he hiked up Mount Tamalpais. And he was the man who took the lead in helping to set aside stately sequoia trees in Muir Woods as a memorial to Franklin D. Roosevelt, then recently dead, when others were suggesting more formalized tributes to the late President.

The Muir Woods episode symbolizes to me the feeling which Stevenson has for the majesty of the American West. Mourning for FDR still continued when the UN organization began. Roosevelt, after all, had been the architect of the United Nations. The gathering in San Francisco was his conception. Many were the proposals for honoring this great man – to dedicate the Opera House or Civic Center to his memory, to stage a grim parade of silent marchers, to bring Churchill from afar to deliver a never-to-be-forgotten eulogy ...

Then some humble bureaucrat in the National Park Service mentioned a noble grove of *Sequoia sempervirons* in Muir Woods, trees centuries in age and more than 250 feet in height. Stevenson snapped his fingers triumphantly. "That's the idea!" he exulted. "Besides, Roosevelt loved trees and he would have wanted that kind of a tribute." Stevenson babied along the scheme and he hovered paternally in the background when the ceremony at last took place in the long shadows of the slender coastal redwoods.

But best of all I liked the fact that Stevenson had a ready reply when Secretary Stettinius, Field Marshall Smuts and others praised him for the success of the Muir Woods undertaking. "It didn't orig-inate with me at all," said Stevenson. "A chap in the offices of the Park Service thought it up. He's the man who deserves the credit."

In my opinion, Adlai Stevenson has a genuine feeling for the wide open spaces of his country. After our Cascade Mountain excursion in 1947, he wrote an indignant protest of the vandalism which was de-stroying signs, rest shelters and public cook stoves in the National Forests. He also said he could not understand a resident of the beau-tiful Northwest who flipped a lighted cigarette from an automobile. This may have been standard nature-loving material from a politi-cian, but it was uttered long before Stevenson became a candidate for office.

This campaign of 1952 will be one in which Eisenhower is por-trayed as the man of action, of vigor and of characteristic American vitality. Stevenson, on the other hand, will be the intellectual, the thinker, the visionary. Can anyone with red blood doubt where his interests will lie?

If we would not substitute the word for the deed, I believe the real conservationist will rest his welfare with Stevenson. True, Stevenson is not an outdoorsman in the Coolidge sense of the word, holding gingerly at arm's length a Dolly Varden fished from a scoured and cleansed creek. Rather, he has the approach of a Thoreau or a John Muir to the wilderness. With him, the outdoors are an adventure of the intellect, the spirit and the mind. He didn't hesitate to cross the hazardous snowfield on Mount St. Helens because the summit, to him, was a natural challenge and an invitation.

Did we think Stevenson was ticketed for destiny? How dreadful, in a way, if a friend made you think he possessed possibilities of cosmic stature? How much better, really, if he was just a friend? My wife took pictures of Stevenson and me hiking across a glacier, eat-ing lunch and trying to boil adequate backwoods coffee. I snapped photos of her and Stevenson swimming in Spirit Lake. We kept the snapshots but threw away the negatives. To what conceivable use could they possibly be put?

Somehow, we are glad that Adlai Stevenson affected us in this way. The negatives are gone, the prints stay in our scrapbook. This is the routine we have followed with ordinary, everyday plain American citizens who are our outing friends and whose company we enjoy. We also regard it as valid evidence that Stevenson is not as completely the man of townhouse and midnight study as some would have us believe.

One need not pose with slabs of beef and warrior chiefs to demonstrate affinity for pine and sage. It can be done in a more genuine way – Adlai Stevenson's way, for example.

Herbert H. Lehman: A Profile in Courage

The Progressive, JUNE 1958

Herbert H. Lehman (1878–1963), one of Neuberger's closest friends in the U.S. Senate, was one of the Lehman Brothers of the investment banking house. Franklin D. Roosevelt tapped him as his lieutenant governor of New York in 1928. And, when FDR was elected to the presidency in 1932, Lehman was elected as governor of New York, serving four terms. Lehman defeated two of the biggest names in GOP history, Thomas E. Dewey for governor in 1938, and John Foster Dulles for the U.S. Senate in 1950. In 1959 Lehman joined with Eleanor Roosevelt in a successful campaign to destroy the remnants of the old Tammany Hall Democratic organization.

IN THE DENVER *Post* Roscoe Fleming recently described George W. Norris of Nebraska as the one authentically great Senator of modern times. Undoubtedly the mold was broken with "Uncle George," who came from the crunching poverty of a stump farm to pioneer for the TVA and to defy lynch-mobs because of his hatred of war. Yet to his illustrious name I should like to add that of another great Senator – a man whose leave-taking of Congress early in 1957 received far too perfunctory recognition. In contrast to Norris, this man came from wealth and from the metropolis. But he combined in himself the qualities which I am certain must have helped to make Norris great – sublime political courage, personal unselfishness, a gentle and kindly nature, and an understanding of people and their frailties.

Herbert H. Lehman has just marked his 80th birthday anniversary. He left the Senate while he was ahead. He did not stay there to vegetate with age. He voluntarily withdrew, in full possession of all his faculties. Characteristically, on his 80th birthday he asked for not gifts or presentations. Instead, to commemorate the start of his ninth decade on earth, he gave a check for $5,000 to one of his favorite "causes" – Brandeis University. It also was in keeping for this singular man to talk about a topic appropriate to his own career. He discussed courage, particularly the capacity to place principle above politics, to think of future generations rather than of future elections.

Herbert Lehman's devoted friend and sponsor, Franklin D. Roosevelt, once described Senator Norris as "the very perfect gentle knight of American progressive ideals." It was a description which fit like a satin glove. But Norris is gone now, and nobody is so qualified to inherit the glowing phrase as former Senator Lehman. Politics can be a brutal game, full of haranguing and personal abuse. Both Norris and Lehman have been men capable of fervent advocacies and creative ideas, without ever resorting to assassination of the reputations of their political opponents. I knew Norris, I know Lehman – two of the greatest privileges I have ever enjoyed. Not once have I ever heard either of these truly noble Americans deride an adversary or run down an antagonist. Such tactics have not been their nature.

I shall never forget Herbert Lehman as he was on the day that I became a Senator, back in January of 1955. He had called a conference in his office of all liberal Senators to thrash out civil rights legislation. Around the room ranged a wide spectrum of Senate liberals from all sectors of the nation. As newcomers, Pat McNamara of Michigan and I stood in a remote corner. Lehman, alone of the entire group, wanted to wage a stubborn fight, then and there, to change Rule XXII of the Senate, which permits unlimited debate. For varying reasons, none of the others chose to support his stand.

"Gentlemen," said Herbert Lehman, "you are making a very serious mistake. You are trying to postpone something which cannot be postponed."

Many times later I was to hear men like Senators Douglas, Murray, Hennings, and Humphrey admit that Lehman had been right. The significant thing was that Lehman himself never rubbed it in. He never even called the episode to memory. It would not have been in character for him to do so. This was never a man to inflict personal hurts.

Politics, alas, is a self-centered game. Acts of nobility are rare. Why take the risk? Men eye their own constituencies with a fixed stare, but with only a side glance for the other fellow's bailiwick.

Fortunately, there are isolated exceptions to this. I remember the night we were debating the Hells Canyon bill in July of 1956. At nearly 10 o'clock, the late Senator Herman Welker of Idaho was criticizing the proposal for a high government dam. I looked around me on the Senate floor. There we sat, all the interested parties: Senators Magnuson and Jackson of Washington, Dworshak of Idaho, Watkins of Utah, Murray and Mansfield of Montana, Morse and Neuberger of Oregon. It was our fight, on one side or another. Our states were directly involved. The stakes for us were as vast as the great canyon itself. Then I turned to the rear of the chamber. An elderly man sat there in solitary exhaustion, at that weary hour of the evening – Lehman of New York, representing a state 3,000 miles from Hells Canyon.

At the age of 78, he was gray and tired. His eye twitched with fatigue.

"What are you doing on the floor, Herbert?" I inquired. "You're the only Senator here who isn't from the Northwest."

His reply was in keeping: "I thought you and Wayne and Scoop Jackson might need me, so I decided not to go home."

And when our bill was under discussion to protect the resources of the Klamath Indian Tribe, Herbert Lehman volunteered an interest in it on several occasions. This was an issue so remote from the Empire State that a Senator from New York could barely communicate with it by smoke signals. Yet these Indians were people, and Herbert Lehman was concerned about people, especially people who needed help.

Personal embarrassment meant nothing to him if he could serve his friends. When the bill was before the Senate to increase Congressional salaries, a long speech had just been made against it by a wealthy Republican Senator. With typical candor, Lehman said he had been fortunate enough in life not to need the higher pay. Indeed, he confessed that the increased salary would merely add to the federal income taxes collected from himself and his wife. But he declared that the U.S. Senate should not be open only to rich men but to all American citizens, regardless of financial status.

Such a speech could not have been calculated to help Herbert Lehman politically in New York. But it helped to pass the Congressional pay bill, and Lehman felt that some of his impecunious friends in the House and Senate desperately needed the increase.

In or out of the Senate, he never did the corny thing. When he was interviewed by Edward R. Murrow on "Person to Person," Lehman was asked which deed of his long career in Congress had given him the greatest satisfaction. He might have referred to any of a dozen bills that provided projects or brought funds to the State of New York. Instead, he referred to his fight against McCarthyism and to his efforts to protect men and women who had been unjustly or unfairly accused of a lack of patriotism. And from the way Edith Lehman nodded her handsome white head in vigorous assent, viewers knew one reason why Herbert Lehman had never lacked for courage on his travels through life.

Cruelties in politics might put to shame the Mau-Mau.[12] Herbert Lehman always has seemed just the opposite from the politician who tries to torment his foes. When he and his New York colleague, Senator Irving M. Ives, were engaged in caustic debate on the question of public versus private acquisition of kilowatts from Niagara Falls, I remarked to Lehman that Ives had not made a particularly effective presentation.

"Irving has been quite ill lately," Lehman answered. "I imagine that is why his speech may have lacked fire or forcefulness. Irving is really a very able man. Don't underestimate him."

And I wondered how often so generous an opinion was ever vouchsafed in politics about a man of another party, with whom one had just been debating an issue of major importance.

I think it was typical of Herbert Lehman that he left the Senate with pennon flying. He refused to wait until he nodded at his desk or bumbled in debate. He never needed Harry S. Truman's admonition, delivered in February, that some men do not know when to quit. Yet departing from the solemn prestige of the Senate has not meant for Lehman a musty retirement. He has not been one to sulk because his own vote-getting career is at an end. At the 1957 San Francisco conference of the Democratic Party, he made the most militant speech of all about the need for a fighting party dedicated to active and affirmative liberalism. In this year of 1958 he has been honorary chairman of another cause which claims his complete allegiance, the 10th anniversary of the founding of the Republic of Israel.

Yet it is civil rights legislation with which the name and career of Herbert H. Lehman are most inextricably identified. It has been a passion with him that neither the color of a person's skin nor the manner of his worship shall interfere with access to the "life, liberty and the pursuit of happiness" which Jefferson enshrined in our Declaration of Independence.

Whenever fundamental bills dealing with civil rights reach the Senate calendar, I know that I shall look back at the desk along the wide center aisle, in the very rear of the Senate chamber. In my mind's eye, no matter who sits at that desk, I know that I will see the balding, gray-fringed old man with the gentle smile and the kindly eyes. I will hear again his solemn warning to us that this is an issue which liberals cannot delay or postpone, regardless of the political difficulties it might precipitate.

And when finally the great government of the United States guarantees the liberties of all its citizens, I will have no doubt as to whom much of the credit really belongs. Herbert Lehman may not participate in these epochal roll-calls, but the victory and the glory will be his, nevertheless.

Warren: Nice Man in Rough Company

The Progressive, APRIL 1952

Earl Warren (1891–1974) was a three-term California governor when Neuberger wrote this profile about him as a 1952 presidential possibility. Although Warren lost the presidential nomination to Eisenhower, he became Chief Justice of the Supreme Court in 1953. Neuberger thought that Warren achieved greatness on the high court but gave him mixed, though mostly favorable, reviews as governor of California.

ON THE NIGHT that Harry Truman announced he would not run again for President, the innate human friendliness of Earl Warren showed itself to the nation. Warren was engaged in a grim grapple with Senator Taft and Harold Stassen for delegates in the Wisconsin Republican primary. To the bulk of these voters, Harry Truman was anathema. He epitomized the political foe who had to be overcome. Taft and Stassen hurriedly took advantage of this, with barbed statements aimed at the President who was retiring from the position they sought so avidly.

But Earl Warren saw back of the dramatic announcement a flesh-and-blood person named Harry Truman, a man with a wife and daughter who loved him and with the same fears and frailties as other individuals. "I understand the President's decision," said Earl Warren. "I wish him and his family the best of luck."

This amiable gesture to the departing Democratic President could

not possibly have been calculated to help Warren in a Republican primary election, then nearing its bitter climax. But it did a good deal
to reveal Warren's character, in contrast with that of Taft and Stassen,
and it made newspaper reporters wonder whether a man as basically
warm-hearted and friendly as this third-term Governor of California
can win the GOP sweepstakes in the critical election year of 1952.

Warren has been a good but not great governor of the country's
second most populous state during its period of most intensive
growth. He has been nearly as popular among Democrats as within
his own party. This was vividly demonstrated in 1950, when Warren
not only won the GOP gubernatorial nomination but nearly defeated
Jimmy Roosevelt for the Democratic nomination. In the Democratic
primary Roosevelt polled 969,433 votes and Warren was close behind with 719,468. Earl Warren's bi-partisan appeal may best be
understood when it is known that California, a state full of migrants
in the lower-income tax brackets, has 3,062,205 registered Democrats as compared with 1,944,812 Rebublicans. Yet Warren, a nom-
inal Republican, has reigned as Governor of this preponderantly
Democratic domain without ever encountering a serious contest. In
fact, in 1946 he ran off with the nominations of both parties. And in
the general election of 1950 his margin of victory was 1,100,000
votes, and over a Democrat with the magic name of "Roosevelt" at
that!

The man who achieved these political miracles might seem to be a
natural for the Presidency. How could he be kept out of the White
House? Yet today, at the age of 61, Earl Warren is trying for the second time for the nation's biggest political bonanza, and his chances
of striking the mother lode may be regarded as only marginal, at
best.

Warren is the logical compromise candidate if the GOP convention
becomes cemented in a stalemate between Taft and Eisenhower. His
strong showing against Taft in Wisconsin accentuates this possibility. Without a formidable organization, with poor advance prepara-
tions and with only a few pennies for every dollar spent by the Taft
forces, Warren nevertheless finished a redoubtable second in Wisconsin and actually won several strategic Congressional districts.

Indeed, some people firmly believe that, by election day in November, Warren could be a stronger candidate than Eisenhower. To begin with, he would not carry on his shoulders, like the Old Man of the Sea or Sinbad the Sailor, the spectre of a lifetime spent in the Army. In addition, he has been experienced in civilian government. Furthermore, he is committed on most of the major issues of the era, and Eisenhower has yet to speak out in anything except the most tenuous generalities.

But a genuine stalemate between the two Republican leaders is Warren's one chance for first prize, although either Taft or Eisenhower probably would be delighted to have this tall, handsome native of California as a running mate.

Why has Earl Warren been so often a bridesmaid but never a bride? One reason is a suspicion nationally that his continued leadership in California may be as attributable to the weakness of his enemies as to his own affirmative powers. A person would have to search with the Lick telescope to find a less healthy political organism than the Democratic Party in the state of California. It could not even function when FDR was sweeping the state almost 2 to 1.

In California the Democratic Party has been a vast goulash of migratory Dixiecrats, Communist fellow-travelers, well-meaning Hollywood do-gooders, opportunistic Johnny-come-latelys and shrewd lawyers with their bi-focals firmly fixed on Federal judgeships. Sincere liberals generally have been outnumbered by this motley crew. Democratic voters, seeing a handsome man of forthright views on their ticket, have hungrily voted for him, whether he was a Democrat or a Republican. This was climaxed in 1946 when Republican Earl Warren seized the Democratic gubernatorial nomination from Robert W. Kenney by a margin of 63,000 votes.

Yet Earl Warren is a name rather than an identifiable human being to most Californians. No tall tales are told of him. Legends have not accumulated. Many citizens say he is a fine man, a good man, an able man. But the word "great" invariably eludes them. All except a few die-hard Tories like the Governor. He probably could remain in the gubernatorial chair, if he willed it, as long as Mulley Doughton of North Carolina has been in Congress. But it is by no means a foregone conclusion that he could carry California for President against a Democratic nominee with real political sinews.

Although Warren is the only man in California history ever to be elected Governor three times, his personality has curiously made no profound impact on the state. Men still talk of Hiram Johnson and how "old Hiram" fought the Southern Pacific to its knees. The public is aware of Warren's photogenic family and his sun-tanned daughters with their pixie faces, but Warren himself is not a vivid image in the minds of the citizens of California.

The elder La Follette in Wisconsin, Norris in Nebraska, Floyd Olson in Minnesota, even Huey Pierce Long in Louisiana – these political figures, both good and bad, were genuine creatures of protoplasm and molecules to the citizens in whose realms they functioned. The people knew that if these men were pricked, they would bleed. They were more than names in the paper. They were *their* spokesmen in government.

But Earl Warren is merely a big, good-natured individual against whom only a handful of extreme reactionaries nurse a real grievance. On San Francisco cable cars or in Los Angeles orange-juice stands, the wayfarer rarely hears Warren mentioned. No elation was felt on the park benches in Union Square the morning after his magnificent race against Taft in Wisconsin. Never is Warren referred to as a "fighter" or as a champion of causes that stir people. On occasion Hiram Johnson may have been more foam than beer, but he succeeded in arousing Californians to a fighting pitch against the railroad octopus. Earl Warren dislikes corrupt lobbyists and oil barons, but he has yet to induce any substantial following to buckle on shield and armour for the fray.

It is not Warren's nature to become passionate over issues. Fervor and zeal are beyond his ken. He is not a crusader. High emotions fail to synchronize with his body chemistry. This is why he can win California's votes for Governor but not its undying allegiance in some far-off foray beyond the borders of the state. It reveals why Warren could lick a woefully-split California Democratic Party three consecutive times for the governorship and yet could not carry California for his running mate, Tom Dewey, against a militant and aggressive Harry Truman in 1948.

Furthermore, although Warren has earned the enmity of a hard core of GOP conservatives, he has not corralled a corresponding measure of adherence from the state's liberals, who continue to eye him somewhat suspiciously.

This undoubtedly stems back to an episode which occurred in 1940, when Warren was serving as Attorney General. It is the most disturbing and perplexing passage in Warren's long public career and one which many of his admirers would like to forget. Culbert L. Olson, California's first Democratic Governor in half-a-century, had appointed Professor Max Radin of the University of California Law School to a vacancy on the State Supreme Court.

Immediately, witch-hunters all over California sprang to the attack. Radin had defended many trade-union organizers whose civil rights he believed had been violated, in the lettuce fields, in the Sequoia woods and along city sidewalks. He had publicly urged clemency for several social workers found in contempt of a "Little Dies" Committee of the state legislature. On top of all this, he lent himself to anti-Semitic whisperings, for he had been born in Central Europe and was the son of a Jewish rabbi.

Warren, as a member of the Judicial Qualifications Commission, which had to review the Radin appointment, opposed the nomination. He never was a part of the anti-Semitic murmurings, but he could not have been unaware of them. California's leading newspaper, the pro-Republican San Francisco *Chronicle*, endorsed Radin from the start. "His nomination," declared the *Chronicle*, "should be confirmed with no more of the scurrilous attack which arises from the inability to distinguish between liberal faith and subversive character...."

The extremely cautious president of the University of California, Robert Gordon Sproul, himself to be under assault nearly a decade later for approving the university's loyalty oath, was unreserved in his approval of Professor Radin: "He is not a Communist, does not believe in communism and never was a Communist." And Justice

William O. Douglas of the u.s. Supreme Court contended that "Max Radin follows the tradition of Tom Paine and Thomas Jefferson. He is part of the tradition of Cardozo in his influence on the law."

Yet Radin, a lumbering little man who looked like a Koala bear, was rejected. He had written many distinguished books – *The Trial of Jesus of Nazareth*, *The Law and Mr. Smith*, *The Day of Reckoning*. It was possible to indict him by lifting sentences out of context. He was a controversial character who spoke his mind on public questions. Earl Warren acted as spokesman for the opponents of Professor Radin. He brought to the commission meeting the documents which presumably were determining in the case. That Radin had won a silver medal for outstanding legal scholarship from the Commonwealth Club, which included San Francisco's most prominent business and industrial figures, evidently made no impression on Warren in Radin's favor.

No one ever has quite known why Warren emerged so out of character in this situation, for it never has been natural for him to move vigorously on the attack. His friends still insist that, in spite of the impressive conservative sponsorship of Professor Radin, Warren sincerely regarded the university teacher as unfit for the bench. The GOP *Chronicle* ventured another explanation and it did Warren no credit: "It was an anti-Olson move by the commission's two Republicans."

The move was successful, for Warren replaced Olson in the gubernatorial chambers in 1942. He won by a whopping 343,000-vote majority. Three years later an unobtrusive announcement came from the Capitol building. Governor Earl Warren had reappointed Professor Max Radin to the California Commission on Uniform Law. Radin died in 1950 at the age of 70, his ambition to be a judge unfulfilled. One wonders if Warren thought of Radin during the California loyalty oath controversy when the same witch-hunting faction which had opposed Radin for the Supreme Court, with the active assistance of Earl Warren, was denouncing as pro-Communist not a humble university law professor but the Governor of California, Earl Warren.

Many Americans have acquired stature when they gained responsibility. Power has mellowed rather than hardened them. Warren seems to be such a man. Another characteristic of American politics is that platforms are to be run on rather than to stand on. Was it not FDR who assailed Hoover for reckless government spending? Thus Earl Warren, who came to the governorship by doing some witch-hunting of his own, later took a position against the witch-hunters on the board of regents of the nation's largest state university.

As district attorney of Alameda County and later as attorney general of California, Warren was not particularly distinguished as a public official. Folks thought well of him. He was completely honest. No breath of scandal ever touched his career. But he was largely a do-nothing official. His service as Attorney General coincided with many organizational drives by both the AF of L and the CIO. California long had been an open-shop state. Buckets of tar and threats of a noose awaited union organizers in many small towns. The Associated Farmers said there would be no organization of agricultural workers, who had been among the most exploited groups in the West. Warren could have turned his office into a shield for the defense of civil liberties. Instead, he carefully kept out of the seething labor situation.

Unlike some of his Democratic adversaries, Warren has never joined up with the Townsendites, Ham and Eggs and similar California "movements." Yet in the 1942 gubernatorial campaign he delivered himself of a pension pledge which gave these forces great encouragement. He said:

> I do not believe a senior citizen should have to be in need in
> order to secure a pension. I do not believe he should be forced to
> relinquish any outside income he may have or property he may
> have acquired. I don't believe he should be forced first to look to
> his children for support.

A man as intelligent and well-informed as Warren probably knew at the time that this pledge was impossible of delivery. Without a "means test" Federal matching funds would have been withheld from California. Old-age assistance actually would have gone down – unless the state were to be saddled with a tax burden unequalled by any individual state in American history. The main effect of the promise was to get Warren the votes of the pensioners, but also to arouse in these elderly men and women many false and cruel hopes which never were fulfilled.

Election as Governor of a great state worked wonders for Earl Warren. Pomp and power occasionally bring out the worst in men. To quote Lord Acton's time-honored axiom, "Power always corrupts, and absolute power always corrupts absolutely." In Earl Warren, however, power and authority inspired new standards of official honesty and ethics. He had arrived. The Radin episode, the pension pledge – these were gone by the wayside. He traveled the high road now. Nor did prominence and importance shake his basic personal modesty. He never had been Up-Beacon-Street and he did not begin in the Executive Mansion at Sacramento. He still was friendly and amiable and sometimes surprised that the son of a Southern Pacific brakeman had gone so far.

Earl Warren undoubtedly has been California's best Governor since Hiram Johnson. In many essentials, he is an improvement over the legendary Johnson. While Hiram threw his weight around against the vested interests, he never was long on administrative detail. He couldn't be bothered. Warren, not a vigorous fighter, has had plenty of time to poke into state departments and clean out waste and dead wood. Although the Chicago *Tribune* assails him as a spendthrift, he actually has streamlined government and effected many economies. "He beat Dewey of New York to the billion mark," claims the *Tribune*, referring to Warren's budget of $1,185,000,000, which knocked many big California taxpayers for a loop.

What the self-styled "world's greatest newspaper" did not add is that California has experienced a 53 percent population increase since 1940. Most of the newcomers have been in the younger age groups. This has meant 600,000 additional school children in a short period of time. Rather than let a whole generation of youngsters suffer from inadequate schooling, Warren put through a program of state aid to financially-distressed school districts.

Warren also has increased California's old-age assistance payments until they average second in the nation, being exceeded only by Colorado, where constitutionally all excise revenues must go to "senior citizens." Of course, he has not kept his famous pledge of 1942 to pay pensions as a matter of right. Quite the contrary, in fact, Warren now boasts that he has "improved the state's machinery for detecting chiselers." This has endeared him both to the general run of taxpayers and to the old folks who are genuinely in need. It is unlikely that Warren ever again will bow in the direction of those who demand that pensions go to all over a particular age, regardless of personal financial circumstances.

Throughout the nation Warren is widely known for his program of pre-paid state medical insurance, which would assure necessary hospital and medical services to every family. This was only the most gingerly-ventured type of program, but the American Medical Association, allergic even to suggestions that the government supervise mosquito control, immediately sounded off that Warren was a Socialist, or worse. In the home state of the AMA propaganda team, Whittaker & Baxter, Warren has taken a constant verbal pounding from the extreme right wing of the GOP In the opinion of some observers, this has made him seem more liberal than he actually is.

Sincere and conscientious though Warren may be, he adheres to party regularity when some truly basic decision is at stake. Unquestionably his most important appointive opportunity came in 1945 after the death of U.S. Senator Hiram Johnson. Warren chose an undistinguished state senator named William F. Knowland. The report was current at the time that the Governor was paying off an old political debt to Knowland's influential father, Joe Knowland, publisher of the Oakland *Tribune*, which supported Warren unremittingly when he was district attorney of Alameda County.

It is significant that Warren and Senator Knowland now do not wholly agree on the policy with which the latter is most identified in the public mind. Because of his zealous sponsorship of Chiang Kaishek, Knowland is sometimes called "the Senator from Formosa." But during the Wisconsin primary Warren said, "I doubt if 320,000 Chinese from Formosa are going to re-conquer China. It would be up to us to see the war through if we started it. I have never been able to persuade myself that we should start that kind of a war."

This was characteristic of the way in which Warren frequently starts off on the conservative side of an issue and then ends up taking the liberal position. "He learns fast and he is intellectually honest," commented a San Francisco reporter who often covers the Statehouse at Sacramento.

Yet the Governor rarely will fight an issue through to the finish. As a result of tremendous population gains, California was given seven new Congressional seats all at once last year, the greatest such prize in American history. It was up to the legislature to draw up new Congressional boundaries. This the legislature did, in typical gerrymandering fashion. Urban districts were discriminated against in favor of rural constituencies. Although the Federal constitution required all the districts to be approximately equal in population, one had 228,812 people and another a population of 415,322.

The bill reached Warren's desk, with such independent newspapers as the Sacramento *Bee* and the *Chronicle* of San Francisco openly calling it a "gerrymander." The Governor held a seven-hour-long public hearing, during which he gravely and courteously listened to the bill's adversaries. But in the end he signed it into law, adding a rather typical Warren concession. If the opponents cared to invoke a referendum by petition, he would immediately call a special election so that the issue could be settled by the voters at the polls.

Some of Warren's finest supporters point to such events as this to explain why he is not a flesh-and-blood character to the people of California. The gerrymander bill was tailored to fit for a fighting Governor. It sold short the residents of the vast metropolitan areas – Los Angeles, San Francisco, San Diego. It was a rap at the citadels of the trade unions, now potent in California. Much more important, the bill was undemocratic. It violated the old Jeffersonian concept of "one man, one vote." Had Warren applied the veto and hurled back the bill to the legislature, he would have been a hero with thousands of voters all over the state. And he would have confronted the legislature with the dilemma of either writing a decent and fair districting bill or having all 30 California Congressmen elected at large, which would have been a merry shambles. But Earl Warren did not operate in this fashion. He is the plodder, not the crusader. He failed to ruffle perceptibly when Artie Samish, the beer-king lobbyist, was quoted as saying, "Earl Warren may be the Governor of California but *I* am the Governor of the legislature." After the *Chronicle* and *Collier's* magazine had exposed Samish's dominance at Sacramento, a stringent lobbyist-registration act was shoved to passage. But Warren never took shape as a strong participant in this effort to restore legislative respect and sovereignty.

A similar twilight zone of gubernatorial influence surrounds the abortive loyalty oath at Berkeley, seat of the University of California. Warren was quoted as opposing the oath. His principle appointee to the board of regents, Admiral Chester W. Nimitz, likewise was against the oath. But Warren never fully used the great sounding board of the governorship to sound off on the issue. One professor on the campus observed, "The Governor's position against the loyalty oath is almost a secret." Yet had Warren taken a bolder position, it ultimately might have paid off generously in political dividends, for the courts and later the public rallied in opposition to the test pledge exacted of faculty members.

Earl Warren today is at a crossroads in his career. After having served as California's Governor for 12 years, it is hardly likely that he would run again in 1954. No Senatorial seat is open to him, because the Knowland seat is up this year and the other California niche was filled only recently, in 1950. He might be an ornament in any President's cabinet, either as Attorney General or as Secretary of the Interior. Yet it would not be easy for a man who had been monarch of all he surveyed in California, to serve at the behest and orders of another. If any individual could make this transition, it would be a man as essentially plain and humble as Earl Warren.

In all the state departments at Sacramento, honest men and women look forward with regret to the day when Warren leaves the Capitol building. Some of these people remember the halcyon era of the special interests, when "Sunny Jim" Rolph and his fellow Republicans ruled the roost in California. They look back with disfavor on many of the political hacks whom Culbert Olson brought to Sacramento, rather than the Democratic liberals he had promised. Earl Warren, in

the estimate of most of these persons, is the best California has offered in their lifetime.

"The nicest, friendliest man I have to deal with is the Governor,"
comments Edmund G. (Pat) Brown, the present California Attorney
General and the state's only major official who is a Democrat. "I
only wish he were a Democrat all four years, instead of just once
every four years – when he is running for election."

Whether Warren would settle for the Vice Presidency or a place in
the Cabinet is not definitely known. He rose once from mediocre Attorney General to be a good Governor of the nation's most mercurial
and turbulent state. His adherents believe he could rise again, from
being a good Governor to being a great President.

Richard and Maurine Neuberger at the state capitol in Salem, Oregon.

(RAY ATKESON)

REFLECTIONS

I Run for Office

Harper's, FEBRUARY 1947

Neuberger maximized the benefits from his dual careers. His political activities brought a fresh perspective to his reporting. And his articles about himself in national magazines greatly enhanced his political standing in Oregon. After losing a 1946 election for the Oregon State Senate, Neuberger wrote this account for *Harper's*.

I HAD NOT REALIZED what quest of political office was doing to me until I received an invitation to speak in a neighboring city across the Columbia River. As I looked at the water through the trusses of the railroad bridge, I suddenly remembered that I had passed into another sovereignty. This was the state of Washington. Oregon's soil – and voters – were behind me.

For the first time in many weeks I would not be talking to people who could vote on my candidacy for the state Senate. Within the limits of taste and decency, I could say what I pleased. I might challenge the prejudices of my listeners and still be safe from retribution at the polls. No longer would fear and hesitation, those abject sentinels, mount guard over each word and syllable.

If I blurted out my true feelings on the sales tax of postwar military training in the colleges, I would not need to review the episode in terms of the school bloc or the Legion vote. An honest expression on state rent control would not inevitably be followed by cold sweat over housewives or landlords striking my name from the sample ballots. And if after the meeting I failed to listen attentively for half an hour to some crank's plan for correcting the evils of the money system, the sequel would not be a sleepless night worrying about his influence in Precinct 144.

Yet before indulging this new-found freedom of speech, I carefully examined the audience to make certain that no constituents had crossed the Columbia to eavesdrop on what I would say in alien surroundings.

Twice in my thirty-three years I have been nominated for public office in Oregon at the Democratic primaries. This experience has run a gamut of sorts for I have both won and lost. In 1940 I was elected to the Oregon House of Representatives on President Roosevelt's coattails. In 1946 I was defeated for the state Senate in the Republican comeback. The pursuit of votes in a great democracy should prove exhilarating. I have not found it so. I have learned much, and I commend the undertaking to students of political science – in fact, to all who would better understand their country. But the temptation to pussyfoot, to evade and parry rather than to voice one's candid opinion, is so overwhelming that the experience will surely torment any except the flintiest conscience.

The candidate commences with one or two issues on which he declares himself as forthrightly as he dares. From such positions he does not withdraw – although I have met politicians who can retreat as skillfully as Marshal Ney. But the candidate knows that these issues form his reputation. They are the basis of his publicity in the newspapers. He utters them over and over again. He becomes recognized as a friend of labor or a champion of free enterprise. He is for or against public ownership of electric power; perhaps he decides to premise his campaign on keeping communism out of the American home or freeing the farmer from Wall Street.

Once away from the few questions on which he has decided to take a stand, the candidate twists and turns like Katooshka fleeing across the steppes ahead of the wolf pack. The electorate seems to him ready to rend him limb from limb should he falter in his personal behavior, family life, or economic concepts. If politicians are moral cowards – and I believe they are – it is partly because the public has made them so. Two campaigns for office have convinced me that the American people are essentially cynical about candidates. This cynicism breeds a curious sort of hostility. At many public gatherings I have felt that the audience waited tensely to deny me support if I should utter one phrase contrary to the predilections of the group I was addressing. Charity definitely does not begin at the political meeting.

I recall the leader of the longshoremen who admitted my one hundred percent record on labor legislation, but declared his union could not possibly back me because I had expressed doubt, in answer to a question from the floor, whether we should share the atomic secret with the Soviet Union. His attitude may have been due to communist leanings, but the same could not be said of the clergyman who conceded our full agreement on social problems, yet advised worshippers to vote against me because of an article my wife had written for the *Oregonian* about a local art group which hired females to pose in the nude.

Had I been aware originally of the desire to embarrass candidates rather than to tolerate in them the shortcomings common to the human race, I confess that I probably would have ducked the atomic question and told my wife to refrain from reference to the unclad models.

Candidates are timid and evasive because such conduct is politically profitable. I might say we are cowards literally in self-defense. The politician siding with a particular organization on nine issues out of ten is scorned for the tenth. Blunt speech in campaigns has always cost me votes – whether the topic involved was ridiculous or sublime. When I inveighed against the billboards cluttering Oregon's roads, farmers renting barns and highway parkings to sign companies mobilized for my opponent. After I had denounced the persecution of returning Japanese-American war veterans, the American Legion commenced gunning for my political hide.

Minorities determine many elections, particularly in the primaries, and this is why equivocation pays. I have faith that a substantial majority of the voters approved my stand both on billboards and the attacks against the Nisei. But the majority was unorganized, while the Legion and the farmers with signs on their land were marshaled for action; and politicians know that one active enemy, constantly at the telephone or buttonholing acquaintances, can do damage to a candidacy which twenty indifferent supporters never offset.

As a writer on politics I liked to think romantically that forthrightness meant victory. I thought of George Norris, and forgot that he was the exception and not the rule. As a candidate, I am aware that forthrightness generally must be its own reward. The political retort perfect is that which sounds strident but offends nobody. "Say nothing, and say it well," I was advised by a United States senator who interested himself in my embryonic political career.

When I spoke in colored neighborhoods for civil rights legislation, I incurred the wrath of wealthy Negro night-club operators who did not want their people allowed to patronize public places frequented by whites. But when I cautiously straddled an old-age pension proposition on the Oregon ballot, I found that I picked up votes from both sides. Before even so sophisticated an organization as the League of Women Voters, outright endorsement of a new school tax did not return the same political dividends as approving the measure "in principle, with certain reservations." This was a way of riding two chariots – and also of convincing the disillusioned candidate that Barnum was right.[13]

At the peak of the campaign, aspirants for all jobs from governor to constable traveled a circuit, addressing trade unions, women's clubs, pension groups, and Izaak Walton Leagues. Most of the candidates thought nothing of telling a property owners' association at eight o'clock that taxes had to come down, and before the evening was over promising a rally of old people the $24,000,000,000 Townsend Plan. When I remarked to a fellow candidate that this seemed a trifle inconsistent he growled, "Well, they're so darned anxious to trip us up that I don't really mind fooling 'em a little. I even kinda think they like it."

Maybe they do, for he had been on the public payroll nearly twenty years.

II

I prefer to believe that I crawfished less than other candidates. Yet crawfish I did, and ironically I wonder now whether such behavior can save a politician when the national trend is going heavily against his party. Shrewd silence and high-sounding abstractions unfortunately result in votes, but not enough votes, in my opinion, to stem the Republican torrent of 1946 or the Democratic tides which ran when FDR was at the height of his popularity.

The fact is I doubt if millions of Americans are very interested in the race for any political office except that of the President of the United States. Their ignorance of other contests is often amazing – as, for example, the high school teacher who had to withdraw from my committee near the end of the campaign when she suddenly discovered, to her great embarrassment, that my opponent was the husband of her best friend.

The apathy toward most political tussles can be demonstrated mathematically. In Oregon 283,000 people voted in the off-year election of 1942, but 479,000 went to the polls for the Presidential contest two years later. Similar proportions prevail throughout the country. The 1946 total of votes was 14,000,000 less than during the Roosevelt-Dewey rivalry of 1944. This means that many of the men and women who vote in Presidential years are concerned with the outcome of only one contest. They are confronted with a ballot listing innumerable other offices, but on those offices they vote almost wholly in accordance with their sentiments on the Presidency.

I fear that this holds true in off-years as well. People decide how they feel about the man in the White House and let that feeling determine who will be district attorney and lieutenant governor. Politicians weasel and equivocate because it seems the safe course and because party primaries frequently go to the cagiest contender; but the bulk of general election contests in my state have been influenced far more by the prevailing attitude toward the occupant of the White House than by local issues and personalities.

Indeed, two campaigns for a seat in the Oregon Legislature have made me wonder whether people really care much at all about local government. Have we thought about the atomic bomb to the exclusion of the schoolhouse on the corner? Are we so eager to have the federal government control prices or crack down on labor unions that we neglect the instrumentalities for economic and social action closer to home?

My adversary and I debated before three hundred and fifty students in the Reed College Commons and then subjected ourselves to cross-examination by the students. At least a score of questions were asked; not one concerned a problem indigenous to the state of Oregon. All involved national or international issues. Yet we were running for an office which could not possibly, by the most fantastic stretch of the imagination, bring the Marines home from China or admit displaced persons to the United States. After the meeting, Reed's president, Peter H. Odegard, said to me: "The kids haven't been thinking about the Oregon school bill or county utility districts. They appear to have a cosmic rather than a local bent." Their elders, too.

I spoke at more than five hundred meetings during the 1946 campaign and found no genuine interest in the problems of our home town. People wanted England to do something about India and Palestine, but would do nothing themselves to clean up the pollution choking the salmon in the river which flowed through the center of our city. The atomic bomb and our relations with Russia were exciting; sewage disposal in the Willamette River was humdrum – and, even more depressing, it required the assessment of local taxes. In fact, when I mentioned pollution at one or two meetings, people dismissed the topic with a single comment:

"We'll get a federal grant to take care of it."

I am a New Deal Democrat, but the perennial looking to Washington, either in hope or dismay, seems to me one of the most discouraging features of contemporary politics. For years the voters think that one man, FDR, will fix everything – and thus their own responsibilities are ended. He will succor France, hold prices, and cope with John L. Lewis. Then the people decide that one man, Harry Truman, can't fix anything, and perhaps a new fixer is required. Beyond this one man the voters are unable to see.

"Had enough?" the Republicans asked in Oregon, as well as elsewhere, during the 1946 campaign. I argued with audiences that in our state, surely, such an argument would signal the end of the Republicans, where they controlled every major office in Oregon. The argument proved a complete dud. The people with whom I talked blamed all their woes on one man: President Truman. For high prices, the lack of sugar, communism, the shortage in housing – he was the guilty party. Republican governors, senators, and congressmen shared none of the responsibility. Truman was a Democrat; therefore vote against all Democrats. That's the way it went with my audiences. Oregon voted more preponderantly Republican than any state outside New England.

The time may come when a Republican President and his followers will regret this approach to the ballot box. I believe both parties have fostered it: the Democrats by making the name Roosevelt the alpha and omega of all public questions, the Republicans by paying lip service to states' rights but neglecting state duties. Oregon has a Republican governor who speaks constantly against federal encroachment, but when the schools faced a recent financial crisis he rushed to Washington to beg for federal funds to keep the kindergartens running.

I want to comment briefly on the fact that in 1940 and again in 1946 I was the only Jew on the ballot in Oregon. Ours is not a state with a large Jewish population; there are approximately 12,000 among 1,300,000 people. This may be the reason that I encountered virtually no religious prejudice. During both campaigns by friends, Jew and Gentile alike, warned me of the anti-Semitism which might lessen my chances. I know that many people believe such feeling is rampant all over America. I am no sociologist and cannot assay the truth of this, but I do know that the fact I am a Jew did not keep me from being elected in 1940, nor did it prevent me from heading the Democratic ticket in 1946.

Only once did I run into an active outburst of anti-Semitism. At a pension rally last October a retired Lutheran minister assailed Jews in general and me in particular. Angry and tense, I was about to jump to my feet in answer, when a leader in the pension club, a man over seventy with a leonine head, got up and said very quietly:

"I figure we're all Americans, every one of us here. Our friend Neuberger found that out in the war we've just ended. I found it out in the Spanish-American War." And he sat down.

I am sure the incident actually reacted to my benefit. Afterwards practically the entire audience lined up to shake my hand. They were obviously embarrassed for fear my feelings had been hurt. I know some of them redoubled their efforts to make certain I carried that neighborhood – which I did.

III

As a candidate one learns to suspect many of the shibboleths and axioms accepted as truth in high circles. A particularly emphatic watchword with all liberals is that a large vote means a liberal vote. The formula goes like this: the conservatives *always* vote, so the bigger the total vote the more working people have voted; and the more working people who vote, the more liberals will be elected.

The formula overlooks only one fact: workers can vote conservatively, too.

I addressed a crowd of trade unionists near a big sawmill. Many of them wore CIO buttons on their hats and suspender bands. It was one of the most conservative groups I encountered during the campaign. The loggers talked about the law of supply and demand and wondered why Truman didn't decontrol the tons of sugar they had heard were stored in Oregon's beet fields.

"Are these the people," I asked my wife, "we are trying so desperately to get to the polls to prevent the Republicans from winning the election?"

After I had picked myself out of the avalanche, I examined the returns. Working-class neighborhoods, which Democratic leaders predicted could insure a Democratic victory by voting heavily, did vote heavily – for the Republicans. It seems to me that the fallacy of the "big vote, liberal vote" theory has been proved nationally, yet everyone appears to have overlooked the demonstration.

Two experiences as a candidate also have convinced me that labor leaders cannot deliver the vote of their members in nearly as neat a package as they would like politicians to believe. I was one of the few candidates in our city endorsed by both the AFL and CIO, yet I was unable to discover any benefit from this in districts thickly populated by union members. I am not so sure that the endorsements were not an anvil rather than a cane, for although I polled more votes than any other Democrat on the ballot in Portland, I ran behind candidates without the union endorsement in precincts mainly inhabited by laboring men and their families. Perhaps many workers belong to unions by fiat of boss or business agent rather than by choice. This happened in the shipyards when Henry J. Kaiser hustled welders, stenographers, and traveling-crane operators into the protective custody of the Boilermakers' Union before they could be recruited by the CIO. I doubt if these "boilermakers" voted as the officials of their union decreed.

Yet organized labor made a bona fide effort to find out how candidates stood on issues affecting union policy. The AFL asked me a series of intelligent and reasonable question on taxation, unemployment insurance, and compulsory arbitration. This could be said for few other groups. To the contrary, most of us were pestered by political racketeers offering, for a fee of course, to put our names on the "Swedish ticket," or "colored ticket," or "veterans' ticket." Several notorious bigots thus appeared on the "colored ticket," and I swallowed hard when a man with a Ku Klux Klan past ran near the top of the ballot in Negro neighborhoods.

Many ugly designs fit into this same pattern. Heads of veterans' organizations sponsored non-veterans over war heroes, particularly if the non-veterans got on well with the state political machine and the Purple Heart belonged to a man of rebellious tendencies. Old-age pension clubs even endorsed members of the legislature who had fought social security bills with every breath in their bodies.

The foes of pensions were supported ostensibly because they had approved a weasel-worded memorial urging Congress to "consider" the Townsend Plan. Yet these same men voted consistently against every propoal to increase Oregon's niggardly old-age assistance of thirty-one dollars. Many politicians in the Far West, where live a larger proportion of people over sixty-five than in any other region, deliberately keep the old people chasing pie in the sky. These politicians, calling themselves "Townsendites," oppose adequate state pension programs in order to continue capitalizing on the desire of the aged for $200 a month.

It is the cruelest runaround I have seen in politics.

IV

Do I want a political career?

Despite the compromises, the intrigue, and the disillusionment, a man has a faint pulse indeed if he is not stirred by the thought of being a United States senator or the governor of a great state. The opportunity for service – and for glory – undoubtedly compensates in generous measure for the deals and hypocrisy of the political race.

Each time that I shilly-shallied while standing before a hostile audience or inquisitive panel, I inwardly assured myself that immortal figures had committed the same sin. Did not Lincoln temporize on the slavery issue, and could not Jefferson be quoted on both sides of innumerable arguments? And what of the silence of FDR on Franco?

I also looked about me and saw contemporary candidates for office (unhappily, the bulk of them successful) demanding no appeasement of Russia in one breath and immediate abandonment of the military draft in the next.

So I was not alone in my political trimming, and I must deny that it was fear of the loss of integrity which made me hesitate when I had my chance to run for major office. Another and more selfish consideration entered my mind last April, at the time the Democratic State Committee asked me to be the party's nominee for governor of Oregon. I was pledged a clear field in the primary.

As events developed I would have lost in November, but the Republican landslide had not broken perceptibly over the rim rock seven months ahead of the election. The offer in itself was an honor, or so I liked to think. I would have been the youngest gubernatorial nominee in the history of the state. In addition – and evidently in defiance of the prevailing opinion of the moment – I consider the Democratic party a great institution and the party most likely to act in behalf of the average citizen. I would have been proud to be its nominee.

I declined, and for only one reason – because of what politics does to people, especially its castoffs. Ring Lardner once said that the most pathetic people he knows were former star athletes. Ex-politicians, or perhaps I should more correctly say discarded officeholders, fit this description – and probably the explanation is similar. Like men who have hit home runs and scored touchdowns, they have heard the acclaim of the crowd and then had it withdrawn. Recent objects of 'attention and flattery, they abruptly find themselves neglected.

A page boy called me out of the legislature one afternoon. A lean, nervous man waited in the lobby. He wanted my vote on a bill in which a client was interested. As I looked at him, standing there in a suit with frayed elbows and worn cuffs, I thought: "This man for four years was governor of Oregon.[14] He sat under this dome with power of life and death, the majesty of our state behind him. He was the most progressive governor in Oregon's history, and Lincoln Steffens and Ida Tarbell came to tell the country of what he had done. Now he stands here, dilapidated and seedy, lobbying for small-time clients, and begs a freshman legislator for a vote."

I know many men who have held high political office and then been defeated. I doubt if one of them ever has been satisfied or content in any future role. They spend most of their time trying to come back. They run repeatedly for judge, for Congress, for county commissioner – for any job which will invest them again with the trappings of office. Often a place on the payroll is a consideration, too. Yet as for the prizefighter who must pick himself up off the canvas, the comeback trail in politics is hard. Few travel it successfully. Not even Teddy Roosevelt could do it.

Once the electorate's passion for a politician is spent, it seldom is tempted again. But men who have been the Honorable So-and-so, whose opinions are quoted solemnly in the press, whose good will is servilely cultivated, whose presence is announced by the blare of trumpets and the roar of sirens – these men learn only by repeated rebuffs that their appeal at the polls is gone. The human mechanism is too frail to be surrounded by pomp and power and then to go back willingly to desk, typewriter, or grocery counter.

In fact, many beaten politicians never go back at all. A week after the Republican victory Paul R. Leach wrote in the Chicago *Daily News*, "A lot of defeated members are staying on in Washington. They're looking for lame-duck jobs while the Democratic administration lasts, or joining law and lobbying firms." Washington, D.C., is full of vanquished senators and congressmen who have not returned to their home states.

Two ex-senators and two ex-representatives from Idaho are now living, for example, but not in Idaho. Two are in the national capital, one in Miami, Ohio, and the other in Knoxville, Tennessee. The late Charles L. McNary of Oregon, for many years Republican minority leader in the Senate, used to claim that strong psychological factors worked to keep a man from returning to the constituency which had repudiated him. "As he walks down the street," said McNary, "he believes each person he passes is one of the votes that licked him."

I like Oregon and its rocks and rills, and have no desire to pull up stakes because of reversal in an election. Yet knowing my own frailties, I do not think I am made of any sterner stuff than the politicians who have done just that. I wonder if I could occupy a high office and then live graciously among the people who had tossed me out of it.

I wonder, too, whether the writer can mix his craft with a personal political candidacy. He can support or oppose others, but should he himself run? Those who would govern us, we measure by a special yardstick. I was sharply criticized for being photographed soliciting a vote from a pretty girl in a brief bathing suit. A labor leader did not believe a genuine friend of the common people could drive a car as new as my 1942 Oldsmobile. These are not charges leveled against the butcher, the baker or the candlestick maker.

A writer, if he is to be reasonably honest, must express sentiments repugnant to a good many people. This is not the way to win votes. During one of my legislative campaigns, a loyal friend went to the public library and checked out all the copies of a book I had written because he had heard its contents assailed at a meeting. "Would that mine enemy had written a book," becomes particularly pertinent when the enemy is running for office. Nor is the novelist any safer than the author of non-fiction. In California's 1934 gubernatorial campaign sentences shrewdly culled from the novels of Upton Sinclair were plastered on thousands of billboards from the Klamath Basin to Mexico.

As long as the business of rounding up votes dominated my thoughts, I discovered an unconscious inhibition on what I wrote. Truth, at least as I saw it, became not the sole test. I speculated on whether my words might antagonize this or that group. Several times, I regret to report, my eraser modified original conclusions so they would be more generally acceptable. This is not a situation in which a writer can do justice to his profession, his topic, or to himself.

And I was seeking only minor office. What might the inhibitions have been if I had glimpsed ahead the prospect of the governor's chair or a United States senatorship?

The case against making politics my career is strong. I accept the case implicitly. Already it has persuaded me against becoming the titular head of the Democratic party in our state.

Yet the argument is only $99^{44}/_{100}$ percent pure. The other fraction disturbs me occasionally. When I see Oregon's teachers paid the lowest salaries on the Coast, when I see a private utility company selling the power from the dam at Bonneville which the people built and paid for, when I see a Japanese-American soldier with forty-one blood transfusions denied a hotel room on a rainy night, when I see a million-dollar race track rising while veterans cannot construct homes – then my blood pressure rises, too, and I wonder if any case is strong enough to impel abdication in favor of those who tolerate these things.

But the slightest return of political ambition brings that degrading fear which is the curse of politics. I even ask myself if I have said too much in these pages.

Confessions of a Candidate

The Progressive, JANUARY 1949

Thomas E. Dewey carried Oregon over President Truman in 1948, helped by a near Republican sweep of the state. U.S. Senator Guy Cordon won reelection and Douglas McKay won the governorship. But a bright spot for the Democratic party was Neuberger's election to the state senate. One of the Democratic candidates recruited by Neuberger to run for the senate, Robert D. Holmes of Astoria, was also elected in a major upset. Eight years later, with Neuberger's support, Holmes would be elected to the governorship. Neuberger wrote about his own successful campaign for *The Progressive*.

I FELT SURE the speech had been a success. After all, school teachers were interested in tenure, academic freedom, and better pay. These issues had been the theme of my talk. But the next day my wife, herself a former teacher, said to me, "The girls liked everything about your speech last night except one thing."

"What's that?" I asked, wondering whether I had pussyfooted on free speech in the classroom or perhaps hadn't suggested a high enough salary scale. "The girls thought you should have worn a white shirt instead of that gray broadcloth. To a lot of them, particularly in the back of the hall, it looked like a work shirt. They thought you should have dressed a little more carefully for a meeting of school teachers."

I dug through my checkbook. The gray shirt had cost the same at the haberdasher as those of impeccable white. But to the teachers I had seemed to be in my garden duds, and that was not good for a young man hoping to represent the 13th senatorial district in the Oregon State Legislature. I had remembered not to be too dressed up when soliciting the votes of truck drivers and longshoremen. I had forgotten a candidate could not be dressed up enough for school teachers.

Ever since election day I have pondered these supposedly trivial details of campaigning. To what extent does the personal equation enter a political race?

Was it Dewey's personal arrogance that decided Nov. 2 or was it the record of the 80th Congress? Was it his failure to discuss issues or was it the episode of the locomotive engineer? Was it high prices and no housing, or was it the smug references in the press to "President-elect Dewey?" How much were farmers in overalls antagonized by the October selection of Dewey as "one of the 10 best-dressed men in America?"

These musings apply to the tenuous realm of human behavior and prejudices. No political seismograph can quite answer them. Dr. Gallup probably never will know whether his poll was upset by 90-cent butter or by the epithet of "lunatic" hurled at an employee of the Louisville & Nashville Railroad. Elmo Roper will be unable to tell whether it was the Taft-Hartley Law or the fact that people sensed the insincerity of the Republican candidate when he tried to assume the common touch.

But my own personal experiences in the recent campaign are at the disposal of Roper and Gallup. They may study and analyze them to their heart's content. They may dissolve them in water, roll them in bread crumbs, and do whatever other mysterious things poll-takers do to the circumstances of life to come up with 54% for Dewey, 37% for Truman, 6% for Wallace, the rest undecided.

I was so far down the Oregon ballot from the Presidential candidates that I could barely communicate with them by smoke signals. Yet I believe people are moved by the same fears, hopes, and conclusions when they vote for a state senator as when they pick a President of the United States.

One evening I went to a turkey dinner put on by the women of a Townsend old-age pension club. It was a good meal and I indulged heartily in a pair of turkey legs and big mounds of dressing and sweet potatoes.

An hour or so later, I addressed a church social. To my surprise, the social was followed by a generous repast – cold meats, deviled eggs, chocolate cake. I had no appetite but attempted to make it appear that the food was as welcome to me as to a shipwrecked mariner. However, women watch carefully when their own handiwork goes under the knife and fork. I was addressed somewhat caustically by the wife of the minister:

"Young man, don't you enjoy our church supper? All these people around you are eating their heads off, but I doubt if you're really enjoying our food."

No votes for me there ...

I decided afterward I should have told the church ladies about the Townsend turkey dinner. That would have been the truth, and it would have been better than pretending to be hungry for the sliced tongue and chocolate cake. And if people can spot Neuberger when he play-acts at having an appetite, perhaps they can get wise to a candidate for loftier office who poses at being friendly.

II

Feeble attempts to prove economic kinship often fall flat. One of my opponents, a man of obvious affluence, used to tell working men's audiences that he once had been a working man himself. Toward this people adopted a "so what?" attitude. Some sensed he was talking down to them. Fortunately for me, my adversary never realized how poorly this condescension on his part went over. But from it I learned a valuable lesson.

At a meeting of 1,200 teamsters I had intended to point out how I had driven a delivery truck when I was in college. Now I thought better of it. Instead, I said that while I was not a working man myself, I had made an effort to understand the problems and difficulties which the average working man faced. I also abandoned a plan to send a postcard to the truck farmers on the fringe of the district, seeking to establish a mutuality of interests by describing the nearby dairy run by my wife and her mother.

Could it be that tales of the farm at Pauling failed to stir rural voters throughout a wider amphitheatre than Oregon?

I am convinced Americans are shrewder at detecting insincerity than some politicians yet suspect. I belong to no lodges. I am not a Mason, an Elk, an Eagle, a Moose, a Woodman or an Odd Fellow. A fellow candidate on the Democratic ticket nearly persuaded me this was fatal. "You've got to sign up in some lodges," he argued. "They control lots of votes." I practically had my hand in my wallet when I wondered what I would think, if I were an ardent and devoted lodge member, when a candidate took the oath a few months before election.

I did not join. My friend signed up everywhere, however, and was badly defeated. After the election a member of the Eagles said to me, "We welcome politicians into the Eagles, but if we think they join just to get our votes, we pass the word along not to vote for them. We don't want our organization belittled that way. We're proud of it, and we resent politicians who try to exploit it."

In politics a great deal depends on *how* a thing is done. President Truman could arrive at an encampment of the Veterans of Foreign Wars, and have a Missouri post overseas cap slapped good-naturedly on his head. But had he come there wearing veteran's accoutrements to achieve a studied effect, the act probably would have back-fired. I think this may have happened with the husband-and-wife affection which the Deweys displayed from the observation platform of their train. History will not record that the voters were won over by Tom with his arm around Mrs. Dewey in public.

Outside a Grange hall one night my wife and I had a strenuous argument over who had the keys to the car. I berated her sternly when she finally found them at the bottom of the debris in her purse. Then I was shocked to discern a good many Grange members listening with fascination in the darkness.

In the morning I telephoned a friend in the Grange to find out if the rumpus in the Neuberger family had jeopardized my chances. "Golly no," said he. "What couple doesn't have quarrels like that? Our people just got a good chuckle out of it."

I contrasted this reaction with that which followed publication of a Signal Corps picture of me in a community newspaper. The photograph had been taken in Alaska during the war. It showed my captain's bars and General's aide shield. I was wearing a muskrat-pelt hat given me by a Canadian Mountie. I gazed skyward grimly. The picture made me look a whole lot more rugged than I really am. And the impression it created was 100% unfavorable.

Some people thought I was trying to capitalize on my military service. Others felt I was boasting of my rank. Still others regarded the pose as corny and full of ham. It made no one think I was rugged and quite a few think I was being stilted and phony. The picture of me in the Arctic hurriedly went into mothballs.

On the other hand, there were two pictures about which I was jittery – and from which the reaction was nothing but good. One picture, snapped by an *Oregonian* camera man, showed me interviewing an extremely pretty girl at Reed College. The girl was wearing a play suit. Another picture, taken of my wife at work posing a Jantzen bathing girl model, was used by the *Saturday Evening Post* after some of her Alaskan photography had been published.

I was afraid that these scenes of the Neubergers in the presence of lightly-clad young women might offend some of the voting public. The fears never materialized. Indeed, a Methodist minister nudged me at a meeting several nights later and said, "Mighty pretty people you and the Missus are keeping company with these days."

I once reluctantly decided straddles were good political technique. The recent campaign has convinced me that, happily, I may have been wrong.

In one precinct I attended a conference of owners of small rental properties. Although I personally favor rent control, I was somewhat less than forthright at this meeting. I said the entire issue should be studied carefully; I suggested that perhaps we could work out a policy which would be "fair to landlord and tenant alike." I doubt if this double-talk proved very profitable. The people at the meeting seemed to know I was trimming. They dismissed me rather coolly, and I trailed in that precinct.

Reviewing the incident, I made up my mind that the next time I was boxed in a tight spot I would tell the whole truth and nothing but the truth.

I got the chance at Vanport College, where a majority of the students are World War II veterans. I was asked my opinion of a bill on the Oregon ballot to pay each ex-GI in the state a bonus of $500. I gulped and said I was against the bill. Although I feared that every word cut me off farther from the votes of the 450 people in the hall, I pointed out that veterans needed a sensible housing program rather than a cash dole and that a $50,000,000 bonus in 1948 would merely add to the inflation.

By now, I have come to the conclusion that this was not only good economics but also good politics. The Vanport registrar, Dr. Putnam, prophesied I would fare better with the student body than would the politicians who promised the bonus and nearly everything else they thought a college audience wanted to hear. On the national scene, I think the performance of Harry Truman with respect to civil rights for Negroes demonstrates that the honest thing is often the best politics. Standing by the fair employment practices proposal bid fair to lose him the Solid South and the election, yet ultimately it may have won him Ohio, Illinois, and California, where the election result was decided.

III

Despite all the shortcomings of the press and radio, the American people are getting more information on public affairs than ever before. They are not as unsophisticated as the Claghorn and Throttlebottom skits would have us believe.[15] Whenever a politician started off with a promise to stand by his convictions "even if I pay for them with my political life," people murmured in audible protest. Unctuousness is disliked, and so is bragging about virtues which many men and women take for granted.

When he is in public, a candidate must be humble but not obsequious. He must be independent but not arrogant. He must be learned but not pedantic. He must be neat in appearance but not ostentatious. Yet frequently the gap is narrow. How much can a candidate supplicate for votes and not be servile. How positive may he be in his opinions without becoming dogmatic?

People are allergic to politicians who talk down to them. Americans want to look up to their leaders in government, but for reasons of achievement and knowledge rather than because of an air of personal superiority. The voter wants to think he is just as good a man as his Congressman or state senator, even if he may not have the politician's college degrees or gift of gab.

Candidates, especially those seeking relatively minor offices, travel from meeting to meeting in a sort of circuit. They come to know each other's tricks and foibles, as vaudeville performers know each other's acts. Although I have no mirror to hold to myself, I am certain the most difficult feat for my fellow candidates was to be a friendly person without being condescending. The "just call me 'Bill'" approach fizzled painfully. And, of course, there were a few aspirants, with an exaggerated notion of their sex appeal, who shook hands with female listeners as though they were about to make love to them. This went over with neither the women – nor their husbands.

I hope I do not sound like Mark Hanna because I have won a small political post in a frontier state. But if there is any advice to give someone else entering politics, it is to be yourself. Don't try to seem humble, or people will surely regard you as pompous. The harder you try to be profound, the more likely folks are to consider you superficial. The American people may take quite a while to get wise to a potential Fascist or Communist, but they can ferret out someone who is essentially synthetic and affected as far away as they can see through the Lick telescope.

A crook, I venture to say, can succeed more readily at the polls than the phony. Our state has elected lawyers who were attorneys for the underworld and men who had been involved in ugly breach-of-promise suits, but the voters made short shrift of the industrialist who claimed he was a farmer because he owned an estate in the country.

I still remember the poor politician who volunteered to help wash dishes after a community-hall potluck supper for 250 people. He toiled in the sink for two or three hours. But afterwards the young woman in charge of the kitchen said to me, "You know, I doubt if I'm going to vote for that fellow. He's a little too obvious, even though he's saving us an awful lot of work. And after all, we're voting for a legislator, not a dish-washer."

My Hometown Is Good Enough for Me

Saturday Evening Post, 16 DECEMBER 1950

Neuberger often wrote about men of the Pacific Northwest who had gained national prominence by moving to the East Coast. *Go East, Young Man* was the title of Supreme Court Justice William O. Douglas's auto-biography, chronicling his life from Yakima to Washington, D.C. Neuberger, too, had opportunities to leave the Northwest. In 1940 he was seriously courted by Henry Luce's *Life* magazine. Later, Ben Hibbs of the *Saturday Evening Post* sought to persuade Neuberger to move to Philadelphia. In this article for the Post, Neuberger explains his decision to remain in Portland.

ONE OF THE DISCOVERIES of the census was that more Americans are on the move than ever before in the country's history. It's become such a national habit that two-thirds of the folks along the Pacific Coast are wayfarers who were brought up elsewhere. I may be hopelessly behind the times, but I can't put in with these millions who have itchy feet.

I live right where I was born and raised. I intend to keep on doing so. What's more, I commend it to all my fellow citizens who can't wait to shake the hometown dust from their oxfords and sandals.

I recall visiting a man and a woman who had left our city shortly after their marriage and gone to New York, where they had prospered greatly. In fact, many of us envied their imposing success. But when

I knocked on the door of their Park Avenue apartment, they fell on my neck and shouted in unison, "How are things back home?"

Home! All my jealousy vanished in that instant. I looked around me at furnishings which probably rivaled the assessed valuation of our neighborhood school district. And yet this splendor wasn't home. To these expatriates home always would be Portland, Oregon – a place three thousand miles away, where the alpine firs marched like a green-clad host up Mount Hood's glacial apron. Through the windows I could see other huge monoliths of New York's most exclusive apartment house district, with lights lit in Pullman rows. I wondered how many people in those luxurious tiers still thought of home as some distant spot far out on the broad expanse of America.

I have had several tempting offers to leave my hometown and toil elsewhere, an opportunity probably commonplace in a land so vast and diverse as the United States. Always these chances promised more money than I had been earning, yet no regret attaches to having refused them. The compensations of living in one's native community cannot be measured in coin of the realm.

When I drive to work, I pass the lot where I first learned the pleasures of one-old-cat and workup, played with an indoor baseball split at the seams. A supermarket stands there now, but it cannot blot spine-tingling remembrance of the afternoon I hit a home run off the neighborhood bully, who was pitching.

A few evenings ago I waited in line at the supermarket with the family groceries. Several places in front of me was the statuesque blonde I never quite could manage to date in high school. She wouldn't even let me buy her a soda. Too many backfield heroes beat my time. A man was with the blonde, meekly pushing a cart loaded with canned goods. He was her husband, I gathered. I studied him intently, and a warm, happy glow swept over me as I realized he was infinitely fatter of paunch and balder of head than I am. Nor could I overlook the fact that the blonde, once statuesque, had widened to the extent that the description no longer applied.

These are petty satisfactions, you may say, and I agree. Yet where could I experience them except in my hometown, and particularly in the exact neighborhood of that town where I was born thirty-eight years ago?

In Portland I have a genuine sense of belonging. The whole atmosphere is *gemütlich*. I am sure I could feel this way in no other place. To begin with, the attachment does not stem from superficialities – political affinity, for example. Indeed, I am a Democrat in the only city of the Far West with a local government that is exclusively Republican. Nor do these roots of mine depend on a propitious climate.

I like to play golf and my wife is an inveterate swimmer; yet all too often neither can be done comfortably outdoors in Portland's interminable drizzle.

The factors in my allegiance are more subtle than this. Everywhere I go in Portland, some scene stirs a remote memory. Here is the store where I wheedled a doting uncle into buying my first electric train; there, down the street, is the bank where my grandfather took me ceremoniously to deposit the first dollar I earned lugging his big leather golf bag. I never pass a shaded building of red brick without thinking of the patient and understanding first grade teacher, who kept a desolate boy from breaking into tears the grim day that his parents went off to the Canadian Rockies without him.

Yet I suppose these adventures in nostalgia would not be sufficient to anchor me, unless I believed that other people also had the feeling that I belonged right where I was.

I have not forgotten the night at a well-attended Community Club dinner that I debated my adversary for a seat in the Oregon State Senate. The opposing candidate spoke first and, perhaps influenced by some zealous cohorts, accused me of every possible crime except the murder of Arnold Rothstein. I could feel the audience eying me suspiciously, if not with actual hostility.

Then came my turn. Almost by rote, I began with the statement: "I was born and raised less than a mile from this hall, and I got my education in the Portland school system."

The tension went out of that meeting like gas out of a dirigible. I had planned replying to my adversary in kind, but suddenly it no longer seemed necessary. If I was a hometown boy, I couldn't be quite so bad as I had been painted. I admit this is irrational, for the native son could make off with the courthouse safe just as readily as the interloper. But blind trust in a product of the hometown is a fact of American life and cannot be ignored. Even on the Pacific Coast, a region of migrants, all the reigning governors boast local school diplomas as part of their political arsenal. And although the nation as a whole may be on the move, seventy-three of the members of the United States Senate can cite representation of their birthplaces as cogent reason for another term in office.

In fact, this residential double standard has been applied to nothing more momentous than the brevity of a dancer's garments. My wife and another high school teacher performed a bare-legged hula as the feature of a PTA benefit. All was serene for both are local girls. When a new teacher, born beyond the state line, shook her hips in a similar costume, the protests of parents and ministers made the school board tremble. My wife now serves with me in the legislature, the first such family representation since Oregon attained statehood, and she says that a firm rooting in local soil tided her over many turbulent riffles during her campaign.

Yet despite the confidence which hometown nativity assures, does not a person owe it to himself to take advantage of opportunity which beckons from afar? How else can he develop his talents and capabilities?

Sherwood Anderson once wrote: "It seems to me that a man like Lincoln would have been Lincoln had he never left Springfield, Illinois; that he grew naturally, as a tree grows, out of the soil of Springfield, Illinois, out of the people about him whom he knew so intimately."

This might have been true of Lincoln, but what of ordinary mortals? Can we afford not to pack the family luggage when the will-o'-the-wisp flutters beyond the horizon?

In 1940 I was offered a job in New York which would have practically doubled my income. At first I was tempted to accept by return wire. Then I looked at my hiking boots in the closet, at the tentative crayon marks I had scrawled on maps of the Cascades and the Olympics. I examined the hateful, rusty lawn mower which I might never curse again. Our friends in Portland came to mind, those with whom we went camping, swapped recipes and argued politics. And I thought of the cold, impersonal glances of all those millions in New York whom we didn't know and who never would know us.

In my dilemma I wrote for advice to a man I had yet to meet, but whose career always has epitomized the American who stayed put and let the world come to him.

William Allen White, born in 1868 in Emporia, Kansas, could have had any editorial position in the land, but he preferred to remain with his *Emporia Gazette*. He died in 1944 only a few blocks from his birthplace, yet his influence had been felt in every part of the globe. His brief letter still is framed over my desk.

"My advice instinctively is don't go East," he began. "Make your name out West. You will find a place out West. As you live longer, you will find that from sheer geography your standing there will be higher up above your surrounding plain than in New York. If you can eat with some regularity and sleep at nights, stick to the West."

My waistline is too tight and I don't need barbiturates, and William Allen White's counsel was sound. I have had fun in my little puddle and there have been rewards. Although my success has been far from spectacular, I have been able to ride for many miles with a President of the United States and go yachting with a famous British industrialist. These men did not know me, but they had read material from my typewriter about regional subjects which interested them. When they came West, they sent word that they wanted to talk to me.

Had I gone to New York, my work would have been lost among the myriad of contributions from journalists far more illustrious than I can ever hope to be. But in Oregon, as the wise old *Emporia* editor foresaw, "sheer geography" has been my ally. The competition is less stern. Furthermore, I know the area as only a native can know it. This gives me that brief start along the base paths which decides many pursuits of a story or topic.

I wonder if this same soul searching does not confront many Americans who are offered impressive opportunities to leave the realm of their youth?

I have a friend named Irving Dilliard whom the *Baltimore Sun* once nearly lured from the *St. Louis Post-Dispatch*. This native son of St. Louis finally sat down with two sheets of copy paper staring up at him from his library table. He listed the reasons for moving to the *Sun* and the reasons for staying at the *Post-Dispatch*.

One reason ultimately seemed to take precedence over all others. Dilliard phrased it in this way: "To live and work in the region in which I was born and which I know best and for which I can speak, upon occasion at least, with some authority; to do what I can to improve that area and to help its people live better lives."

And in his letter to the *Sun* the newspaperman explained, "I have made the decision that William Allen White made many years ago." In this instance it unquestionably was a sage verdict, too, for Dilliard since has become editor of the famous crusading editorial page of the *Post-Dispatch*.

But what if everyone through history had shared these sentiments? Who would have started for Ohio in a canoe or for Oregon in a Conestoga wagon?

Each man to his taste. If I had lived in the era of the pioneers, I probably would not have put on buckskin and braved the frontier. I like to think this would have been attributable to no fear of grizzly bears or Indian hostiles, for the wilderness often calls to me today. But I would have been one of those fellows content with their friends, their books, their pipes and the rather mediocre fishing down at the village creek. Gold in California never would have induced me, even in younger years, to leave behind mother's cooking and all the girls to court at home.

When I am away from Portland now, I compare other communities with Portland, and invariably to their disadvantage. Good Democrat though I am, I miss the Republican editorials in our local papers. If I am in a metropolis of skyscrapers, I note the superior safety of Portland's modest-sized office buildings. But in a city of buildings as flat as sardine tins, I comment on the majestic height of Portland's fifteen-floor rooftops.

Although millions of Americans may be looking for a new address, pride in place still must be a dominant national trait. Once we were pulling trout out of an Alaskan lake like women tugging at a bargain counter. The catch was limited only by the strength in our arms. Yet a homesick lieutenant insisted this couldn't muster up to the fishing back in his native Colorado.

"What?" we yelled accusingly.

"Well," he replied, "the climate's better there, anyway."

I hesitate to leave Portland, even for greater opportunities in money and prestige, for fear I will abnormally romanticize the place I have left behind. This was the case of the married couple I visited on Park Avenue. Their notion of the city of their birth bore no resemblance to reality. This, I imagine, was why they never had returned for a visit. The illusion would be shattered. During the war I was ordered to advise Robert W. Service – who no longer lived in the Far North – that American troops in the Yukon would be delighted to have the author of *The Shooting of Dan McGrew* as a guest. He politely declined.

"I want to remember it the way it was," he explained.

Allegiance to a hometown frequently has little or nothing to do with creature comforts. It relies on such intangibles as memories, friendships and a sense of belonging.

Last summer I visited a retired officer of the Royal Canadian Mounted Police, who was brought up in the bleak solitudes of the Northwest Territories. He lives today in a pleasant green neighborhood of one of Canada's great prairie cities. His routine might be considered idyllic – polo, puttering in a garden of flowers, lunch at an exclusive club, a movie or bridge at night. Yet this man's heart is in the North Country, in the isolated detachments along the broad Mackenzie River – outposts a thousand miles from a theater or a polo field.

"That was where I felt I really amounted to something," he said. "I guess you take to a place where people know you from way back, and you don't have to tell them who you are or what you are."

Recognition is an important human value. We all crave it. What if I go to New York and succeed prodigiously? Who will really care? Should I start all over again to create friendships, I should be an old man before I enjoyed the sort of loyalties I now take for granted. The

Mountie mourned for the distant Arctic, because that was where a trapper's eyes might glisten at mention of his name.

I want to protect myself from this kind of loneliness, which is the worst loneliness of all. The Mountie officer admitted that he was never so alone on the Barren Lands as in a metropolis full of strangers.

So I am staying in Oregon. I may be provincial, but aren't we all? A few years ago a newspaper syndicate conducted a symposium under the heading: What I Like About America. Every preference, without exception, was local. People in Seattle nominated Mount Rainier. Bostonians whooped it up for planked steak at the Parker House. A girl in Brooklyn picked the Dodgers. A Miami resident selected bathing beauties. Californians named Yosemite or the Golden Gate. I chose the Columbia Gorge with its bastions of lava and granite.

Oregon is the place with which I am the most familiar. I studied its history in school and in college. I have driven over its plateaus and hiked across its mountains and rim rock. Whether I write essays or sell life insurance policies, why should I move to a strange locality? A prophet may be without honor in his own country, but I can shoot a hole in one and walk down Portland's streets the next day collecting cigars. I would be eligible for the Townsend Plan before I achieved this same recognition anywhere else.

If I ever was going to rip up my roots, I should have done it many years ago as a boy, when I possessed the flexibility and resilience of youth. But that was before I had any freedom of choice. Now it is too late, and I am glad of it.

When I look out across the slanting ramparts of the Cascade Range to Hood's frosty peak I feel like Antaeus, the mythical giant who gained strength merely by touching the earth. This is my own special corner of my native land. This is where my bearded grandfather came from the Old World in 1870, even ahead of the railroads. Eventually homesickness for a hamlet in far-off Baden drove him back to Germany. One of his descendants wants to avoid that kind of dark, desperate yearning, and so he is just staying put.

A 'Little' Senator on the 'Big' Senate

New York Times Magazine, 4 MAY 1952

Running for his second term in the Oregon Senate in 1952, Neuberger was already weighing the possibility of a future race for the United States Senate. He visited Washington, D.C. and offered these observations on the "Big Senate" for the *New York Times Magazine*.

PEERING DOWN from the gallery upon the United States Senate in action – if you are a member of one of the nation's forty-eight State Legislatures, as I happen to be – is a curious and humbling experience. Here one realizes, are the grand viziers, the nabobs of American public life; by their confident bearing and casual manner on the field of great events, the men below show clearly that they have arrived politically; only the White House stands higher among the honors bestowed by the people's ballots.

The impression is borne home that, by contrast, we solons of the provinces are tense and earnest and far less assured. After all, we have barely begun in politics. We are eager beavers, full of zeal and desperately anxious to please. We would not think, for example, of making our presiding officer rap seven times for order during a single hour, as Vice President Barkley had to do on a recent afternoon. If any of us had to be gaveled into silence as many times as some celebrated United States Senators were that day, we would be in political purgatory all over the state.

These reflections were induced in me by the experience of having looked in on a session of the United States upper chamber recently. If the impression of being a social inferior in such company was strong, it was not by any means the only one. The differences between our "big" and "little" Senators and their ways of doing business are many – and possibly enlightening.

One striking contrast is that the United States Senate is so far removed from the home bases of most of its members. A handful of visitors from Iowa or Oregon may occasionally be in the galleries, and on those occasions the Oregon and Iowa Senators are generally at their desks and possessed with derring-do. But this pressure to be present and accounted for is rare. It explains why only ten or twelve Senators were on the floor listening to the debate over the President's proposal to reorganize the Bureau of Internal Revenue.

True, ninety Senators rushed into the chamber for the final roll-call, because the yeas and nays were what the folks back home in Montana or Texas would learn about. The home folks would never know that their Senators had not been present to hear the oratory leading up to the eventual decision.

We State Senators, on the other hand, pass laws in full view of our constituents. The galleries are jammed whenever we debate a major bill affecting schools or forests or oleomargarine. Buses and auto caravans bring people from all over the state. The voters, seeing with their own eyes, know on what information is founded the verdict that turns a bill into law.

Indeed, whenever two or three of our number are missing during a floor fight, some Senator invokes a call of the Senate, which means that we cannot proceed until all thirty State Senators are accounted for. Once our sergeant-at-arms was compelled to call a Senator, who hailed from the sagebrush, out of a cowboy movie to listen to a school-bill debate. On another wholly regrettable occasion he is said to have interrupted a motor-court liaison which a Senatorial Casanova had arranged with a lady lobbyist.

We of the State Senates must envy the antiseptic surroundings which protect the Senators in Washington from a buffeting by the public. To get in touch with these Senators, one must funnel his calling card through an unknown number of guards, secretaries and page boys. "Big" Senators even have their own private elevators. But in the State Senate, lobbyists press up to the rail to whisper threats or sweet nothings into our ears even before a crucial vote. We have no offices; our desks are on the floor of the chamber, in front of anybody who cares to look over our shoulders as we dictate correspondence.

One morning I found a member of the Governor's staff at my desk, calmly reading a letter I had drafted to a constituent on why I could not go along with the Governor on milk control. Still, in the "little" Senate, perhaps just because we are not so well protected by aides and functionaries, more of the real legislator may glimmer through the political trappings and paraphenalia and make what we mean or stand for clearer to the voters.

Although our State Senate has no speakers to compare with such adepts as Senators Humphrey of Minnesota or Morse of Oregon, oratory in general is more important in our modest domain. This is because our chamber lacks a written journal, like the *Congressional Record*, in which all spoken utterances are taken down. Our speeches must be ends in themselves. They tend to perish as they are spoken. If they lack genuine ideas for someone to remember or for a journalist to quote, they have merely vanished into thin air. A speech in our Senate has to get by on its merits. No Linotype machine waits outside the chamber to immortalize it mechanically

In addition, with us a speech is a speech – possibly because if we wanted to read one, we would have to write it first ourselves. We do not have professional staffs; our sole assistance is stenographic. But, during the Internal Revenue reorganization debate, at least two-thirds of the participating United States Senators read their remarks. In some instances, mainly because of their unfamiliarity with words or phrases, I could not help feeling that these speeches had been prepared by someone else. The fine hand of the ghostwriter seemed plain.

When the discussion was at its height, I noticed that two leading combatants – Senator Millikin of Colorado and Senator Lehman of New York – received promptings from youthful executive assistants who slipped nimbly down the aisle with words of counsel. I could detect no harm in this; who does not need advice and coaching? Yet if it had happened at home, the guilty State Senators would have been marked as "stooges" for "young intellectual whippersnappers." This is too bad – for us.

Partisanship in this Senate debate also was new to me as a "little" Senator. Although the nation as a whole is bipartisan, it is well to remember that at least half the individual states tend to be dominated by one party or the other. I am a Democrat in a state where our party has not had a legislative majority since 1878. We cannot even muster enough Democratic Senators to be set apart by an aisle – our desks being scattered among the overwhelming Republican majority. I envied the healthy party organizations which made possible the two strongly represented sides I saw below me in the Senate.

Most of our "little" Senators share a common aspiration – to be "big" Senators some day. With the experience they might bring with them to Washington, it would seem to be a desirable thing. But how much chance have they? Although the state capital is traditionally supposed to be a starting place for young politicians, the average age of our thirty State Senators is 53 – only five years younger than the average age of members of the United States Senate. In addition not one of our states' Senators in Washington during the past generation was previously a State Senator. Some of my colleagues, as a result, are beginning to feel they have taken the wrong road to the "big" Senate.

"I enjoy this service," said one of my fellow "little" Senators, who has long cherished hopes of graduating to Washington, "but you become committed on so many hot questions that you've got a host of enemies in every county of the state by the time you get ready to try to be a Senator with a capital S."

The Senator Behind the Give-aways

The Progressive, FEBRUARY 1954

Senator Guy Cordon, a native of Texas who rose to political prominence in Oregon, was a pillar of the Senate's establishment in 1954 when Neuberger challenged his bid for a third term. Cordon had wanted to return to his law practice instead of seeking reelection but was talked into running by President Eisenhower who made the argument that his candidacy might enable Republicans to retain their narrow Senate majority. Neuberger made his case against Cordon in this article for *The Progressive*.

Reprints were distributed by Neuberger and the Oregon Democratic party during the 1954 campaign. Former Governor Charles A. Sprague, editor of the *Oregon Statesman*, and no admirer of Cordon, said that Neuberger exaggerated Cordon's faults. But Cordon acknowledged that Neuberger's polemics were a major factor in the outcome of the election.

ON MAY 5, 1953, the U.S. Senate completed action on a bill to give to three or four coastal states a vast treasure-trove in off-shore oil which formerly had belonged in equal quantity to all 48 states. The move imperiled the traditional public-lands policy of the nation which stems from the era of Lewis and Clark. It conferred a gift worth at least $40,000,000,000. It brought joy and pleasure to the great oil companies that always have preferred state to federal custodianship of natural resources.

Guiding this far-reaching measure through the Senate was a gnome-like man with droning voice and self-assured manner. In the cloakroom he gestured truculently with a dead cigar in his hand. He symbolized the oil bill to his colleagues.

A few weeks later, Congress refused by the narrowest of margins to set aside for grade schools and high schools throughout the country the income from petroleum deposits still belonging to the national government. These reserves, beyond the three-mile limit and beneath "the outer Continental shelf," had been saved, providing the give-away went no further. They might have enriched public education by as much as $180,000,000 annually.

Once again, this same gnome-like Senator figured actively in keeping the oil reserves from serving an enlightened social purpose. He was a decisive participant in the conference committees which thwarted a proposal endorsed by nearly every major educational organization in the land. He was able to maneuver this in spite of the fact that his fellow Senators had voted 45 to 43 – over his reiterated protests – for the amendment dedicating the petroleum deposits to the schools.

Guy Cordon, 63, senior U.S. Senator from Oregon, takes pride in the fact that he makes no headlines like his spectacular junior colleague from Oregon, Wayne L. Morse.

Obscurity is welcomed by Cordon, and in his rare case it has become a political asset. Were his Senate record fully known, he might have to get so far from the state he represents that he could barely communicate with it by smoke signals. The fact that Cordon is a shadowy figure, operating largely in the dim and murky background, has made it possible for him to survive as a Senator since 1944, despite his cross-purposes with the basic sentiment of people in his state.

Oregon has not been a fertile field for witch hunters. It is the sole Pacific Coast state without special "test oath" legislation. Yet Cordon votes consistently with the McCarthy-Jenner group and against wheat for India, against the Point IV program, for reducing the authority of President Eisenhower in foreign affairs, against liberalizing the oppressive McCarran Act.

No state is more reliant on the National Forests than Oregon. Yet Cordon is sponsoring bills to permit raids by the big timbermen on these wooded reserves, which give the people of Oregon drinking water, recreation, and a tourist industry worth $120,000,000 a year. Furthermore, Cordon has sided with the huge lumber monopolies and against the small local sawmills that are attempting to gain a permanent foothold in a precarious business.

Public power has been a paramount issue in Oregon for half a century, because the surging Columbia River contains 42 percent of the country's latent hydroelectricity. Yet Cordon is a leading Congressional supporter of the McKay program to turn over damsites and power allocations to the private utilities. A lobbyist for Pacific Power and Light Company sat at Cordon's elbow when an Interior subcommittee of the Senate shaped the Bonneville appropriation bill to the liking of the power companies.

II

Oregon is a state with 214,000 trade-union members among its 1,600,000 residents, yet Cordon has voted persistently for the Taft-Hartley Act and against price controls and cost-of-living studies sought by working men and women.

Agriculture dominates much of Oregon's economy. Its high plateaus and dry grasslands are particularly in need of erosion control. Yet Cordon has been one of the Senators opposing an increase in Soil Conservation funds and benefits. He also has voted *nay* on various phases of the national school lunch program, one of the best hopes for using surplus crops to the benefit of farmers and consumers alike.

Because of a 40 percent population increase since 1940, Oregon is far short of necessary hospital beds to maintain high standards of health. Yet Cordon voted against more generous allotments of federal funds for local hospital construction in crowded and expanding communities.

On top of all this, Cordon is the successor to the late Sen. Charles Linza McNary, a man of kindly humanitarian views, who often sided with George Norris and the La Follettes, father and son, in support of social legislation. Cordon's reactionary voting record is practically the direct antithesis of that compiled by McNary during his 26 years in the Senate.

How, then, has Guy Cordon, proponent of the oil give-away and timber raids, been able to continue as a Senator from the state of Oregon?

"So the people may know" is the slogan of the American press. It is a noble axiom. A good many newspapers strive earnestly to uphold it. This has not been true in Oregon with respect to Senator Cordon. His votes on major bills are as anonymous as snowflakes in a blizzard. The people have yet to be told about their senior Senator's stand on the great questions of the day.

A second factor has accounted for Cordon's political success – huge campaign funds. A preponderance of money often has enabled him to win over opponents of more liberal views and greater capacity for public service. Cordon votes with the special interests in the Senate. He sides with them in committee. He favors them in the bills which he sponsors. *Quid pro quo* – they do not forget him at campaign time. This crucial problem of democracy, a problem by no means confined to Oregon, has helped to saddle Oregon with one of the most right-wing and unenlightened Senators in its 95-year tenure as a state.

Although this disparity in funds is difficult to believe, the Republican State Central Committee spent $211,071 in 1948, when Cordon was reelected to the Senate, and its Democratic counterpart could muster only a trifling $1,025. Nelson Poynter of the *Congressional Quarterly* told me it would be hard to match this contrast anywhere else in the country.

In 1944 Senator McNary died after a long and illustrious career in public life. Some leaders of public opinion hoped that the late Earl Snell, then governor, would name Palmer Hoyt as his successor. Hoyt, a man of liberal outlook (now editor of the Denver *Post*), would have continued the McNary tradition of political independence and humanitarianism. Instead, the appointment went to Cordon.

In the Republican Party primary that year, Cordon was challenged by one of Oregon's outstanding citizens, former Gov. Charles A. Sprague. Although Sprague publishes a broad-gauge daily in Salem,

The Statesman, other papers tried to make it appear as if no genuine issue separated the two rivals.

Actually, a gulf as wide and deep as the Grand Canyon lay between the men. As governor of Oregon, Sprague had been preoccupied with conservation of dwindling forest resources. An internationalist, he later was to serve as a U.S. Delegate to the United Nations. He used his column in *The Statesman*, "It Seems to Me," as a sounding-board for civil rights, for strengthening of civil liberties, and for criticism of witch hunters. He is a sensitive, shy person of intellectual quality, unlike Cordon in personality and temperament.

In the Senate, Cordon associated himself with the isolationist bloc. He refused to modify the Revercomb bill which was aimed at minority religious groups among displaced persons. He opposed extension of Cordell Hull's reciprocal-trade pacts. He voted against moderating the cloture rule, and thus helped to choke off the one real chance to bring the question of civil rights to a decisive roll call.

Cordon had approximately 53 percent more campaign funds than Sprague. Although Sprague had impressive ties with prominent Republican personages in banking and retail trade, the big-business forces in the state evidently had determined that Cordon was their man. His billboards, brochures, and radio time exceeded the broadsides available to his opponent. And Cordon won, 68,666 votes to 63,944. The general election was easy after that, in a state which last elected a Democratic Senator in 1914.

In 1948 Cordon won a full term in the Senate. His Democratic adversary was the late Manley J. Wilson, editor of the CIO *Woodworker*, organ of the men in logging camps and mills. Wilson had been one of the leaders in the fight to rid the Woodworkers of leadership oriented in the Communist direction. But he was handicapped by the perennial woe of Democrats in Oregon. He had no campaign funds. While the Republicans were laying down a blitzkrieg of propaganda in behalf of Cordon, Wilson's forces had to try to reach half-a-million voters by word of mouth. It was like attempting to go up Niagara Falls with an outboard motor. Yet Cordon's victory was not overwhelming – 299,295 votes to 199,275.

III

At the time of the battle between Eisenhower and Taft forces for the Republican nomination in 1952, Cordon and his machine in Oregon were lined up with Taft. But after Ike's victory, it was reported that Cordon would become the next Secretary of the Interior. It turned out that Cordon, somewhat in the role of the man who wrote the Purple Cow couplet, would rather see than be one, so far as Cabinet status was concerned. He preferred to name the Interior Secretary. He told his contacts in the Republican National Committee to have the President pick Governor McKay, of Oregon.

In the Cabinet, McKay has been a willing errand boy for his sponsor. He has pledged government water power for 20 years to the power companies. He has abandoned federal claims to key damsites. He has relinquished partially-completed government transmission lines to power companies. He has set in motion plans to raise the rates charged for Bonneville and Grand Coulee energy, thus diminishing the competitive threat to the private utilities. And Cordon has stood in the wings, occasionally lending a public "amen" to the hurtful work of his protégé.

Some observers in Oregon believe Cordon will not run for a new six-year term in 1954. They premise this prophesy on the fact that no politician, about to face the electorate, could behave so defiantly of public opinion.

Cordon is one of the sponsors of a bill to allow the biggest lumber operators to take nearly any land in National Forests and National Parks in exchange for their own acreage which might be needed for public purposes. The Forest Service has denounced the grab in forthright terms, despite pressure on these foresters to remain silent. And Oregon is a state where the reserves set aside by Teddy Roosevelt and Gifford Pinchot have been of basic importance to the health, economy, and outdoor life of nearly all the people.

Even politicians who oppose trade-union policies make a show of friendly relationship with organized labor, at least on a personal level. The late Senator Taft enjoyed friendship with some of the union leaders whose philosophy he opposed. Cordon bows to none of these amenities. In the city of Portland he found one hotel, the Imperial, picketed by AFL members. That was where Cordon set up his headquarters, back of the picket line.

If Cordon should decide not to run again, his replacement probably will be one of two Republican Congressmen from Oregon, Walter Norblad, 45, or Harris Ellsworth, 54. With respect to issues, they are carbon copies of Cordon – isolationist at the international level, reactionary at the domestic level, witch-hunting in the moral sphere. They voted with Cordon to give away the offshore oil. They collaborate with him in backing up present Interior Department policies to part with the public-power resources belonging to the federal government.

Can Cordon and/or an alter ego be defeated in Oregon?

There can be no doubt that this will be the decisive referendum of 1954 on the effort of the Eisenhower Administration to do away with the public power program which was in effect from 1933 until 1952. To begin with, much of the power struggle centers directly in Oregon. This state has been the principal loser by the abandonment of the Hells Canyon site to the Idaho Power Company. It was in Oregon that the transmission line from Redmond to Klamath Falls was handed over to the California-Oregon Power Company. Finally, it was in Oregon that five utility companies received long-term allocations of federal kilowatts, to the possible detriment of rural electric co-ops and similar systems.

Under the U.S. system, Cabinet officers do not run for office, as they do in the Parliamentary framework of Canada and Great Britain. But the race run by Senator Cordon will be tantamount to a test of the policies of Secretary McKay, for they are the gold-dust twins of the anti-public power forces. Were Cordon to be replaced by one of his stand-ins, the same measuring stick would be applicable. Reelection for the Cordon forces would sign, seal, and deliver the doom of public power in Oregon particularly and in the Pacific Northwest generally.

Cordon (or his substitute) will be running, of course, in a state where the Republican party has ruled like Genghis Khan for many decades. Only Maine, Vermont, and Oregon failed to elect Democratic or third-party Senators while FDR was in the White House.

Cordon and his adherents probably will be able to spend $1 for each penny mustered by his rival. The disproportion in campaign funds is sure to be enormous, particularly in view of the alarm which would rock certain special interests were Cordon to be beaten or even threatened with defeat.

IV

Candor compels me to confess that I am one of the individuals mentioned frequently as a prospective opponent for Senator Cordon.

Nobody can deny the challenge which exists. Here is a man who has voted against Eisenhower on foreign affairs, against the spirit of Pinchot and Ickes on conservation, against the ghost of Gompers on labor legislation, against the welfare of his own state on innumerable specific measures. Yet, partisan politics being what it is, Eisenhower probably will campaign for the man who opposes the foreign policy associated with Eisenhower's name. Will the oil outfits remain passive when the man who did so much for passage of the tidelands bill runs for another term? And how will funds be raised by Cordon's opponents to inform the parents and teachers just what they and their children lost when the federal petroleum reserves were not allocated to education?

On the other hand, if Cordon were miraculously defeated – and it would require a miracle to bring this off in Oregon – would Secretary McKay dare continue with the Hells Canyon abandonment? Could such a referendum be ignored?

I was born in the Northwest. It is my home. To this magnificent region I feel a deep sense of loyalty. I think its economic future depends upon a reversal of the power policies set in motion by the Cordon-McKay faction. The one chance is the election of 1954. The bell tolls, but for whom?

My Wife Put Me in the Senate

Harper's, JUNE 1955

The Neubergers were the best known husband-and-wife team in Oregon political history. Neuberger did not exaggerate the importance of Maurine in the 1954 election for the U.S. Senate. She was her husband's chief adviser, an articulate surrogate campaigner, and his best friend. After Neuberger's election to the U.S. Senate, he placed Maurine's photograph next to his at the top of their monthly newsletter, which was mailed to thousands of Oregon constituents. By sharing credit with his wife, and by building a national image of a political partnership, Neuberger set the stage for his wife's election to the Senate in 1960. Maurine Neuberger was elected by a record vote that has since been surpassed. But she retains the record for the highest percentage of the vote won by a Democratic senator in Oregon history.

POLITICAL ANALYSTS in Washington are still searching for the decisive factor which made me the first Democrat to be elected to the Senate from Oregon in forty years. After all, this might afford a clue to 1956 and even beyond. The correspondents are particularly intrigued because I won what they call "a miracle victory" in a year of only tepid success for my party throughout other areas of the West. But in Oregon people aren't troubled by any such doubts. When they are asked why I won, they invariably reply: "Maurine."

Maurine is my wife.

The issues were, of course, important. Conservation, electric power, the threat of unemployment, the clear need for some kind of federal aid for our schools – all these are questions which mean a great deal to the people of Oregon. If I hadn't fought hard on every one of them, I certainly would have lost. Yet these same issues existed in greater or lesser degree in neighboring states – Idaho, California, Washington, Colorado – where the Democrats *did* lose. The one ingredient which was present in Oregon and was present nowhere else, was Maurine.

Her story is worth telling, because – I think – it offers a lesson for everybody interested in politics. Especially for liberals. It suggests that political blessings sometimes descend unexpectedly on those who don't take their ambitions too seriously. It proves that uninhibited courage can pay off far better than most politicians (including myself) ever dared hope. It also demonstrates that elections are seldom won on The Issues alone. The soundest arguments, the highest principles, the hardest kind of campaigning may not be enough – unless they are combined with one thing more. That one vital ingredient is a personality capable of arousing enthusiasm, trust, and (let's admit it) curiosity among the voters.

When I first swung around the state early in the campaign, I was alone. Strangers kept coming up and asking: "Where is Maurine?" The disappointment in their voices and faces was evident. The had come to see Mrs. Neuberger – but they referred to her as Maurine. Even the cynics who rim newspaper copy desks follow the same practice. In headlines in the Oregon press I am "Neuberger" but she is always "Maurine." This one fact tells a lot about her role in politics.

It would be difficult to find anyone with a less conventional preparation for that role. Although she has become the most phenomenal vote-getter in the history of the Oregon legislature, she was trained as a teacher of physical education and modern dance. Her main interests are out-of-doors – gardening, swimming, farming. When I told her over long-distance telephone that I had been honored at a New York banquet attended by Senator Lehman, Mayor Wagner, and Franklin D. Roosevelt, Jr., she asked: "Was Martha Graham there?"

Maurine would rather cook or sew than draft legislation. If I am out of the city, *The New Republic*, *The Progressive*, and the *Congressional Record* remain in their brown mailing wrappers while Maurine opens *McCall's* and the *Ladies' Home Journal*. On a camping trip we made into the Cascade Mountains with Adlai Stevenson, Maurine chatted with him about fir seedlings, square-dancing, and the comparative merits of swimming in hot or cold water. It never occurred to her to talk politics with this man.

Although Maurine is descended from one of the famous old Republican families in our state – a family claiming kinship with several editors of the properly-Republican *Oregonian* – she has been a registered Democrat ever since she was twenty-one, "because Democrats seem so much more light-hearted and have such a good time." Politics to her has never been grim or ugly. She takes it as casually as if she were teaching a girls' gymnasium class.

This blithe touch was invaluable when I decided to distribute alta-fescue grass seed instead of the usual political book-matches; the seed dramatized our major issue of conservation of natural resources. My wife made a project of lining up Boy Scouts and Campfire Girls all over the state to pour seed into little cellophane wrappers, which then were stapled between cardboard covers that heralded the name "Neuberger" and advised using the seed to re-sow Oregon's upland range while out camping.

Maurine even drafted some young people whose parents are rabid Republicans. "Conservation is nonpartisan," she said with a grin. I doubt if anything caused more gnashing of molars among the opposition – for a lot of these youngsters will just about reach voting age when my Senate term ends in 1960.

In the ten years we have been married, I have yet to see Maurine act deviously. Although caginess is presumed to be a prerequisite for politics, she has marched to the top of the ballot by blurting out exactly what is in her mind. When she was asked to back a bill allocating a portion of dog-racing revenues for 4-H clubs, Maurine scolded her constituents for tying a worthy cause to pari-mutuel gambling. The special interests which she has offended would terrify most politicians – utility companies, dairy farmers, the Bar-Tender's Union, the fairs in all thirty-six Oregon counties, slot-machine operators, the Farm Bureau Federation, even the American Legion.

To public life in our one-party state, my wife has brought a candor that still alarms my friends. Since our party has been a minority almost all through modern times, it would not be unreasonable to expect that Maurine's uninhibited behavior might reduce our status still further. Indeed, such prophecies have been virtually constant. Veteran party officials and self-appointed newspaper sages have shaken their heads dolefully and warned:

"She's really gone and sunk you now."

The extent of that sinking may be judged by election statistics. Maurine first ran for the Legislature in 1950. She said she did so because she became tired of sitting in the gallery and watching men make a botch of things. A woman, she concluded, couldn't do worse. Maurine reached this decision while we were in the wilds of Idaho's magnificent Lochsa River region, writing about the Lewis and Clark expedition. She liked to tell audiences later how she had mailed in her filing from Moscow. When some local witch-hunter would claim that this proved the Republic was in peril, Maurine cheerfully noted that she didn't think it necessary to say "Moscow, *Idaho*" to an intelligent group of Americans.

For her original venture on the ballot, Maurine had to rely on my reputation as a writer and State Senator. She ran a respectable race and was the only woman elected to the House of Representatives. The next time, in 1952, she was running on her own record. This was the year of the Eisenhower landslide. General Ike swept Oregon by one of his largest proportionate margins in the nation. In Multnomah County – which is principally the city of Portland – he polled 132,602 votes. One candidate for the lower house of the Legislature ran ahead of him. Paradoxically, this was a Democrat: Maurine got 133,467 votes.

This might have been in the mind of my Republican opponent, Senator Guy Cordon, when he was interviewed during the bitter Oregon campaign of 1954 by Doris Fleeson, the syndicated columnist. The one time in the interview that Cordon brightened up was when he said with a wry smile:

"At least I have something to be thankful for, Miss Fleeson. I think maybe the easier of the two Neubergers ran against me!"

Cordon could have been right. When I became the second Democrat ever to be popularly elected to the United States Senate in Oregon's ninety-five-year history, I swept Multnomah County with an off-year total of 107,672 votes. My wife's total was 114,560.

After the election I was eating lunch in Portland with a wise and canny man, Lyle F. Watts, formerly Chief Forester of the United States. He had organized a zealous statewide group known as Conservationists for Neuberger.

"Many circumstances contributed to your election, Dick," he said, "but everyone in Oregon realizes that there's one person without whom you couldn't possibly have won your great victory. That person is your wife."

In politics Maurine and I operate in tandem. I make most of the decisions for us on what might be called cosmic issues. These are foreign policy, taxation, agriculture, conservation of natural resources, and civil liberties. Maurine sets the course where she is best informed – schools, public health, consumer problems, social welfare, recreation. Nor does this mean she is a cipher on the other issues. I believe our best speech on public power was Maurine describing how her widowed mother – who lives eighteen miles out of Portland on a farm of 120 acres – had no electricity until the transmission line from Bonneville Dam was erected along the wooded ridge above the north 40.

Campaigning with Maurine is like wearing a hair shirt. Being less concerned about politics, she made it a point of honor to serve constantly as my conscience. The strategy of living to fight another day had no status with her. Either you told the truth about your views or you didn't. There was never a middle ground. So once I had fully made up my mind regarding a public question, Maurine held me to it. The only times during the long Oregon campaign, from March until November, that I saw her get irritated was when she suspected me of pussyfooting. Indeed, before I ever mailed to the state capital the check for $150 which put me on the ballot, my wife exacted two pledges:

1   If I didn't win I would concede that Oregon was impossible for the Democrats and withdraw from politics, letting us live a normal life.

2   Under no circumstances would I conduct a shabby or dishonest campaign.

"A writer's life is an enviable one," she said. "Why stultify yourself to end it?"

At the top of a notebook which I carried around the state to use for speech material, my wife wrote one of her favorite phrases from *Hamlet*: "To thine own self be true." The first test of this came when it was suggested that I use a teleprompter or a set of "idiot boards" for an appearance on television.

Maurine shook her head stubbornly. "Let's tell the people you don't play like that," she argued. So together we worked out a little introduction for my talk. It spoke of the teleprompter as a device to fool the audience into believing a politician was talking extemporaneously when this actually was not the case. If a candidate deceived the viewers about this method of presentation, might he not also be deceiving them about the substance of what he was saying? The introduction added that I was not depending upon facial makeup to conceal beard, bald spot, or jowls.

This returned an immediate bonanza. Secretary of the Interior McKay had been in the state, speaking for my opponent with the aid of a teleprompter. Thousands of voters got the point. Furthermore, radio columnists for the New York *Times*, *Christian Science Monitor*, and other national papers called attention to the forlorn-hope Democratic nominee out in Republican Oregon who was refusing to "stage" his TV appearances. Dollar bills came through the mail in appreciation from men and women all over the land who were weary of candidates being merchandised on the air like comedians or chorus girls.

But Maurine's standards of honesty were not always easy for a hard-pressed candidate to maintain. Near mid-October we were scheduled to address a big farm potluck dinner in the Willamette Valley. The weather had turned brisk and Maurine came downstairs wearing a rich brown ermine coat – a legacy from a well-to-do aunt who recently died in New York City. Maurine quickly noted the petulant look on my face. "What's wrong?" she asked.

"It's extremely unwise politically to wear that coat to a meeting like this," I retorted. "In the first place, it gives a false impression of our income. You never could have such a coat if Aunt Rita hadn't left it to you. It's sure to arouse jealousy and gossip."

Maurine turned around and went back upstairs. I was sure my counsel of caution had prevailed. She came back in a few minutes, clad in the slacks and moccasins she often wore around the house.

"I'm not going," she calmly announced.

"But they're expecting you," I said desperately. "There are certain to be hundreds of women present, just to hear you. What'll I tell them?"

"Tell them the truth," said Maurine. "Tell them I wouldn't stand for any cloth-coat phony business. I've got just the right kind of coat for the weather tonight. If I can't wear that coat because you're a candidate for the United States Senate, you can go to the potluck without me."

I was torn between laughter and anger.

"Okay," I said, reluctantly. "You win. Put on the fur coat."

Maurine ran upstairs and soon returned, luxurious in ermine. I never heard her give a better speech – and I ran stronger than any Democrat had done before in those row-crop precincts.

Lest this episode seem to indicate that Maurine was cavalier about my welfare at the polls, I should add that no wife ever endured a sterner regimen to help make her husband a Senator.

There were days when we started campaigning at 6:00 A.M. and stopped at midnight. We spoke in locomotive roundhouses, we shared chuck-wagon meals with cow punchers, we chatted with Indians in the mist of Columbia River rapids. Maurine did most of the driving and at least half of the speaking. In the beginning we traveled by ourselves, without public-relations men or any other entourage, because we had no funds. Later on, when an exchequer was available, we still campaigned in this way – for we found that Oregon's people took to a husband and wife out on their own, as contrasted with the elaborate retinue of advertising counselors, press agents, and politicians who convoyed my opponent.

I remember the day near Grants Pass when I spoke thirteen times, ending with a big dinner at Fruitdale Grange. It was our plan to drive to Coos Bay after the dinner, calculating we might make it in three hours and get to bed at 1:00 A.M.

Before I fell asleep, utterly bushed, I had said, "Wake me in an hour. I'll take the wheel." When I awakened five hours later she was still driving – inching through the Coquille River Canyon in the worst fog I ever have seen.

Maurine slept two fitful hours at dawn, then stood under the cold shower and appeared – seemingly fresh and buoyant – at a breakfast of trade-union wives. When Mae Barton, the alert Coos County Democratic chairman, told this spartan tale it was worth more votes to us in that salt-water bailiwick than a dozen boners by the opposition.

Perhaps because she would have been completely content to have me return to a writing career, Maurine always was stunning our campaign committee. She had sponsored a bill in the Legislature ending Oregon's thirty-eight-year-old ban on colored margarine. She had even put on an apron and demonstrated to her fellow-legislators what a messy chore it was to color margarine by hand. After that, political orthodoxy dictated that she should stay as far as possible away from the dairy counties during the campaign. Instead, she traveled to the foremost butter-and-cream production areas and stood on her feet for fifty or sixty minutes at a stretch, placidly answering hostile questions. She never got belligerent but she never gave ground. I still can hear her remarking to a defiant dairy man:

"Mister, if it's legal to put artificial coloring into maraschino cherries, into cheddar cheese, into catsup, and even into your butter, why should it ever have been illegal to do the same thing with margarine?"

Nor did she forget to mention that her own mother was in the dairy business; that she herself had milked eighteen cows a day when her brother was in the Army; and that she had been born and raised on Oregon farming soil.... And in the creamery realm, too, I ran far ahead of any Democratic candidate for major office in modern times, although the Republicans had tried to capitalize on Maurine's margarine "blunder."

We never were quite sure what she would do next – and yet everything she touched seemed to turn to political gold. She did not go with me on a trip into southeastern Oregon because the Soroptomists asked her to stay in Portland and model at a charity tea. A day or so later, the Railroad Brotherhood official who was to introduce me to the men in the Southern Pacific freight yards at Klamath Falls inquired if I had seen the paper. "Better get it," he advised.

In the pictures of the fashion tea, one well-known woman was in evening dress, another in lounging clothes – and the wife of the Democratic nominee for United States Senator in skimpy corduroy shorts and sandals. I didn't look up from my cornflakes for a moment or so. "Well, Gerry," I asked the railroad-man, "what do you think?"

His reply became a classic of our campaign. "Dick," said Gerry Rutledge, "it's either very bad or very good."

Maurine also persisted in criticizing the impact of pari-mutuel wagering upon low-income families, despite the fact that the voters had overwhelmingly ratified the racing law at the polls. And when she was invited to help judge the annual bathing-beauty contest at Seaside in July, she turned up at the beach in her own swimming suit, to the delight of photographers and the consternation of Democratic party leaders.

Yet having someone with me who really didn't care too much may have been what saved me. It prevented the violent displays of righteous indignation which scuttle so many candidates. For example, the opposition had a nightly broadcast about me called "Tricky Dick." The program consisted mainly of personal abuse. Maurine persuaded me not to listen to it. "You'll only waste a lot of energy in being mad," she argued. So to this day I have yet to hear "Tricky Dick." Maurine also urged me to include in the official *Voters' Pam-*

phlet, most widely-circulated campaign document in Oregon, a statement commending my opponent's patriotism. "It will make their accusations all the more shameful," she prophesied.

During the entire campaign I saw her really angry only once. It was when the headquarters of my adversary mailed out a broadside heavily tinged with anti-Semitism. A few nights later, Maurine was speaking in a lumber community. In the question period a man friendly to the opposition rose in the audience.

"What religion are you, Mrs. Neuberger?" he inquired. It was obvious what he hoped to get at.

"I'm Unitarian," shot back Maurine. "My husband is Jewish – and what does that have to do with a person's qualifications for public office in a great free country like the United States?"

It was evident from the sustained applause that this was not a fertile furrow for the other side, and six small-town daily papers sharply rebuked the Republicans for trying to introduce bigotry into the contest.

After eleven years in the Senate, my opponent, who was experiencing his first real challenge, abruptly endorsed the old McNary-Haugen farm program, which was favored by many wheat growers of eastern Oregon. Democratic officials in that area felt I should do likewise immediately. Maurine argued: "It would be obvious Dick had just done it for politics. He hasn't had a chance to study the plan. There wouldn't be anything back of his endorsement. The wheat ranchers surely know that the other side has done it only for votes, with no basic belief in the idea."

I followed Maurine's counsel – and carried grain areas never before friendly to a Democrat.

And, as I write these words, I have just phoned my wife in Oregon, where she still is serving in the Legislature, to announce that I have taken a potentially unpopular stand which she long had been urging upon me.

Since 1904 Alaska's insane have been treated at a private hospital in Portland, Oregon. Perhaps necessary in the Klondike era, this remote incarceration is an anachronism today. It is as if New York's mentally ill had to be institutionalized in Butte, Montana. Yet many generations of Oregon politicians have thwarted efforts by Alaskans to secure their own mental hospital. The voteless Delegate from the Territory never has been able to prevail against two Oregon Senators and four Oregon Congressmen. Thus, it has been obvious that a bill for an Alaskan insane asylum might become law only if sponsored by a member of Congress from Oregon – which has had a sizable payroll out of treating wretched Indians, Eskimos, and cabin-wracked prospectors, 2,000 miles from their homes.

When I told my wife, via long distance, that such a bill at last has been introduced, she never even mentioned the possibility that it might cost votes.

Wherever I went campaigning with Maurine, I did much better at the polls than where I stumped the countryside alone. My crowds were larger; their enthusiasm seemed more genuine; the audiences represented a wider segment than the hard core of partisan support which goes to every politician.

I have tried to analyze my wife's amazing political popularity in Oregon. Why should she set new voting records in a state which had been considered nearly as Republican as Maine or Vermont? To some degree I suspect that her performance proves the old maxim that "the best politics is no politics." If anyone ever violated every standard political rule, that person is my wife. A Mark Hanna or a Jim Farley would have been horrified, thinking Maurine had set out deliberately to antagonize most of the state's big pressure groups.[16]

The American Legion, for example, is supposed to be immune from criticism. It is *lèse majesté* for anyone dependent upon popular favor not to stand in awe of our biggest organization of veterans. But when a teachers' oath bill was before the Legislature, Maurine conjectured publicly why Legion spokesmen at the Capitol were actively pushing this bill, while a measure to safeguard the bank accounts of war veterans in mental hospitals languished in committee. Which was more important to the Legion, she asked, imposing an oath on teachers or guarding the assets of men who had lost their sanity fighting for the United States?

Since I also had voted against the teachers' oath in the State Senate, I was told that Maurine's candor assured our retirement from public life. Yet we survived – and wonder of wonders, the Legion was represented at the next session of the Legislature by a State Commander named Karl Wagner, who said a teachers' loyalty-oath was not necessary in Oregon but that the bill to establish legal protection for the estates of incompetent ex-soldiers was a "must."

Perhaps because of her physical-culture training, Maurine disapproves of cocktail bars. After the electorate had voted in favor of liquor-by-the-drink, it was up to the Legislature to pass an enabling act. Maurine voted and spoke against it.

"It'll just mean more money spent on whisky," said she, "and that means less spent on medicine and lamb chops and diapers. I'm going to speak my piece even if it costs us the votes of everybody who ever drank a highball."

What was most unorthodox of all was her active campaign in Portland for the reelection as Mayor of a prominent Republican, Dorothy McCullough Lee.

In between these escapades, Maurine worked desperately hard on the legislation which has been her dominant interest in Oregon politics – setting up pilot courses in the schools for children who are retarded mentally and physically. I remember vividly a meeting of the parents of these poor children; they crowded around her with tears of gratitude in their eyes. I also recall the night I hurried away from a TV broadcast at a studio on top of a mountain outside of Medford. I had to catch a train for Portland, and already its headlights flickered far off in the wooded darkness. I was told a woman in great emotional stress was on the telephone.

"Are you Maurine Neuberger's husband?" the woman asked.

I said I was.

"Tell her," said the woman, obviously under strain, "that my husband and I bless her every night. He is a sawmill worker, and we are the parents of a retarded little boy. He never had a chance to learn to feed himself, to play with other children, or to read and write until your wife got her wonderful bill for pilot classes through the Legislature."

And so at last I came to realize that my wife was someone who always did what it came into her head to do, and that this fact had gotten through to the people of the state. Some certainly disagreed with her. Yet the general impression remained of a woman politician who behaved as if she were not in public life at all.

This was neatly put by a seventy-nine-year-old Republican matriarch, a woman descended from the pioneers who brought the first Conestoga wagons to Oregon over the famous Applegate trail, who had given a tea in her home at Yoncalla because of personal admiration for Maurine.

"I never went into politics myself," Annie Kruse said to me, "and now it's too late. But if I had, I would have hoped to be exactly like your wife."

"And what is that like, Mrs. Kruse?"

"You know what it's like, young man," she replied. "It's like somebody who does just what comes naturally."

When the 1955 session of the Oregon Legislature adjourns this spring, Maurine's active political career will end. There is not a doubt in my mind that she could win any office the state has to offer, including the one which I occupy. But this is not her ambition – and perhaps that is why she could fulfill it. Voters may sense the need in these times of electing people who don't have to win an office to climax their personal destinies.

In 1956 Maurine plans to campaign in all thirty-six counties for the reelection of Senator Wayne L. Morse. She doesn't always agree with him, but she greatly admires his independence and courage. Meanwhile she will work in my senatorial office, without pay. Walter Wanger of Allied Artists – who intends to use our experiences as the basis for a movie about a married couple in politics – also has plans for Maurine. He wants her to play a supporting part in the film – the role of a lady legislator who mixes margarine in marble halls, wears bathing suits, and invariably speaks her mind.

But I hope Maurine's movie career will not be permanent, for I need her urgently in Washington, at suite 348, Senate Office Building.

Mistakes of a Freshman Senator

American Magazine, JUNE 1956

Neuberger struck many of his colleagues as a bit brash when he arrived in the Senate in January of 1955. His remarks were so partisan during an appearance before a Washington press club that the wife of a Republican senator booed him. Neuberger seemed to be vying for the role of gadfly when he criticized President Eisenhower for the removal of squirrels from the White House grounds and senatorial colleagues for relying too much on ghostwriters. In this article, Neuberger describes his education as a freshman senator. Within a short time, Neuberger changed his tactics and gained acceptance into the Senate establishment.

I MADE MY FIRST MISTAKE as a member of the United States Senate shortly after taking the oath of office in what has been called "the most exclusive debating society on earth." It occurred when I was sponsoring an amendment to the upper Colorado River bill to eliminate approval of Echo Park Dam, a project which many conservationists feared would drown out scenic canyons and gorges within our National Park system.

Senator Arthur V. Watkins of Utah, a white-haired Republican, was my principal opponent. Under a special rule limiting debate, he had used up all his allotted time, but I still had about half an hour of my quota to spare. An excerpt from the Congressional Record will reveal what happened:

Mr. Watkins: *Mr. President, will the Senator from Oregon yield two or three minutes of his remaining time, so that we may complete the discussion we started yesterday?*

Mr. Neuberger: *I think there was ample time for the discussion yesterday. I yielded sufficiently then.*

Mr. Watkins: *I thank the Senator.*

No sooner had my negative reply to Senator Watkins' request popped out of my mouth than I realized I had blundered. The atmosphere in the chamber seemed to change at that moment. Kindly GOP Senator Jim Duff of Pennsylvania confirmed this a few minutes later. He was supporting my position on the National Park issue, but he said, "Dick, you shouldn't have done that. You hurt your cause. If you had given Arthur Watkins a little of your time, it would have strengthened you with other senators. Now, some of them will wonder whether you were afraid of his ammunition."

"Senator Duff," I confessed, "I know you're right. I find in the Senate that you have to make decisions about as rapidly as a shortstop waiting for a hot ground ball with the score tied and the bases loaded. I just didn't figure out soon enough which base I was going to throw to, and I committed an error."

As the youngest of the new senators who were sworn in by Vice-President Nixon last year, I have discovered that it's easier to take the wrong corner in the world's most famous parliamentary body than in any other place I have ever been, including narrow horseback trails hugging the ramparts of mile-deep chasms back home in the Northwest. Decisions come at you hard and fast in the U.S. Senate. Many of them involve stern, unyielding pressures – from close friends, from zealous constituents, from political enemies, from importuning lobbyists, from press and radio correspondents who demand unequivocal answers.

This was not what I had expected when I became Oregon's first Democratic senator in forty years. I felt I was coming to a leisurely way of life, where decisions might be made at ease and where tensions and strains could be forgotten. Perhaps I still had a vision of my old friend and counselor from Idaho, the great Senator William E.

Borah, with his flowing mane of hair, sonorous voice, and measured walking pace. Haste was foreign to him. Surely, the chamber where Borah flourished would be anything but frenzied and hurried!

Instead, I found myself rushing down the marble steps to the Senate Restaurant one day with Democrat J. William Fulbright of Arkansas. I hoped to pry loose ten minutes for a cheese sandwich and glass of milk between quorum calls.

"How do you like your new way of life?" inquired this former Rhodes scholar and university president.

"Senator," I answered, "I find it hectic – most hectic."

"If there's any more hectic spot on this globe," replied Fulbright, "I don't ever want to be there!"

Indeed, the decisions, duties, and public functions which crowd in upon a senator frequently preclude thinking through a question until it is virtually too late. One day, when I thought I had voted incorrectly on a bill to establish a compulsory military-reserve system in America, a shaggy bruin of a man in a nearby Senate seat noticed my dejection.

"What's the trouble, young fellow?" he asked. The late Alben W. Barkley, Democratic senator from Kentucky and ex-Vice-President of the United States, was thirty-six years older than I am, so he could call me "young fellow" with impunity.

I told Barkley that compulsory drills every week seemed an unfair intrusion into the personal affairs and civilian lives of ex-GIs who already had given two years of full-time Army service, and I believed I should have voted against the bill.

"Well, get up and say so, then," Kentucky's elder statesmam advised me. He also added something more: "If you meet a man here in this chamber who advises you he never has made a mistake as a senator, you have met an Ananias – a liar. There are only two things to do about mistakes – learn from them and don't let them spoil your sleep."

I have found this to be sound counsel. To begin with, mistakes in the Senate generally can be redeemed, in one way or another. I felt certain I had made an effective apology to Arthur Watkins, for example, when I turned out to be the only Democratic senator who praised the stand taken for conservation of timber in the Al Sarena "tree-mining" case by the Agricultural Department under Watkin's intimate friend, Secretary Ezra Taft Benson. And I followed Barkley's advice by doing just what he recommended. I got recognized by the chair, and admitted that my original vote on the military reserve bill had not, in my opinion, been the right one.

Nor is it only junior senators like myself who learn that the driving, grinding pace often makes impossible proper judgments on the first time around. Even though I have been a member of the Senate for only 17 months, I have heard many of my colleagues confessing to a change of heart and mind on basic issues. I listened to Republican Senator Dirkesen of Illinois telling how he had shifted from being a foe of foreign aid to one of its confirmed supporters, and to Democrat Lyndon B. Johnson of Texas describing his transformation from hostility to endorsement of strict government control of campaign expenditures.

In the hurly-burly of the Senate, considered verdicts are a rare luxury. Snap judgments are required by the schedules which yoke most senators to at least a twelve-hour working day. I had expected deliberation. Instead, I have found haste and even a certain amount of frenzy.

I remember the afternoon I was sitting in Interior Committee hearings on Federal forest policies, a matter of prime importance to my lumber-producing state. This was the second successive day we had listened to technical testimony for five or six hours in a row. Close attention was essential if one was to understand the detailed information being presented. All at once the bells clanged for a Senate vote. We hurried out of the big caucus room, with its chandeliers of crystal and brass, and rushed by subway car to the carpeted chamber beneath the Capitol dome. The reading clerk already had reached the "L's." I inquired what we were voting on.

"A resolution to set up a special Senate committee to investigate lobbying and campaign contributions," answered my burly Irish seatmate, Democratic Senator Patrick V. McNamara of Michigan.

Every one around me was intoning *Yea*. Almost instinctively, I did likewise. Less than five minutes later I wished I had voted *Nay*. After all, could the Senate investigate itself?

The New York *Times* had reported that it cost $1,000,000 in campaign funds to be elected a senator from a populous state, as much as $200,000 from an average state. This meant that senators were involved in the situation under fire. The Senate would not permit a government agency to inquire into its own behavior. Why, then, should the Senate have this privilege? Could any senators, myself included, perform such a function with complete detachment? Might not an outside commission, appointed by the chief justice of the Supreme Court be the ideal way to get an impartial study of the entire lobbying, campaign-spending dilemma?

But these were merely afterthoughts. When I arrived in the chamber to vote, my head had been full of figures about timber acreage, National Forest stumpage, and Indian fir allotments. I literally had not had time to analyze the investigation problem. Later, when I introduced a resolution to create a special lobby-study commission chosen by Chief Justice Earl Warren from people beyond the realm of politics, I had to swallow my own roll-call vote favoring a Senate undertaking in this field.

Most of the senators I have met are honest, conscientious men – plus one charming and outstanding woman, Mrs. Margaret Chase Smith, Republican of Maine. But all of them are badgered and harried from dawn until midnight, and perhaps into the small hours of the morning besides. I receive an average of twenty-five speaking invitations a week, some from as far off as Los Angeles or New Orleans. I could not accept half of them, even if I abandoned my Senate duties completely. I rarely ever enter my office when there are not so many callers waiting to see me that they overflow our cramped waiting room into the corridor. My mail contains approximately 250 letters a day, and I realize that senators from states with greater populations than Oregon receive infinitely more.

Just before a big football game or prize fight, athletes are kept in seclusion; not even close friends can visit them; nothing must disturb their tranquillity. But when United States senators make ready to decide issues that affect the peace and welfare of mankind, they are button-holed by lobbyists, besieged by well-wishers, and stormed by a blizzard of mail, petitions, and telegrams.

At the height of debate over the 1956 farm bill, one Republican senator from the Middle west confided to me, "I'm just about groggy and out on my feet from the torrent of advice descending on all of us. I'd like to be alone just to have a few hours to myself, to do some clear thinking about this proposition."

During the same period, I asked a Democratic senator why he had opposed an amendment seeking to grant more plantings to small cotton farmers. His answer was candid: "I guess I'm nearly punch drunk after so many long sessions on the farm question. I actually don't know why I voted as I did, but I'm going to do my best to see if it can't be reversed before we get through with the bill. Probably my present schedule is more than flesh and blood can endure."

Knowing my own schedule, I could only nod in agreement, particularly because I realized that this senator is a more celebrated legislator and thus subject to sterner pressures than I am. While sitting in the Democratic cloakroom waiting for a 10:30 P.M. roll call on a grain amendment, I found myself next to the dean of the Senate, Democrat Walter F. George of Georgia, whose service began in 1922. He looked tired and ashen. I knew that Senator George was 78 years old, and that he carried the sorrow of having lost a son in action during World War II.

"Was it always as tense and intense as this, Senator George?" I asked.

"No, it was not," answered the dean of the Senate. "Government for a long time was small. Its financial outlay except in time of war, was modest. It impinged on few lives. We did not even need air-conditioning in the Capitol Building, for we were not here in the summer months. But now Government has become vast and complex. It touches every citizen. Often the only avenue by which the citizen can contact or approach the Government is through his senator or congressman. Thus, 96 of us in this chamber and 400-plus in the House are the focal point for over 160,000,000 people."

Because I anticipated so slow and deliberate a pace in the Senate, it may be that I am too acutely conscious of the feverish haste which surrounds our work. Of that, I am willing to let the reader be the judge. While I was writing this article, my wife and I selected a day on which to set down my schedule in detail. We deliberately made it a normal day, rather than one which would be inordinately crowded. This was my schedule for a typical working day during this 1956 session of Congress:

6:45–7:45 A.M. Rise, read *Congressional Record* of previous day which was left on doorstep during night, also two daily newspapers.

7:45–8:30 A.M. Take orange juice with my wife, drive to Capitol building.

8:30–9:30 A.M. Have breakfast with leader of Railroad Brotherhoods from Oregon and his wife; take them onto Senate floor and show them my desk – which is permitted only when Senate is not in session.

9:30–10 A.M. Confer with administrative assistant and others on my staff about day's agenda, scan important letters and telegrams.

10–12 A.M. Attend Senate Public Works Committee hearings on government water-power policies.

NOON. Go to floor for opening of the day's Senate business, make two-minute speech urging adherence to Supreme Court ruling in school-segregation cases.

12:30–1:30 P.M. Relieve Senator George, president pro-tem in chair, and preside over Senate.

1:30–2:15 P.M. Have as guests in Senate Restaurant college coed from Oregon who is studying drama in New York City and her girlfriend, a delegate to Young Republican meeting. (Because I was late for lunch as usual, my wife was present to get our guests started.)

2:15–3:15 P.M. Attend Senate session and participate in debate on amendments to farm bill. Called off floor four times for interviews with delegations from "home" and once to be questioned by Associated Press reporter about campaign spending bills.

3:15–4:30 P.M. Preside again over Senate, relieving Democratic Senator Bible of Nevada in chair.

4:30–5:30 P.M. Dictate to secretary in alcove just off Marble Reading Room, answering personally more than forty letters and telegrams.

5:30–6:30 P.M. Return to office to sign mail and be briefed by staff about information and messages brought by steady stream of callers during day.

6:30–6:45 P.M. Phone government officials at their homes about matters of vital importance to my state.

6:45–7:30 P.M. Return to Senate floor to make insertions in *Record* of several editorials from Oregon papers, prior to close of day's debate.

8:00–10:00 P.M. Dinner at downtown Washington hotel with Oregon's Chancellor of Higher Education, in city for conferences with Veteran's Administration on GI training.

10:00–12:00 P.M. Return home with briefcase full of documents, work in study for two hours on draft of major Senate speech urging reduction in Social Security age for women.

12 MIDNIGHT to 1:00 A.M. Go to bed, discuss with wife events of the day, ask her advice on policy questions involved. Read magazines until turning off light.

Furthermore, in the interval between bedtime and the clanging of the morning alarm, the telephone can ring at any moment, and often does. I have been awakened by a constituent who wanted me to facilitate his bidding on a Defense Department contract, by an Oregon GI who had run afoul of MPs in Louisiana for alleged drunken driving, and by a female voter 3,000 miles away who wondered if my wife, a member of the Oregon State Legislature, would be good enough to compute her income tax if the woman sent us her payroll slips and check stubs.

Probably the reader will be surprised to note that a freshman senator presides frequently over the august United States Senate. This surprised me, too, until I learned that this was one of the chores expected of a fledgling member. The task is distasteful to veteran senators in many instances, because the occupant of the chair is immobilized during debate. I recall how I writhed one day on the rostrum while a natural-resource issue, on which I had strong feelings, was debated when I thus was restricted to the side lines.

Yet adventures can befall an occupant of the presiding officer's chair, although not always pleasant ones. I wielded the gavel on a day when Republican Senator McCarthy of Wisconsin delivered a long address critical of the President's brother, Milton Eisenhower. A hubbub occasionally rose on the floor, and Senator McCarthy several times asked me to rap for order. Finally, he became critical not only of Milton Eisenhower but also of me, because the confusion continued. I told McCarthy I was doing my best to maintain order and for him to get on with his speech. After this passage at arms, a number of little chits were passed up from senators on the floor, telling me to stick to my guns and not be bullied.

But a new senator does not always know all the rules, and the big leather chair below the silken American flag is a rough place to learn them. During a debate over a totally different subject, Republican Senator Williams of Delaware suddenly obtained the floor and began discussing internal-revenue violations and inefficiencies in Philadelphia, Pa. I reminded him from the rostrum that this was not the topic under discussion. Senator Williams retorted, in effect, that he would jolly well discuss any subject he pleased. Who was I to tell him what to talk about?

Charles L. Watkins, the veteran and trusted parliamentarian of the Senate, looked up at me elfishly and commented in his dry, crackling voice: "He's absolutely right, Senator Neuberger. There is no rule here that speeches have to be germane to the bill being debated. Senator Williams can talk on any subject he likes. The chair has no right to limit what he says."

Of course, Charlie Watkins, who knows the Senate Rules by heart, was right and I was wrong. Once a senator gains recognition from the chair, he can talk about shoes or ships or sealing wax – or ballet dancers, or labor unions. A bill dealing with the pay of Federal judges can be before the Senate, but a senator, if he desires, may talk for three or four hours about the comparative merits of whitefish and eels.

I am aware of the importance of unlimited free speech in the Senate, yet I believe speeches should have to be addressed to the subject at issue, as in the British and Canadian Parliaments, and as in most U.S. State legislatures. This was impressed upon me late in the 1955 session of Congress when we were under pressure to pass vital foreign-aid bills and other crucial measures. In the early afternoon two of the younger senators rose and made lengthy speeches on wholly extraneous matters; one of these speeches lasted for two hours, the other for an hour and forty-five minutes.

That night we were still on the floor at 10:45 P.M., trying to grind out urgently needed legislation. The two younger senators who delayed us with their speeches had long since gone home, to frolic or to bed. But still in their chairs, grim with fatigue, sat Senators Green (D.) of Rhode Island, 88; Murray (D.) of Montana, 79; Barkley (D.) of Kentucky, 78; George (D.) of Georgia, 78; Lehman (D.) of New York, 78; and Martin (R.) and Duff (R.) of Pennsylvania, 77 and 73, respectively.

Ever since that night, when I saw how inconsiderate youth could be to age in the Senate – and get away with it – I have been opposed to rules which allow the legislative machinery of the United States to be halted at any time when some senator wants to throw into the gears a four-hour speech on a totally unrelated question. Perhaps some of my strong feeling in this respect stems from the obvious fact that a good many Senate speeches are "ghost-written." At the mere drop of a lead pencil, a senator can get a competent speech on almost any side of any issue from the national headquarters of the particular pressure group involved, be it business, labor, or transportation. He need not even write in the salutation of "Mr. President" or pertinent references to his home state. They will be there, too.

With the brashness that undoubtedly goes with a lack of understanding of all aspects of a problem, I had boasted early in my Senatorial career that I would never rely on anyone else to prepare my words for me on the floor of the Senate. One of the senators who can speak fluently without a note in his hand, Paul H. Douglas, Democrat of Illinois, observed gently but with a touch of remonstrance in his voice: "You may not believe this, Dick, but no senator can take care of all his duties and obligations, and still write all his own utterances for Senate delivery – unless he somehow can arrange for expansion of the day into more than twenty-four hours, or perhaps can contrive to do without any sleep whatsoever."

And then Senator Douglas went on to advise me how much of my time would be spent performing errands and chores for the people out in Oregon. I was skeptical as I listened to his words, but I believe him thoroughly now. In fact, he even may have understated the case when he prophesied that at least half my waking would be devoted to handling missions for the home folks. In a single typical day, for example, I have worked on these assignments for constituents:

1   Trying to relocate in Oregon a Navy ordnance depot unwanted by the Californians.

2   Having an Oregon county wracked by floods listed as a disaster area, so it could obtain priority in bidding on Federal contracts.

3   Attempting to secure a hearing and fair treatment for an Oregon letter carrier charged with being a security risk.

4   Urging the State Department to facilitate adoptions by Oregon families of half-caste orphans left behind in Korea by American GIs.

5   Seeking additional Agricultural Department lunch funds for children in Oregon schools.

These are all challenging missions, but they left little time on the day's calendar for legislating. Being a senator, I have discovered, is not so much to enact laws as to be an ambassador for one's state. Members of the House of Representatives tell me they have the same problem. Strange as it may seem, I actually have received letters reminding me that Oregon needs diplomatic representation quite as much as England, because Oregon is almost as distant geographically from Washington, D.C. as is London!

The degree to which senators and representatives are often local or regional spokesmen first and national lawmakers second has been another amazing feature of my service. Many of my fellow liberals were critical of the Democratic majority leader, Senator Lyndon B. Johnson, because he pushed so vigorously for the bill exempting natural-gas producers from Federal controls. Although I spoke and voted against the gas bill, I have not echoed this criticism of Senator Johnson. The gas bill was important to Texas. Senator Johnson represents Texas in the Senate. He was doing what his state wanted. It has seemed to me, a newcomer, that this is common practice. Most of the Democratic liberals, for instance, come from states where dairying is vital. They militantly opposed repeal of the 10-cents-per-pound Federal penalty tax on butter's competitor, colored margarine, although the tax was a levy on the same urban consumers whom the liberals were trying to protect in the fight over the gas bill.

This characteristic in Congress prevails alike among Republicans and Democrats, among liberals and conservatives, and among Northerners and Southerners. Its intensity has amazed me. Some senators vote for 90 percent of parity on the farm product grown in their own state, and against 90 percent of parity on the product grown in the other fellow's state. They will support high protective tariffs on goods manufactured inside the borders of the state they represent, but will favor reciprocal trade agreements involving goods manufactured elsewhere.

I know one bloc of prominent senators who have promoted a Federal power project costing $780,000,000 in their own region, and yet denounce as "Socialism" a $350,000,000 Federal power dam in another region! Senators from states with toll roads demand special toll-road credits in the highway bill, and senators from states without toll roads are equally adamant on the opposite side. When I introduced a bill to rename a national forest in another state for historical reasons, one of the senators from that state claimed I had no business intruding into its affairs. Yet each national forest belongs to the people in all 48 states. I decided sadly that the word "national" will lose its meaning if we insist upon dividing ourselves so completely into tight little compartments, each determined on its own sectional and provincial interests.

A solution, in my opinion, would be for each state to have a business agent or field representative in the national capital. This person, out of partisan politics and under Civil Service, would be trained in liaison and contacts with Federal agencies. He would be the equivalent of a city manager in a metropolitan community. He would be expected to take care of the purely local projects, errands, and missions of a particular state. This might help to leave the senators free to legislate from the perspective of the national welfare. Such a proposal may seem visionary, but I believe it would be preferable to having U.S. senators weighted down with such chores as finding out why some crosspatch's mail is delivered late or what happened to the missives a lovelorn young woman insists she hasn't been receiving from her boyfriend in the Marine Corps.

Next to attending to all of one's responsibilities, I find that the most difficult phase of serving in the United States Senate is to be one's natural self. No effort is spared to make a senator feel important, to think he is of a class apart. Where else, except in the Presidency, do 95 men and one woman exercise such power and authority in the free world? Senators are treated sycophantishly by many who come seeking favors. A senator can buzz three times, and all Capitol elevators must come forthwith at his command. If a senator is a passenger along with other people, the elevator must go to his floor first and the rest later. Policemen require average folks to relinquish their seats on a crowded subway car for a busy senator. Each state furnishes its senators with special license plates, which have a VIP significance in the District of Columbia. Mine heralds me thusly: "Oregon – U.S. Senator 2." This indicates I am the junior senator from Oregon.

At dinners and banquets in Washington, senators are the object of much bowing and scraping. When I planned to divide into two parts my big office with the marble fireplace, because my poor staff workers are so jammed in their bulging rooms, I was advised that this would be inappropriate. A senator, it seemed, had to receive his visitors ceremonially in large and fancy quarters. And although nearly everyone on my staff is a long-time personal friend of mine from Oregon, I learned further that there had been some criticism because they addressed me as "Dick" rather than as "Senator Neuberger."

Indeed, in view of the flattery and subservience which most senators receive, I marvel that they retain their perspective as well as they do.

But this atmosphere has disturbed me, because I fear it could be a heady wine. I am certain that I can be a good and faithful senator, from the standpoint of all the people, only if the office itself means so little to me personally that I am not afraid to lose it. If I ever think in my own mind that it would be intolerable to cease being a senator, then I have lost much of my capacity to serve without selfishness and without fear. Threats and pressure can move me, as I see it, only when I am frightened of defeat.

Although I have been a senator only a comparatively short time, I have learned that many of my best friends are protective to the point of wanting to make me over. After I had admitted to the annual banquet of Portland's Retail Trade Bureau that I was wearing the first tuxedo I had ever owned, several advisers counseled that this was too "unsophisticated" a remark to come from a member of the United State Senate.

In the Oregon State Legislature, where both my wife, Maurine, and I were members simultaneously, we worked together as a team. We have tried to continue this teamwork in Washington. We send a weekly newsletter to constituents, written and signed jointly by the two of us. On our weekly radio program, Maurine and I appear together discussing issues of significance to Oregon families. A good many of my political counselors have warned that, while it may be all right for a mere state legislator to seem politically dependent on his wife, this definitely was out of keeping for a United States senator. My reply to this was brief and, I trust, to the point. I said I was identically the same person as a United States senator that I had been as a state senator, and I intended to stay that way, if at all humanly possible.

The Tyranny of Guilt by Association

The Progressive, SEPTEMBER 1955

Senator Joseph R. McCarthy of Wisconsin, who rode the issue of domestic Communism to national notoriety in 1950, was a powerful force in American politics. He was the boldest demagogue of the postwar era, appealing to prejudice and mob hysteria. Two presidents of the United States were held hostage by McCarthy and six senators were defeated for reelection in part because of McCarthy's opposition in states where he enjoyed a large following. Neuberger abhorred McCarthyism and linked Cordon with McCarthy in the 1954 campaign for his tacit support of the Wisconsin demagogue. Edward R. Murrow of CBS News aired a devastating portrait of McCarthy in 1954. Soon afterward, McCarthy was humiliated when his charges of espionage activities at Fort Monmouth, New Jersey were exposed as a hoax during the Army–McCarthy hearings. A month before Neuberger took his senatorial oath, McCarthy was censured by two-thirds of the Senate. McCarthy's legacy, though, inhibited political dissent in the United States and encouraged a hard line in American foreign policy with Communist nations. Neuberger never backed down to McCarthy and his allies.

The son shall not bear the iniquity of the father, neither shall the father bear the iniquity of the son. EZEKIEL, XVIII, VERSE 20.

THE HYPOCRITICAL Pharisees murmured centuries ago that Jesus was "gone to be a guest with a man that is a sinner." Ever since, guilt by association has served well those who prefer to judge a person not by his own deeds but by the deeds of others. The Russians, whom our American devotees of guilt by association supposedly detest, have refined the doctrine into a cruel art.

In the United States, guilt by association poses a strange thesis. I was presiding temporarily over the Senate the day Joseph R. McCarthy, Wisconsin Republican, made his speech attacking Milton Eisenhower, who is highly trusted by his brother, the President. The charge was that Milton Eisenhower allegedly had corresponded with individuals whom McCarthy considered "security risks."

I did some hasty calculating while sitting in Vice President Nixon's big leather chair. My office gets about 250 letters a day. We try to answer them all. If we had to run a security check which would satisfy Senator McCarthy concerning each correspondent before preparing an answer, we would need the combined services of Scotland Yard, the Royal Canadian Mounted Police, and the FBI.

Guilt by association is a curious kind of guilt. The contagion often works in only one direction. It is as if the prevailing winds, which spread the germs, never changed.

President Eisenhower has been engaging in a lengthy personal exchange of letters with his "old friend," Field Marshal Georgi K. Zhukov. If this correspondence can hasten world peace, why shouldn't the President try it? Yet one needs no lively imagination to guess at the outraged cries from a certain side of the aisle in the U.S. Senate if the President writing personal and undisclosed letters to the Soviet Minister of Defense had been named Harry S. Truman rather than Dwight Eisenhower.

A suggestion that Japan trade more extensively with Red China recently came from Senator Walter F. George, Georgia Democrat. The author of this proposal is the senior member of the U.S. Senate, chairman of the Foreign Relations Committee, one of the most respected conservatives from the old South. Yet how many Congressional sleuths would be off on their own private witch-hunts if the recommendation for greater commerce between Japan and Red China had come not from the distinguished Walter F. George but from one listed as a liberal?

Conservatives, by and large, seem to have a strong immunity to

guilt by association. *Pravda* on many occasions has praised the isolationist views of Herbert Hoover. Yet, casual references in the *Daily
Worker* were used to indict the patriotism of Helen Gahagan Douglas
in the California Senatorial campaign in 1950.

In Oregon last year, I was accused of radicalism, and worse, because contributions from my typewriter had appeared in *The New Republic*, *The Nation*, even in *The Progressive*. Ironically, no such
thing as innocence by association seemed equally possible. I had
also written extensively for the *Reader's Digest*, the *Saturday Evening Post*, and similar periodicals. But, while writing for a "radical"
magazine might make me a radical, few ever suggested that writing
for a "conservative" magazine could make me a conservative.

Speaking in the Oregon seacoast town of Coos Bay, my wife ventured a sane comment on the whole nonsense. "Dick also has written
for some of the leading women's magazines," said she. "What are
they going to say about that?"

One of the healthiest occurrences in the entire guilt-by-association
hysteria took place on April 16, 1955, in New York City when Sen.
William L. Langer, Republican of North Dakota, addressed a group
known as the Emergency Civil Liberties Committee. The group was
averred to be subversive. Presented with this claim by a reporter for
the New York *Herald Tribune*, the ranking minority member of the
powerful Judiciary Committee replied:

"As a member of the United States Senate, I feel free to address any
group of American citizens."

II

That answer by Senator Langer is the voice of free and courageous
Americans speaking once again. What other position can a self-
respecting man take? Must he cringe and parry – yes, and investigate
– each time he is asked to speak to a public meeting, write for a magazine, or correspond with an individual? Since when did an American become responsible for anybody's loyalty and personal behavior
except his own? I may be my brother's keeper, but I not necessarily
his stand-in.

I can write for a "radical" magazine without becoming a radical.

I can write for a "conservative" magazine without becoming a conservative. I can write for a Canadian magazine without transferring my citizenship. I can write for a woman's magazine without being a woman. William L. Langer, Republican of North Dakota, can address a "subversive" group without becoming a subversive. And Dwight Eisenhower, Republican of the United States, can write to a Communist war lord without becoming a Communist. Yes, and Dorothy Jones, a voteless government typist in the District of Columbia, can sit in a "subversive" meeting without being subversive.

If we are to return to Jefferson's old-fashioned idea that guilt is an individual matter, then liberals as well as Tories are going to have to exercise restraint in hitting people over the noggin with the tomahawk of guilt by association.

One Viorel Trifa, as chaplain *pro tempore*, pronounced the invocation in the u.s. Senate on a recent day. A fearful ruckus ensued when Trifa turned out to be a renegade European clergyman who is a notorious anti-Semite. Liberals looked for heads to decapitate because of guilt by association with Trifa. Who had rubbed elbows with the bigot?

It soon developed that Senator Pat McNamara, Michigan Democrat, had introduced Trifa to the regular Chaplain of the Senate, the Rev. Frederick Brown Harris, who invited Trifa to give the opening prayer. Pat McNamara sits in the chair next to mine on the floor of the Senate, and a finer and kindlier man I never met. Of course, he had known nothing of Trifa's background. It was all perfectly innocent. When Chaplain Harris learned who Trifa was, he exclaimed, "My Lord, I must start checking on the people to whom I turn over the pulpit."

This remark was made to Herman Edelsberg, able director of the Anti-Defamation League of B'nai B'rith, which fights anti-Semitism in the United States. Edelsberg gave the Reverend Harris a wise reply. "No, Chaplain," he said, "don't start putting proposed chaplains through a full field investigation. It is better to make a mistake once every 10 years than start questioning routine Senatorial recommendations."

Is this not the only sane answer to guilt by association? The harm of one anti-Semite preaching briefly to the U.S. Senate, of the President's brother corresponding with a "security risk," of a Senator addressing a "subversive" group – these perils are trivial compared to a compulsive need to put through the third degree every human being with whom we exchange nods and letters.

A few months ago I visited Christ Church in Alexandria, Virginia, where George Washington worshipped. As I left the old churchyard, I rejoiced that guilt by association had been temporarily in abeyance during a critical period of General Washington's life. The father of our country trusted a traitor. The traitor was his friend and comrade in arms. He gave to the traitor a crucial military mission. How easy it might have been for Washington's political foes to tar him with the guilt of treason by reason of his association with Benedict Arnold. But there was no charge of "four years of treason," and Washington's name has come down to us unsullied.

Yet Washington himself fretted that unscrupulous efforts would be made to spread the fear of further disloyalty. In the fifth volume of his monumental work *George Washington*, Douglas Southall Freeman has written:

> In the conviction that Arnold had no partner in perfidy, Washington was anxious that suspicions should not be indulged. When he heard from the Board of War that a notorious informer, whom he suspected of being a double spy, had alleged that Robert Howe was in British pay, he protested.
> "It will be the policy of the enemy," he wrote, "to distract us as much as possible by sowing jealousies, and if we swallow the bait, no character will be safe; there will be nothing but mutual distrust."

One only can wonder what the squire of Mount Vernon would have thought of those today who scatter the seeds of guilt by association.

III

Guilt by association has spawned two rather unprepossessing offspring. They are (1) guilt by inheritance and (2) guilt by contamination.

Guilt by inheritance works simply. If any one of your ancestors were guilty of Communism or of being security risks, then you are guilty too. This doctrine reached a climax in the case of Corporal Walter W. Kulich of Aberdeen, Wash., who was tendered an "undesirable" discharge from the Army because of charges that his father was a Communist. After two Washington Congressmen, Don Magnuson, a Democrat, and Russell V. Mack, a Republican, had voiced strenuous protests, the discharge was held up.

Just as guilt by association smacks of roundups by the Russian secret police, guilt by inheritance is a throw-back to ancient Inca rites when beautiful maidens occasionally were buried alive with their dead parents. If one now must suffer all the penalties of Communism because one's father was a Communist, what will happen if one's father was a murderer? Must then the innocent son or daughter share the electric chair? And if you are unfortunate enough to be the descendant of a man who embezzled from a bank, will you automatically occupy the same prison cell? Yet this is almost precisely what happened to Corporal Kulich – disgrace, shame, and an "undesirable" discharge from the Army not because of anything he himself had ever done, but merely because of charges against his father.

Guilt by contamination is slightly more subtle than guilt by inheritance. Its operation is best illustrated by what has happened to Amendment V to the Constitution of the United States. This is the clause against self-incrimination. Because alleged Communists and security risks have been invoking this clause, it has fallen onto evil days. It is contaminated in spite of undoubted authorship by the illustrious father of our Constitution, James Madison. The phrase, "Fifth-Amendment Communist" has become a commonplace.

A former right-wing member of the Senate, Harry P. Cain, Washington Republican, has warned us, however, that those "who use 'Fifth Amendment' as an adjective of disapprobation modifying the noun 'Communist' are as guilty of disrespect to the Constitution as any Communist could be."

Because a Communist invokes the amendment, does that make it either obsolete or shameful? Communists unquestionably make use of the First Amendment, too, which guarantees freedom of speech and of the press. They orate from soap boxes and print their *Daily*

Worker. Shall the existence of these "First-Amendment Communists" induce us to jettison Amendment I as well as Amendment V of our Constitution?

Cain, now an Eisenhower appointee to the Subversive Activities Control Board, has said it is preferable to maintain the basic American principle "that an individual shall not be required to convict himself" than to punish "a few who hide behind the privilege without justification." Why set the whole kitchen on fire to fry the breakfast eggs? After all, the Fifth Amendment cannot be revoked merely with respect to Communists. Once it has been wiped off the Constitution, we may be delivering an entire generation of 165,000,000 Americans over to police confessions won by the third degree.

Although the modern practitioners of guilt by association proclaim themselves as the most militant foes of Communism, are they not actually encouraging the Communists to hold veto power over our own lives and institutions?

Let Communists shield themselves behind the bulwark of our Constitution, and our land rings with the demands that integral sections of the charter of our liberties be indiscriminately destroyed. Naturally, the Constitution would be destroyed for us, also, in the process. One of my colleagues in the Senate has gone so far as to suggest that "if the Communists take a unanimous stand for anything, it would be a pretty good rule to be against it – even if it does contain some good features." Adoption of this idea, of course, might allow the Communists to prevent us from chlorinating drinking water, using smallpox serum, or manufacturing paper from woodpulp. All the Communists would have to do is "take a unanimous stand" in favor of these practices. And did anybody ever hear of a Communist stand which was not unanimous? The firing squad and the long one-way train ride on Trans-Siberian are powerful inducements to conformity and unanimity.

Indeed, at one stage in the lengthy struggle over the vast hydroelectric resources of Hells Canyon, adherents of the Idaho Power Company claimed that public development of the chasm could not possibly be sound because the *Daily Worker* was alleged to endorse it. *Ergo*, half-a-million kilowatts at Hells Canyon had to be sacrificed for all time. Could the *Daily Worker* accomplish a greater service for the Soviet Union than this? Energy resources may decide the ultimate weapons race between the major powers. Russia is harnessing the mighty reaches of the Volga and Yenesi Rivers. Yet Russia's satellite newspaper in the United States can perhaps, with a single editorial, persuade Americans to follow a policy which will result in the permament loss of immense quantities of electrical energy in the depths of Hells Canyon.

Where does it all lead? We transfer to Russian puppets control over our own ideas. We make sons suffer for the sins of fathers and we consider gutting our great Constitution because Communists hide behind its gleaming ramparts.

The most hopeful thing one can say about guilt by association is that each day fewer Americans are being fooled by it. When this misguided doctrine is employed in an effort to indict the patriotism of an intimate brother of the most popular Republican President of the United States in half a century, even some original backers of the doctrine must be sorely shaken. They discover that tyranny, like a tiger, does not always discriminate between victims.

Guilt by association may be on the way into the vasty deep, but the residue lingers on. To my office each week come many pitiful letters from men and women who have been summarily discharged from the civilian or military arms of the federal government because of suspected disloyalty – almost always stemming from some form of guilt by association.

My limited staff cannot even begin to run down all these leads. But one case in particular stands out in my mind. It involves an Oregon GI who was jolted with a dishonorable discharge only four weeks before his two years of drafted military service was to end. His career was in ruins. He had been shut off from all Veterans' Administration benefits. Could he ever explain what had happened? I took up his problem because a Protestant minister in Oregon, in whose integrity I have personal confidence, vouched for the boy's character. The discharge, of course, involved alleged subversive association.

There is not space here to go into all the sorry details, nor do the details belong in this story. Shortly after I interested myself in the matter, the Army took a long second look. It discovered that the two key "witnesses" against the GI were people of instability and unreliability. As a consequence, the dishonorable discharge was quickly rescinded.

The episode has left me with two distinct impressions: (1) that of profound relief and gratification that the Army moved so promptly to correct an injustice and (2) a gnawing worry that this boy might have spent his entire life in the thwarting shadow of a dishonorable discharge if a U.S. Senator had not taken an active and persistent interest in the case.

The second impression still lingers in my mind.

Principles or Party?

Christian Century, 18 JULY 1956

O regon is a state with a long tradition of nonpartisanship. As in most western states, there have never been strong political party organizations in Oregon. Elections for major offices since World War II have been decided by issues and personalities rather than by party. In such an environment, Neuberger gained politically by appealing to nonpartisanship. Neuberger, in fact, was much more of a Democratic regular than his contemporaries Wayne L. Morse, a Republican-turned-Democrat, whose support of Mark Hatfield, a Republican, proved to be decisive in a 1966 Senate election; and Edith Green, who crossed party lines in 1976 to support her old friend President Gerald R. Ford. Before his election to the Oregon State Senate, Neuberger had voted for such Republicans as Morse and Charles L. McNary. But when Neuberger gained Democratic party leadership positions, he was a stalwart party man.

Compared with the importance of America, the importance of the Democratic Party, the importance of the Republican Party, the importance of every other party, is absolutely negligible.

WOODROW WILSON

A CONSTITUENT OF MINE wanted to know what I, as a liberal Democrat in the United States Senate, would do if my party adopted a platform which favored segregation and inequality among the races of mankind. My reply to her was, I hope, unequivocal and to the point:

"I trust the Democratic party never will sanction any kind of discrimination based on race, creed, religion, sex or color. If it should do so, I would crusade as hard and stubbornly as I could against any such plank. I would try my best to eliminate it from Democratic doctrine. If I failed utterly in this effort over a reasonable period of time, I would leave the Democratic party. No man or woman should ever subordinate principles and ideals to mere political party membership. A political party is not a goal in and of itself. It exists simply to advance and promote certain ideas of government, through candidates who presumably favor those ideas. When a party begins promoting the wrong ideas, it has terminated its usefulness."

As I review this letter now, I do not see how an American can have any different code. Can a political party become the be-all and end-all of existence? It is perhaps possible, in the name of national survival, to justify the Stephen Decatur doctrine of "My country, right or wrong," but surely this degree of tolerance need never be extended to a political party, which involves none of the patriotic or traditional elements of the nation itself.

I

The question of party allegiance is made unusually pertinent in this mid-year of 1956 by three significant developments now stirring the country: (1) the dilemma that confronts the Democrats over the searing and crucial civil-rights issue, which tends to divide the party at the Mason and Dixon line; (2) the sensational disclosure in a friendly new biography, *Eisenhower – the Inside Story*, by Robert J. Donovan, that the President gave "prolonged thought" in 1953 to forming a third party because of his dismay over bitter opposition from right-wing Republicans; and (3) the campaign of excoriation being conducted in Oregon against Senator Wayne Morse, who was elected to the Senate in 1944 and again in 1950 on the Republican ticket but in this election is seeking a third term as a Democrat.

For a number of reasons I am particularly conscious of these situations. To begin with, I zealously favor a strong and genuine program of civil rights. And, although I am a lifelong Democrat, I have voted far more consistently for President Eisenhower's foreign policy, according to the *Congressional Quarterly*, than the three Republican congressmen from my state. In addition to this, I am Senator Morse's junior colleague.

All at once I have become aware that party membership can be either a strait-jacket or a loose cassock. How should the garment be tailored? What are the real obligations of a political figure to his party, of the party to the person? When, if ever, should he bow to the party mandate, and on what kind of matters? Is it in the national interest for party control to require suppression of individual views? Furthermore, how can prevailing attitudes within any party ever be accurately assayed at regular intervals?

It is my own opinion that partisan rancor has soared to new and unfortunate heights in the United States during recent years. This probably originates in several sources. Men of great wealth and power have felt themselves threatened by labor's increasing political role. Such political pawns as the tidelands oil reserves and natural gas regulation involve enormous sums. The vast stakes of American politics are symbolized by the estimated $80 million spent on the presidential campaign of 1952 and by the $160 million likely to be spent this year. Custodianship of natural resources, favoritism in tax policy, military contracts, the trappings of pomp and power – these things largely depend on the caprice of political fortune. So each new phase of the partisan combat takes on a cutting edge.

II

We think of England as a land of extreme party discipline. But our current political malevolence shames us and makes Britain's good-tempered party rivalry seem mild indeed. Consider the career of England's most illustrious statesman, Winston Churchill, and ask if his changes of party would be even remotely tolerated in our present political atmosphere. In 1900 Churchill was elected to Parliament as a Conservative. In 1904 he found himself at odds with his party over the issue of free trade, which he favored. Without resigning his seat, Churchill strode across the chamber and joined the rival Liberals. He soon ascended to dominance in his new party and was First Lord of the Admiralty in the Liberal cabinet of Lloyd George. After World

War I he broke with the Liberals and was for several years a political independent. In 1924 he returned to the Conservative party, which he served during World War II as a famous and embattled prime minister. One of Churchill's most celebrated biographers, Philip Guedalla, has said that "a man who did not follow his opinions into the party which believed in them was a tragic failure."

Far greater party obedience than this is demanded of our public figures. Because he had been a Democrat as late as 1938, Wendell Willkie was never wholeheartedly accepted by many Republicans as the party's standard-bearer in 1940; in fact he was not even invited to the 1944 national convention. I have some Democratic friends who can be equally enslaved by party bondage. In 1948 they advocated replacing Harry S. Truman with General Eisenhower as the Democrats' presidential candidate. Four years later, when Dwight Eisenhower had cast his lot with the Republicans, these same people declared that a military man without political experience should never occupy the White House.

This intransigence is being demonstrated in Oregon today. Senator Morse, a former Republican, is running on the Democratic ticket. He has said that he regards present Republican policies in the field of public power and natural resources as a repudiation of the program of Theodore Roosevelt and Gifford Pinchot, eminent Republicans of the past.

Almost overnight, Morse's former supporters now revile him as an apostate and renegade. One might think he had resigned from the human race instead of merely from a political party. In the recent primary one of Morse's Republican adversaries told an audience: "If I thought there was a chance that I would become as cold, as grasping, egotistical and self-centered as some of the politicians I have known – and I refer, specifically, to Senator Morse – I would cut my throat before I would seek this office." This speaker had been one of Morse's ardent backers and campaign managers when the latter was a Republican. In his mind, Morse became "cold, grasping, egotistical and self-centered" only after he had changed his party affiliation from Republican to Democrat.

III

What makes intelligent Americans behave like this? Why was my wife, Maurine, who is a member of the Oregon state legislature, chastised by one of her sister Democrats because Maurine had commented favorably in a speech on Senator Margaret Chase Smith, the Maine Republican? "Please do be discreet, my dear," the Democratic lady admonished Maurine. "Never forget that Mrs. Smith is one of the opposition. Do not be taken in. You might be embarrassed some day for having praised her so generously. What if she ever were to become the Republican candidate for President?" Maurine answered: "I would support Margaret Smith against a Democrat who was less sympathetic to social welfare, public health, education and old-age security."

Nor have I forgotten the bald, belligerent man who called at my campaign headquarters in the 1954 campaign to determine the truth of the rumor that I, a Democrat, had given public approval to a re-election effort of the late Senator Charles L. McNary of Oregon, who served for many years as Senate Republican minority leader.

"The report is true," I told him. "Senator McNary was a public servant of integrity and ability. He advocated Bonneville dam and other federal projects on the Columbia River. He fought for rural electrification. He sponsored the Clarke-McNary act for improved forestry methods. He tried to pass the McNary-Haugen bill to aid our wheat farmers. In all these vital realms of policy I considered Senator McNary as considerably more liberal and enlightened than his Democratic opponent. So I supported Senator McNary." My caller was equally forthright. "Then I can't vote for you for the Senate," he said. "You backed a Republican, even a leading Republican. You're not my idea of a good Democrat. You're not loyal to the party."

I sat in moody reverie after the man had left my office. To him, being a Democrat did not mean allegiance to any fixed set of principles. It meant giving unquestioning support to anyone whom the party nominated – and against any Republican, regardless of how enlightened that Republican might be. Can such slavishness possibly result in the success of free government? And if I, in the name of mere party regularity, had stumped for an anti-public power Democrat against a pro-public power Republican like Senator McNary, would I now be on sound moral grounds in criticizing the present national administration for its hostile attitude toward such projects as Bonneville, Grand Coulee, and Hells Canyon?

We look with contempt, and properly so, on American Communists, who revise their views at the push of a button from Moscow. They subserviently cry that the "Yanks are not coming," or press for arms for Hitler's foes, or hail or revile Stalin, or praise new theories of heredity. It makes no difference that these positions are totally in contradiction with earlier ideas expressed by the same people. Consistency in principle becomes infinitely less important than hewing to the party line, no matter how suddenly or erratically that line may change.

Yet it is always easier to diagnose somebody else's frailties than to be even aware of our own. We look with scorn upon the enslavement of the Communists to party doctrine. But do we ourselves constantly strive to maintain personal independence? Liberals in the Democratic party surely have no choice save to oppose segregation, regardless of what the party platform may proclaim in this respect. Equality among races and religions is an immutable goal. While it may not be attained between dawn and dusk, it cannot be compromised. No Democrat of good will and high ideals can possibly accept a platform or plank which suggests that segregation is compatible with basic American principles.

IV

Party thralldom has no role in a land which declares that man is created in the image of God and that minds and souls must be unfettered. Some have expressed shock that, when Republican right-wingers in Congress were chopping his foreign policy to pieces, President Eisenhower once contemplated a third party. Yet why not? What was wrong with this showing of political independence? Mr. Eisenhower's coattails have always seemed more inviting to some members of his party than have his policies. The Republican legislature of my own state, for example, memorialized me to oppose the

President's reciprocal-trade program – a plea I ignored. The Wisconsin state Republican convention has just rejected Senator Alexander Wiley for another term because he has backed such international commitments of President Eisenhower's as foreign trade, the United Nations and mutual security. Was it not a great Republican political leader, Theodore Roosevelt, who organized the Bull Moose party because of his dissatisfaction with the conservative tenets of his GOP successor in the presidency, William Howard Taft?

One of the genuine needs in America today is for more political maturity. The herd instinct makes us submissive, willy-nilly, to any party fiat, regardless of its wisdom. The dignity of man pulls us in the other direction, toward true intellectual emancipation. I sit in the Senate with Harry F. Byrd of Virginia, who bolted the Democratic party to speak and vote for General Eisenhower in 1952. I have never agreed with the wisdom of Senator Byrd's choice in this matter, but his lack of party fealty has not diminished my respect or friendship for him. He did not concur in Adlai Stevenson's whole approach to social and economic issues. Why, then, should he support Stevenson? I am quite certain I would reach a similar decision were the Democrats to nominate for President a candidate who defended segregation and opposed such legislation as minimum wages and Social Security. The right of a conservative to bolt his party presupposes the same right on the part of liberal, and vice versa.

V

Let me emphasize that I am not advocating irresponsibility or recklessness in party membership. Political parties, by their very nature, are coalitions in which some measure of give and take is required. Few of us ever quite get the nominee and platform of our choice. Frequently we must swallow hard on some aspects of the party's preference. But this is totally different from accepting a candidate who offends one's deepest convictions. To be specific, let me point out that I never would support a Democratic ticket which included Governor Shivers of Texas, who, in my opinion, has catered to many of the most inflammatory and bigoted elements in his state. However, although he might not be my first choice, I feel far from this way about Senator Lyndon Johnson, also of Texas. While I have not agreed with Senator Johnson on every issue, he did not sign the so-called "Southern Manifesto" on segregation and he has taken a liberal position on questions like Hells Canyon, Niagara Falls, civil service and tax policy.

The issue of Niagara Falls, which faced the Senate this May, served to dramatize that our major parties are, after all, coalitions in the broadest sense. At stake was the proposal to let the state of New York develop the thundering hydroelectric power of America's greatest cataract. The only alternative was surrender of the site to an amalgamation of private utility companies. The Lehman bill, authorizing state priority, passed the Senate with the support of about 80 percent of the Democrats and 20 percent of the Republicans. This fusion kept Niagara Falls as public property. About one-fifth of the Democratic senators opposed the prevailing public-power concept of their party and a similar proportion of Republican senators opposed the prevailing private-power doctrine of their party. Things are rarely all black or all white in either party. That is why, when I addressed the famous Oberlin College mock Democratic convention this spring, I referred to the Democrats not as the "best" party but as the "better" party. Modern-day politics seldom give cause for honest superlatives.

Party ties rest but lightly on the average American. This, in my estimation, is as it should be. The typical voter has none of the rigidity and intolerance of the political potentates, who spurned Mr. Willkie and Senator Morse as "traitors" because they moved across the party moat. Yet, under existing circumstances, would it be possible for an American political leader to enjoy as unconventional a career in the no-man's land between our major parties as Winston Churchill has had? I doubt it, and I think this is too bad. As the Democrats have moved closer to the trade unions and the Republicans nearer an alliance with industrial corporations, the pull of each party on its "hard core" has tightened. The untrammeled and defiant behavior of such proud mavericks of the past as George Norris, William E. Borah, Edward P. Costigan and the La Follettes, father and son, is rarely duplicated in the Senate of today.

Too many people look upon defection from a party as the equivalent of political heresy. They forget that abandonment of one's own inner convictions and ideals is an intellectual felony. Compared with this, resignation from a political party ought never to rank as more than a misdemeanor. Indeed, under certain conditions, it could well merit the red badge of courage.

A Senator's Case Against Seniority

New York Times Magazine, 7 APRIL 1957

Neuberger's criticism of the seniority system is still valid. In 1987, Senator Jesse Helms of North Carolina, whose foreign policy views are simple-minded in the extreme, deposed the respected Richard Lugar of Indiana as the ranking Republican member of the Foreign Relations Committee by virtue of Helms's seniority. Democratic members are currently restless with Majority Leader Robert Byrd's performance but are hesitant to replace him with a fresher face.

ALTHOUGH I HAVE SERVED in the Senate only since January, 1955, it has become my firm conviction during this period that seniority should not continue to be the sole determinant of Congressional sovereignty and influence as reflected in committee chairmanships and committee assignments. As I see the question, seniority is wrong on three fundamental counts:

1   It attaches little or no significance to the special abilities and experience of an individual, but only to the duration of his service.

2   A committee chairman never can be removed, even if the national interest is jeopardized by his continuance in that post.

3   Seniority rewards those states with one-party systems and, conversely, penalizes states in which two robust and equally matched political parties fight it out at the ballot box.

The reasons for these objections to seniority are so obvious, it seems to me, that they can be regarded as practically self-explanatory. What can be said for a method of operating Congress that will give an ordinary layman with long political tenure a greater opportunity to serve on the Joint Committee on Atomic Energy than a famous nuclear physicist who might come newly to House or Senate? A man may be the leader of the bar in his state, but will he attain the Judiciary Committee if he lacks seniority? Senator Thurston Morton of Kentucky was President Eisenhower's Assistant Secretary of State, but the inexorable rule of seniority has given him a seat on the District of Columbia Committee rather than on the Foreign Relations Committee, where his training in the State Department could be put to practical use.

After their defeats for the Presidency, both Thomas E. Dewey and Adlai Stevenson were surrounded by rumors of Senatorial ambitions. Why should men of their distinction and oratorical gifts not aspire to the Senate chamber? Yet, it later was reported that they had decided against essaying the humble and unrewarding roles of freshmen Senators. Surely the decision of men of their caliber not to try to run for the Senate was a loss to the whole nation. Under a similar system in England, Winston Churchill would have had to be content with back-bench status after he dropped out of Parliament for a time and thus relinquished his seniority.

In these days of crisis, Government must be flexible to meet new situations. The earth is moving at a mad pace. Emergencies are omnipresent. Never so true was the couplet from James Russell Lowell's "The Present Crisis":

> New occasions teach new duties,
> Time makes ancient good uncouth.

Yet the Congressional rule of seniority is the direct antithesis of this. It is rigid, inflexible and unyielding – particularly in the vital realm of committee chairmanships. An isolationist may head the Armed Services Committee at the height of American involvement in a world-wide conflict, and in that post he stays if seniority put him there. If seniority installs a foe of conservation as chairman of the committee charged with protecting America's dwindling supply of natural resources, draft horses and wainrope cannot drag him out of this seat. And if the allies or beneficiaries of special interests become the heads of key committees responsible for regulating those same special interest – well, that is seniority.

Ought Congress be laced into such a straitjacket? If Senators can be trusted to pass on matters as crucial as war and peace, why is it unsafe to let them pick their own committee chairmen?

This is not to claim that able men of integrity rarely rise to Congressional dominance through the seniority system – far from it. For instance, Senator James E. Murray of Montana, an ardent conservationist at the age of 80, presides today over the Interior Committee. I have been amazed at the details concerning fiscal matters known to Senator Carl Hayden of Arizona, 79, who wields the gavel in the vital Appropriations Committee.

But the point is that, even if Senator Murray were not so ardent a conservationist and if Senator Hayden possessed far less familiarity with the Federal budget, they still would head the Interior and Appropriations Committees, respectively. Their qualifications are secondary to their seniority. I wonder if this is a wise set of priorities, particularly when we consider that men critically ill have ruled strategic committees for years *in absentia*. As long as breath remained in their bodies, the seniority rule could not be breached. They had to retain their chairmanships.

Furthermore, under such an arrangement, seniority often becomes an end in and of itself. Electorates are told that they must keep in office a certain individual not necessarily because he is sound on the burning issues confronting America and the rest of the world, but simply because he has so much seniority on deposit in Senate vaults.

In 1954, when I ran for the Senate as a Democrat in a state which had not elected a Democratic Senator for forty years, my opponent was an incumbent Republican who, through the inexorable workings of the seniority process, had become chairman of the Interior Committee. This is the most powerful Senate committee in dealing with problems affecting the Western states. The special advantages and benefits to Oregon of my opponent's seniority became a leading issue of the campaign. Indeed, at times it subordinated all other issues!

I shall never forget a conversation I had with an enlightened and able editor of a small-town daily newspaper whose support I was seeking. This man is an internationalist and a fervent defender of civil liberties. I cited to him my opponent's roll-call votes in the Senate against ratifying the North Atlantic Treaty Organization, against extending reciprocal trade, against Point Four, against any moves toward rebuking Senator McCarthy, against confirming such appointees as Chester Bowles and David E. Lilienthal, against positive Federal action in the realm of civil rights.

"Everything that you charge about your opponent's voting record is undoubtedly true," said the editor, whom I long have respected and admired. "I can't defend that record. Yet I still would hate to see our state lose all that valuable seniority in the United States Senate, as well as on some of its most important committees."

And, near that climax of the campaign, this internationalist, liberal-minded editor endorsed for the Senate an isolationist and adversary of civil rights.

I am convinced that such incidents are by no means uncommon. Yet an endless and self-serving circle is thus created. A one-party state produces seniority for its Senators because they serve without serious challenge to their tenure. Then, this seniority is relied upon as an all-persuasive argument for continuing the state's one-party standing.

This constitutes my principle complaint against the seniority system. It provides an argument and shield for people who fear the real workings of democracy. Despite all our vaunted devotion to the two-party system, grassroots competition between strong political parties is virtually unknown in approximately half the states of the Union. In fact, the absence of genuine political competition in so many states may be at the root of the undue emphasis on prolonged tenure in office. Such tenure is inevitably a by-product of one-party rule.

Occasionally some of the one-party states may be breached by a Presidential nominee of the other party who possesses overwhelming personal popularity or glamour – Franklin D. Roosevelt or Dwight Eisenhower, for example. In some distressing cases, as with the religious bigotry of 1928 directed against Alfred E. Smith, a one-party state may reverse itself.

But these exceptions seldom register any lower on the ballot. Mr. Hoover, once, and Mr. Eisenhower, twice, successfully invaded much of the Deep south. Yet they brought to victory with them not a single Republican Senator from that region. Mr. Roosevelt carried Oregon decisively four times, but the state never elected a Democratic Senator on such occasions. For offices like United States Senator or the governorships, no fewer than twenty-eight states may be regarded as nearly impregnable strongholds of one party or the other. These are the states which ascend most often to dominance in Congress under the seniority system.

What is a one-party state? I admit the term is susceptible to no hard and fast definition. Yet some specific standards of measurement are possible.

I have based this measurement on Senate seats because they are generally the offices fought over the hardest and national significance is most likely to attach to the results. I have gone back only to 1914, when some states first began to experiment with the direct election of Senators. Prior to that time all Senators were chosen by state Legislatures, with railroads and timber companies and steamship monopolies often more influential in the choice that the will of the electorate.

With this in mind, I believe it is fair and accurate to describe as a one-party state any in which one party has held, since 1914, a preponderance of Senatorial election victories of three to one, or more.

I find that in twenty-eight states the nominees of one party have regularly won Senate seats in three elections out of four, or better. This is considerably more than half the states of our nation. Some of these one-party states, especially in the South and Southwest, have been traditionally Democratic. Other states, particularly in New England and the Corn and Wheat Belt of the Middle West, have been steadfastly Republican.

In only twenty of the states have Senate seats been divided somewhat evenly between the two parties since the direct election of Senators began to replace the appointment method. They are: Colorado, Connecticut, Delaware, Idaho, Illinois, Indiana, Iowa, Kentucky, Maryland, Massachusetts, Minnesota, Missouri, New Mexico, New York, Ohio, Rhode Island, Utah, Washington, West Virginia and Wyoming.

It is true that these states today hold five chairmanships among a total of fifteen permanent Senate committees. But it is also true that the chairmanships belong to the five among the two-party states that are the closest to being one-party states. In this category is New Mexico, whose senior Senator serves as chairman of the Public Works Committee. New Mexico has had its Senatorial seats occupied by Democrats for a 13 to 5 supremacy during the past forty-three years. This is narrowly below the three-to-one ratio which would add New Mexico to my list of one-party states.

Furthermore, states where the two parties are as closely matched politically as New York and Illinois have not held major Senate chairmanships for a considerable number of years, despite their vast populations and their importance to the national economy. I can think of no more compelling reason for modifying the seniority rule than the manner in which seniority must inevitably discriminate against great two-party states such as these.

Fortunately, there has been some slight recent erosion of seniority. This has occurred not in the disposition of committee chairmanships, but in the place where reform ought logically to begin – in the assignment of new Senators to committee seats.

Some weeks ago, Representative Stewart L. Udall of Arizona, in an able defense in this magazine of the seniority rule, stressed the change in the methods of committee assignments as a hopeful sign that seniority is losing its ironclad aspects. I agree with his satisfaction over this development. However, Representative Udall neglected to point out that this curtailment of seniority has applied thus far to only one of the two major political parties.

Upon becoming Democratic leader of the Senate in 1953, Senator Lyndon Johnson laid down the policy that no member of the party, regardless of his seniority, would receive a second top committee seat of his choice until every Democratic Senator had been given at least one such assignment. Up to that time, senior Senators had monopolized nearly all the prized committee posts. Newcomers were relegated to minor committees, which usually meant Rules or Post Office or District of Columbia. This is still often the fate of junior Republican Senators, because the Johnson doctrine has yet to spread across the center aisle after four years of operation.

Immediately after their elections, Senators Mike Mansfield of Montana and Stuart Symington of Missouri were seated by the Democrats on the Foreign Relations and Armed Services Committees, respectively, because of their long backgrounds in those fields. Senator Wayne Morse of Oregon, who once taught international law, received a Senate Foreign Relations Committee place from the Democrats even while he was still an Independent. Yet no Republican seat on the committees operating in the realm of diplomacy has gone to Senator John Sherman Cooper of Kentucky, even though he has come to the Senate fresh from experience as President Eisenhower's envoy to India.

Two years ago I entered the Senate as a freshman and was assigned by the Democratic leadership to the Interior and Public Works Committees, both vital to natural-resource management in my Pacific Northwest constituency. By contrast, Senator Clifford Case of New Jersey, an Eisenhower Republican who entered the Senate with me, has been given only such typically minor berths as Post Office and District of Columbia because members of his party senior to him had laid claim to all the committee chairs of his preference.

What is to be done about the whole thorny question of seniority in Congress and of the penalty it imposes open two-party states?

Stubborn issues rarely respond to easy or pat solutions. However, I have three specific remedies to propose:

1   Relate committee assignments in Congress far more to geography and to specific state problems than to seniority.

2   Permit committee members to elect a chairman by secret ballot, rather than having this decided only by seniority.

3   Convert as many of the present one-party states as possible into two-party states.

Let me explain what I mean by the first proposal.

The people of the State of New York pay about 20 percent of all the taxes collected by the Federal Government. There should always be one Senator from New York on the Finance Committee, where taxation matters are decided. The Agricultural Committee should be balanced as fairly as possible among members from the cotton states of the South, the grain states of the Middle West and the specialty-crop states on both seacoasts. This balance does not prevail today. Among the committee's fifteen members there is not one Senator from the immense rural area between the Great Plains and the shores of the Pacific Ocean.

It is my belief that, once assignment to committees has been removed from the realm of seniority, it will soon follow that each committee will be able to elect its chairman. In the Senate committees on which I serve, the chairmen thus selected undoubtedly will be the same Senators who have occupied the head chair through seniority. But this would not be automatically the case in every committee, and the two-party states would find themselves at least participating in the choice; their total exclusion from such decisions might end.

My third suggestion may seem illusory and farfetched. How do you change a one-party state into a two-party state? Let me offer my own state as a prime demonstration that the feat can be accomplished.

While Franklin Roosevelt was President, only three states – Maine, Vermont and Oregon – failed to elect Democratic Senators or third-party Senators aligned with the Democrats. The last Democratic Senator from Oregon had been elected in 1914, the last Democratic Governor in 1934, and two of Oregon's four House seats had never in history been won by Democrats. Today, Oregon has two Democratic Senators, a Democratic Governor and three out of its four Congressional seats are occupied by Democrats.

The significant feature of Oregon's emergence from entrenched one-party status is the circumstance that two out of three Democratic Senatorial victories have occurred in 1954 and again in 1956. Oregon never elected a Democratic Senator during the twelve years that the White House was occupied by Franklin D. Roosevelt, most popular of Democratic Presidents. Paradoxically, Oregon today has two Democratic Senators who were elected during the four years that the White House has been the residence of Dwight D. Eisenhower, most popular of Republican Presidents.

What was responsible for this?

The principle ingredient in the political upheaval in Oregon has been the refusal of the Democrats to be daunted by the deeply rooted political monopoly of the Republicans. Democratic leaders in every Oregon county decided there was no valid reason why Oregon should be the exclusive property of the Republican party. Spirit and persistence accounted for the change.

I discuss Oregon merely as a case in point. There are other one-party bastions and they, too, can be carried by a formidable political assault. Pennsylvania, with a fourteen-to-four preponderance of Republican Senatorial victories throughout its modern history, is succumbing to change. Joseph S. Clark, Jr., is the first Democratic Senator from Pennsylvania in many years. And, now that President Eisenhower himself has twice breached many of the Democratic redoubts in the South, his party is looking southward for victories at other levels on the ballot.

Any invasion of a political stronghold, be it Republican or Democratic, is to the eventual advantage of democracy and progressive government. As one-party citadels fall, seniority will lose much of its attraction and influence in Congress. And as seniority is gradually modified, there will be less temptation for a state to continue suppliantly in the clutches of one political party. Both of these changes will help the nation – inside the halls of Congress as well as far beyond the Capitol dome.

Who Polices the Policeman (Congress)?

New York Times Magazine, 23 FEBRUARY 1958

Since Neuberger's article, Congress has made more serious efforts to police itself. Former Senator Harrison Williams of New Jersey was reprimanded by colleagues for accepting a payoff from a federal undercover agent. Williams was later convicted and resigned from office. Two congressmen were censured in 1983 for their relationships with teenage pages. Senator Mark O. Hatfield of Oregon was investigated in 1986 by a Senate ethics panel in connection with promoting an energy pipeline for one of his wife's real-estate clients. Hatfield was embarrassed but exonerated. Former Senator Adlai E. Stevenson III of Illinois, who chaired the Senate ethics panel, said it was a thankless task.

ONCE AGAIN the disturbing question of "conflict of interest" is racking the city that is our seat of government. This time those involved are predominantly members of powerful quasi-independent regulatory commissions, with particular emphasis on the personnel of the Federal Communications Commission, which allocates licenses for radio and television outlets. Some of these men have been charged by Congressional committees with accepting entertainment, travel expenses, speaking fees and reception equipment from various segments of the industry that they are supposed to supervise. Wives and other members of their families are also said to have shared in this hospitality. Certain of the charges have been challenged, but the basic issue continues as one of the thornier problems confronting representative government like ours.

How can private obligations be squared with one's responsibility to the public?

In these cases conflict of interest has been interpreted to mean that federal commissioners may not be able to exercise their regulatory powers fairly and judicially when they are indebted for financial or social favors to those whom they must regulate. A television channel, after all, is a highly valuable piece of property. The dispensing of such property should never be influenced by any conflict of interest which stems from the showering of gifts upon the dispensator. Such is one crucial facet of the conflict-of-interest controversy.

Conflict of interest does not always take this form. Frequently it derives from a person's own acquisitions, rather than from offerings pressed upon him. During the very recent past, Senate committees investigating the qualifications of various Cabinet appointees of President Eisenhower have suggested that these men sell their stocks in industries negotiating contracts with the Government. Such suggestions have affected the corporate holdings of Presidential selections from the business world like ex-Secretary of the Treasury George M. Humphrey and his successor, Robert B. Anderson, and ex-Secretary of Defense Charles E. Wilson and the man who succeeded him, Neil H. McElroy.

The implication has been that an inevitable conflict of interest occurs when the head of a government department must rule or pass upon contracts with a firm in which he himself retains an equity. It evidently would be taxing human nature too strenuously to expect strict impartiality in such circumstances.

Whenever the conflict-of-interest issue is raised on the floor of the Senate or House, or before a committee of either chamber, the public stirs uneasily. The taint of corruption or shady dealings is sniffed in the land. Murmurings come from the political opposition, and often in highly inflammatory terms. The slurs over baked hams and deep freezes in the Truman Administration still rankle Democrats and have not been forgiven. My Senate colleague from Oregon, Wayne Morse, has declared that President Eisenhower himself is guilty of a conflict of interest by accepting gifts of cattle and farm machinery for his Gettysburg estate.

The claim of conflict of interest, whether brought against Republican or Democratic regimes, invariably makes people commence to suspect that government has departed a long way from the ideals of Thomas Jefferson, who said, "When a man assumes a public trust, he should consider himself as public property."

Yet, as a member of the United States Senate, I have some uneasy feelings of my own over the entire conflict-of-interest question, especially because the voicing of this question in any particular episode almost always begins in the halls of Congress. Congress has set itself up to scrutinize the ethics and morals of the Executive branch of government. But who watches Congress with respect to conflict of interest? Is the sentry unsullied? In other words, who polices the policeman?

Many different statutes pertain to the general matter of conflict of interest. One of these laws stipulates that "no person appointed to the office of Secretary of the Treasury shall directly or indirectly be concerned or interested in carrying on the business of trade or commerce, or be owner in whole or in part of any sea vessel, or purchase by himself, or another in trust for him, any public lands or other public property, or be concerned in the purchase or disposal of any public securities of any state, or of the United States...."

This is all well and good. The Secretary of our Treasury must be above suspicion. No conflict of interest should ever attach to him. Yet the Secretary merely carries out the broad policies of taxation, or maritime customs and arrangements, of tariffs, of banking procedures, which are fixed for him by Congress. Why, then, do not these restraints apply to members of the Senate and the House? They can own a "sea vessel," buy any securities they please, negotiate to run their grazing herds on public lands, and be very much interested indeed "in carrying on the business of trade and commerce." Furthermore, they can accept speaking fees. Some of these fees not only run to $1,000 or more, but are offered by organizations and groups directly interested in issues pending before Congress.

What is the theory behind such a double standard of morality? Can it possibly be the settled notion of the American people that an appointee of the President, serving as Secretary of the Treasury, is likely to be motivated by his own financial self-interest but that an elected Senator or Representative will be immune to any of these temptations? Is Congress a law unto itself?

"You can't make a Senator do anything!" exclaimed a Senator, Karl E. Mundt of South Dakota, during the dispute between the Army and the late Senator Joseph R. McCarthy in 1954. This seems to be the situation which lurks behind Congressional exemption from the code imposed on Executive agencies. A Senator, or his counterpart in the House of Representatives, can do no wrong. This may have been what was meant by Dr. George Galloway and his collaborator, Cabell Phillips, when they wrote five years ago, in a book about the legislative process: "No one ever investigates Congress."

Yet I fear that it has a corroding effect on government generally, when a member of the President's Cabinet can be ordered to jettison his corporate portfolio by Senators who themselves may be dabbling in oil, cotton futures, television, hotel chains or uranium. If Federal commissioners are to be pilloried for accepting hacienda suites at Palm Springs or airplane tickets to Palm Beach, how can Senators and Representatives continue profitable associations with law firms retained by banks, railroads, labor unions and utility companies?

I want to emphasize that my thesis implies no criticism of any specific Senators or members of the House. All are only doing what comes naturally. This is a matter of group behavior and not individual sin. The pattern has become accepted over the years. Most of our law-makers are fundamentally honorable and trustworthy, but custom and habit apparently justify many contradictions. Although celebrated careers as Congressional investigators have been built by looking for fly specks in governmental bureaus, our country's annals record few instances when conflict of interest ever was applied to a Senator or Representative.

In fact, Daniel Webster of Massachusetts has just been selected by a bipartisan Senate committee as one of the five greatest Senators of our history, to be heralded in a special portrait gallery at the Capitol. The choice of Senator Webster was recently eulogized on the floor of the Senate. But Webster once wrote to Nicholas Biddle, president of the controversial Bank of the United States: "I believe that my retainer has not been renewed or refreshed as usual. If it be wished that my relation to the bank should be continued, it may be well to send me the usual retainers."

This was conflict of interest with a vengeance – even at the point of blunt threats. The Bank of the United States was in need of a Federal charter at the moment. Yet Senator Webster has been chosen in our own time as one of the Senate's immortals. Why, in view of this, should lesser legislators worry about owning "sea vessels" or acquiring radio and television outlets?

I am encouraged by the fact that I am by no means the only member of Congress troubled by the double standard surrounding the current crisis over conflict of interest. Senator Paul H. Douglas of Illinois has lamented many times that members of the House and Senate may accept valuable gifts or speaking fees which could be the downfall of a bureaucrat in one of the Executive departments. Senators Thomas C. Hennings Jr. of Missouri and Albert Gore of Tennessee have sought to provide far closer scrutiny over funds spent for lobbying, influence-peddling and other avenues to Congressional favor. And Representative Thomas M. Pelly, a Republican sent to the capital by the populous Seattle district, recently told his colleagues:

"I raise the question as to whether bankers should be on committees that consider matters of benefit to banks? Should members who own farms frame legislation to support the prices of crops they raise themselves? ... It is pretty obvious that if I owned an oil well, I should not be free to participate in setting the rates for depletion. Members of Congress have raised their eyebrows and also their voices, at times, over situations involving the ethics of members of the Executive branch of government. It seems to be the standard we have set for ourselves is not as high as the standard we have set for others."

As a member of the Senate Committee on Post Office and Civil Service, I have heard Presidential appointees to the Postal Department asked if they had any properties which might benefit from special classes of mailing rates. Of course, a conflict of interest was at stake in their replies. Yet a good many members of Congress are engaged in daily or weekly newspaper publishing, and no question ever seems to be raised when they vote on the second-class mailing schedules that apply to newspapers.

I am the author of quite a few books, but I can participate without criticism in Senate discussions deciding the fate of the separate mailing rate for book publishers. As a Senator, I am free to file for a radio-station wave length, to bid on national forest timber or to prospect for minerals on Federal land. Yet, as a presidential appointee to the agencies handling these matters, I would be forbidden under the conflict-of-interest statute from any such undertakings. Ironically, the Senate and the House form the supreme policy-making arm of our country, which sets the rules for all these responsibilities of government, and many more, besides.

However, it is not even in this realm that I regard Congress as being the most paradoxically immune to the conflict-of-interest standard by which it measures Federal bureaus. I think the greatest degree of irony and contrast is to be found in the freedom of candidates for the Senate and House to collect huge campaign funds.

William S. White of the New York *Times*, author of the Senate analysis, *Citadel*, has written that it requires a $200,000 exchequer to win election as a senator in a state of small population and at least $1,000,000 in a large industrial state. This, it seems to me, narrows to a *reductio ad absurdum* the spectacle of a Senate committee breaking a poor Presidential appointee on the wheel because he owns some General Motors stock or is married to a woman who manufactures military uniforms.

To begin with, I believe that the native integrity of the average human being is most jeopardized by favors he has accepted from somebody else rather than because of any holdings which have long been his own. Our political system being what it is, most successful Senatorial candidates take the oath of office after having received substantial benefactions from the political-action funds of labor organizations or from the owners of distilleries, sawmills, gas corporations, power companies, breweries, airlines and mines.

If this is not conflict of interest, what is it? Such groups are as involved in legislation as was the Bank of the United States during

Webster's era. Can it be that a Federal Communications Commissioner is susceptible to the "loan" of a color television set, but a Senator or Representative incurs no commensurate obligation because of a $5,000 campaign contribution from a leading stockholder in a broadcasting chain?

What is the solution to all this? Must we continue standards of behavior for the Executive and Legislative branches of government under which one is expected to observe antiseptic purity while the other may fare forth every two years in quest of campaign treasuries of ever-increasing size? It is estimated that all the major political contests of 1956 cost at least $200,000,000 for radio and television time, elaborate headquarters, paid managers and agents, signboards along miles and miles of trunk highways, and prodigious quantities of buttons, badges, ballons and similar gadgets. This sum is sufficient to create more conflict-of-interest dilemmas than could be unearthed by Scotland Yard, the Royal Mounties and the Federal Bureau of Investigation combined.

My recommendations for correction are these:

1   The Executive and Legislative wings should be governed by conflict-of-interest laws as nearly similar as their differing structures and composition will permit.

2   Neither administrative appointees nor members of Congress should be required to divest themselves of their corporate holdings or other possessions. The mere public listing of these equities annually ought to be enough in a democracy to assure that such ownership will not be subject to abuse.

3   This public listing should include a record of any speaking fees larger than $100, of any travel reimbursement from private sources higher than this amount, of any gifts greater than this value except from members of one's own family.

4   President Theodore Roosevelt's recommendation of 1907 should be put into effect, which would liberate political candidates from the necessity of raising large purses from private donors by authorizing the Federal Government to finance each major party with a contri-

bution of 20 cents per voter in Presidential years and of 15 cents in the "off-year" elections.

5   Enforcement of these statutes should be removed as far as possible from politics, through a special non-partisan agency in the office of the Comptroller General, which would supervise all laws dealing with conflict of interest or corrupt practices.

6   The net financial worth of a Federal administrator or member of Congress should be disclosed at the start of his public career, in much the same manner as Adlai E. Stevenson revealed his holdings in the Presidential campaign of 1952. I am convinced this kind of yearly accounting would do far more to curtail favoritism or pocket-lining than any number of artificial limitations, such as forbidding a Secretary to own a "sea vessel" or trying to prevent a Senator from establishing a law-firm connection in his home state.

7   Adequate provision should be made by the government for the office expenses and travel needs of members of Congress, so they will not be under compulsion to compete for questionable speaking fees and otherwise feel an urgency to augment their incomes. I know that many Senators exhaust their $1800 stationary allowance and $300 fund for postage stamps long before the year is ended. After that, these supplies are paid for by the member himself. In addition, one round trip annually between the national capital and a legislator's home state is rarely sufficient and plane or train fares across the continent to California, Oregon or Nevada are expensive.

These proposals, in and of themselves, will not promote honesty in government. The stain of corruption or careless ethics is not thus easily removed. Nor are rules ever a substitute for men and women of character and enduring integrity. But such a code would have the great virtue of placing the Executive and Legislative branches on the same moral footing. And one of its genuine additional benefits would be to provide for enforcement outside the ordinary political zones of government. The Comptroller General is appointed for fifteen years; that fact furnishes insulation from the hazards of each passing election.

Today, for example, we have statutes dealing with the disclosure of campaign contributors, but such laws are honored principally in the breach. My 1954 campaign in Oregon was comparatively under-financed. My Republican adversary outspent me by at least 75 per-cent. I had not one billboard. I had a small two-room office near the top of an unpretentious building, only two poorly paid employees and few printed brochures. My campaign had only limited television time – a few one-minute spots and a single fifteen-minute program with my wife, who was a candidate for the Legislature, on the night before the election.

Imagine my consternation, therefore, when I discovered that the Senatorial contest in sparsely settled Oregon had reported a much larger expenditure to the Secretary of the Senate than extravagant campaigns in some of the states of greatest population. I decided, then and there, that few United States Attorneys or Attorneys General cared to invoke the rather ambiguous Corrupt Practices Act against United States Senators.

But until we end this double standard, until we make a Senator as scrupulous about conflict of interest as a Cabinet member must be, we shall merely be shadow-boxing when we talk about coming to grips with shabbiness in government. Nor will we be dealing fairly with Congress itself unless we promote affirmative and enlightened steps to free the average Senator or Representative from the humiliating necessity, every few years, of collecting a well-filled purse to finance his continuance in public office.

They Never Go Back to Pocatello

from *Adventures in Politics*, 1954

Neuberger's best-known contribution to the language of American politics was his reference to former senators and congressmen who don't go back to their hometowns. The line about Pocatello was inspired by former Senator Glen Taylor of Idaho, who doomed his political career by running for the vice-presidency on Henry Wallace's 1948 Progressive party ticket. Taylor later moved to California. After his loss to Neuberger, Senator Cordon stayed in Washington, D.C., instead of returning to Roseburg. Morse, too, retained his posh Watergate apartment until the end of his life. Former Idaho Senator Frank Church preferred to live in Washington, D.C., following his 1980 defeat for reelection. So did former House Ways and Means Committee Chairman Al Ullman of Oregon, who was defeated for reelection in 1980 partly because he had lost touch with his Eastern Oregon district. There have been notable exceptions to the rule, however, including former Oregon Congressman Bob Duncan, who now lives in Yachats, and Maurine Neuberger of Portland. Had Richard L. Neuberger lived beyond his Senate term, there's little doubt that he would have come back to Oregon.

IN THE DUSK OF evening I swung down from my Pullman in the Union Pacific's streamlined City of Portland at Pocatello and picked my way across the tracks, while the yellow diesel-electric locomotive was being serviced with fuel and lubricating oil.

Idaho's dark sagebrush uplands bulked like battlements above the sprawling brick station. At the ticket office I went through the local telephone directory once, and then I glanced up nervously at the sound of couplers bumping in the yards.

"Looking for someone, mister?" asked a lanky man with a green eyeshade behind the grille of the window. "Maybe I can help you."

I told him that I wanted to phone a friend of mine who had been a United States Senator from Idaho until a few years back. I once had gone fishing with the Senator and I hoped to say hello to him.

"Heck, mister," said the Union Pacific station agent, "I ain't seen him since he got licked for reelection. Knew him pretty well, too. Used to fix up his tickets for him. But he don't live here any more. Those guys never come back to Pocatello."

Idaho citizens in general have decided that neither do they come back to Twin Falls, Boise, or Coeur d'Alene. Nor is this situation confined to Idaho. Men sent to Congress by Casper, Salt Lake City, Los Angeles, Des Moines, Charleston, and innumerable other places have also absented themselves permanently from the localities they formerly represented in the Senate and House of the national government.

It is one of the ironies of American politics that men who have been clogging the *Congressional Record* with tales of the glories and blessings of their constituencies take repulse at the polls as the signal never to look on those constituencies again.

On defeat, they vanish from local ken as completely as Ichabod Crane. Occasionally these vanquished politicians do not even return to crate the family possessions, trusting this chore to the impersonal hands of a moving crew.

Idaho, ribbed by lofty ranges and white-riffled rivers, has magnificent attractions, but evidently not for the individuals who have spoken for Idaho in the Congress of the United States. Three Idaho ex-Senators and three Idaho ex-Representatives still live, and some of them have roamed the continent – managing the Tennessee Valley Authority, constructing housing projects in Alaska, teaching in Ohio. These places are a far piece from the state which once hallowed them with Congressional authority.

Practically every state – especially states in the Far West and on the Middle-Western prairies – has lost former members of the Federal House and Senate through self-imposed exile. The exiles are an impressive tribe. They count four warriors even from sparsely settled Nevada. They include such formidable figures as Elmer Benson, ex-Governor and ex-Senator from Minnesota and Henry F. Ashurst, for 28 years a Senator from Arizona.

This would seem to be entirely a Federal problem. After all, the statesmen disappear from their home states only when their Federal tenure is at an end. Yet, peculiarly enough, it is even more a dilemma for the states in general and for state government in particular.

There goes on continually a sluicing off of many of the most able people in state politics. The process involves three distinct stages: (1) the man or woman of appeal at the polls quits his position in state government to seek a seat in the Federal Congress; (2) eventually he or she is separated by the voters from the Congressional seat; (3) the defeated member of Congress stays on in Washington, D.C., or some other distant place and never returns to the home state.

This drain of talent never stops. It is perennial. The Governor or State Senator asks himself why he should be struggling with such matters as a new cell block for the penitentiary when he could be deciding the more exotic issues of war and peace, wire tapping, and FBI appropriations.

The Governor's wife asks questions, too. Part of the lure of the national capital is unquestionably social, which means the distaff side of the politician's family. Standing in the reception line at a typical hotel in a state capital city of perhaps 35,000 population, the home-town girl whom the Governor married long ago has visions of the Sulgrave Club, of tea at the White House, of cocktails at the British embassy, of a bearded ambassador from a strange land gravely kissing her manicured hand.

With these notions in mind, the wife of the Governor comes to look upon the state capital as pretty small potatoes. Why should her talents be limited to this cramped social domain? Should she not operate in a wider, more glittering realm? Accompanying her husband to a potluck supper of the Pitchfork Union suddenly seems drab and unglamourous, when she might be gracefully declining hors d'oeuvres proffered by the servants of European nobility.

Such pressures few politicians can resist, for they frequently are husbands first and public servants second. If mamma wants to go to Washington, then state government abruptly becomes less important to the Governor than Federal government. State's rights are urgent, but only in political speeches. Mamma's rights – and wishes – are with him at mealtime, in the boudoir, and at many places in between.

So he heads for Washington, and state government has lost a capable leader. Worst of all, he never comes back.

II

After nearly three decades as a Senator from Arizona, Henry Ashurst told his colleagues that he would return "to the starry stillness of an Arizona desert night, the scarlet glories of her blooming cactus, the petrified forest which leafed through its green millenniums and put on immortality seven thousand years ago."

Yet Senator Ashurst did not get farther west permanently than the Wardman Park Hotel in Washington, D.C., and the closest that he approached to the petrified forest was the fringe of foliage between the Wardman Park and the busy traffic along Connecticut Avenue.

In choosing to make his full-time residence in the country's capital, the Arizona statesman was following the standard practice. His decision was not abnormal in any respect.

The march of political talent from the states to Washington is all in one direction. And if the defeated politician does not remain in Washington, he generally picks out some sanctuary that is equally distant from the state where he got his political start.

Most of these storm cellars were not dug on the spur of the moment. Their occupants thought about them during many years of statesmanship. "I always realized," said Professor Burton L. French of Ohio's Miami University, who had been Congressman for twenty-six years from the forests of Northern Idaho, "that persons in elective political offices are subject to shifts of sentiment. With this idea, over the years I kept in close touch with educational work. I felt that when my work in Congress would be over I should go to some university faculty as a professor of government."

"My inclination and desire is naturally to return to my home city of Twin Falls, Idaho," admitted Addison Smith, another ex-Idaho Congressman, "but as I know of no way to be profitably occupied there, and am doing very well in Washington, D.C., I must forego the pleasure of being among my Idaho friends."

Jonathan Bourne, Jr., first Senator to be elected by a direct vote of the people, never went back to Oregon, because he frankly confessed that Washington, D.C., seemed "a whole lot more like home."

Some of the reasons for such a situation were hinted at by Senator Estes Kefauver of Tennessee, when he said that "people here on Capitol Hill, particularly those from the far-off Western states, are away from home so long that they are in danger of losing touch with their constituents. They get in an ivory tower, so to speak." And Representative W.R. Poage, of Texas, suggested that members of Congress be paid "a regular mileage and regular per diem," so they can go back to their districts more frequently. He is opposed to the present system, under which Congressman receives twenty cent a mile for approximately one trip a year, but the rest of the time must pungle up for his fare. He believes that most people think Senators and Representatives get the twenty-cent rate for every trip. "It is embarrassing to return home," says Poage, "and have the folks think, 'Well, he is just grafting on the Government.'"

Senator Bourne, a rich man, simply conceded he had more friends in Washington than in the state which had sent him there. But many Congressmen stay on in the national capital because it offers greater possibilities of paying the grocery bill. Before the recent upping of their salaries and a generous expense allowance, a lot of them complained that they ended up their political careers in the red because of money they had to pay out of their own pockets for clerk hire.

Some Congressional rejects get Government plums, others crab apples. At the end of eight years in the House, Bernard J. Gehrmann, a Progressive from Wisconsin, went to work for the Farm Security Administration at $3800 annually. On the other hand, Harry H. Schwartz, New Deal Democrat from Wyoming, became a member of the National Mediation Board at $10,000, after his defeat for re-election to the Senate in 1942.

Seats on numerous boards and commissions call for compensation approximating that of a Senator or Congressman. "If you get trimmed while your party is in power and you've been regular," observes one ex-Senator, "you can stay in Washington with your standard of living undisturbed. But if the other crowd is in the saddle, you probably will have to move into a clerk's office and a smaller house."

After Oklahoma's voters ended the tenure of Josh Lee as their Senator in 1942, President Roosevelt appointed the silver-tongued New Dealer to the Civil Aeronautics Board, where he continued to enjoy a senatorial pay level. A former Democratic Senator from Nevada, seventy-three-year-old Charles B. Henderson, became chairman of the RFC. Bennett Champ Clark, turned down for a third senatorial term, was able to avoid a return to Missouri when his erstwhile colleague, Harry Truman, appointed him to the Court of Appeals for the District of Columbia.

Bountifulness to repudiated legislators does not flow only from the White House. Senators and Representatives reserve a tender spot in their hearts for defeated comrades. "There, but for the grace of God, go I" is a prevalent Congressional emotion whenever the election-day wreckage is inventoried.

Wall Doxey, sergeant at arms of the Senate under the Democrats, was once a Representative and later a Senator from Mississippi. A clerk of the House, South Trimble, served three terms as a Congressman from Kentucky. Melvin Mass, former Representative from a St. Paul district, became chief investigator of the Naval Affairs Committee on which he sat as a member. Other ex-legislators occupy liaison and legal posts on Capitol Hill.

Lobbying, of course, offers a snug refuge for many powerful Congressional figures whose constituents have tired of their services. They represent every element from the CIO to the Republican National Committee. Some merely are counselors-at-law, speaking for such clients as choose to knock on their glass-paneled doors. A few of the friends of the late Robert M. La Follette, Jr., one of the great luminaries of Wisconsin politics, believe that his tragic suicide may have stemmed from the fact that he stayed on in the national capital as a representative of various private clients, rather than returning to Wisconsin to carry on the political fight against McCarthyism and other forces traditionally abhorrent to the La Follette family. Despondency may have followed this retreat.

Yet to return to one's home state after a defeat at the polls could mean starting all over again at the bottom of the political staircase. It would be tantamount to Johnny Mize or Joe Di Maggio beginning once more in sandlot or high-school baseball. What would a man who had been State Senator, Governor, Congressman, and U.S. Senator think in his inner thoughts if he had to struggle to be even a State Senator for a second time?

It is easier to stay on in Washington, where the rewards total up to more financially and perhaps even more politically. After the Democrats had retired him from the United States Senate, John A. Danaher of Connecticut became a Congressional lieutenant on the staff of the Republican National Committee at $20,000 a year. When the Republicans eventually came back into national power, President Eisenhower named Danaher to be a Federal judge. Remaining in Washington had paid off far more durably than a return to Connecticut possibly could have promised.

William A. Ekwall, Republican Representative from Portland, Oregon, delivered a speech telling his constituents that even if they defeated him, he wished nothing better than to return and dwell among them for the rest of his days. They took him at his word. He now lives in Bronxville, New York, having been appointed by President Franklin D. Roosevelt as a minority member of the United States Customs Court.

Albert G. Simms of Albuquerque, New Mexico, was one of the Congressmen who did go home after defeat. He thought the reason he went back to the wide open spaces may have been that he was only a one-termer. "It is my observation," he said, "that some members of Congress who have had long tenure of office gradually lose their contact with the home people, and so Washington then becomes home for them."

The late Senator Charles L. McNary of Oregon used to claim that strong psychological factors worked to keep a man from returning to the constituency which repudiated him. "As he walks down the street," said McNary, a shrewd observer of politics, "he thinks each person he passes is one of the votes that beat him. In addition, Washington has an intoxication for many people. You rub elbows with the mighty. You feel important. It is not easy to buy a ticket to Podunk after being at the center of things. One's self-esteem takes an awful drop."

III

But the tendency to rush to Washington – and then never to return – adds up to bad news for state government.

Probably the Governor or State Senator is right who decides that his political talents, having been fully developed, are needed at the level of government where the most important decisions are to be taken. These, of course, are decisions in the international sphere. Yet, after defeat, is he justified in staying away forever from the state which gave him his start?

In Canada, I have observed, there is great flexibility between the national and provincial spheres of government. It is not uncommon for a member of the Federal Parliament to retire as an MP in order to try to rehabilitate his party's fortunes within the province. Then, if successful, he becomes the provincial Premier, a position comparable in authority and duties to the Governor of a state. Many Premiers and cabinet ministers in the ten provinces of Canada are men who once sat under the soaring Gothic spire of the Peace Tower in Ottawa, where the national House of Commons convenes. Canadians do not regard a withdrawal from the Federal to the provincial echelon of government as at all out of the ordinary.

This has happened so rarely in the United States that an exception only serves to prove the rule. James F. Byrnes was U.S. Senator from South Carolina, Supreme Court Justice, and Secretary of State. Now he is the Governor of South Carolina. Yet this occurred not as part of a traditional political career, but because Byrnes broke completely with the Democratic Party, which had sponsored these high honors in his behalf.

Yet Byrnes was willing to go back to his home state to live, and for this he deserves a measure of credit. The capital city of Columbia was not too small for him after the glamour of Washington and the chancellories of Europe.

Few other politicians follow this route. Once Mon Wallgren had been counted out for re-election as Governor of the state of Washington, he took off for Palm Springs, California. An ex-Georgia Congressman became executive vice-president of the Air Transport Association, and ex-Virginia Congressman became head of the American Plant Food Council, and an ex-Massachusetts Congressman became counsel for Transcontinental & Western Airlines. Naturally, these tempting positions required the presence of the former statesmen in Washington, D.C. No retreat to state politics for them!

Once a man or woman has left the State Legislature or the gubernatorial chambers for a fling at Congress, he or she is gone for good. In this essential, state government is worse off than the minor leagues in baseball. The minors train recruits for the major leagues. But after a baseball player has finished his period of usefulness in the big show, he usually totes his ailing arm or slowing legs back to the Pacific Coast League or International Association for a few seasons of moderate usefulness.

This almost never takes place in politics. After a politician has left the state capitol building for Congress, he is seen no more at his old haunts – except possibly on a fleeting outdoor trip to catch steelhead or rainbows with other assorted VIPs. And because he fails to return to the home state to make his residence, he is not even available to advise the next generation. The constant loss of talent and experience does state government no good in the long run.

Yet perhaps Harry S. Truman may be setting an example which others, some time, will choose to emulate. In all the welter of abuse directed at Truman, it is forgotten that he went back to Independence, Missouri, while Herbert Hoover went not to Palo Alto, California, but to the Waldorf Towers on New York's Park Avenue.

Harry Truman was not too proud or too big for his britches to return to his home state. All the abuse by the Jenners and Brownells and McCarthys cannot erase this bright spot from the ex-President's shield! He was loyal enough to Independence to go back there to make his home.

In Defense of the Politician

New York Times Magazine, 2 NOVEMBER 1958

Neuberger believed that politics was an honorable profession and sought to encourage new people to participate. This article was written in the wake of a major political scandal, the forced resignation of White House chief of staff Sherman Adams, who had accepted favors from a Boston industrialist and then had intervened in his behalf with federal regulatory agencies. The Democratic party was helped by Adams' fall and by the 1958 recession.

In his opening paragraph, Neuberger is referring to Senator Edward Bartlett of Alaska, a former prospector; and the New York battle of the millionaires in which Republican Nelson A. Rockefeller ousted Democratic Governor W. Averell Harriman.

THE QUEST for public office in the United States enlists every segment of the vast mosaic of American life. This year in the nascent state of Alaska, for example, a former prospector for "colors," or gold, in the creeks is an overwhelming favorite to be elected to the United States Senate. Two of the wealthiest men in the country are competing in New York for the honor of governing their country's most populous state.

Yet, despite the fact that political leaders come from varied backgrounds like the rest of Americans, as a group they do not rank high in the esteem of the average voter. On all too many occasions I hear candidates spoken of as low and undignified creatures who will stoop to any shabby trick or maneuver to get themselves elected.

Americans are always ready to believe the worst of those who aspire to operate their government, whether at the local or state or national level. In fact, a poll of a few years ago revealed that a mere 20 percent of American parents would like to see their own sons make a career of politics. Seventy percent were definitely opposed to such a prospect, and the remaining 10 percent were undecided. This is not an encouraging outlook for a nation whose fate may depend upon the quality of its political leaders.

I am convinced that a great deal of this distaste for politics stems from the excesses and exaggerations of political campaigns. A warlike atmosphere prevails at most party headquarters as the zero hour nears. Genuine hostility often exists against the opposition. Furthermore, candidates often are surrounded by public-relations specialists who tend to look upon victory as an end in itself, rather than as a means of advancing broad programs in the public interest. Ethics, accuracy and propriety mean less to these men than winning a majority on Election Day.

The average American thinks of his political ideal as a citizen of great dignity, of grandeur. He recalls from his textbooks scenes of Jefferson and Lincoln, and he has thrilling memories of FDR. All too frequently, the horseplay and the frivolities of modern politics make him believe that these illustrious men were of a vanishing breed, who never again will be seen in the land. He forgets, of course, that Jefferson, Lincoln and FDR were practical politicians who had to participate to considerable degree in the political maneuverings and compromises of their eras.

My wife and I like to speak to college and high school audiences whenever possible. This is where we find the cynicism about politics and politicians especially disturbing, because people of education and scholarship are needed more in public life today than ever before. Issues have become incredibly complex and detailed.

Young people tell us they are reluctant to enter politics for two principal reasons. One is what they consider the undue emphasis on political partisanship. The other is the character assassination which has increased alarmingly during recent years. For example, I have had cited to me on several occasions the bitter fight which certain Republican Congressmen carried on recently against the bill providing pensions and office allowances for former Presidents of the United States, merely because one of the beneficiaries of the proposal would be Harry Truman, an active and ardent Democrat.

I always try to tell these audiences that there generally is another side to each such incident. When the proposed Presidential pension was in trouble in the House of Representatives, it received a strong endorsement from the only other living ex-president, Herbert Hoover, a Republican, although he himself is a man of independent wealth and thus not in need of such an annuity from his Government. Mr. Hoover specifically mentioned the heavy burden of correspondence carried on by Mr. Truman as one of the justifications for the bill.

In addition, the country witnessed during the last session of Congress the two leading Democrats, Speaker of the House Sam Rayburn and Senate Majority Leader Lyndon B. Johnson, putting aside partisanship to sustain the Republican Administration on the politically unpopular question of not providing across-the-board cut in income taxes.

In politics, the American people have an impulsive tendency to judge from the particular to the general, especially if the judgment is inclined to be unfavorable. Let a prominent politician accept a deep-freeze or an expensive garment from a friend in difficulties with the Government, and the public will immediately believe that all individuals in public life are rogues. No such sweeping verdicts are arrived at in other avenues of endeavor.

The Internal Revenue Service has reported that in 1957 some 377,000 business firms pocketed over $300 million which had been withheld from the paychecks of their employes for income taxes. Announcements like this rarely are followed by indignant remarks that no business man is to be trusted any more. Only the politician is measured, by the worst of his clan.

Another element in the public's view of the politician is the failure to realize the extent of his industry and his devotion to his job. I have never observed people who work harder than politicians. Their day is never done. Constituents and lobbyists are after them from dawn until bedtime. During the closing days of the Eighty-fifth Congress, the Senate was often in session from 10 in the morning until midnight.

On August 14, Senator Carl Hayden of Arizona, chairman of the Appropriations Committee, was on his feet in the Senate chamber, hour after hour, explaining and discussing the intricate details of the Supplemental Appropriations Bill. Senator Hayden is 81 years old. Yet when the bill was tied up late at night in heated debate over the widely publicized amendment to forbid any study of possible "surrender" of the United States, Senator Hayden characteristically said:

"Mr. President, I am of an age when I do not need as much sleep as others do. However, there are younger members of the Senate I know would like to proceed with the pending business. I wonder if it would be possible to obtain a vote on the pending amendment."

I have seen Senators like Theodore Green of Rhode Island, 91, and James E. Murray of Montana, 82, so tired on the Senate floor that one feared for their health. Yet they would not quit their seats late in the evening because an important roll call might be imminent.

Almost by rote, the voter thinks of a politician as somebody ruled completely by expediency and self-interest. I believe this conception is belied by numerous events of recent years.

Congress, prodded by both Presidents Truman and Eisenhower, has voted many billions of dollars for programs of foreign aid which are frequently misunderstood at home. Such programs are vulnerable to demagogic attack by unscrupulous opponents. Yet the professional politicians who make up the membership of the Senate and the House have consistently voted funds for these policies, which certainly set a new international standard for responsibility and realistic altruism.

Individual acts of political bravery are constantly taking place – and with comparatively scant recognition. Senator William Knowland, facing the stiffest kind of political competition in his home state, voted against an amendment to boost Social Security increases from 10 to 25 percent, which hundreds of thousands of elderly residents of California might believe would otherwise have gone to them. Despite much virulent sentiment in Texas against the school desegregation decisions of the Supreme Court, Senators Lyndon Johnson and Ralph Yarborough voted in opposition to those who would have fettered the Court in its future authority to review such matters.

Regardless of how one looks upon the merits of these acts, one can only respect the political independence and courage shown in them.

Demagogues there are, of course, who vote against every tax and for every appropriation; who orate against the specter of a Communist conspiracy at home and vote against funds for the military and diplomatic struggle against Soviet expansion abroad. Yet these men are conspicuous by the sheer fact that they consititute so small a minority.

How can the politician in America be given greater stature and dignity? What can be done to heighten his prestige? The best that America has ought to be available for posts in local, state and Federal Governments, but this will happen only if politics wins new esteem as a career.

In my opinion, these positive steps would help profoundly toward the attainment of such a goal:

1   Schools and universities should place far more emphasis on the purely political aspects of government. Students must be made to realize that the founders and the saviors of the nations were, in their day and time, politicians. Emphasis ought to be placed on the fact that anybody who seeks office is, *ipso facto*, a politician. Jefferson, Lincoln and Theodore Roosevelt, Gifford Pinchot, Cordell Hull and Charles Evans Hughes were politicians, and politics can be a noble calling in our own generation, too.

2   Greater responsibility should be lodged in a relatively few top policy-making elective officials rather than diffused among literally hundreds of petty offices on the ballot. Politics and politicians often suffer the most in prestige in those states where so many candidates appear on the ballot that even the worst buffoon has a chance to be elected, because of voter's boredom or confusion.

If a President of the United States can be trusted to appoint a Secretary of Defense, with his immense powers over the country's treasure and over America's youth, then Governors should be able to appoint all their administrative assistants, and county commissioners to appoint purely technical local officials.

3   Political elections should be limited to top officials responsible for major policy decisions on administration, and administration as such should be left to administrators. If this could be done, then maybe someday these officials could escape the time-hallowed maxim that unswerving attention to constituents' personal problems is the key to political success.

In Congress, this means that Representatives and Senators are expected to turn from legislation affecting millions of people, in order to lend weight to the special claims or wishes of individuals before Federal agencies. On another level, members of Congress have been criticized for intervening on behalf of local interests in matters before the Federal Communications Commission, the Civil Aeronautics Board or the Interstate Commerce Commission.

The responsibility for this lies with the American public as much as with elected officials. Regardless of occasional public indignation over "political influence," the legislator who sticks to legislation and leaves the execution of the laws to administrators can expect to have his dereliction exploited as a political issue by his opponent in the next election. In no large modern government is the elected representative so personally the property of his constituents as he is in the United States.

4   The American focus on the personality of the politician, rather than on the policies for which he and his party stand, also distorts our political life. The candidate, rather than his program, is "sold" to the electorate.

I believe that the purely public relations carnival of political campaigning should be discouraged and restrained as much as possible. More mature attention to issues rather than personalities, through education and press coverage, can contribute to this. To accomplish such a goal, it is also essential to reform our present system of financing elections so as to remove the competitive opportunities for "outselling" the opposition.

To assure all bona fide candidates of a fair hearing and at the same time reduce these opportunities for abuse, I believe we should adopt the recommendation made to Congress in 1907 by President Roosevelt for federal financing of basic election campaign needs as an essential cost of democratic self-government.

In the first place, this would make reasonable means of access to the electorate available to all candidates on equal terms, sparing them the unpleasant and undesirable chore of having to go, hat in hand, to big contributors for campaign donations. Secondly, the auditing and potential withholding of such public campaign funds would be a far more effective means than unenforceable criminal penalties for limiting privately collected contributions to small amounts and keeping a ceiling on total campaign spending.

5   All public officials should be reimbursed adequately enough to make such jobs attractive to able men, and to remove any temptation from offers of unwise or possibly improper gifts. This means not only that salaries should be sufficient, but that allowances for staff, office operation, mail, travel and similar expenses must likewise be adequate.

As a Senator, I find that my office expenses frequently are at least $500 a month over and above what I am allowed by the Government. Not being a person of private wealth, I must earn this money by writing or speaking for fees, giving away to colleges in my state any speaking fee from an organization with specific legislative interests. Members of Congress should be entirely liberated from many of these financial necessities.

6   An impartial and nonpartisan body, outside of government and politics itself should have the function of discouraging character blackmailing and name-calling in public life. It would operate along the lines of the Fair Campaign Practices Committee, whose work was described by its chairman, Charles P. Taft, in a recent issue of this magazine. But it should make sure that any candidate who goes too far in besmirching the reputation of an opponent is called to account.

Obviously, I do not advocate censorship, for that would be incompatible with our traditions of freedom of speech. But if deliberate indulgence in character assassination were discouraged through citations from a highly respected tribunal, I believe that our politics might be greatly raised in the public esteem.

All the blame for a nation's ills cannot be put upon its politicians. An informed and vigilant electorate is essential, too. Have we attained that goal when some 40 million adult citizens did not even take the trouble to go to the polls and vote in the 1956 Presidential election?

A member of a celebrated political family, Robert E. Merriam, now Deputy Assistant to the President for Interdepartmental Affairs, has written: "The brutal fact is that we still take this wonderful human invention – the free election – for granted.... We are loud in our protests when it does not work to suit us, louder still when someone tries to snatch it from our grasp.... If things go awry, we are quick to blame the wickedness of the other fellow, but the fact is that we are collectively responsible if the rascals take over."

Press, schools, pulpit, civic organizations, business groups, trade unions – all these have an obligation to inform and educate Americans on their duty to take a more active interest in political affairs.

The best of American talent, ability, knowledge and integrity is needed in every level of government. Will we be able to tap our reservoir of skills and honor if young Americans and their parents mistrust that process known as politics by which a mighty democracy has selected its public officials for nearly two centuries?

How Oregon Rescued a Forest

Harper's, APRIL 1959

Perhaps Neuberger's most notable legislative accomplishment for Oregon was his role in protecting the vast Klamath forest and marshland. Before Neuberger's election to the Senate, Congress had already passed legislation providing for the termination of the Klamath Indian Reservation. Like many liberals of the time, Neuberger supported termination as a step toward autonomy and self-determination for Native Americans. Termination of the Klamath tribe in Oregon and the Menominee tribe of Wisconsin in the 1950s proved to be a major setback for the Indians. Maurine Neuberger said in 1987 that her husband would have worked with Indian leaders to come up with a better alternative had he lived into the 1960s.

THE KLAMATH INDIANS of Southeastern Oregon – like most American Indian tribes – have an old history of sorrow. During the first years of the Eisenhower Administration, the Klamaths seemed fated for new disaster – not only to themselves but to the whole state of Oregon. But their story has turned into one of the few almost-bright chapters in what former Secretary of the Interior Douglas McKay caustically called "the Indian business." The turn came last summer, at the end of the 85th Congress, when a group of stout-hearted Republicans and Democrats joined forces in a rare bi-partisan action to conserve our natural resources.

In 1954 Congress had passed a bill terminating the reservation status of the Klamath people, and in due order the Klamaths, numbering some 2,133 men, women, and children, voted by a 77 percent majority to withdraw from the tribe and take, each and every one, his share of the assets. According to a surprise provision of the federal bill, every Klamath could collect $58,000 in cash. A family of four might end up with almost a quarter of a million dollars, snugly secure from income tax.

Yet these claims, totaling nearly $120 million, would not only destroy by auction sale one of the world's great forests of ponderosa pine and endanger a precious and rare waterfowl refuge; they would beggar the timber economy of the state of Oregon. What termination might do to the Klamath people themselves was summed up by Elnathan Davis, stern-faced secretary of the Tribal Council, one of the 23 percent minority who voted to remain in reservation status:

"It'll be like throwing a steak to the dogs. Too few of us are prepared to handle these things. The money might do us a lot more harm than good."

As matters now stand, the Klamaths will still get their money, for good or for ill, but the forests and the wildlife will be guarded by and for the American people. Here is how it happened.

When Douglas McKay was appointed as the first head of the Interior Department under the Eisenhower Administration, one of his declared objectives was to commence the process of ending federal trusteeship over the country's 350,000 Indians. This obligation was costing the Treasury at least $150 million annually. Opinions on the effectiveness of the reservation system were, to say the least, sharply divided. It made good political propaganda, along orthodox Republican lines, to be shutting down so expensive an undertaking.

Furthermore, many Indian tribes seemed to be deteriorating under this benevolent paternalism. Alcoholism was on the rise, the general level of education often on the wane. Indians, especially reservation Indians, were rarely able to share in the increased living standards and economic activity which had benefited so many Western states. Indeed, Robert W. Chandler, editor of the Bend, Oregon, *Bulletin*, had said of the Klamaths themselves that only sixteen had graduated from high school during a thirteen-year period, and but one of these had gone on to college. "This is the fault of the system imposed upon the Indians many years ago by the federal government, which is their guardian," Chandler added.

The original Klamath termination bill looked innocent enough. It provided for a long, orderly period in which the Klamaths would be prepared for life in the outside world, beyond the stately tree-stockaded reservation. No specific plan for managing the assets of the tribe could be put into effect until approved by the government. Presumably a private trust, overseen by some responsible bank, would replace the Bureau of Indian Affairs as supervisor of the property – nearly a million acres – which the Indians had been given at carbine point by treaty with their blue-clad cavalry conquerors in 1864.

But, at the eleventh hour during consideration of the termination bill, there was unobtrusively slipped into the legislation a provision allowing any tribal member to claim his proportionate share of the value of the reservation. Records of Senate and House committees leave amazingly vague exactly how this clause got into the bill. Some of us have always suspected that certain lumber operators, eager for a quick financial killing, knew about its origin. A greater mystery is why the Interior Department let the President of the United States sign a piece of legislation which had been so drastically transformed in character without any real explanation on the floor of either chamber of Congress – legislation, too, which held the fate of more than $100 million worth of Indian tribal property.

After President Eisenhower had approved this dubious law, a survey by the Stanford Research Institute revealed that over three-fourths of the members of the Klamath Tribe would elect to withdraw from the tribe under the moot provision and take their cash. But cash could result only if the trees were sold, and speedily. All at once, the timber economy of Southeastern Oregon faced the ugly prospect of boom and bust. And it would not be boom and bust for a few years. It would be for keeps.

In the Klamath Basin, many of the ponderosa pines are as tall as twenty-story office buildings, six feet in diameter. To stand in a grove of ponderosas is like being among the Corinthian columns of some cosmic temple. Because of careful management by trained foresters of the Indian Bureau, the prodigious Indian forest had survived in a region where much of the other privately-owned timber had long since vanished. Over the years logging operators, bidding competitively on the stumpage, had taken 4.6 billion board-feet of finest-quality pine off the reservation. This was enough lumber to house all the residents of the Pacific Coast metropolises of San Francisco, Portland and Seattle. Each tribal member collected $1,100 annually, tax free, from the sale of this timber. Yet prudent harvesting of only the ripe and mature trees had left some 4.2 billion board-feet of pine still standing. Patrolled by the same wise policies, 80 million feet of logs could have been taken off the Indian reservation each year in perpetuity, keeping Oregon sawmills in operation and Oregon lumberjacks on the payroll. Their paychecks would ring the cash registers of merchants in Klamath Falls, Bend, Medford and other nearby communities.

But now this had come to an apparent end. With at least 75 percent of the Klamaths pulling up stakes from the tribal society, a minimum of 3.3 billion feet of the ponderosa forest had to be liquidated virtually overnight to satisfy the legal claims of the withdrawing Indians. Oregon's lumber market was already as shaky as aspic because of the adverse impact of stiffening interest rates on the national demand for housing. Unemployment in Oregon had led the country during the previous three or four years. Now, the dumping of 3.3 billion board-feet of Indian timber could break apart a depressed lumber industry. A few opportunist operators might get the Indian forest for a song, because genuine competitive bidding would be practically out of the question when forty times the normal annual cut was put up for sale in one frantic grab.

But these operators would be the sole beneficiaries. Dr. Richard E. McArdle, chief of the U.S. Forest Service, pointed out that the flooding of the market could cost nearby National Forests in Oregon and northern California some $49.7 million in stumpage receipts. Inasmuch as one-fourth of this amount – about $12.4 million – would ordinarily have been allocated for the financing of schools and roads in ten counties, the chaos might thread all the way down into the classroom and ranch turnpike.

Nor did even this begin to encompass all the possible ravages to the region. The Klamaths' preserve is contiguous to Crater Lake National Park, although five or six times the size of that majestic mountain wonderland. For epochs the high Indian forest had soaked up rain and snow like a sponge, letting it run off gradually into Upper Klamath Lake, largest in Oregon, and through the gorges and canyons of many roaring rivers. The water sustained a huge 303,000-acre irrigated agricultural economy of potatoes, alfalfa, and diversified row crops. The Williamson River was unparalleled for trout fishing, and the Klamath River nurtured the important hydroelectric plants of the California-Oregon Power Company in both states. With the stripping bare of the Indian pine forest, all these beneficial uses could be imperiled by a shortage of water. The rhythmical capillary flow of the drainage from the uplands would be replaced by flash floods – and then choking drought.

The Indian reservation also contained the continent's most intensively used waterfowl marsh outside the refuge systems of the wildlife services of the United States and Canada. Such protection had never been essential as long as it sprawled within the cordon of safety assured by the Indian reservation. Eighty-five percent of the birds traveling the Pacific Flyway nested and fed on this fabulous marsh. I have seen redheads, canvasbacks, ruddies, and mallards rising from off its glistening surface in undulating waves that made the heart beat faster. But if the reservation had to be liquidated financially in order to pay each migrating Klamath $58,000, it was obvious that the marsh would no longer serve as a sanctuary for waterfowl. Peripatetic ducks and geese carry no wallets. Millions of nomadic birds, finding their nesting place drained for grazing purposes or farmland, might be driven by hunger to foraging on fields and crops. The inevitable out-of-season slaughter by growers would be bloody, and when would the birds come again – if ever?

It was obvious that somebody had goofed, and that somebody had to be the government of the United States – Interior Department, Senate, House, and President.

Amid the mounting anxiety, a thunderclap sounded. Secretary McKay had appointed three of his personal friends, all staid and reliable Republican businessmen, to handle the liquidation of the Klamath reservation at a salary of $1,000 monthly apiece. Now the chairman and dominant member of the three, sixty-eight-year-old Thomas B. Watters of Klamath Falls, imperturbably announced there was only one solution. The government itself had to buy the Klamath Indian reservation, and fast. Then the marsh could be made a game refuge, and the timber could be harvested under the same perpetual-cutting practices which had successfully guided the operation of the reservation for so many years. Any other alternative, added Watters, would result in "an economic disaster for our area that is too disturbing to contemplate."

Oregon was stunned. With much fanfare, termination of government supervision over the Klamaths had been heralded as a tremendous victory for free enterprise. Immense sections of land – formerly under the quasi-public status of the reservation – of course would be placed on the taxrolls as private timber holdings. The government would be saved millions in Congressional appropriations. The Indian Agency office could be permanently closed. What finer way to please Senator Byrd, then Secretary of the Treasury Humphrey, and the Hoover Commission in one fell stroke?

Yet Secretary McKay's hand-picked appointee was proposing that the government reverse the whole procedure and add the entire reservation to the already extensive federal holdings in Oregon – with the U.S. Treasury, of course footing the bill. For many decades, conservatives in Oregon politics had made a lively issue of the fact that the federal government owned half the land area of the state. But here was the former Republican Mayor of Klamath Falls warning that this government domain had to be increased, or the direst of calamities would occur.

"At first we thought Tom Watters might be touched in the head," I was told by Frank Jenkins, exuberant and forceful publisher of the Klamath Falls *Herald and News*. "Yet the more we studied the situation from every possible angle, the more we saw he was entirely right. The clear cutting of the Indian forest would have been a monstrous catastrophe for our state. But who could prevent it except the government?"

And so I introduced a bill early in 1957 to provide for federal purchase of the Klamath reservation, with the funds to be used for reimbursement of the 77 percent of the Klamath tribal members who wanted to leave their traditional bivouac grounds. The pine timber would be added to nearby National Forests, for sustained-yield management by the Forest Service. The marsh would become a refuge supervised by the Fish and Wildlife Service. In the meanwhile, as chairman for the Senate Indian Affairs Subcommittee, I had secured passage of an emergency measure delaying, until August of 1958, the time when the timber and the waterfowl marsh had to go on the auction block to satisfy the claims of withdrawing Indians. We had that much elbow room in which to save vast watersheds and natural resources in Southeastern Oregon. The patient Klamaths had agreed to the delay. Their sympathy with the white man's plight was truly heroic.

A dilemma was posed for Secretary McKay's successor at the head of the Interior Department, Fred A. Seaton. He could not allow destruction of the Indian marsh, forest, and uplands. Yet he hesitated to repudiate his predecessor's position completely. So Mr. Seaton, with the collaboration of the Agricultural Department, recommended an alternative to my bill. In essence it was this:

The Indian timber first would be offered for sale in huge blocks to private mills, at competitive bids. The successful buyers would have to agree to pay an appraised price which would be fair to the Indians, and also to cut the timber under strict government supervision. This, of course, would mean that sustained-yield policies would keep the yearly cut in balance with new growth. Any timber not bought by private operators by April of 1961 would be purchased by the government and turned over to the Forest Service as National Forest land. Under this proposal, the marsh would become a wildlife sanctuary.

Now the dilemma was mine. If I insisted on my own bill and it bogged down in a partisan political debacle, the economy of my native state would suffer grievously. I desperately needed the unified backing of all my colleagues on the Indian Affairs Subcommittee if we were to have any chance of success with the Senate as a whole. And if only one or two large blocks of Indian timber were purchased privately under the Interior Department's bill, its total cost would be $90 million as contrasted with $120 million under my original bill. This was decisive with me, for I knew that many of my fellow Western Senators – rebuffed on relatively small reclamation and public-works projects in their own states – would wonder why scores of millions of dollars were necessary to buy an Indian reservation in Oregon.

I took the bill which Secretary Seaton had sent to me and dropped it in the Senate hopper "by request." If I had not crossed the Rubicon, I at least had crossed Upper Klamath Lake. It was my bill now.

A few weeks later the National Lumber Manufacturers Association began a bitter and abusive attack against even this bill. They denounced it as a threat to the American system of government and to free enterprise in the lumber industry. To its credit, the largest operator in the Klamath Basin, the Weyerhaeuser Timber Corporation, declined to join in this massive assault. Five of my colleagues helped particularly to bring the measure to passage – James E. Murray of Montana, Clinton P. Anderson of New Mexico, and Frank Church of Idaho, all Democrats; and Arthur V. Watkins of Utah and Barry Goldwater of Arizona, both Republicans.

The crisis came when lobbying by the National Association of Lumber Manufacturers succeeded in eliminating in the House of Representatives all the language guaranteeing sustained-yield management of any of the ponderosa timber which might be privately purchased. This could have been ruinous. We had to restore the lost language in conference between the two chambers. At this juncture there came to the rescue a man who is not customarily a hero with liberals – Ezra Taft Benson, Secretary of Agriculture. He sent to the conference a strong letter detailing why the Forest Service (which is in his Department) could not accept responsibility for supervising the timber effectively unless it had full legal authority to keep the forest from being recklessly cut. This meant that sustained-yield policies had to be assured. Benson's letter carried the day.

And so, as these words are written, biologists of the Fish and Wildlife Service are measuring off the acreage their agency soon will acquire in the Klamath marsh. Foresters of the Indian Bureau and the

Forest Service are preparing for sale some 617,000 acres of the great ponderosa groves – with $90 million in purchase funds already approved by Congress for National Forest acquisition in the event private buyers do not materialize.

And a valuable lesson has been learned all around – albeit an expensive one. Secretary Seaton now insists that it would be "absolutely unthinkable" for any Indian tribe to be "forced" into a termination proceeding without its full understanding and consent. Mr. Seaton also has said that it would be "incredible, even criminal, to send any Indian tribe out into the stream of American life until and unless the educational level of that tribe was one which was equal to the responsibilities it was shouldering."

Although Oregon is essentially a conservative and cautious state, practically every element of Oregon society had rallied to the cause of federal rescue of the Klamath reservation – press, pulpit, industry, banking, labor unions, conservation and outdoor groups, women's clubs, farm groups, education organizations. Few of these influential citizens believe the Klamaths measure up to the standards prescribed by the Secretary for merging with "the stream of American life." Yet the egg cannot be put back into the shell. Legal rights have been vested and each withdrawing Klamath is entitled to his share of the tribal assets, which might conceivably be reduced to $45,000 because of a new appraisal of the timber that reflects a declining lumber market. The amount of the exact sum due every Klamath may yet end up before the Indian Claims Commission. Fervent thanks are offered daily, however, that neither the $58,000 nor the $45,000, multiplied many times, is to be at the expense of the lumber, water, and wildlife economy on which Oregon is so utterly dependent.

But nobody in our state talks very much these days about getting the United States government out of "the Indian business."

The Best Advice I Ever Had

Reader's Digest, JUNE 1959

As Neuberger got older, he mellowed a bit, while not softening his principles and commitment. "You can say this for Dick," a longtime associate told The New York *Times* in 1957. "You can disagree with him, even to the point where there is real anger on both sides. Yet perhaps a year or so later he may encounter you and, with a broad smile, tell you, 'Well, I guess that time you were right.'"

I STILL REMEMBER my encounter with a band of silent and forbidding Chipewyan Indians, building longboats in a primitive shipyard along the Athabaska River. They stared at me hostilely until I mentioned that I was a friend of Inspector "Denny" La Nauze, a member of the Royal Canadian Mounted Police in these Northern solitudes. With that, their hospitality knew no bounds. Afterward on the trip, whether at a trapper's lonely bivouac or in a remote mission hospital, the same magical result occurred whenever I mentioned my friendship with La Nauze.

Later, at his home in Calgary, I asked the famous man-hunter of the Mounted how he accounted for such affection, rarely given to a man with the stern task of upholding the law. La Nauze looked at me out of pale-blue eyes that had squinted across bleak miles of frozen tundra. "Dick," he replied, "I suppose those people in the North Country still think well of me because I followed a rule that I would recommend in all human relationships. No matter how decisive things seemed to be on my side, I always kept in mind one thought: *The other fellow may be right.*

Perhaps because of the impressive dignity of the man, his advice has lingered in my memory and guided me. It has given me second thoughts in situations where once I felt all too sure of myself.

Not long after my last visit with La Nauze I spoke to a convocation at Oregon State College. It was during the 1954 Senatorial campaign. A member of the faculty asked a question challenging the consistency of a position I had taken on inflation and taxes. Instead of retorting belligerently, as I was tempted to do, I hesitated for a moment, then answered, "I never thought of it that way before. I believe you are right. My stand isn't wholly consistent."

After the election the president of the college, Dr. A.L. Strand, said, "Nothing that happened won you as many votes on our campus as that answer. Too many politicians are certain they are right on every issue. You made your best impression with that simple admission of human fallibility."

This has not invariably been easy advice to put into practice. On one occasion I was debating on the Senate floor with my former colleague, Arthur V. Watkins, of Utah, over a bill proposing a huge storage dam in Dinosaur National Monument. He had used up his allotment of time; I had about half an hour left. When he asked if I would yield him a little of my time, I obeyed an impulse to press my advantage and replied testily that I thought the Senator had spoken long enough.

From the rustle which went through the Senate Chamber, I knew I had said the wrong thing. I also realized that Watkins might be right in his request. If his argument was so effective that I could not afford to be generous about granting him 10 to 15 minutes more did I deserve to triumph in the debate?

I wrestled this over in my conscience and then admitted publicly that I had been wrong and arbitrary in my attitude. Not only did the submission make for me some personal friends out of Senators who had merely been acquaintances before, but it won an invaluable ally in Arthur Watkins. A year later, when the Klamath River watershed in my state needed urgent legislation to protect timber and waterfowl marshes, he gave it strong support.

Denny La Nauze's rule, it seems to me, can benefit almost anyone. How many times in casual conversation are we led into quarrels because we bristle up and stubbornly refuse to admit that the other fellow may have a case? How often a parent confuses a youngster by insisting that father knows best when a textbook has just proved the old man wrong. Whenever I hear some dubious claim arrogantly advanced, I wonder how many humiliations might be avoided and friendships saved if we could always remember the Mountie's simple rule. I, for one, have found it far easier and happier to go through life willing to grant that – *the other fellow may be right!*

When I Learned I Had Cancer

Harper's, JUNE 1959

He neither smoke nor drank. Neuberger worked out regularly in the Senate gymnasium as he had in climbing mountains and backpacking in the Northwest. Both of his parents were living and in the prime of health. Neuberger received a jolt, though, when he returned to Oregon after the 1958 summer congressional recess and took a routine physical examination. The disclosure that he had cancer stunned Neuberger's state and the nation. With courage, he fought back and appeared to be making a strong recovery. This article reflects Neuberger's optimism. But Neuberger lost his brave fight in March of 1960. Two other great senators of the postwar era, Robert A. Taft and Hubert H. Humphrey, also fell victim to cancer. But because of Neuberger's relative youth, his death was much more of a shock than the passing of distinguished elder statesmen.

MY GRANDMOTHER died a lingering death at the age of fifty-seven. I then was twelve years old and devoted to her, since she took my part whenever parental discipline threatened. On the day of her death I was brought into the bedroom. "Richard," she told me, "Grandma's dying."

Afterwards, frightened and trembling, I asked the nurse what had caused my grandmother's death. "She had cancer," the nurse replied. Not until then had I been trusted with this information. My grandmother had never known the nature of her illness, and the family had feared I might betray the secret to her.

Perhaps because of the emotional impact of this episode, I have been deeply concerned with medical-research legislation ever since I entered the United States Senate in 1955. Under the tutelage of Senator Lister Hill of Alabama, the pioneer legislator in this field, I helped to get approval of increases in research grants for the National Cancer Institute from $21 million to $75 million. Many times during those debates I mentioned that forty million Americans now living were destined to suffer from cancer. I believe I stressed it on the afternoon last spring when Senator Hill, Senator Hubert Humphrey, and I welcomed delegates from the Cured Cancer Congress, who dramatically thronged the Senate galleries.

Yet none of this prepared me for the day last August, in Portland, Oregon, when our family doctor – who is also my closest friend – told me that I probably had cancer. Ironically, I had gone to him merely to ask him to look at a sore in my mouth, which turned out to be trivial. The malignancy had produced no symptoms.

While I lay on the table waiting for a specialist from the University of Oregon Medical School to confirm the diagnosis, my mind kept insisting that this could not possibly be. This was the kind of thing which always happened to somebody else, but never to me. I soon would awaken from the nightmare, the cold chills would subside, my heart would stop pounding – and my wife and I would be driving through evergreen forests to our annual vacation on the seacoast.

But when I did awaken, it was after surgery at the Teaching Hospital. The little lump in my testicle, caught miraculously early, was nonetheless malignant. There was no doubt about that. I lay back, physically and psychologically exhausted, and wondered how soon I would die. Then I heard the doctor, who earlier had been so candid with me, saying:

"We think you're going to be all right."

Through the haze of anesthetic which had not yet worn off, I remember that I answered, "You're just telling me that to keep me from being overcome by panic. It's not true."

The doctor's reply was dogmatic: "If the permanent histological sections tomorrow confirm the frozen sections study in surgery today, we're very hopeful that you are going to have a complete recovery."

I still suspected that, like my grandmother, I was just another cancer patient who was being drugged with lies.

And so began the long and patient effort of my physicians to teach a layman – even a layman who had been sponsor of cancer-research legislation – that cancer is not one disease, but many. If my tumor had turned out to be any of several other types, my outlook would have been hopeless. These types, explained my doctors, were not responsive to radiation, and it was on radiation that my life now depended. Fortunately, my cell-type was that of a tumor long regarded as susceptible to destruction by radiotherapy.

"Was there spread?" I inquired fearfully.

Yes, admitted my doctors, there was spread. This tumor almost invariably metastasized early. Rapid dissemination was one of its characteristics. There were indications of cancer in both my lungs. They added that the spread was "minimal" – so little, in fact, that they had missed it on the first x-rays. But it was there, a very small spot on the periphery of each lung. If not destroyed, the spots would grow until they were the size of baseballs or larger. After that, they would eventually spill out of the lung, reaching to the brain and other vital organs. This, of course, would be the terminal stage of the disease.

This candor encouraged me. If my doctors were so truthful with me about the spread of the illness and its fatal possibilities, would they be lying about the vulnerability of the tumor to radiation? This glimmer of hope was strengthened when medical texts came down from the shelves and I was shown, like a schoolboy, that the cell-type named in my pathological report had been proven destructible by radiation over a long history of medical cases.

I will never forget the afternoon I spent in a rowboat on a quiet mountain lake with the radiologist who was to treat me.

"Cure is not inevitable," he began, and I felt perspiration creep over my body. "But if we get any breaks at all," continued the radiologist, "we think you're going to be cured."

"What do you mean by breaks?" I asked.

"First," he answered, "you must be able to tolerate the treatment so the necessary number of roentgens can be applied to the affected areas. That's a whole lot easier with cobalt than with the old-style x-ray therapy. Second, we hope that additional new lesions do not appear throughout your chest in such numbers that we would have to apply a high dose of radiation to your entire lungs – for that cannot be done safely. To a limited area in the chest, definitely yes; to the entire chest, no."

As I started my brief daily treatments beneath the cobalt-60 cone, my doctors pared down my speaking schedule. They let me keep some speaking engagements in Oregon, because they felt it would be better for my mental outlook to be moderately active rather than to become a semi-invalid. They made me warn each sponsoring group, however, that my appearance might be canceled at the last moment because of radiation reactions. During five months of treatment, I spoke fifty-three times. In addition, I presided at six Senate hearings, some as distant from Portland as San Francisco and Kalispell, Montana. Not one had to be canceled. This indicates not only how I tolerated the cobalt treatments but also the skill with which I was treated.

Hope lives by example, and I think one of my main sources of strength during a long period of anxiety was to meet other men who had suffered the same malignancy and gone onto full recoveries. Several were in the little lumber town of Lebanon, Oregon, and called themselves "the club." My spirits soared when William C. Doherty, president of the National Association of Letter Carriers, told me one of his sons had recovered from a testicular tumor six years ago. And I read at least a dozen times a letter from a talented Portland doctor my age, who was teaching in the medical school at Djakarta on the Indonesian island of Java. "Eight years ago I traveled the same path you are traveling now," he wrote. This kind of encouragement to a cancer victim cannot ever be measured.

From the beginning, my friends in the East were greatly alarmed that I was receiving therapy in a place which, to them, seemed so remote and even primitive. Why wasn't I at the Mayo Clinic, or the National Institutes of Health, or the Harvard Medical Center? Several friends generously offered to pay the travel and medical bills to any center of international renown. I know that throughout my entire therapy they worried over the quality of my care. A member of President Eisenhower's staff wanted to help arrange for treatment at Walter Reed.

Yet my own decision was never in doubt. I had complete personal confidence in my doctors in Portland. I think this is enormously important with a disease that imposes such heavy psychological stress. Furthermore, I was meeting people day after day who had survived malignancies more serious than mine, and they had received their care in Oregon.

This faith in my own doctors was justified when, midway during my treatments, one of the nation's great cancer specialists visited Portland – Dr. Sidney Farber, director of the Children's Cancer Foundation of Boston and chairman of many of the chemotherapy panels of the National Cancer Institute. He and I had become intimate friends through my sponsorship of legislation for medical research. He studied my case thoroughly.

At the Portland airport, as he made ready to fly back to Boston, Dr. Farber said to me, "If I had been in the least dissatisfied with your care you would be on the Mainliner with me tonight, en route East. But you must stay here. You are being treated with skill and wisdom. I am impressed with your doctors as real medical scholars. In fact, I think you should let them complete your therapy in Portland, even if it extends over into the start of the next session of Congress. Don't transfer your case."

As Dr. Farber's plane took off, my hopes stood higher than at any time since I had heard the bad news in August. I had also been confirmed in my belief that many talented doctors are scattered all over the United States and not concentrated in one or two celebrated medical centers.

Dr. Farber left with my doctors a supply of actinomycin – one of the new chemical agents recently developed for the treatment of cancer. Administered by itself, actinomycin often must be used in such large quantities, in order to have an effect on tumors, that it comes as a toxic reaction. But, used in conjunction with radiation, even small doses of actinomycin have helped to make the radiation far more effective on certain types of tumors. My particular type of lesion happened to be one of these.

My doctors took chest films from week to week, as they applied the cobalt rays and injected actinomycin into my arm. The feared mass-seeding of my lungs had not occurred. This, in itself, was a source of jubilation to the doctors. Yet I still worried. What if the original pathology had been wrong? What if the spot in each lung proved resistant to the cobalt beams and continued to grow? And would my doctors tell me the truth if this should happen? Many times I awakened in the night and imagined I could feel the lesions expanding within my chest.

In the daylight, fantasy yielded to reality. No one could have feigned the relief and satisfaction of my doctors when the lung lesions began to show signs of growing smaller relatively soon after the cobalt treatment started – indeed, far earlier than they had dared to hope. They lost their hard outlines on the X-ray film and appeared fuzzy and ghostlike. The time was to come when a trained radiologist, taking films for a routine checkup in Washington, could not discern the exact location where the lesions originally had been.

So the pathology done at the Teaching Hospital was confirmed. Equally significant, my doctors felt that the worth of the actinomycin, as a so-called "potentiating" agent with the cobalt, had been clearly proved. And I recalled the day before Senator Hill's Subcommittee on Health Appropriations when Dr. Farber and his brilliant medical associate, Dr. I.S. Ravdin, had testified that, in their opinion, chemotherapy offered the single most promising avenue for hastening our ultimate conquest of cancer. While I may overdramatize my own case, I thought it was an extraordinary coincidence that a Senator so actively interested in cancer-research legislation should himself, at the age of forty-six, have been treated by all three methods thus far discovered – surgery, radiation, and chemotherapy.

I imagine all sensitive people have wondered about the mental outlook of somebody who has cancer. Of course, such reactions are highly individualistic. "Cancer finds us as we are," Dr. Farber has said. "It does not make the weak strong or the strong weak." Futhermore, my own case, from its earliest stage, was regarded as hopeful – although my doctors had a trying time convincing me of this.

Yet a change came over me which I believe is irreversible. Questions of prestige, of political success, of financial status, became all at once unimportant. In those first hours when I realized I had cancer, I never thought of my seat in the Senate, of my bank account, or of the destiny of the free world. I worried over my cat Muffet. Who would take care of him? What would happen to my wife when I was gone? And how would it feel to die?

My wife and I have not had a quarrel since my illness was diagnosed. I used to scold her about squeezing the toothpaste tube from the top instead of the bottom, about not catering sufficiently to my fussy appetite, about making up guest lists without consulting me, about spending too much on clothes. Now I am either unaware of such matters or they seem irrelevant. In their stead has come a new appreciation of things I once took for granted – eating lunch with a friend, scratching Muffet's ears and listening for his purrs, the company of my wife, reading a book or magazine in the quiet cone of my bed lamp at night, raiding the refrigerator for a glass of orange juice or slice of coffee cake.

For the first time I think I actually am savoring life. I realize, finally, that I am not immortal. I shudder when I remember all the occasions that I spoiled for myself – even when I was in the best of health – by false pride, synthetic values, and fancied slights.

Politically, I have changed too. I doubt if ever again I could be wholly partisan. The response of the people in Oregon to my illness reflected no party lines. Republicans as well as Democrats offered us the use of their beach cottages or mountain cabins for convalescence. The press, without exception, was friendly and concerned. The Republican state chairman wrote a glowing letter about what a good Senator I had been. Another Republican politician telephoned my sister, offering to give blood if a transfusion were necessary. Senator Barry Goldwater sent a telegram from a remote Arizona town, telling us that he and his wife Peggy were praying for me. Other Republican or Conservative Senators, including George Aiken of Vermont, Margaret Chase Smith of Maine, and Alan Bible of Nevada went by my suite in the Senate Office Building frequently to inquire about my health. On the other hand there were some fellow Democratic liberals from whom I never received so much as a postcard during the five months of my treatment.

Under such circumstances it becomes hard to bristle at people for political reasons. At the treatment center, each patient receiving radiation had a separate little shelf for his or her linen smock. Here were the names of a Republican banker, a Democratic Senator, a liberal college professor, a socially prominent housewife. We might be separated on questions of balancing the budget or public power, but we were united by something more fundamental: a realization that life itself is a privilege and not a right.

I am glad that I insisted upon my doctors' disclosing publicly from the very start, the nature of my illness. The medical profession and the press are not the most congenial of companions, and doctors often think that what affects their patient is none of the public's business. I disagree, when the patient is a public official of any prominence. Several times during recent years, major officials in Oregon have suffered from cancer but no announcement of the fact was made except posthumously. This contrasts with the commendable candor surrounding the illness of John Foster Dulles. Beyond all this, I believe that a heavy obligation rests on any individual who has recovered from cancer, particularly somebody who is in the public eye.

Leaders in the American Cancer Society have told me that cancer has such horrifying connotations to many people that thousands, even after they recognize their symptoms, still refuse to seek prompt medical treatment. They fear their case is hopeless and that they will be hurt by doctors to no purpose. Time for successful treatment may run out for these people while they hesitate.

They find it difficult to believe that 30 percent of cancer cases are being saved right now, even though no major breakthrough has yet been made. But this fact can be given dramatic impact whenever a person of prominence is included in the 30 percent. When I was welcomed back on the floor of the Senate, the Senator from Idaho, thirty-four-year-old Frank Church, revealed that he had suffered from the same sort of cancer when he was a student at Stanford University eleven years earlier.

From my experience, an old word has come to have new meaning for me. It is "serendipity." It was coined by Horace Walpole to describe the three wandering princes of ancient Serendip (Ceylon), who were always making lucky and unexpected finds by accident. If there is any one issue about which I long have felt strongly, it is the fact that our total investment in cancer research – federal and private – falls far short of what we spend on permanent waves or even pari-mutuel wagers. It is less than 2 percent of what we spend on cigarettes and barely more than 1 percent of what we spend on liquor. Two out of three American families will be afflicted by cancer; yet the federal treasury pours out sixty-five times as much money on price supports for six favored crops as it does to investigate the causes of and possible cures for cancer.

Now I can talk about this situation more effectively to my colleagues in Congress. For I can tell them that I, myself, am alive today because of medical research. What would have happened in my case without cobalt radiation and actinomycin?

Like the princes of Serendip, I was in quest of one thing and I found something else. I sought desperately a restoration to health and I discovered, along with it, the opportunity to symbolize a cause which may help in the future to bring health to countless others.

Should a Public Man Write?

Saturday Review, 9 APRIL 1960

In this article, published after his death, Neuberger answered in the affirmative. For Neuberger's hundreds of thousands of readers, the only disappointment in his dual role as politician and journalist was that his byline appeared much less frequently after his election to the U.S. Senate. No prominent public official since Neuberger has left a comparable literary legacy.

EDITOR'S NOTE: Richard L. Neuberger, who died on March 9, was known primarily as a free-lance writer before he was elected United States Senator from Oregon in 1955. Among the national publications for which he frequently wrote was *Saturday Review*, to which he contributed numerous articles and book reviews over a period of two decades. The following article represents his last effort as a writer. Written in response to attacks on his literary activities, it was in process of revision at the time of Senator Neuberger's death; it is printed here without the final alterations he had planned.

After the 1959 session of Congress, I returned to Oregon to discover that the state chairman of the Republican Party had decided to make a major political issue out of the fact that I occasionally contribute articles about public matters to such periodicals as *The New York Times Magazine*, *Harper's*, *The Saturday Evening Post*, *Reader's Di-*

gest, and *Saturday Review*. He claimed this literary activity meant I was neglecting my job as a Senator.

To say the least, I am nonplussed. In the first place, the lead article – some thirty-five pages long – in the December number of the *National Geographic Magazine* was entitled "Russia as I Saw It," by Vice President Richard M. Nixon, who presumably qualifies as a Republican in good standing. Furthermore, it evidently is quite all right for members of the United States Senate to be in the oil business, cattle business, television business, banking business, and department-store business. There is apparently nothing wrong if Senators retain affiliations with law firms that represent coal mines, distilleries, or labor unions.

But let a Senator write books or magazine articles, and that is "moonlighting" which demonstrates he is not attending properly to his public duties. All of this has me puzzled. If a Senator spends his spare time raising and selling Black Angus herds, no complaint attaches. But if a Senator should devote a weekend to composing an article about civil rights for The New York *Times* or about the plight of Indian tribes for *Harper's*, there is a presumption of original political sin on his part.

And yet I have found the reaction in my state to these attacks both encouraging and refreshing. In a word, the attacks have not gone over – not even in the Republican Party, whose chairman initiated them. The people have refused to buy the charge that a Senator is unfit for service because he spends some of his time writing for publication. For example, here is the verdict of one of Oregon's most eminent former Governors, Charles A. Sprague, himself a Republican, as expressed in the editorial columns of the *Oregon Daily Statesman* of Salem:

> When one who has a certain capacity for speaking or writing becomes a public figure his talent is not allowed to rust, and shouldn't be.... The written communications of those high in public office contribute to public understanding of issues. Even those written from party bias present "one side" in a controversy and provoke response from the "other side." Thus articles by

Neuberger dealing with his observations of political life from his rare vantage point serve a wider purpose than just to supplement his salary, which he says wouldn't stretch to cover expenses....

Other Oregon dailies, most of them of Republican affiliation, have commented in a similar vein. On top of all this, my office has received numerous letters from leading Republicans in Oregon, expressing indignation over a "confidential" memorandum circulated by their party's state chairman, outlining his plans for making my writing proclivities a dominant issue against me in the 1960 campaign. One former Republican county chairman, in a key county politically, said he had donated his last contribution to the Republican State Committee because of this type of attack. And in more than 100 speeches this past fall to groups as varied as Rotary and Kiwanis clubs, Chambers of Commerce, labor unions, and Izaak Walton Leagues I have yet to be asked a hostile question about my writing. In essence, the attack has proved a total dud. It fizzled. The fuse flickered out.

At the height of the McCarthy era, it often was easy to ridicule a public man for reading, much less writing. Why did this particular denunciation of me fail in Oregon?

To begin with, Oregon is a highly literate state with an excellent school system. During the Korean War, 97 percent of Oregon's GIS passed the intelligence tests given by the Army. Only one state ranked higher – Minnesota, with 97.3 per cent. Oregon ranks near the top, proportionately, in such categories as book purchases, magazine subscriptions, and library borrowing. All of these things had their influence, of course, when a prominent political leader tried to equate writing on the part of a Senator with high crimes and misdemeanors.

Yet a number of more or less fortuitous circumstances also have been of material assistance to me in this situation. It so happens that Oregon probably will have the most strategic of all Presidential preference primaries this year. Every potential candidate will be placed on the Oregon ballot, willy-nilly, whether he likes it or not. Thus Oregon is virtually infested with pilgrimaging aspirants for the highest elective office in the land. One of these is the very attractive Senator John F. Kennedy of Massachusetts, who owes a good deal of fame to the remarkable popularity of his book *Profiles in Courage*, an account of bygone politicians who put priniciple first and survival at the polls second. With a spectacular bid for the White House pinned in no small measure on literary success, it became difficult for Oregon voters to see why their own Senator should be downgraded because he sometimes put pen to paper.

Indeed, I was told by a schoolteacher in the Columbia River salmon-fishing community of Astoria, "The students in my classes like Senator Kennedy best and you next, and you'd never guess the reason why. They're a whole lot more awed by people who can write than by those who can get elected to office!"

Furthermore, right at this time a national controversy arose over the writing of books and articles by celebrated members of the armed forces. Whether or not Admiral Hyman G. Rickover could copyright his stimulating speeches became a heated issue. The Pentagon also objected strenuously to the publication by General Thomas S. Power, commander of the Strategic Air Command, of his book, *Design for Survival*, which gave scant comfort to current defense policies. These episodes helped to emphasize the fact that elective officials are not the only Government employees engaged in occasionally putting their ideas on paper. And my friends in Oregon circulated widely a speech by Senator Stuart Symington of Missouri, an ardent partisan of General Power, whic`ḥ pointed out that such well-known American military leaders as Dwight D. Eisenhower, Mark Clark, and Omar N. Bradley had prepared their memoirs while on active military duty.

Yet the entire situation in Oregon has made me do a good deal of thinking about the question of public officials writing for publication. After all, why shouldn't they? If Vice President Nixon presented for the television networks a discussion of his journey to the Soviet Union, is there any valid reason why he should not write for *The National Geographic* on the same fascinating subject?

Many Senators and Representatives receive handsome speaking fees from groups like Knife and Fork Clubs, NAM chapters, Bonds for Israel, banking and utility conferences, and labor-union conventions. Some of these organizations have been known to lobby actively for specific legislative proposals, which is rare in a magazine or book publisher – although not completely out of the question. This is why Senator Clifford P. Case of New Jersey and I are sponsoring a bill to require that members of Congress and policy-making executive officials must list publicly all substantial outside income, including their speaking and writing fees. We see no objection whatsoever to speaking or writing for pay on the part of public officials, so long as the electorate can evaluate the connections or obligations thus created. After all, it was an unwholesome situation when Federal Communications Commissioners were being paid clandestinely to address broadcasters whom they were supposed to regulate.

Only once did I ever think a possible conflict of interest was involved even remotely in any of my writing. I had sold an article to *American Heritage* about the settlement of the Oregon frontier, in connection with our state's 100th anniversary. A few months later, the publisher of *American Heritage* sought second-class mailing privileges for his excellent periodical. These had been denied because *American Heritage*, unlike most magazines, has a stiff cover. I successfully sponsored legislation which admitted *American Heritage* to the same postal rate as other magazines. Although there was no connection whatsoever between the sale of my article and the meritorious bill dealing with the mailing fees assessed *American Heritage*, I felt – under all the circumstances – that I should donate the $500 which I had received in payment for the article to Portland State College as a scholarship in Oregon history.

Yet had I actively opposed this legislation, instead of sponsoring it, I am certain that my writings still would have been welcome in the pages of *American Heritage*. A public man incurs less obligation in writing than in any other form of activity which might widen his field of influence or augment his income.

Some political figures flinch from committing themselves to print for several reasons. They remember the comment in the Book of Job: "My desire is ... that mine adversary had written a book." The printed word cannot be called back, but a controversial speech can frequently be labeled as a misquotation. The *Congressional Record* may be doctored and edited even after the transcript has been prepared. But the periodicals indexed in *Reader's Guide* are inflexible. On top of all this, a political figure speaking from the stump often can get by on oratory and rhetoric. Sound and fury become substitutes for substance. Editors are sterner critics than the populace who crowd in front of the lectern or speaking stump. Most political speeches are insufferably dull to read. However, the politician who writes for a periodical of stature must have something worth while to say. I have labored far harder and longer on a magazine article which paid me $250 than I know I would have had to do on a lecture engagement offering $1,000, plus plane or train fare.

So as a practitioner of the habit, I fervently defend politicians and other public officials who are willing to commit themselves to paper. I know of no more effective or enduring way in which to inform the electorate. And each of us can persist in hoping that he will turn out to be the American version of Sir Winston Churchill – victorious most of the time politically and always eloquent and persuasive in print.

Endnotes

1 Alfred Rosenberg (1893–1946) was a German Nazi leader and writer. His writings gave Hitler the spurious philosophical and scientific basis for the racist doctrines of the Nazi party. He was hanged as a war criminal.

2 Nicholas Murray Butler (1862–1947) was president of Columbia from 1902 to 1945 and won the Nobel Peace Prize jointly with Jane Addams in 1931. He was a leading member of the Eastern intellectual establishment for half a century.

3 William S. Hart (1872–1946) was an American actor who made his name in stage and screen Westerns.

4 Jim Farley (1888–1976) was chairman of the Democratic National Committee from 1932 to 1940. He was U.S. postmaster general 1933–40 but resigned to protest Roosevelt's third term.

5 Prior to this time the party controlling the legislature elected one of their own to the Senate rather than allowing for direct election by the people.

6 The Wheeler-Rayburn Act forced the break-up of national utility holding companies, limiting them to regional holding companies.

7 John Llewellyn Lewis (1880–1969) became president of United Mine Workers from 1920 and in disagreement with AF of L policies orga-

nized the Congress of Industrial Organization (CIO) in 1935. Phillip Murray (1886–1952) was vice president of the United Mine Workers (1920–1942) and succeeded Lewis as president of CIO. Harry Lloyd Hopkins (1890–1946) was an administrator and politician who held many different positions in the Roosevelt administration. Harold Ickes (1874–1952) was U.S. secretary of the interior from 1933 to 1946. Cordell Hull (1871–1955) was secratry of state from 1933 to 1944 and received the Nobel Peace Prize in 1945. Raymond Moley (1886–1975) was a member of FDR's brain trust, an editor of *Today* magazine and a professor of government and public law.

8 Quarantine was and is an attempt to isolate hostile nations through economic sanctions, trade embargoes and other punitive actions.

9 As governor of Indiana, 1933–37, Paul McNutt used force to break a strike.

10 When United Mine Workers President John L. Lewis threatened a wartime strike, the Roosevelt administration did not call the bluff but acquiesced to their demands.

11 His grandfather was Adlai Ewing Stevenson, vice president 1893–97 with Grover Cleveland serving as president.

12 The Mau-Mau were terrorists or freedom fighters in Kenya. Composed of members of the Kikuyu tribe, they led an armed rebellion against the British from 1952–1956 that came to be known as the Mau-Mau emergency.

13 "There's a sucker born every minute."

14 Neuberger is referring to former Governor Oswald West (1911–1915), who became a lobbyist in his post-political career. State officials of his time did not receive pensions.

15 Senator Claghorn was a character from the Fred Allen radio show, a parody of a wind-bag, know-nothing Southern senator. Johnathan P. Throttlebottom ran for president in the musical *Of Thee I Sing*, music and lyrics by George and Ira Gershwin, book by George S. Kaufman and Morrie Ryskind.

16 Mark Hanna (1837–1904) was the powerful Republican national chairman at the turn-of-the-century. See NOTE 4 for information on Jim Farley.

Selected Bibliography
The Writings of Richard L. Neuberger

This bibliography was compiled by Paul Pitzer while attending the University of Oregon in the pursuit of a PH.D. in History. The word "draft" found occasionally in the citations below refers to the fact that draft copies of various final articles (some were never published) were found among the Richard L. Neuberger Papers in the Special Collections Library of the University of Oregon. Citations with question marks signify that the date listed could not be verified.

BOOKS

An Army of the Aged: A History and Analysis of the Townsend Old Age Pension Plan, co-authored with Kelley Loe. Caxton Press: 1936.

Integrity: The Life of George W. Norris, co-authored with Stephen B. Kahn. Vanguard: 1937.

Our Promised Land. Macmillan: 1938.

The Lewis and Clark Expedition. Random House: 1951 (children's book).

The Royal Canadian Mounted Police. Random House: 1953 (children's book).

Adventures in Politics: We Go to the Legislature. Oxford University Press: 1954.

ARTICLES

1933
4 October 1933, "The New Germany," *Nation.*
15 November 1933, "Germany Under the Choke-Bit," *New Republic.*

1934
11 July 1934, "Hooverism in the Funnies," *New Republic.*
22 August 1934, "President Comes to Our Town," *New Republic.*
25 August 1934, "Political Laboratory Chief," *Today.*
7 November 1934, "The Northwest Goes Leftish," *New Republic.*

1935
7 August 1935, "Just Paddle 'em Down the Road!" *Nation.*
20 August 1935, "Home Folks Have No Doubt About Borah," *New York Times Magazine.*
September 1935, "The Shouting and the Tumult Die," *Everybody's Business.*
October 1935, "Fascist Labor Bills in Oregon," *American Federationist.*
30 October 1935, "Townsend Plan Exposed," *Nation.*

1936
February 1936, "Behind the Borah Boom," *Current History.*
March 1936, "Old People's Crusade (The Townsend Plan)," *Harper's.*
March 1936, "Six Martyred Senators," *Real America.*
4 March 1936, "Will Borah Be Re-Elected to the Senate?" *Pacific Weekly.*
13 May 1936, "Political Notes from the Northwest," *Nation.*
June 1936, "Transaction Tax," *American Federationist.*
9 August 1936, "Battle of the Idaho Titans," *New York Times Magazine.*
19 August 1936, "Oregon's People Confront the Military Drill Issue," *Christian Century.*
22 August 1936, "Zioncheck: An American Tragedy," *Nation.*
September 1936, "Power as an Issue," *Current History.*
October 1936, "Politician Unafraid," *Harper's.*
22 November 1936, "O'Neill Turns to New Horizons," *New York Times Magazine.*

1937

1937, "Sign Here, Please," *American Magazine* – draft.

February 1937, "Biggest Thing On Earth," *Harper's*.

February 1937, "Oregon Votes for Drill," *Social Frontier*.

7 February 1937, "C.E.S. Wood Remains a Non-Conformist," *Sunday Oregonian*.

7 February 1937, "Lusty Seattle, Pioneer at Heart," *New York Times Magazine*.

20 March 1937, "Biggest Thing on Earth," *Scholastic*.

27 March 1937, "The New Oregon Trail," *Collier's*.

16 May 1937, "Power Giants of the Far West," *New York Times Magazine*.

30 May 1937, "Labor Unrest Invades the Deep Forests," *New York Times Magazine*.

June 1937, "America Talks Court," *Current History*.

26 June 1937, "C.I.O.: Far West Front," *Nation*.

August 1937, "Senator Wheeler's Plight," *Current History*.

28 August 1937, "Wheeler Faces the Music," *Nation*.

29 August 1937, "The Red Demon That Eats Forests," *New York Times Magazine*.

September 1937, "Who's Laughing Now?" *American Mercury*.

12 September 1937, "Western Deserts Made to Bloom," *New York Times Magazine*.

26 September 1937, "Roosevelt Goes to See a Vision Made Reality," *New York Times Magazine*.

November 1937, "Roosevelt Rides Again," *Current History*.

7 November 1937, "Climb, Fish, Climb!" *Collier's*.

14 November 1937, "Prophet of a New 'Promised Land' of Power," *New York Times Magazine*.

20 November 1937, "Just Call Me Babe," *Collier's*.

December 1937, "The Last Frontier," *Coronet*.

5 December 1937, "The West Rejects Eastern Gloom," *New York Times Magazine*.

1938

January 1938, "World's Greatest Engineering Wonder," *American Magazine*.

20 February 1938, "State of the Slapstick in Politics," *New York Times Magazine*.

March 1938, "Labor's Overlords," *American Magazine*.

2 April 1938, "Goon Squads, Halt!" *Collier's*.

25 May 1938, "Bonneville," *New Republic*.

June 1938, "Don't You Cry For Me," *Country Home Magazine*.

June 1938, "Labor's Cycle in Seattle," *Current History*.

26 June 1938, "What Makes a Great Varsity Crew," *New York Times Magazine*.

July 1938, "Mormons Find A Way," *American Mercury*.

July 1938, "Oregon Strikes Back," *Collier's* (also *Reader's Digest*, March 1939).

2 July 1938, "Some Like Roosevelt," *Nation*.

17 September 1938, "Townsend Racket, New Phase," *Nation*.

6 October 1938, "The President Goes Traveling," *Ken*.

22 October 1938, "Power Play," *Collier's*.

29 October 1938, "Ballot Poison for Labor," *Nation*.

19 November 1938, "Gridiron G-Man," *Collier's*.

December, 1938, "J.D. Ross, Northwest Dynamo," *Survey Graphic*.

15 December 1938, "Sovereign of the West," *Ken*.

1939

January 1939, "They Love Roosevelt," *Forum*.

18 January 1939, "Colossus in the West," *New Republic*.

26 January 1939, "New Deal Hatchet-Man," *Ken*.

March 1939, "Liberalism Backfires in Oregon," *Current History*.

March 1939, "Oregon Strikes Back," *Reader's Digest*.

18 March 1939, "Power Dams and Politics," *Nation*.

27 March 1939, "New Oregon Trail," *Collier's*.

April 1939, "Bad Man Bridges," *Forum*.

April 1939, "Hells Canyon, the Biggest of All," *Harper's*.

April 1939, "Mr. President – Your Forgotten Frontier," *Common Sense*.

April 1939, "Refugees from the Dust Bowl," *Current History*.

May 1939, "Seattle's $4.05 Week-end," *The Coast*.

May 1939(?), "What's Wrong With Our Legislatures," *Everybody's Digest*.

5 May 1939, "Laski Says Roosevelt Hasn't Gone Far Enough," *Oregonian*.

14 June 1939, "America and the Next War," *New Republic*.

July 1939, "Columbia Flows to the Land," *Survey Graphic*.

July 1939, "The Man Who Made Grand Coulee," *The Coast*.

8 July 1939, "Young Man With Two Horns," *Saturday Evening Post*.

September 1939, "What the Home Folks Say About Events Abroad," *Harper's*.

September 1939, "Who Are the Associated Farmers?" *Survey Graphic*.
October 1939, "Decision," *Collier's* – draft.
21 October 1939, "Unhappy Fishing Ground," *Collier's*.
November 1939, "Borah of Idaho," *The Coast*.
November 1939 (?), "30,000 Candidates and Why They Run," *Everybody's Digest*.
25 November 1939, "Lewis and the Third Term," *Nation*.
December 1939, "America's Biggest Ditch," *The Coast*.
December 1939, "Prairie Senator," *Survey Graphic* (also *Reader's Digest*, December 1939).
December 1939, "Should Our Government Own Our Utilities? Power Belongs to the People," *Forum*.

1940

January 1940, "Uncle Sam's Sun Valley," *The Coast*.
5 February 1940, "Columbia River Power," *New Republic*.
24 February 1940, "The Two Fisted Champions," *Collier's*.
23 March 1940, "Putt and Take," *Collier's*.
1 April 1940, "Trouble in the Tall Timber," *New Republic*.
May 1940, "Wheeler of Montana," *Harper's*.
1 June 1940, "Miracle in Concrete," *Nation*.
15 June 1940, "How Much Conservation?" *Saturday Evening Post*.
25 June 1940, "Canyon Conqueror," *Collier's* – draft.
August 1940, "Last Frontier," *Free America*.
12 August 1940, "McNary of Fir Cone," *Life*.
September 1940, "Private Power," *Survey Graphic*.
28 September 1940, "Where McNary Heads the Ticket," *Nation*.
26 October 1940, "Wilkie Sets in the West," *Nation*.
9 November 1940, "Purity League," *Collier's*.

1941

February 1941, "Go West Young Man," *Survey Graphic*.
February 1941, "Public Domain," *Survey Graphic*.
February 1941, "West Needs People," *Survey Graphic*.
1 February 1941, "Our Gerrymandered States," *Nation*.
March 1941, "Our Greatest Exploration," *Reader's Digest*.
16 March 1941, "Mightiest Man-Made Thing," *New York Times Magazine*.
April 1941, "The Mercer Girls," *Reader's Digest*.
May 1941, "Vacations for the Adventurous," *Esquire*.

June 1941, "Buy British," *Reader's Digest.*

23 June 1941, "Wilderness Battleground," *New Republic.*

July 1941, "I Go to the Legislature," *Survey Graphic.*

5 July 1941, "Grand Coulee – Industrial Kingdom," *Christian Science Monitor.*

15 July 1941, "Grand Coulee – Industrial Kingdom," *Christian Science Monitor Magazine.*

23 July 1941, "An Idealist in the Legislature," *St. Louis Post-Dispatch.*

6 September 1941, "Kilowatt Battlefront," *Nation.*

13 September 1941, "Conservationist," *Saturday Evening Post.*

13 September 1941, "The Great Salmon Mystery," *Saturday Evening Post.*

21 September 1941, "Out on the Trail with a Forest Ranger," *New York Times Magazine.*

27 September 1941, "Men, Lakes and Railroad Detours," *Christian Science Monitor Magazine.*

29 September 1941, "On Delaring War," *New Republic.*

9 November 1941, "Trees for our Arsenal," *New York Times Magazine.*

20 December 1941, "Reveille in the Northwest," *Nation.*

20 December 1941, "Water Gals," *Collier's.*

1942

January 1942, "What God Hath Wrought," *Common Sense.*

February 1942, "Alaska, Northern Front," *Survey Graphic.*

21 February 1942, "Wilderness Defense: Abridged," *Saturday Evening Post.*

March 1942, "Progressives in Congress," *Common Sense.*

April 1942, "America's Burma Road," *This Week.*

April 1942, "Seeing the Northwest," *Harper's.*

12 April 1942, "Alaska, Our Spearhead in the Pacific," *New York Times Magazine.*

19 April 1942, "Much-Discussed Bill Douglas," *New York Times Magazine.*

May 1942, "Deepest Canyon on the Continent," *Travel.*

16 May 1942, "New War Horses," *Collier's.*

23 May 1942, "War and Public Power," *Nation.*

31 May 1942, "Where Auto Racing Really Bites," *New York Times Magazine.*

June 1942, "Decentralize the War Effort – Now!" *Free America.*

June 1942, "Japanese in the Aleutians," New York *Times* and *Oregonian.*

June 1942, "Pacific Coast Morale," *Asia*.
August 1942, "Alaska, Our Spearhead in the Pacific," *Science Digest*.
August 1942, "Mr. Justice Douglas," *Harper's*.
August 1942, "Other Things Besides Fight," *Esquire*.
August 1942, "Our Battlefront in the Wilderness," *Reader's Digest*.
9 August 1942, "Man's Greatest Structure," *New York Times Magazine*.
5 September 1942, "Gentleman from Alaska," *Collier's*.
24 October 1942, "Mail Carrier of Hell's Canyon," *Saturday Evening Post*.
24 October 1942, "On the Warpath," *Saturday Evening Post*.
November 1942, "American Indian Enlists," *Asia*.
12 December 1942, "Hollywood's No. 1 Hideout," *Saturday Evening Post*.
19 December 1942, "Mountain Air for the Navy," *Collier's*.

1943

February 1943, "Alcan Epic," *Yank* and *Philadelphia Bulletin*.
February 1943, "Salvaging the Salmon," *Coronet*.
27 November 1943, "Highballing at Sixty Below," *Saturday Evening Post*.
December 1943, "Haines Highway," *Alaska Life*.

1944

19 February 1944, "Yukon Adventure," *Saturday Evening Post*.
17 September 1944, "For Pioneers of the Years Ahead," *New York Times Magazine*.
19 September 1944, "Alaska's Future: Home for Veterans," *Washington Post*.
15 October 1944, "Alaska: Land of Promise for Battle Vets," *Sunday Oregonian*.
November 1944, "Skyway to Russia," *Coronet*.
23 December 1944, "Go North, Young Man!" *Collier's*.
24 December 1944, "Modern Noah," *This Week Magazine*.

1945

8 January 1945, "Choking Our Rivers," *Washington Post*.
February 1945, "Discovered: The Northwest Passage," *Coronet*.
February 1945, "Great Salmon Experiment," *Harper's*.
17 February 1945, "Eskimo Guerrillas," *Saturday Evening Post*.
March 1945, "Army Outwits Arctic Weather," *Science Digest*.
26 May 1945, "Marginal Notes at San Francisco," *Saturday Review of Literature*.

23 June 1945, "Gander Man," *Collier's*.

14 July 1945, "The Delegates Were Amazed," *Christian Science Monitor*.

30 July 1945, "Grandeur of America Belongs to All the People," *Progressive*.

26 August 1945, "Highballing Over the Big Hump," *New York Times Magazine*.

14 October 1945, "City Folks Did It," *This Week Magazine*.

November 1945, "Arctic Cradle of the Atom," *Liberty*.

November 1945, "West Wants Regional Redistribution," *Forum*.

3 November 1945, "Nobody Hates the Umpire, Yet," *Collier's*.

December 1945, "Our Vanishing Resources," *Common Sense*.

9 December 1945, "Land of New Horizons," *New York Times Magazine*.

1946

January 1946, "Royal Canadian Mounties," *Harper's* (also *Reader's Digest*, March 1946).

19 January 1946, "What Do the People Think of Truman?" *Nation*.

26 January 1946, "Big Things Are Stirring the Mighty Northwest," *Liberty*.

16 February 1946, "Wisconsin's Tough Old Man," *Saturday Evening Post*.

March 1946, "Wizard of Billiards and Ballots," *Liberty Magazine* – draft.

3 March 1946, "Wonders of the Northwest," New York *Times*.

9 March 1946, "Men, Not States, Run For President!" *Saturday Evening Post*.

16 March 1946, "Sons of the Wild Jackass," *Nation*.

April 1946, "C.T.C. On the Old Oregon Trail," *Signalman's Journal* – draft.

13 April 1946, "Want to Name a Mountain?" *Saturday Evening Post*.

27 April 1946, "Rocky Mountain Boy," *Saturday Review of Literature*.

25 May 1946, "Fish Run," *Saturday Review of Literature*.

June 1946, "The Land of New Horizons," *Digest* and *Review*.

June 1946, "Political Upheaval in the West," Washington *Post* – draft.

June 1946, "Travel Lure With a Capital 'L'," *Signalman's Journal*.

22 June 1946, "Great American Snout Count," *Saturday Evening Post*.

6 July 1946, "Danger 'Round the Bend," *Saturday Evening Post*.

22 July 1946, "Cross-Country," *New Republic*.

28 July 1946, "This is a World I Never Fought For," *New York Times Magazine*.

August 1946, "Can You Drive to Alaska?" *Holiday* (also *Saturday Evening Post*, 5 July 1947).

3 August 1946, "Big Nick," *Liberty*.

10 August 1946, "Their Brothers' Keepers," *Saturday Review of Literature* (also *Reader's Digest*, November 1946).

11 August 1946, "Wilderness Boss," *This Week Magazine*.

18 August 1946, "Westerner Tells What We Miss," *New York Times Magazine*.

24 August 1946, "Cowboy on Our Side," *Nation*.

September 1946, "Come and Get It," *Holiday*.

14 September 1946, "They Never Go Back To Pocatello," *Saturday Evening Post*.

October 1946, "I'm Happiest in My Home Town," *Your Life*.

October 1946, "Telegraph Trail," *Harper's*.

October 1946, "What's Wrong With Alaska," *Reader's Digest*.

5 October 1946, "Woodmen and the Trees," *Nation*.

6 October 1946, "Should We Move the Capital to the Rockies?" *New York Times Magazine*.

13 October 1946, "Nick Bez: Immigrant Salmon King," *Oregonian*.

November 1946, "The Nisei Come Back to Hood River," *Reader's Digest*.

2 November 1946, "Pacific Northwest," *Nation*.

2 November 1946, "What Some People Do To Vote!" *Saturday Evening Post*.

3 November 1946, "Alaska Looks Toward Statehood," St. Louis *Post-Dispatch*.

December 1946, "Democrats from the Northwest," St. Louis *Post-Dispatch* – draft.

1947

19 January 1947, "They're All for Lower Taxes, But –," *New York Times Magazine*.

February 1947, "I Run for Office," *Harper's*.

8 February 1947, "Highballing with Kilowatts," *Nation*.

March 1947, "Will Killowatts Replace Oil Out West," *Railroad Magazine* – draft.

1 March 1947, "Cities of America," *Saturday Evening Post*.

1 March 1947, "Portland, Oregon," *Saturday Evening Post* (also *Changing Times*) – draft.

8 March 1947, "Reading in the Backwoods," *Saturday Review of Literature*.

26 April 1947, "Looting the National Forests," *Nation*.

4 May 1947, "Spring Thunder of the Falls," *New York Times Magazine*.

7 June 1947, "Curtain Raiser for '48," *Nation*.

15 June 1947, "Lone Woman of the Mountains," *New York Times Magazine* (also *Reader's Digest*, September 1947).

July 1947, "Wallgren – Hometown Boy in Politics," New York *Times* – draft.

July 1947, "Wayne Morse: Republican Gadfly," *American Mercury*.

6 July 1947, "Etiquette of Eating West vs. East," *New York Times Magazine*.

13 July 1947, "Our Urbane Civilized Frontier," *New York Times Magazine*.

19 July 1947, "America's Most Isolated Family," *Saturday Evening Post*.

19 July 1947, "Rim Rock Boy," *Saturday Evening Post*.

19 July 1947, "They've Gone Wild and Love It," *Saturday Evening Post*.

19 July 1947, "Tribal Town," *Nation*.

26 July 1947, "Alaska Arms Again," *Nation*.

13 September 1947, "Flight for Freedom in the Arctic," *Nation*.

27 September 1947, "Who Wrecked Bonneville?" *Nation*.

28 September 1947, "High Prices? Everybody Has A Theory," *New York Times Magazine*.

30 August and 1 November 1947, "Fish and Politics," *Nation*.

October 1947, "Gruening of Alaska," *Survey Graphic*.

5 October 1947, "Land Rush, GI Style," *New York Times Magazine*.

1 November 1947, "It Always Rains in Ketchikan," *Saturday Evening Post*.

15 November 1947, "Political Void in Oregon," *Nation*.

December 1947, "How the Trapper Braves the Snowy Fastness," New York *Times* – draft.

December 1947, "Insurgent Senator Comes Home," *Salute*.

December 1947, "The Olympics – Cockpit of Controversy," *American Forests*.

December 1947, "Scourge of the North," *Survey Graphic*.

20 December 1947, "Girls Do All Right Up North," *Saturday Evening Post*.

20 December 1947, "Save the Public Domain!" *Nation*.

1948

11 January 1948, "Battle of the Family Budget," *New York Times Magazine*.

February 1948, "State of Alaska," *Survey Graphic* (also *Reader's Digest*, May 1948).

7 February 1948, "Seattle Ponders a Bad Dream," *Saturday Evening Post*.
15 February 1948, "Trappers' Season," *New York Times Magazine*.
March 1948, "British Columbia Electric Rolls On," *Railroad Magazine*.
March 1948, "Glen Taylor: Evangelist in Politics," *Progressive* – draft and article, April 1948.
4 March 1948, "Farmer Is Worried About His Future," *New York Times Magazine* (also New York *Times*, 14 March 1948).
13 March 1948, "Monopoly at Alaska's Throat," *Nation*.
April 1948, "Great Canal Fiasco," *American Mercury*.
11 April 1948, "It Costs Too Much to Run for Office," *New York Times Magazine*.
17 April 1948, "Beating the Arctic Bush," *Collier's*.
17 April 1948, "North Country Limited," *Saturday Evening Post*.
8 May 1948, "Bonneville: The First Ten Years," *Nation*.
14 May 1948, "Showdown for Dewey in Oregon," *Washington Calling* – draft.
22 May 1948, "Stassen vs. Dewey, Second Round," *Nation*.
25 May 1948, "Bonneville," *New Republic*.
6 June 1948, "30,000 Americans Can Be Wrong," *New York Times Magazine*.
12 June 1948, "One of Our Cities Is Missing," *Nation*.
19 June 1948, "Idaho's Fantastic Millionaire," *Saturday Evening Post*.
July 1948, "Cowboy on Our Side," *Nation* – draft.
July 1948, "The Great North Road," *Progressive* (also *Catholic Digest*).
July 1948, "Politics Is Your Business," *Foreign Service*.
July 1948, "Seattle," *Changing Times*.
September 1948, "Glen Taylor: Crooner on the Left," *American Mercury*.
September 1948, "We Have Nothing but the Earth," *Survey Graphic*.
12 September 1948, "Changing the Face of the West," *New York Times Magazine*.
25 September 1948, "He's Our Meat Now," *Saturday Evening Post*.
October 1948, "Ah, Wilderness, New Style," *Harper's*.
October 1948, "It's a Circus – But We Love It," *Foreign Service*.
9 October 1948, "My Current Reading," *Saturday Review of Literature*.
10 October 1948, "Juneau, 50 Years After the Gold Rush," *New York Times Magazine*.
16 October 1948, "Petersburg Goes It Alone," *Saturday Evening Post*.

16 October 1948, "Slow-Bell Campaign in the Northwest," *Nation*.

24 October 1948, "To the West, Water is Life and Death," *New York Times Magazine*.

28 November 1948, "Booming Bruins," *New York Times Magazine*.

December 1948, "Mountains of the West," *Ford Times*.

4 December 1948, "C.I.O. Convention," *Nation*.

1949

1949, "The Columbia – A Wilderness River," *Holiday* – draft.

January 1949, "Confessions of a Candidate," *Progressive*.

January 1949, "Last of the Breed," *Collier's*.

January 1949, "Portland, Metropolis on the Columbia," *Holiday*.

29 January 1949, "Daring Young Man from the West," *Nation*.

30 January 1949, "I Am a $5.00-a-day Senator," *This Week*.

February 1949, "Ski Whiz," *Liberty*.

6 March 1949, "It's a Woman's World Anyway in Alaska," *New York Times Magazine*.

12 March 1949, "Hail Fellow Well Met," *Nation*.

April 1949, "News at the Legislature," *Nieman Reports*.

30 April 1949, "There's No Boat Like the Minto," *Saturday Evening Post*.

May 1949, "A Doolittle Raider Returns," *The Link*.

May 1949, "I Am a $5.00-a-day Senator," *Reader's Digest*.

1 May 1949, "Timber Graveyard," *New York Times Magazine*.

15 May 1949, "River Authority for the Northwest," St. Louis newspaper (unnamed).

June 1949, "America Surges Westward," *Survey*.

June 1949, "The Columbia: With Biographical Sketch," *Holiday*.

21 June 1949, "Kilowatts Out to Sea," *The Reporter*.

July 1949, "CVA, Order on the Frontier," *Survey*.

July 1949, "My Favorite Town: Enterprise, Oregon," *Ford Times*.

30 July 1949, "Plutonium and Problems," *Nation*.

31 July 1949, "Country Slicker vs. the City Yokel," *New York Times Magazine*.

August 1949, "How to Keep Warm at 81 Degrees Below," *Progressive*.

28 August 1949, "Frontier of the Atomic Age," *New York Times Magazine*.

October 1949, "House on the Glacier Highway," *Ford Times*.

8 October 1949, "Solid West," *Nation*.

November 1949, "How to Keep Warm at 81 Degrees Below," *Science Digest*.

November 1949, "Who Shall Control the West," New York *Times* (?) – draft.

22 November 1949, "The Battle of Chilkoot Pass," *The Reporter*.

December 1949, "Boss of the Royal Mounted," *Holiday*.

December 1949, "Where Names Come From," *The Argus*.

1950

1950, "I Stay In Oregon," *Saturday Evening Post*.

1950, "Pulverizing the Highways," *Railway Progress Magazine*.

January 1950, "Canyon Creek Lodge: 1938," *Progressive*.

January 1950, "The Press and the CVA," *Nieman Reports*.

January 1950, "You Can Have Skiis—I'll Take Snowshoes," *Ford Times*.

14 January 1950, "Morse Versus Morse," *Nation*.

18 January 1950, "The Diesels Take Over," New York *Times*—draft.

31 January 1950, "Tribulations of a State Senator," *The Reporter*.

February 1950, "Our Rotten-borough Legislatures," *Survey*.

5 March 1950, "Are You Tougher than Your Wife?" *This Week*.

2 April 1950, "Again a Land Battle in the West," *New York Times Magazine*.

8 April 1950, "Washington's Dry Run Primary," *Nation*.

8 April 1950, "Where There's No Place Like School," *Saturday Evening Post* (and *Reader's Digest*, September 1950).

16 April 1950, "Day of the Diesel," *New York Times Magazine*.

30 April 1950, "Northwest Giant," *New York Times Magazine*.

May 1950, "Hoyt of the Post," *Frontier*.

May 1950, "I'd Rather Not Be a Governor," *Progressive*.

May 1950, "Moscow, Idaho," *Eagle Publications*.

20 May 1950, "Glen Taylor Rides Again," *Nation*.

20 May 1950, "Mr. Mac Shocks 'Em," *Collier's*.

June 1950, "The Oregon Trail Still Calls," *Nation's Business*.

July 1950, "Let's Take Our Children West," *Survey*.

30 July 1950, "They Still Go West, Young and Old," *New York Times Magazine* (also *Reader's Digest*, November 1950).

30 July 1950 "Why Not Admit DP's to Alaska?" *This Week*.

August 1950, "Government by Petition," *Butcher Workman*.

August 1950, "Regional Theater," *Theater Arts*.

12 August 1950, "Cities of America," *Saturday Evening Post*.

12 August 1950, "Edmonton, Alberta," *Saturday Evening Post*.

27 August 1950, "When Grangers Throw a Party," *New York Times Magazine*.

September 1950, "Oregon: Promised Land in the West," *Ford Times*.

September 1950, "Price Tags in Politics," *Progressive*.

2 October 1950, "Farmers in the Saddle," *New Republic*.

14 October 1950, "Outlook for November," *Nation*.

14 October 1950, "Stand-Off in the Northwest," *Nation*.

November 1950, "Government by the People," *Survey*.

November 1950, "Out of the Water's Reach," *Railway Progress*.

November 1950, "The Stronger Sex," *Progressive*.

November 1950, "They Knew What They're Fighting For," *Foreign Service*.

5 November 1950, "Frank Frankenstein," *New York Times Magazine*.

December 1950, "Land of Grandeur and Glory," *The Argus*.

16 December 1950, "My Home Town is Good Enough for Me," *Saturday Evening Post*.

23 December 1950, "What Labor Unions Forget," *Nation*.

31 December 1950, "When the Big Snow Shuts out the World," *New York Times Magazine*.

1951

1951, "Pendleton, Oregon," *Eagle Magazine*.

January 1951, "Why People Live in Alaska," *Tomorrow* and *Magazine Digest* (May 1951).

March 1951, "Why People are Moving to Town," *Survey*.

18 March 1951, "Lament for the Trolley Car," *New York Times Magazine*.

24 March 1951, "Big Damn in a Big Pit," *Nation*.

April 1951, "Confessions of a State Senator," *Tomorrow*.

April 1951, "States in Strait Jackets," *American Magazine*.

April 1951, "What Labor Leaders Forget," *Reader's Digest*.

22 April 1951, "Canada Lightly Talks Union with Us," *New York Times Magazine*.

May 1951, "Why Men Should Envy Women," *Science Digest*.

27 May 1951, "Footnotes on Politics by a Lady Legislator," *New York Times Magazine*.

June 1951, "America; Where Stands She Now?" *Survey*.

June 1951, "Seattle: City of the Last Frontier," *Chrysler Events*.

3 June 1951, "Justice Comes Too Late," *This Week*.

July 1951, "State Government in America," *English-Speaking World*.

August 1951, "Can the Salmon Survive?" *Catholic Digest*.

August 1951, "Canada's Bonus for Babies," *Butcher Workman*.

August 1951, "This Bus Rolls Through the Sky," *Popular Science*.

22 August 1951, "Canada Lightly Talks of Union with Us," *New York Times Magazine*.

September 1951, "Justice Comes Too Late," *Reader's Digest*.

September 1951, "Playground of the Inland Empire," *Ford Times*.

8 September 1951, "Oregon Goes to the Dogs," *Nation*.

23 September 1951, "Last Frontier Road," *Sunday Oregonian*.

October 1951, "Border Detachment," *Ford Times*.

October 1951, "The Case for Intertie," *Frontier*.

27 October 1951, "Aluminum Squeeze," *Nation*.

27 October 1951, "Aluminum," *Nation*.

November 1951, "Engineers Invade Another Wilderness," *Popular Science*.

November 1951, "Seattle," New York *Times*—draft.

24 November 1951, "When MacArthur Remained Silent," *Nation*.

December 1951, "Our Rotten Buroughs," *Progressive*.

2 December 1951, "Seattle: New York By and By," *New York Times Magazine*.

1952

1952, "Land of the Last Frontier," *Lifetime Living*.

1952, "More Americans Must Vote," *Eagle Magazine*.

1952, "When is a Gift Not a Gift?" *Nieman Reports*.

January 1952, "The Camas Prairie: Frontier Railroad," *Railway Progress*.

January 1952, "Seattle Station Crisis," *Railroad Magazine*.

6 January 1952, "World's Biggest Waterpower System—etc.," St. Louis *Post-Dispatch*.

26 January 1952, "Sprague, Conscience of Oregon," *Nation*.

28 January 1952, "George W. Norris, Statesman Unafraid," speech made in Calif.

February 1952, "Gruening of Alaska," *Frontier*.

March 1952, "County Unification," *This Week Magazine*.

March 1952, "Trek of the Rod Maker," *Ford Times*.

April 1952, "The Greatest Migration of them All," *Redbook*.

April 1952, "Lake Chelan—Playground of the Inland Empire," *Ford Times*.

April 1952, "Warren: Nice Man in a Rough Country," *American Magazine*—draft.

April 1952, "Westward the Land is Bright," *Redbook*.

April 1952, "When is a Gift Not a Gift?" *Nieman Reports*.

6 April 1952, "Canada's 'Baby Bonus,'" St. Louis *Post-Dispatch*.

25 April 1952, "School for Smart Young Things," *Saturday Evening Post*.

27 April 1952, "Canada's Social Security System for Children," *Reporter*.

May 1952, "America's Biggest Cat," *Science Digest*, and Toronto *Star Weekly* (1948?).

May 1952, "Canada: The West," *Esquire*.

May 1952, "Canada's Unknown Realm," *The English-Speaking World*.

May 1952, "Not Too Many Clothes," *The Quill*.

May 1952, "It's Summer and Time to Head West," *Butcher Workman*.

May 1952, "Trouble with You Canucks Is . . ." *New Liberty*.

4 May 1952, "Little Senator on the Big Senate," *New York Times Magazine*.

18 May 1952, "A New Frontier Dawns in the Far West," *Everyday Magazine*.

June 1952, "How VIP are the veeps?" *American Magazine*.

June 1952, "Hydro Power Drives Biggest Electric Engine," *Popular Science*.

June 1952, "Lady Who Licked Crime in Portland," *Coronet*.

June 1952, "Not Too Many Clothes," *Reader's Digest*.

June 1952, "Old Men for Council, Young Men for War," *Harper's*.

23 June 1952, "Let's Limit all Terms in Office!" *New Republic*.

July 1952, "The Lewis and Clark Highway," *Ford Times*.

July 1952, "National Forests in Danger!" *New Republic*—draft.

July 1952, "Re: Non Partisan Legislatures," *Reader's Digest*—draft.

July 1952, "Whose 'Home' State," *Frontier*.

6 July 1952, "From the Sod to the Sidewalk," *New York Times Magazine*.

August 1952, "Lure of the Pacific Northwest," *Lifetime Living*.

August 1952, "Pendleton Round-Up: The West's Big Show," *Chrysler Events*.

August 1952, "Surrender in Oregon," *Frontier*.

9 August 1952, "Fish and Concrete," *Nation*.

11 August 1952, "Senate Struggle in the West," *New Republic*.

September 1952, "She's Been Working on the Railroad," *Railway Progress*.

September 1952, "Stevenson the Man," *Frontier*.

13 September 1952, "Wile and Wandering," *Saturday Review*.

14 September 1952, "Northland Nonesuch," *New York Times Magazine*.

28 September 1952, "Democracy in Danger," *This Week*.

October 1952, "Canada's 49'ers Move North," *Science Digest*.

October 1952, "Hell's Canyon," *Holiday*.

October 1952, "Who Shall Pay for our Roads?" *Harper's* (also *Reader's Digest*, December 1952).

11 October 1952, "Jackson vs. Cain," *Nation*.

25 October 1952, "School for Smart Young Things," *Saturday Evening Post*.

26 October 1952, "Toward Restoring States' Rights," *New York Times Magazine*.

November 1952, "Economy Begins at Home," *National Municipal Review*.

November 1952, "Economy Begins at Home," *National Municipal Review*.

November 1952, "Government by Petition," *English Speaking World*—draft.

November 1952, "Let's Get Rid of Coat-Tailing," *Progressive*—draft.

November 1952, "My Wife Succeeds in Politics," *Coronet*.

November 1952, "The Pride of the Northwest—SP&S," *Railroad Magazine*.

November 1952, "You're a Stranger, Mr. President," *New Liberty*.

17 November 1952, "West, Eyes on Korea," *New Republic*.

Late 1952, "Senate Titanic in the West," *New Republic*—draft.

Late 1952, "Cain vs. Jackson," *Nation*—draft.

1953

1953, "It Is the Country's Most Scenic Road," *Empire Magazine*—draft.

January 1953, "Campaign Spending in the United States," *English Speaking World*.

January 1953, "Is the Independent Journalist Obsolete?" *The Quill*.

January 1953, "Kitimat: Colossus of the Northwest," *Harper's* (also *Reader's Digest*, March 1953).

January 1953, "McKay: New Boss of the West's Vast Resources," *Frontier*.

January 1953, "Mounties Become Mechanics," *Popular Science*.

February 1953, "Toward Winning States' Rights," *National Municipal Review*.

1 February 1953, "Two-party Blues in One-party State," *New York Times Magazine*.

March 1953, "The Neubergers: Oregon's Political Paradox," *Frontier*.

March 1953, "New Habits for Salmon," *Science Digest*.

30 March 1953, "Season for Plunder," *New Republic*.

April 1953, "Strange Story of Senator Morse," *American Magazine*.

26 April 1953, "There Oughtta Be (and Often Is) a Law," *New York Times Magazine*.

May 1953, "Can We Control Campaign Spending?" Berkeley Conference.

May 1953, "Fun-time in the Rockies," *American Magazine*.

May 1953, "Let's Swap," *New Liberty*.

May 1953, "The West Uneasily Eyes Its Vast Resources," *New York Times Magazine*—draft.

10 May 1953, "We're Democrats and Human," *Sunday Journal Magazine*.

30 May 1953, "Season for Plunder," *New Republic*.

June 1953, "New Horizons for the Article Writer," *Writer*.

June 1953, "What Will Happen to Wayne Morse?" *Frontier*.

July 1953, "Betrayal at Hell's Canyon," *Progressive*.

July 1953, "He Builds America's Finest Wagons," *Popular Science*.

6 July 1953, "Venus Vanquished," *Time*.

27 July 1953, "The House, a Second Senate?" *New Republic*.

August 1953, "Canada's Mechanized Mounties," *Science Digest*.

August 1953, "What's a Treaty with an Indian Worth?" *Christian Herald*.

6 August 1953, "Dining-Car Commissary Manager," *Railway Progress*.

29 August 1953, "Another G.O.P. Grab," *Nation*.

September 1953, "Let's Strengthen our State Legislatures," *Butcher Workman* draft.

September 1953, "The Schizophrenia of Secretary McKay," *Reporter*.

6 September 1953, "Wide Open Debate on the Wide Open Spaces," *New York Times Magazine*.

October 1953, "Decay of State Governments," *Harper's*.

October 1953, "Is Grand Canyon's Rival Deeper?" *Popular Science*.

October 1953, "Let's Control Campaign Spending," *Eagle*.

October 1953, "Senator Morse: The Life of Any Party," *Everybody's Digest*.

13 October 1953, "Secretary McKay Looks in the Wrong Dam Places," *Reporter*.

November 1953, "We Need More Young Lawmakers," *Redbook*.

13 November 1953, "Are You Fit for Political Office? How Can We Get Better People Into Politics," *Collier's*.

7 December 1953, "Westerner Against the West," *New Republic*.

20 December 1953, "Profile of the Real Mounties," *New York Times Magazine*.

1954

January 1954, "The Northern Alberta Railway," *Railway Magazine*.

January 1954, "Wanted: More Christians in Politics," *Christian Herald*—draft.

February 1954, "High Lava Country: The Klamath Wilderness," *Lincoln-Mercury Times*.

February 1954, "The Senator Behind the Give-Aways," *Progressive*.

27 February 1954, "Limits of the West," *Saturday Review*.

Spring 1954, "A Tribute to Joseph Kinsey Howard," *Montana: the Magazine of Western History*.

March 1954, "America's Toughest Railroad," *Popular Science*.

March 1954, "Sourdough—The Wilderness Yeast," *Ford Times*.

March 1954, "The U.S. and Canada: Union Someday?" *Everybody's Digest*.

April 1954, "From SF to Portland on the Shasta Daylight," *Railway Progress*.

April 1954, "Oregon's Coast—Sublime Meeting of Land and Sea," *Chrysler Events*.

April 1954, "The Wetbacks: Menace to the American Standard of Living," *Butcher Workman*.

10 April 1954, "They're Taming the Lolo Trail," *Saturday Evening Post*.

27 April 1954, "Canada's Social Security System for Children," *Reporter*.

May 1954, "Ladies in High Places," *Ford Times*.

May 1954, "Northwest, Tailored to All Tastes," *Harper's*.

May 1954, "Seeing the Pacific Northwest," *Harper's*.

May 1954, "Taming America's Wildest River," *Popular Science*.

9 May 1954, "I Will Believe," *This Week*.

June 1954, "Want to Climb a Mountain?" *Popular Science*.

Summer 1954, "The Lochsa: Realm of History and Grandeur," *Montana: the Magazine of Western History*.

July 1954, "David Among Goliaths," *Ford Times*.

3 July 1954, "Baron Munchausen's Dam," *Nation*.

13 August 1954, "Two Thousand Miles from his Company's Rails," *Railway Progress*.

September 1954, "Missoula of the Mountains," *Ford Times*.

September 1954, "Wanted: More Churchmen in Politics," *Christian Herald*.

12 November 1954, "Candidates Size up the Election: Interview," *U.S. News*.

December 1954, "Eating on the Cars: A Great American Adventure," *Butcher Workman*.

25 December 1954, "They've Been Plowing out the Railroad," *Saturday Evening Post*.

1955

1955, "Family Allowances: A Step Forward in Social Legislation," *Harper's*—draft.

17 January 1955, "State of the Union; Resources," *New Republic*.

17 January 1955, "Two for the Show," *Time*.

5 February 1955, "Does Familiarity Breed Wisdom?" *New Republic*.

24 February 1955, "Partnership vs. Public Interest," *Reporter*.

5 March 1955, "Unfruitful Acres," *Saturday Review*.

April 1955, "Lewis and Clark 150 Years Afterward," *Progressive*.

May 1955, "Is the President's New Highway Program Sound?" *Congressional Digest*.

May 1955, "Wayne L. Morse: 1956 and Beyond," *Fortnight*.

9 May 1955, "Professional Touch," *New Republic*.

28 May 1955, "Go, Thou, and Do Differently," *New Republic*.

June 1955, "My Wife Put Me in the Senate," *Harper's*.

June 1955, "Why I Do Not Drink," *Christian Herald*.

14 June 1955, "Social Security for Children: Next Step," *Congressional Record*.

July 1955, "Partners in Plunder," *Progressive*.

July 1955, "Rail Travel," *Railway Progress*.

4 July 1955, "Making a Scapegoat of Lyndon Johnson," *New Republic*.

14 August 1955, "The Larceny at Hells Canyon," *New York Post*.

September 1955, "Family Allowances: A Challenge to the Eagles," *Eagle Magazine*.

September 1955, "The Tyranny of Guilt by Associations," *Progressive*.

6 October 1955, "Trek Was Pinnacle of U.S. Exploration," Lewiston *Morning Tribune*.

November 1955, "Begin Women's Benefits at Age 60," *Eagle*.

20 November 1955, "Vote for the West," New York *Times*.

December 1955, "Excerpt from Report from the Nation's Capital," *Congressional Digest*.

1956

January 1956, "Our Parks and Forests Are in Trouble," *Chrysler Events*.

January 1956, "Registration: Our Passport to Democracy," *Butcher Workman*.

25 January 1956, "Federal Funds for Party Coffers," *Christian Century*.

February 1956, "Westward on the Empire Builder," *Railway Progress*.

March 1956, "A Visit to Capitol Hill," *Lincoln-Mercury Times*.

March 1956, "Aids for the Legislator," *National Municipal Review*.

April 1956, "A Family Allowance for America," *Grail*.

April 1956, "And Beyond is America," *Railway Progress*.

April 1956, "Way Over People's Heads," *Progressive*.

29 April 1956, "Power and Politics," *The American Forum*.

May 1956, "Schools, Subsidies and Segregation," *Progressive*.

June 1956, "Mistakes of a Freshman Senator," *American Magazine*.

3 June 1956, "Who Should Pay for Political Campaigns?" *New York Times Magazine*.

July 1956, "The Neubergers—Oregon's Only Legislative Family," *Listen*.

18 July 1956, "Principles or Party," *Christian Century*.

August 1956, "Al Sarena Case," *American Forum*.

August 1956, "Political Union Spending," *Facts Forum News*.

August 1956, "Portland's Forest Park," *Ford Times*.

August 1956, "Shadow and Substance at the Ballot-Box," *Saturday Review*.

August 1956, "Super Continental of the Canadian National," *Railway Progress*.

August 1956, "Washington Lobbyists: The Third House of the Legislature (Lobbyists and What to Do About Them)," *Coronet*.

August 1956, "Welfare Goals for America," *Progressive*.

13 August 1956, "A Humanitarian View of Animal Welfare," *Washington Religious Review*.

13 August 1956, "Principles Over the Brink," *New Republic*.

20 August 1956, "Roll Calls, School Children and Politics," *New Republic*.

September 1956, "Political Courage vs. Political Cowardice," *Christian Century*.

October 1956, "Reply to Article by Sidney Lens," *Progressive.*

27 October and 29 December 1956, "Isn't There a Better Way to Elect a President?" *Saturday Review.*

25 November 1956, "Monument on the Pacific," New York *Times.*

December 1956, "Let's Practice What We Preach," *Adjust Student.*

18 December 1956, "Oregon Feels Pinch as U.S. Prospers," New York *Times.*

26 December 1956, "Let's End Discrimination Against Northwest History," *Oregonian.*

1957

January 1957, "Winning the West for Democrats," *Progressive.*

14 January 1957, "When Rule XXII Swallowed Itself!" *New Republic.*

February 1957, "Crash Program for Health," *Eagle.*

24 February 1957, "To Protect Our Interstate Highways From Billboards," New York *Times.*

27 February 1957, "Memorandum on Reforms in Campaign Spending."

13 March 1957, "God's Resources and Ours," *Christian Century.*

Spring 1957, "Oregon's Economy: No Share in the Boom," *Northwest Review.*

April 1957, "Morse for President," *Progressive.*

7 April 1957, "Senator's Case Against Seniority," *New York Times Magazine.*

May 1957, "The Nature of the Crisis Confronting Democrats," New York *Times.*

11 May 1957, "Family Allowances," *America.*

June 1957, "Beauty vs. Billboards," *County Officer.*

June 1957, "Signboards vs. Scenery," *Oregon Democrat.*

June 1957, "Time for an All Out War Against Cancer," *Family Weekly Magazine.*

7 July 1957, "Democrats' Dilemma: Civil Rights," *New York Times Magazine.*

14 July 1957, "What Do Senators Read? Very Little," *New York Times Book Review.*

21 July 1957, "Reading Time is Stolen From Hours of Sleep," New York *Times.*

August 1957, "Madison Avenue in Politics," *Esquire.*

August 1957, "The Tax that Chokes the West," *Railway Progress.*

24 August 1957, "Oregon Must Let Mind Be Bold and Seek Industries," *Oregon Journal*.

Fall 1957, "We Need More Social Welfare," *IUD Digest*.

September 1957, "Let's Strengthen Social Security," *Eagle Magazine*.

September 1957, "Rigging the Record," *Progressive*.

4 September 1957, "Cigarettes and Price Supports," *Christian Century*.

24 September 1957, "Frontier of the Future, Beaver State," *Retirement Life*.

October 1957, "Can You Change the World?" *Legion Magazine*.

October 1957, "Should Private Enterprise Do the Major Job of Developing Water Power?" *Legion Magazine*.

9 October 1957, "Country Placed Ahead of Party," *Oregon Journal*.

9 November 1957, "Outdoor Advertising: A Debate," *Saturday Review*.

December 1957, "Economic Situation in Oregon and PNW," *Oregon Journal*—editorial.

December 1957, "Portland Builds a Railroad," *Railway Progress*.

December 1957, "Power Struggle on the Canadian Border," *Harper's*.

31 December 1957, "Industrial Power Priority Proposed for Bonneville," *Oregonian*.

1958

1958, "No Discrimination of Government Contracts," *Eagle Magazine*.

January 1958, "Pilgrimage Through the Far West," New York *Times*.

January 1958, "Oregon Economic Situation," *Oregon Journal*—editorial.

8 January 1958, "You Meet Such Interesting People," *Oregon Journal*.

February 1958, "The Greatest Killer of Kids," *Progressive*.

February 1958, "Power is Slipping Through Our Fingers," *Power Industry*.

23 February 1958, "Who Polices the Policeman (Congress)?" *New York Times Magazine*.

March 1958, "Why I 'Saved' the White House Squirrels," *Parade Magazine*.

2 March 1958, "Oregon Lays Groundwork for its Centennial," New York *Times*.

29 March 1958, "Sternest Crisis in 111 Years," *Star Weekly Magazine*.

April 1958, "The Buck Stops Here," *New Republic*.

April 1958, "Solving the Stubborn Klamath Dilemma," *American Forests*.

19 April 1958, "Solving the Stubborn Klamath Dilemma," *American Forests*.

19 April 1958, "A Milepost Through the Billboard Jungle," *Izaak Walton League Magazine*.

20 April 1958, "Congressional Record is Not a Record," *New York Times Magazine*.

30 April 1958, "No National Lottery!" *Christian Century*.

May 1958, "The Buck Stops Here!" *The Reporter*—draft.

May 1958, "The Miracle of the Rivers," *Progressive*.

June 1958, "Herbert H. Lehman: A Profile in Courage," *Progressive*.

June 1958, "How I Got My First Job," *Alliance*.

June 1958, "My Wife on Her Own," *Parade*.

July 1958, "Next—IMY: International Medical Year," *Progressive*.

27 July 1958, "When Influence is Good and Bad," *New York Times Magazine*.

August 1958, "Bloody Trek to Empire," *American Heritage*.

19 August 1958, "Report on Political Campaign Contributions in the 1956 Election," *Congressional Record*.

September 1958, "Guest Column on Conflict of Interest," New York *Herald Tribune*.

September 1958, "Subsidies for Children," *Parents Magazine*.

6 September 1958, "Night the Senate Didn't Surrender," *Saturday Review*.

25 September 1958, "Subsidies for Children," *Parents*.

18 October 1958, "Neuberger Proposes Oregon Billboard Law," *Oregonian*.

19 October 1958, "Subsidy or Actual Public Operation May be Needed to Save Rail Transportation," *Oregonian*.

20 October 1958, "Neuberger on Tax Cuts," *New Republic*.

22 October 1958, "No Surrender Law: Moral Aspects," *Christian Century*.

30 October 1958, "No National Lottery," *Christian Century*.

2 November 1958, "In Defense of the Politician," *New York Times Magazine*.

23 November 1958, "15 Point Policy Program for Democrat Congress," *Sunday Oregonian*.

1959

January 1959, "Auto Racing Must be Outlawed," *Mechanics Illustrated*.

January 1959, "Conservation During 50 Years of 'The Progressive,'" *Progressive*.

January 1959, "Listen Pattern for Progress," *National Journal of Better Living*.

January 1959, "Our Resources—Human and Natural," *Childhood*.

1 January 1959, "Senator Asks 'End to Political Invective,'" *Oregonian*.

4 January 1959, "Conservation: Prospects for 1959," New York *Times*.

February 1959, "Oregon Celebrates a Birthday," *Kiwanis Magazine*.

February 1959, "Oregon Celebrates 100 Years of Statehood," *Retirement Life*.

1 February 1959, "West Puts its Brand on Congress," *New York Times Magazine*.

11 February 1959, "I Always Felt That It Would Be Someone Else," Washington *Daily News*.

25 February 1959, "President's Budget Bad for Oregon," *Oregon Journal*.

March 1959, "The Greatest of All Oregon Adventures," *Oregon Horizons*.

March 1959, "Seminars in Government," *NEA*.

9 March 1959, "Unfinished Business Outdoors," *New Republic*.

29 March 1959, "Oregon Celebrates Its Centennial Year," New York *Times*.

April 1959, "A New Fisheries-Power Partnership," *Outdoor America*.

April 1959, "How Oregon Rescued a Forest," *Harper's*.

14 April 1959, "Preference Clause Change in Power Bill is Fair and Moderate," *Oregonian*.

May 1959, "Oregon's Second Century," *Christian Science Monitor*.

May 1959, "Ross," *Holiday*.

9 May 1959, "Senator Surveys the Land of the Braves," *Saturday Review*.

12 May 1959, "Health Research: Plea for Funds," New York *Herald Tribune*.

June 1959, "Best Advice I Ever Had," *Reader's Digest*.

June 1959, "The Legacy of Lewis and Clark," *Think Magazine*.

June 1959, "Make Mine Oregon," *Pageant*.

June 1959, "Oregon at 100," *Sports Afield*.

June 1959, "Oregon's Big Birthday Party," *Eagle Magazine*.

June 1959, "The People vs. Billboards," *Garden News*.

June 1959, "The Struggle for a Liberal Senate," *Progressive*.

June 1959, "When I Learned I Had Cancer," *Harper's*.

August 1959, "The Dangerous Decline in Doctors," *Progressive*.

23 August 1959, "Are the People Ahead of their Leaders?" *New York Times Magazine*.

30 August 1959, "Plan for Shoreline Parks," New York *Times*.

October 1959, "Reflections on a Brush With Death," *Think Magazine*.

1960

January 1960, "Let's Build a Crash Program to Beat Cancer," *Coronet*.
25 January 1960, "The Pacific Northwest and Alaska," *This Week Magazine*.
February 1960, "Adlai E. Stevenson: Last Chance," *Progressive*.
21 March 1960 "High Trail to Reform," *New Republic*—reprint.
9 April 1960, "Should a Public Man Write?" *Saturday Review*.

1963

June 1963, "Winema, the Memorial Forest," *American Forum*.

Index

Richard Neuberger in the West Hills of Portland looking out over the city.
(RAY ATKESON)

Colophon

They Never Go Back to Pocatello is set in Mergenthaler Times Roman, a photo-composition typeface based on the hot-metal face originally commissioned in 1931 by *The Times* of London for its newspapers. The design was supervised by Stanley Morison for the Monotype Corporation. The display type is also Times Roman.

They Never Go Back to Pocatello is printed on 60 lb. Warren's Olde Style. The jacket cover color is PMS 292. The endpapers are 80-lb. Gainsborough Blueweave. The binding is Holliston Roxite 53549.

The production of *They Never Go Back to Pocatello* was accomplished through the cooperation and professional skill of the following:

TYPESETTING: Wilsted and Taylor, Oakland, California
PRINTING: Print Tek West, Salem, Oregon
BINDING: Lincoln and Allen, Portland, Oregon
PAPER: The Zellerbach Paper Company, Portland, Oregon

Produced and designed by the Oregon Historical Society Press.

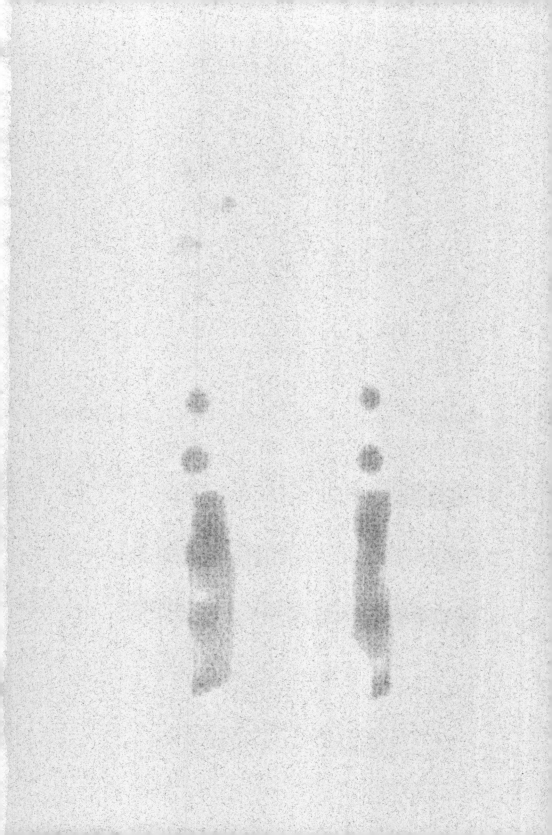